INTRODUCTION
TO PASCAL:
Including Turbo Pascal

INTRODUCTION
TO PASCAL:
Including Turbo Pascal®

RODNAY ZAKS

BERKELEY • PARIS • DÜSSELDORF • LONDON SYBEX®

Cover art by Eduardo Jonquieres
Technical illustrations by j. trujillo smith.

Apple II is a trademark of Apple Computer Inc.
CP/M is a trademark of Digital Research Corp.
IBM PC is a trademark of IBM Corp.
Turbo Pascal is a trademark of Borland International Inc.
UCSD Pascal is a trademark of the Regents of the University of California.
WordStar is a trademark of MicroPro International Corp.
SYBEX is not affiliated with any manufacturer.

Every effort has been made to supply complete and accurate information. However, SYBEX
assumes no responsibility for its use, nor for any infringements of patents or other rights of third
parties which would result.

Library of Congress Card Number: 85-63778
ISBN 0-89588-319-8
Printed by Haddon Craftsmen
Manufactured in the United States of America
10 9 8 7 6 5 4 3 2

Acknowledgments

The manuscript of this book has gone through many phases, and has been shown to many people, the final form benefitting from the comments and suggestions of all. I am particularly indebted to the following educators or Pascal programmers who have provided valuable criticisms or opinions on the original manuscript: Michael Farr, Joseph Faletti, Jacques Tiberghien, Michael Powell, Eric Novikoff, and Elein Mustain. The first version of this book was published as an *Introduction to Pascal, including UCSD Pascal* and I am grateful to David Carroll for his essential contribution to the Turbo Pascal material. Thanks too to the others who worked on the Turbo Pascal version of this book: David Kolodney, Supervising Editor; Bonnie Gruen, Editor; Dave Clark and Olivia Shinomoto, Word Processing; Nick Wolfinger and Keith Gruen, Technical Support; Sharon Leong, Book Design; Donna Scanlon, Typesetting; and Eileen Walsh, Proofreading.

Contents

3 SCALAR TYPES AND OPERATORS _____31

4 EXPRESSIONS AND STATEMENTS _____53

5   INPUT AND OUTPUT _____ 65

6   CONTROL STRUCTURES _____ 79

10 RECORDS AND VARIANTS _____191

11 FILES _____217

12 SETS _____ 253

13 POINTERS AND LISTS _____ 267

Preface

I have written many books on computers, ranging from the introductory (*Your First Computer*) to the highly technical (*A Microprogrammed APL Implementation*). Yet, this was one of the most difficult to write, as this book was designed to be read and understood by everyone, whether novice or experienced programmer, who wants to learn how to program in Pascal.

Pascal is a powerful language, equipped with highly sophisticated facilities. Explaining all of the features simply and progressively, without losing the novice or boring the experienced programmer, was a significant challenge.

The arrangement of the chapters will lead the reader from simple concepts to complex data structures and all aspects of Pascal are covered progressively.

The first five chapters present the basic definitions needed to use and understand Pascal. After studying them, the reader will be able to write simple programs. Specific techniques and data structures are presented next, allowing the reader to write more complex programs.

Pascal is a powerful programming language requiring actual practice to learn well. Many exercises are provided throughout the book to test the reader's skills and comprehension while learning. Answers to selected exercises appear at the end of the book.

The original definition of Pascal by Niklaus Wirth has been formalized by the International Standards Organization as ISO Pascal, and is referred to in this book as Standard Pascal. A more recent version of Pascal, from Borland International, known as Turbo Pascal, has gained widespread acceptance for use on microcomputers. Each chapter describes Standard Pascal, as well as the differences and special features of Turbo Pascal, where applicable. The more complex aspects of Turbo Pascal are described in a special chapter at the end of the book.

The extensive appendices provide a listing of all symbols, keywords and rules of syntax for programming in both Standard and Turbo Pascal. These appendices provide a concise summary that can be used as a reference.

How to Read This Book

This book is designed to be used primarily as a tutorial on Pascal, and also as a reference text. Designing a book as a tutorial requires a linear presentation: each concept must be defined before it is used. Designing a book as a reference text requires a modular organization: all information pertaining to a topic must be included in that section.

The approach chosen for this book is a tutorial one: concepts are carefully defined, each in turn. Even those who have never programmed before will be able to understand the entire book.

Since the reader may need to refer back to specific chapters when programming, each chapter has been structured so that it may also be used as a reference later on. The most simple concepts are presented at the beginning of each chapter; more complex information is systematically presented at the end of the chapter. Other sections in the book are included for reference.

The more complex concepts presented at the end of most chapters, as well as the special features and differences of Turbo Pascal, may be omitted during a first reading. Later on, once the reader has acquired programming practice, these sections may be consulted as useful references.

The following sequence is recommended for the reader who wants to learn to program in Pascal as quickly as possible.

First phase:

— Read Chapters 1 through 6 carefully.
— Try to solve the exercises.
— Read Chapter 15.
— Ignore the information of Turbo Pascal within the chapters.

The most important task for the reader, at this point, is to write many real programs and execute them. The first six chapters may be used to help accomplish this.

Second phase:

— Read Chapters 7, 8, and 9.
— If you are using Turbo Pascal, read all of the pertinent sections.
— Write as many programs as possible.

At this point, the reader will have learned most of the techniques required to write common Pascal programs.

Third phase:

— The specific data structures required for complex programs are presented in Chapters 10, 11, 12 and 13.
— Advanced features of Turbo Pascal are presented in Chapter 14.
— The program development process is described in Chapter 15.

The time required to learn a programming language varies from one person to another. The author can only express the hope that this book will make it possible for everyone to learn Pascal quickly and enjoyably.

A final point, for the convenience of the reader the programs in this book are available on a Turbo Pascal compatible disk. Please see the last page for details.

CHAPTER **1**

BASIC CONCEPTS

INTRODUCTION

The basic concepts of computer programming in the Pascal language will be introduced in this chapter. Actual programs will be presented and explained in order to give the reader realistic programming examples. The more formal concepts and definitions of the Pascal language will be introduced in Chapter 2.

COMPUTER PROGRAMMING

A *computer program* is a sequence of instructions designed to be executed by a computer in order to obtain a specific result. For example, computer programs may be written and used to play games, perform scientific calculations, or execute business-oriented tasks.

Internally, a computer can only execute a limited set of instructions, which must be expressed in a *binary* code, i.e., as a sequence of zeroes and ones. Unfortunately, programs written in binary are difficult and time-consuming for most users to write or read. To alleviate this problem, a number of programming languages have been invented to facilitate the writing of programs.

A *programming language* is a subset of the English language that allows the programmer to give unambiguous commands to the computer. Of course, the most desirable way to give instructions to the computer would be in English (or any other human language). Unfortunately, studies have shown that none of the common spoken languages, including the English language, are adequate for this purpose. The English language is *ambiguous*. Statements may be interpreted in many ways, depending upon the context. Therefore, so-called "natural languages" may not be used to program a computer. Only a restricted and well-defined subset of this language, i.e., a programming language, may be used. Hundreds and perhaps thousands of programming languages have been proposed for computers.

Two different types of programming languages exist: assembly and high-level languages. *Assembly language* is a symbolic representation of the binary instructions the computer understands. This language is difficult to use, as the programmer must specify internal registers and detailed internal operations. Assembly language is used whenever execution speed is essential. However, it makes programming difficult.

High-level languages have been developed to facilitate writing computer programs in specific environments such as: scientific, business or educational.

Pascal is a high-level language. In order to be executed on a computer, a high-level language requires a special program, called an interpreter or a compiler, which will translate the language into a sequence of binary instructions that a computer can understand.

Now that we understand how languages are used, let us look at the way in which a computer program is created.

ALGORITHMS AND DATA STRUCTURES

A computer program is created either to automate a process or to solve a given problem. The sequence of steps or operations that must be followed in order to solve a specific problem is called an *algorithm*.

An example will serve to clarify the concept of an algorithm. The problem to be solved is that of "preparing a soft boiled egg." A possible algorithm for this task is:

1. Fill the pan with water.
2. Bring the water to a boil.
3. Place the egg in the pan of boiling water.
4. Remove the egg three minutes later.

This algorithm is a step-by-step specification of the process that will solve our problem. Written for a human, it is somewhat loosely specified. For example, extra steps could be added to indicate:

1. The amount of water to be placed in the pan.
2. The way in which the egg should be lowered into the pan (gently).
3. The act of placing the pan on the range and then later removing it.

This method of first defining the algorithm loosely, and then defining it in detail is often called "top-down design" or "stepwise refinement." It will be discussed in Chapter 15.

Let us look at another example of an algorithm. The problem to be solved in this case is the specification of directions necessary to locate a specific building in Berkeley, California, assuming that the person driving is coming from San Francisco.

A possible algorithm for locating the building at 2344 Sixth Street in Berkeley is:

1. Go over the Bay Bridge.
2. Follow Highway 17, North.
3. Take the University Avenue exit in Berkeley.
4. Turn right onto Sixth Street at the first traffic light.
5. Proceed to the intersection of Sixth and Channing Way. The building is on the northwest corner.

This simple algorithm specifies the sequence of steps required to reach the building. It is clear and unambiguous.

To be solved by a computer, all problems must first have a solution expressed as an algorithm. Then, in order for the computer to be able to execute the algorithm, the algorithm must be translated into a program by a programmer using a programming language.

In addition, one other task may have to be performed: often *data structures* must be defined to represent the required information. The information or data used by a program must be organized by the programmer in a logical and efficient manner. This is called designing data structures.

In summary, *programming* involves designing an *algorithm* and using the appropriate *data structures*. Specifically,

— An *algorithm* is a step-by-step specification of a sequence of instructions that will solve a given problem.

— A *data structure* is a logical representation of information. Examples of data structures are tables, lists and arrays. They will be described in other chapters of this book.

The Pascal language has been designed to facilitate the conversion of algorithms into programs, as well as the construction or representation of data structures. The origin and nature of the Pascal language will now be described.

PASCAL

Pascal evolved from the search for a programming language that would be complete, yet simple to learn and easy to implement on a computer. The properties of Pascal reflect these aspirations.

Reviewing the history of programming languages, we find that one of the earliest languages to be defined was FORTRAN (FORmula TRANslator). FORTRAN is one of the most often used languages in the field of scientific computation. Because it was an early programming language, FORTRAN has, over time, become a complex collection of "facilities" that are useful but cumbersome to learn or use on computers.

An attempt was made to define a simple language directly inspired by FORTRAN which would be easy to learn and could also be executed in an interactive (conversational) manner. The result was BASIC (Beginner's All-Purpose Symbolic Instruction Code). The BASIC language is easy to implement on a computer and requires only a small amount of memory. Because of these two advantages (ease of implementation and ease of learning), BASIC has become the most widely-used language on microcomputers. However, it has many limitations due to its rules of usage (its "syntax") and is often inadequate for writing complex programs.

Another language, ALGOL (ALGOrithmic Language) resulted from an attempt to define a computer language other than FORTRAN that would be consistent and well-suited for use with complex algorithms. ALGOL gained great popularity in educational circles yet was never widely used by industry. Although the ALGOL language provides an excellent tool for describing algorithms, it is somewhat complex to learn, and difficult to implement on a computer.

Pascal was inspired by ALGOL and PL/I, and represents an attempt at defining a programming language that is simple to learn yet well-suited for the specification of algorithms and the definition of data structures.

Pascal was created by Niklaus Wirth of the ETH Technical Institute of Zurich in 1970-1971 (upon his return from Stanford University). Pascal gained acceptance in educational institutions as a good tool for learning how to program. In addition, because Pascal is relatively simple and highly coherent, the Pascal compiler (required in order to use the language on a computer) can be implemented in a small amount of memory. As a result, when low-cost microcomputers equipped with limited memories appeared in the late 1970's, a number of Pascal implementations became available, bringing Pascal within the reach of almost anyone.

The name of the language is a tribute to the French mathematician Blaise Pascal who in 1690 at age 18 invented the first mechanical calculating machine.

TURBO PASCAL AND OTHER PASCALS

The original Pascal language was defined by Niklaus Wirth and Kathleen Jensen in the *Pascal User Manual and Report* (reference [1] in Appendix K) first published in 1974. The language definition was later formalized by the International Standards Organization as Level 0 ISO Standard Pascal (ISO dp7185) in 1980. The ISO Standard was also accepted (with extremely minor changes) in the United States by the American National Standards Institute (ANSI) and the Institute of Electrical and Electronics Engineers (IEEE) as a standard for the "American National Standard Programming Language Pascal" in 1983 (ANSI/IEEE770X3.97-1983). In fact, ISO Standard Pascal is almost identical to Wirth's original Pascal, but it is much more precisely defined.

ISO Standard Pascal will be called *Standard Pascal* throughout the text for simplicity. There are, however, a number of extensions and variations of Standard Pascal in existence today.

As new implementations of Pascal were released, changes to the original definition began to occur. Features were added to the language, and operations were interpreted in different ways when ambiguities existed.

As with any programming language, Pascal has become implementation-dependent. In theory, learning Pascal involves not only learning "Standard Pascal," but also learning the features and differences inherent in the version being used at a specific installation.

Fortunately, in practice, all versions of Pascal to date implement "Standard Pascal" with some additional features, as well as a few changes.

In order to learn Pascal, the best procedure is, therefore, first to learn

Standard Pascal, and then to learn the advanced features as well as the differences inherent in the specific implementation being used.

Pascal was originally designed for use on a traditional "batch-oriented" computer, where a progam is submitted on a deck of cards, and data are submitted on cards or stored on tape.

As Pascal gained popularity, the language became available on time-sharing systems and microcomputers, where a user has direct access to a terminal.

Because of the greater user-computer interaction possible on such systems, additional features became desirable, and one version called UCSD Pascal became widely used. This version was developed at the University of California at San Diego (UCSD), and was available for many small computers including the Apple II by 1978. It featured several extensions to Standard Pascal, including an easy to use screen graphics technique called *Turtle Graphics*. UCSD Pascal was described in previous editions of this book.

In 1983, Borland International released Turbo Pascal, a sophisticated Pascal compiler for CP/M, IBM PC-DOS, and MS-DOS computers. Turbo Pascal is a powerful, low cost, high speed, native code compiler featuring built-in error detection and a WordStar like program editor. Together, these elements make up the *Turbo Pascal Programming Environment*. Turbo Pascal has been very successful and over 400,000 copies have been sold through 1985. It has been adopted by over 400 universities and colleges for their introductory programming classes. Because of its importance, Turbo Pascal is included in this book.

Many other versions of Pascal exist. For a comprehensive description of these versions, the reader is referred to reference [11].

A SIMPLE PASCAL PROGRAM

The basic concepts of computer programming have now been described, and a short history of the Pascal language has been presented. Let us now examine an actual Pascal program. This example will serve to illustrate the features of the language and will provide a basis for the additional definitions that follow.

Here is our first Pascal program:

```
PROGRAM GREETING (OUTPUT);                               (1)
(* THIS IS A SIMPLE PASCAL PROGRAM *)   (* COMMENT *)     (2)
BEGIN                                                     (3)
    WRITELN('HELLO')              (* STATEMENT *)         (4)
END.                                                      (5)
```

When executed, this program will print 'HELLO'. It may be surprising that the program requires five lines for this simple action. This is because the program has been formatted for clarity. This same program could be written in one or two lines. This example will serve to introduce some of the basic concepts in Pascal. Let us look at it more closely. The first line of our program is:

PROGRAM GREETING(OUTPUT);

This line is the *program definition* or *program heading*. It tells the computer (or more exactly, the *compiler*) that the lines which follow the heading form a program called 'GREETING'. In addition, this line contains a *file declaration:* 'OUTPUT'. Whenever a program must access data outside the program itself, it will read or write on or from a *file*, and this file must be declared in the program heading. *Input* refers to the transfer of data to the program. *Output* refers to the transfer of data from the program, by the program. INPUT and OUTPUT are considered as special cases of files. In this program example, this declaration warns the compiler that the program will be performing an output operation, i.e., it will be printing or displaying information. Standard Pascal requires that such file declarations be made at the time of the program definition.

Note that the word 'PROGRAM' appears in boldface type. This is done to help the reader differentiate the word 'PROGRAM' from the word 'GREETING'. PROGRAM has a predefined meaning for the compiler, while GREETING is a word defined by the user. Predefined words in Pascal are called either *reserved words* or *standard identifiers*. In the actual program listing produced by a printer, both PROGRAM and GREETING would be printed in exactly the same way. However, when reading a book, it is helpful to have reserved words differentiated from other words. Therefore, all reserved words within a program are shown in boldface type in this book.

In Pascal, either lowercase or uppercase letters may be used interchangeably. For example, the first line of our program could be written:

program greeting(output);

However, some implementations may impose restrictions.

Finally, note that this line is separated from the rest of the program by a semicolon. The function of the semicolon is to separate two consecutive statements or declarations. In this way, for example, two statements (terminated by '';'') may be written one after the other on the same line. However, not all statements need to be terminated with a semicolon. In particular, the semicolon is optional before an END.

The second line of the program is:

(* THIS IS A SIMPLE PASCAL PROGRAM *)   (* COMMENT *)

This line is called a *comment*. Comments are ignored by the computer, thereby allowing the programmer to write explanations anywhere within the program that will clarify what the program is doing. A comment must be preceded by (* or { and terminated by *) or }, as in our example.

Blank lines, indentations, and extra spaces are also ignored by the computer. Like comments, they are used to clarify programs.

Now let us look at the body of the program:

BEGIN
      WRITELN('HELLO')   (* STATEMENT *)
END.

This program contains only one executable statement, WRITELN('HELLO'), which is preceded by BEGIN and followed by END. This section of three lines is called a *program block*. Every *program heading* must be followed by a *program block*. The actual instructions of the program, called *statements*, are listed between the reserved words BEGIN and END. Pascal has been designed to encourage programming in blocks. Other examples of blocks within a program will appear throughout the text. For this reason Pascal is said to encourage *structured programming*.

The single *executable statement* in our program is:

WRITELN('HELLO')

This statement means "write 'HELLO' on the output device and skip to a new line." The output device is usually the CRT terminal or a printer. The only action taken by this particular program is to display or print the characters 'HELLO'. WRITELN also does one more thing: this command terminates the line by moving the cursor (in the case of a screen) or the printhead (in the case of a printer) to the beginning of the next line.

Let us now summarize the important aspects of our first Pascal program. Each statement in the program is separated from the next one by a semicolon. To improve program readability, comments and indentations are used. For example, the body of the program may be written:

BEGIN WRITELN('HELLO')   (* STATEMENT *) **END**.

This line was written in a "block format" in our example:

```
BEGIN
        WRITELN('HELLO')          (* STATEMENT *)
END.
```

Writing a program in "block format" is a recommended practice, but not a mandatory one. The purpose of this practice is to identify clearly each block bracketed by the words BEGIN and END. To achieve this, the corresponding BEGIN and END are aligned vertically. The statements within that block are indented.

Finally note that the word END, followed by a period, indicates the end of the program.

A SECOND PROGRAM EXAMPLE

Let us look at another Pascal program:

```
PROGRAM SUM(INPUT,OUTPUT);
VAR A,B,TOTAL : INTEGER;
BEGIN
        WRITELN('ENTER TWO NUMBERS TO BE ADDED...');
        READ(A,B);
        TOTAL := A + B;
        WRITELN('THE SUM OF ', A ,' AND ', B ,' IS ', TOTAL)
END.
```

This program is more complex than the first one and will introduce several new concepts. When the above program is executed, it will type or display:

ENTER TWO NUMBERS TO BE ADDED...

Two integers, called A and B in the program, must then be typed in at the keyboard, separated by blanks. The program will automatically add these two integers and print on the next line:

THE SUM OF (first number) AND (second number) IS (total)

Before describing this program further, let us follow the correct procedure when designing any program. For reasons of clarity, the three steps are labeled A, B, and C:

A. The *problem* to be solved is the following: read two integers and add them.

B. The corresponding *algorithm* is:
1. Read the first integer.
2. Read the second integer.
3. Add both integers and display the result.

A new problem is introduced by this algorithm: the two integers must be "remembered," i.e., stored in memory, before they can be added.

C. A simple *data structure* will be used to solve this problem: the two integers will be represented internally by two *variables* of *type* integer.

The total will also be represented by an integer variable. The concepts of *variable* and *type* will be clarified as we use them. Let us now examine this program in detail.

The first line is the program heading:

PROGRAM SUM(INPUT,OUTPUT);

This program is called SUM. The word PROGRAM is shown in boldface type because it is a reserved word. Recall that reserved words in Pascal have a special meaning to the Pascal compiler; thus, the word 'PROGRAM' can be used only in the context of a program heading. Note that a program may not be called "PROGRAM", since the word 'PROGRAM' has a special meaning in Pascal, and would immediately be flagged as an error by the compiler. Reserved words may only be used as authorized by the rules or *syntax* of Pascal.

In the above program, the program heading specifies '(INPUT,OUTPUT)'. This means that the program will both read from the keyboard (an input operation) and print on the printer or display on the CRT (an output operation).

The second line of the program is:

VAR A,B,TOTAL : INTEGER;

This statement is called a *variable declaration*. It performs two functions. First, it tells the Pascal compiler that the symbols A, B, and TOTAL are variables. Second, it states that these variables are of type INTEGER. This allows the compiler to reserve an adequate amount of memory for each of the three variables.

Let us first clarify the concept of a *variable,* and then the concept of *type.* Each variable has a name, a type and a value. In this program, the symbol A will be used as the name of a variable that stores the value of the first integer. The variable named B will be used to stored the value of the second integer. The variable named TOTAL will be used to store the value of the sum. A variable can contain any (reasonable) value. The value may vary during execution of the program.

When this program is first executed, A might receive the value "2" and B might receive the value "11." When this program is executed another time, A might rceive the value "251" and B might receive the value "3." Thus, the actual values to be stored in A and B may vary with each program run. Accordingly, A, B and TOTAL are called program variables. The characters or the sequence of characters A, B and TOTAL are *names* assigned to internal memory locations. This concept is illustrated in Figure 1.1.

Initially, the contents of A, B and TOTAL in Figure 1.1 are undefined. Later, assuming that the values "2" and "11" are typed in, the contents of A and B will be as shown in Figure 1.2.

For clarity, the values shown as "2" and "11" in Figure 1.3 are represented internally in the memory in a binary notation (with 0's and 1's). If no value has yet been assigned to TOTAL, TOTAL is still undefined at that stage.

Let us now go back to the variable declaration:

VAR A,B,TOTAL : INTEGER;

This declaration declares the symbols A, B and TOTAL as variables,

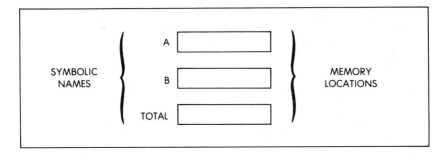

Figure 1.1:   A Variable is the name of a memory location

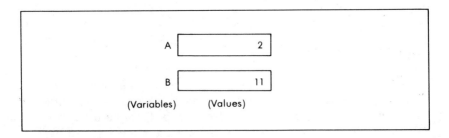

Figure 1.2:   Variables with Values

thereby automatically reserving memory locations to store their values later on. In addition, this declaration specifies that these three variables are of type integer.

The name of a variable is called an *identifier*. Identifiers will be formally defined in the next chapter. We have introduced the concept of *variable*. We will now explain the concept of *type*. A type declaration has two advantages. First, it simplifies the design of the Pascal compiler. Second, it assists the programmer in preventing or detecting errors. Let us examine these two points.

Once a variable has been declared, the compiler must allocate storage to it. Internally, different numbers of bytes (a byte is a group of 8 bits) are allocated to each type of data. For example, a character may be allocated one byte, while an integer may require two bytes, and a decimal number may require four bytes. It is therefore very helpful for the compiler to know ahead of time how much storage must be reserved.

Once the type of a variable has been declared, the compiler can easily detect a number of obvious errors. For example, integers may be multiplied together, while characters may not. If two variables were declared of type 'char' (character), an attempt to add them will be automatically detected as an error by the computer. A character is a letter like 'F', 'X', or 'T', or any other symbol on the keyboard, like '.', '?' or '5'. When a digit like '5' is declared as a character, it is not represented in the same way as when it is declared as an integer. A character is generally represented as a byte (8 bits) in the ASCII code, while an integer is represented in two or more bytes, using a different internal code.

Returning to our program example, since A and B are declared as integers, any attempt to type illegal values, such as "TRUE" or "D" at the keyboard, will be automatically rejected.

In summary, variable declarations simplify compiler design and enhance programming discipline. It is possible, however, to design language compilers that do not require such declarations. The disadvantages may be an increased complexity in compiler design and greater probability of errors in the program.

Pascal requires type definitions. This requirement is often viewed by programmers as a nuisance, especially if they have programmed in BASIC before. However, this feature is part of Pascal's overall philosophy of disciplined programming, and enhances the probability of successful program design.

Having clarified the concepts of variable and type declaration, we now enter the body of the program with the reserved word 'BEGIN'. The lines that follow the VAR declaration are:

BEGIN

WRITELN('ENTER TWO NUMBERS TO BE ADDED...');

We have already encountered this instruction in our previous example.

It will display or "type" the text: 'ENTER TWO NUMBERS TO BE ADD-ED...'. Note that the actual text to be displayed is simply enclosed in single quotes (apostrophes) in the program. This sequence of characters is called a *character string*. This statement is terminated by a semicolon.

The next line in the program is:

READ(A,B);

This line means "read two numbers from the keyboard and call them A and B." At this point, the program will wait for the user to type the numbers at the keyboard. If the numbers are not typed, nothing will happen and the program will continue to wait. Once the two numbers have been typed, this instruction will have been satisfied and the program will proceed. A and B are *names* of variables. 'A' will contain the first number typed. 'B' will contain the second number.

As explained before, A and B are called *variables* because their values may be changed later on in the program, or may be different during another program run. In this program, A and B have been declared of type INTEGER in the second line of the program. As a result, the compiler will verify that any value given to A or B is indeed an integer. Throughout this program, A and B will be integers, and the compiler will check this every time A or B are referred to.

This particular feature is characteristic of Pascal: the type of each variable must be declared prior to using the variable, and must be respected throughout the program.

The next line in the program is:

TOTAL := A + B;

This statement means "compute A + B and call the result TOTAL." This instruction is called an *assignment* statement. The symbol of the assignment is ':='. This symbol is created by typing ':' followed by '=', and is called the *assignment operator*. This operator assigns the sum of A plus B to a new variable called TOTAL. If we had typed 2 and 3 as the values of A and B to be added, the resulting sum 5 would be assigned to the variable TOTAL.

Naturally, the sum of two integers is an integer, and it can be verified that TOTAL was declared to be of type INTEGER in line 2 of the program.

'A + B' is an addition. This sequence of variables and operators is called an *arithmetic expression*. The rules for creating such expressions will be presented in the following chapters.

The next line of the program is:

WRITELN('THE SUM OF ', A ,' AND ', B, ' IS ', TOTAL)

This instruction will display the following line on the CRT:

THE SUM OF 2 AND 3 IS 5

Again, note that any text to be printed is simply enclosed in single quotes (this is called a character string). Also, note that the value of the variables A, B, and TOTAL is printed when their names are used. The name of a variable always stands for the value that it contains.

The program body is terminated with the usual END followed by a period.

This program is longer than the previous one, and should be examined carefully until you are thoroughly familiar with its meaning.

SUMMARY

The basic concepts of computer programming, including the concepts of algorithm, data structure, and program, have been introduced and illustrated with actual examples.

The Pascal language was described as a high-level language designed for disciplined programming, ease of use, completeness, and convenience of implementation.

Another advantage often claimed by Pascal is *portability*. The term "portability" is used to indicate that a program written in Pascal may be transported to another computer and executed without change. However, this is true only if both of the computers being used execute exactly the same version of the language. Thus, true portability has disappeared as various versions of Pascal have been introduced. Some changes are usually required when using a different Pascal compiler.

Two simple programs were presented in this chapter in complete detail, and additional concepts relating to Pascal programs were introduced within the context of these examples. These concepts included program headings, program blocks, the comment, variable declaration, input and output instructions, the assignment statement, arithmetic expressions and reserved words.

Here are examples of these concepts taken from the second program presented in this chapter:

program heading	**PROGRAM** SUM(INPUT,OUTPUT);
variable declaration and type definition	**VAR** A,B,TOTAL : INTEGER;
program block	**BEGIN** ... ... **END**.

comment	(* THIS PROGRAM ADDS TWO NUMBERS *)
input and output	READ(A,B); WRITELN(TOTAL);
assignment	TOTAL := A + B;
arithmetic expression	A + B
reserved word	**PROGRAM**

It is essential that these concepts be thoroughly understood. All of the important concepts required to write and understand Pascal programs will now be reviewed systematically in Chapter 2.

EXERCISES

1-1: *Modify the program SUM so that it prints the product of A and B (the multiplication symbol is *).*

1-2: *Modify the program SUM so that it reads three numbers A, B, C, and computes their sum.*

1-3: *Can a variable be used without being declared?*

1-4: *What is a program? What is an algorithm?*

1-5: *Is the following a legal statement?*

TOTAL (* THIS IS THE SUM *) := A (* 1ST NBR *) + B (* 2ND *);

1-6: *Is an algorithm the same as a program?*

CHAPTER 2

PROGRAMMING
IN PASCAL

INTRODUCTION

In Chapter 1 the concepts of algorithm, data structure, and program were introduced and two simple Pascal programs were examined in detail. In this chapter, we will describe the organization of a Pascal program and introduce the concepts of syntax and modular program organization, or "structured programming." Our goal is to learn the basic rules of the Pascal language so that we can start solving simple problems with Pascal programs.

Three special entities—identifiers, scalars and operators—are defined by the syntax of Pascal and must be understood before writing a simple Pascal program. Once these three entities are understood, expressions may be constructed, and Pascal statements written.

Identifiers will be presented in this chapter. Scalars and operators will be studied in Chapter 3. Expressions and statements will be studied in Chapter 4.

WRITING A PASCAL PROGRAM

Once the solution to a problem has been specified in the form of an algorithm, the algorithm must be transformed into a Pascal program. After the program is written, it will be translated by the compiler and executed. Various other programs such as the editor and the file system can be used on an interactive computer to facilitate this process. These programs are described in Chapter 15.

From now on, we will concentrate on the task of translating algorithms into programs and data structures. The set of rules for constructing a valid Pascal program is called the *syntax* of Pascal. We will learn all of the syntactic rules of Pascal, one at a time. The first use of these formal rules will be presented in this chapter.

THE SYNTAX OF PASCAL

Pascal is a high-level language. Pascal allows the programmer to specify instructions in a language that is similar to the English language, but is highly restricted. In order to avoid any ambiguity, and to facilitate the translation of the program by the compiler into binary instructions, the syntax of the language imposes strict rules.

Programming may require ingenuity and intelligence, but it also requires a strict *discipline*. Every instruction or statement in a Pascal program must strictly follow the rules of the Pascal syntax. Any instruction that violates the rules will cause the program to fail. There are no exceptions. It is therefore essential to understand and strictly adhere to the rules of the syntax. A single misplaced dot or comma will cause the program to fail. The single largest source of failure in all computer programs is negligence. The importance of following a highly disciplined approach toward computer programming cannot be emphasized enough.

The rules of Pascal can be described in many ways. For example, they can be described by using words, the BNF (Backus-Naur Form) notation, or syntax diagrams. Throughout this chapter, the syntax will be described by using words. Then, in the following chapter, syntax diagrams will be introduced to provide a concise and accurate representation of the rules. Examples of BNF notation will be provided as well.

FORMAT OF A PASCAL PROGRAM

Pascal has been designed to encourage modular programming. Thus, each step or logical group of steps within the algorithm can generally be translated into a Pascal module. Pascal modules are called *blocks, functions* or *procedures,* depending upon the way they are used. (These modules will be described in turn later in the book.)

In addition, the syntax of Pascal requires that all of the declarations and definitions must appear at the beginning of a program. The resulting overall organization of a Pascal program is shown in Figure 2.1.

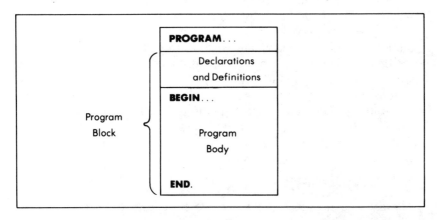

Figure 2.1:   Overall Organization of a Pascal Program

As shown in Figure 2.1, all declarations appear at the beginning of a program. The declarations are followed by the main block, which is bracketed by the words BEGIN and END.

Let us now consider the organization of each of these modules in more detail. A detailed description of a Pascal program is shown in Figure 2.2.

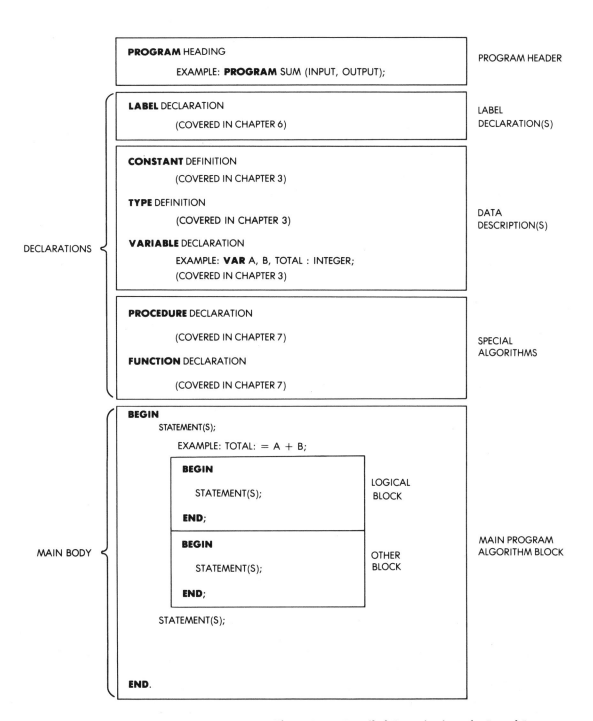

Figure 2.2: Detailed Organization of a Pascal Program

Let us look more closely at the declarations and the main body.

DECLARATIONS

The various kinds of declarations in Pascal must appear exactly in the order in which they are shown in Figure 2.2: first, the labels, then the constants, etc. However, declarations are all optional. For example, in our first program example:

```
PROGRAM GREETING(OUTPUT);
(* THIS IS A SIMPLE PASCAL PROGRAM *)
BEGIN
      WRITELN('HELLO')
END.
```

there were no declarations. This program included only the program header, followed by the main executable body. Recall that comments do not count: they are ignored by the compiler.

Usually, any Pascal program that has more than a few lines uses variables and must include one or more variable declarations. For example, our second program was:

```
PROGRAM SUM(INPUT,OUTPUT);
VAR A,B,TOTAL : INTEGER;
BEGIN
      WRITELN('ENTER TWO NUMBERS TO BE ADDED...');
      READ(A,B);
      TOTAL := A + B;
      WRITELN('THE SUM OF ', A ,' AND ', B ,' IS ', TOTAL)
END.
```

This program includes the program header and the variable declaration, followed by the main executable body.

Referring back to Figure 2.2, labels are seldom used, and functions or procedures are generally used only in long programs. The only three declarations required for short programs are: CONSTant, TYPE, and VARiable. They will all be described in Chapter 3. The remaining declarations will be described in Chapters 6 and 7.

THE EXECUTABLE PROGRAM BODY

The program body, shown in Figure 2.2, contains the sequence of statements that will execute the proper algorithms. Several types of statements can be used in Pascal. The three most important types of statements are:

1. Assignment statements (described in Chapter 4)
2. Input and output statements (described in Chapter 5)
3. Control statements (described in Chapter 6)

Other types of statements include procedure calls, 'GOTO', and 'WITH' statements. These statements will be described in subsequent chapters.

PROGRAM ORGANIZATION SUMMARY

In summary, each Pascal program must contain at least a program heading and a statement. In addition, a program may contain several declarations or definitions following the heading (in the proper order), as well as any number of statements. Comments, additional blanks, and indentations may be placed anywhere in a program to improve readability.

FORMAL ORGANIZATION OF A PROGRAM

For those readers who can already read syntax diagrams, the formal syntax of a Pascal program is shown in Appendix F.

The corresponding program organization is shown in Figure 2.3.

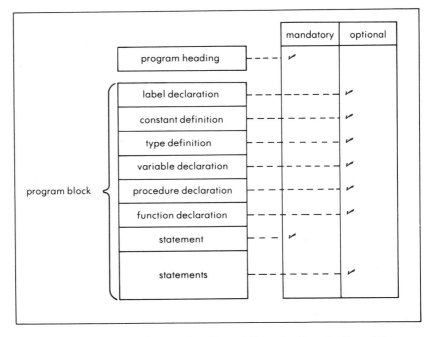

Figure 2.3:   Formal Organization of a Pascal Program

Note that, using the formal definition, a ''program block'' refers to everything that follows the heading, including the declarations.

THE SYMBOLS OF PASCAL

All of the symbols in the alphabet available on your computer installation may be used in a Pascal program. Most computers use the ASCII code (shown in Appendix G), and provide 128 characters. However, it should be noted that many of these characters, or sequences of characters have a special meaning for Pascal, and may be used only for specific purposes.

These special symbols will be described in this section. Then the rules for constructing additional symbols or identifiers will be presented.

RESERVED SYMBOLS

The reserved symbols used by Pascal are shown in Figure 2.4.

+	−	*	/	: =	.	,	;
:	/	=	< >	<	< =	> =	>
(	)	[	]	(* or {	*) or }	↑	..

Figure 2.4:   Reserved Symbols

Most of these symbols are used to denote operations such as +, −, * (multiply), / (divide). Other symbols are used for specific syntax purposes. For example, '';'' has already been used to separate statements, and ''(*'' with ''*)'' have been used to enclose comments. These symbols and others may be used freely within a *text* processed by a program, but not within a program itself. Within a program, these reserved symbols have a well-defined (pre-defined) meaning.

RESERVED WORDS

In addition to the reserved symbols, a number of predefined words have a special meaning within a Pascal program. Some of these words called *reserved words* may not be redefined by the programmer. Others may be redefined by the programmer and are called *standard identifiers*.

The reserved words of Pascal are shown in Figure 2.5. Some reserved words are used to denote operations: AND, OR, NOT, DIV. Other reserved words are used for declarations or definitions: PROGRAM, CONST, VAR, TYPE. Still others are used as part of statements: IF, WHILE, REPEAT.

AND	**END**	**MOD**	**REPEAT**
ARRAY	**FILE**	**NIL**	**SET**
BEGIN	**FOR**	**NOT**	**THEN**
CASE	**FORWARD**	**OF**	**TO**
CONST	**FUNCTION**	**OR**	**TYPE**
DIV	**GOTO**	**PACKED**	**UNTIL**
DO	**IF**	**PROCEDURE**	**VAR**
DOWNTO	**IN**	**PROGRAM**	**WHILE**
ELSE	**LABEL**	**RECORD**	**WITH**

Figure 2.5: Reserved Words

Reserved words are always shown in boldface type in the programs contained in this book. Remember that these words may never be used by the programmer in any other way than as reserved words. For example, a program may not be given the name ''PROGRAM.'' We will now show the ways the reserved words are used by the compiler.

Let us review again the first program introduced in Chapter 1 illustrating a simple Pascal program:

```
PROGRAM GREETING(OUTPUT);
BEGIN
      WRITELN('HELLO')
END.
```

The three words shown in boldface in the program are reserved words.

The reserved word PROGRAM must appear at the beginning of every program. Once this word is recognized, the compiler expects the next word to be the name of the program. Then, if any parentheses are found, the compiler is told that the program will use files. The file used in this case is OUTPUT. The word OUTPUT is not a reserved word, but it has a predefined meaning. This type of word is called a *standard identifier* and will be described in the next section. Finally, the program header is terminated by a ';'.

Next, the compiler finds the reserved word BEGIN. This tells the compiler that one or more executable statements follow.

The only executable statement in this program is:

WRITELN('HELLO')

where WRITELN is called a standard identifier, and 'HELLO' is called a string of characters.

The program is terminated with the keyword END. Every program must be terminated with the word END followed by a period.

We will see in Chapter 6 that blocks of statements delimited by BEGIN and END may appear in various locations within the program. However, the last END written in a program is the only one that is followed by a period.

Having explained the meaning and role of reserved words, let us examine the standard identifiers, such as WRITELN and OUTPUT.

STANDARD IDENTIFIERS

Standard identifiers are words that have a predefined meaning in Pascal, but that may be redefined by the programmer to take on a different meaning. These words are shown in Figure 2.6.

The novice or intermediate programmer is strongly advised not to redefine these standard identifiers within a program. Standard identifiers are *not* shown in boldface type in the programs.

The facility to redefine these identifiers should only be used by the advanced programmer in highly specific cases, i.e., when the standard identifier does not do exactly what is required by the program.

In practice, standard identifiers should be treated in the same way as reserved words, unless there is a very good reason not to treat them this way.

Let us look again now at the second program example introduced in Chapter 1:

```
PROGRAM SUM(INPUT,OUTPUT);
VAR A,B,TOTAL : INTEGER;
BEGIN
      WRITELN('ENTER TWO NUMBERS TO BE ADDED...');
      READ(A,B);
      TOTAL := A + B;
      WRITELN('THE SUM OF ', A ,' AND ', B ,' IS ', TOTAL)
END.
```

The reserved words in this program are:

PROGRAM, VAR, BEGIN, END

The *standard identifiers* are:

INPUT, OUTPUT, INTEGER, WRITELN, READ

```
STANDARD IDENTIFIERS
FILES:
        INPUT       OUTPUT


CONSTANTS:
        FALSE       TRUE        MAXINT


TYPES:
        BOOLEAN     CHAR        INTEGER     REAL        TEXT


FUNCTIONS:
        ABS         EOLN        PRED        SUCC
        ARCTAN      EXP         ROUND       TRUNC
        CHR         LN          SIN
        COS         ODD         SQR
        EOF         ORD         SQRT


PROCEDURES:
        DISPOSE     PACK        READ        REWRITE     WRITELN
        GET         PAGE        READLN      UNPACK
        NEW         PUT         RESET       WRITE
```

Figure 2.6: Standard Identifiers

Finally, one more type of identifier called a *user-defined identifier* is used in this program. The user-defined identifiers in this program are:

SUM, A, B, TOTAL

The role and meaning of identifiers will now be explained.

Identifiers

An *identifier* is a name. This name may be given to a variable, program, type, constant, function, procedure, etc. Three types of identifiers are distinguished in Pascal:

— Reserved words
— Standard identifiers
— User-defined identifiers.

Reserved words and standard identifiers have already been described. User-defined identifiers will now be explained.

Four examples of identifiers appear in the second program example in Chapter 1. These identifiers are:

— The name of the program: SUM
— The names of the three variables: A, B, TOTAL

An identifier must start with a letter, can contain any combination of letters and digits, and can be any length. In Wirth's definition of Pascal, only the first eight characters were significant, but Standard Pascal considers all characters significant. An identifier can never be a reserved word, since a reserved word already has a special meaning for the compiler.

Here are examples of valid identifiers:

    A
    B
    Alpha
    Alpha1
    Numberofemployees
    Numberofcustomers

Listed below are examples of invalid identifiers:

FIRST-A	(includes a "-")
2nd	(starts with a digit)
program	(reserved word)
BETA 2	(includes a blank)

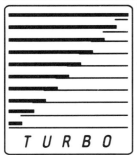

TURBO PASCAL COMMENTS

A comment may be bracketed by (* . . . *) or by { . . . }, inter-changeably. Whenever a comment begins with (*, it must terminate with *). When a comment begins with {, it must terminate with }.

For example, the following comments are legal in Turbo Pascal:

(* THIS IS A {SPECIAL} PROGRAM *)
(* THIS IS A (* SPECIAL PROGRAM *)

In the first example above, the { and } characters are ignored because the comment begins with a "(*." In the second example, note that the first "(*" triggers the "comment mode." All subsequent characters are ignored by the compiler (including the second "(*") up to the matching "*)."

However, a $ in the first position of a comment is interpreted as a compiler command. Compiler commands are specific to the Turbo Pascal version and operating system used.

TURBO PASCAL PROGRAM HEADINGS

Unlike Standard Pascal, Turbo Pascal does not require file parameters such as (INPUT, OUTPUT) in the program heading. In fact, the entire program heading is ignored.

For example, in Turbo Pascal

        BEGIN

and

        PROGRAM TEST;
        BEGIN

are valid ways to start a program and are equivalent to

        PROGRAM TEST (INPUT,OUTPUT);
        BEGIN

which is also valid.

Although not required, inclusion of the program heading is strongly recommended in Turbo Pascal programs to aid documentation and to maintain program compatibility with other compilers.

TURBO PASCAL DECLARATIONS

Turbo Pascal relaxes the Standard Pascal requirement that declarations and definitions in program blocks occur either not at all or only once and in a specific order. This allows declarations or definitions of related objects to be grouped together for clarity.

TURBO PASCAL SYMBOLS

Turbo Pascal recognizes the dollar sign ($) symbol as hexadecimal integer notation and the number (#) symbol as an ASCII ordinal character prefix. For example:

```
A := $FF80; (* signed integer value  −128 or 65408 *)
C := #07; (* bell character *)
```

TURBO PASCAL RESERVED WORDS

Turbo Pascal has eight additional reserved words that are not included in Standard Pascal. They are:

```
ABSOLUTE
EXTERNAL
INLINE
OVERLAY
SHL
SHR
STRING
XOR
```

TURBO PASCAL STANDARD IDENTIFIERS

In addition to the 40 standard identifiers in Standard Pascal, Turbo Pascal 3.0 provides over 100 additional "built-in" identifiers representing the many extensions provided. These are made up of additional constants, procedures, and functions. A complete list of these identifiers is provided in Appendix J.

Turbo Pascal does not support the following Standard Pascal identifiers:

```
GET
PACK
PAGE
PUT
UNPACK
```

User-Defined Identifiers

Unlike Standard Pascal, Turbo Pascal user-defined identifiers may include the underline character (_) which can be used to add to the clarity of long identifiers (for example: BIGTABLE compared to BIG_TABLE). User-defined identifiers may be of any length up to the maximum line length of 127 characters, and all characters are significant. Also unlike Standard Pascal, they can contain embedded reserved words without conflict.

SUMMARY

The overall structure of a Pascal program has been described in this chapter. Each program starts with a program heading, followed by optional declarations, and one or more statements bracketed with BEGIN and END.

Three types of identifiers are used in Pascal: reserved words, standard identifiers, and user-defined identifiers. Each of these three types was described in this chapter.

By this point in the text, the reader should easily follow the organization of the first two program examples that were introduced in Chapter 1. In order to construct more complex programs in Pascal, we must first study the rules that will allow us to perform computations. We will now study the way that numbers are represented and the operations that may be performed on them.

EXERCISES

2-1: Are the following identifiers legal in Pascal?

   1: A   2: 2B   3: A1B3D2   4: ALPHA+1   5: SIMPLE NAME

2-2: What will be the effect of using the following three identifiers in a program?

   PERSONNO1,   PERSONNO2,   PERSONNO3
   Are these identifiers legal?

2-3: Without looking at the examples provided in the text, write a simple Pascal program that will print 'HELLO', followed by your name.

CHAPTER **3**

SCALAR TYPES
AND OPERATIONS

INTRODUCTION

In order to design simple Pascal programs, we must first learn the rules relating to data, as well as the rules relating to the operations that may be performed on data.

In Pascal, there are *four* fundamental *data types* which are called the *standard scalar types: integer, real, character* and *Boolean*. These four types and the rules that apply to them will be studied in this chapter. Once these data types and the corresponding operators are understood, we will then be able to assemble them into *expressions,* and write program *statements.*

There are two kinds of scalar types in Pascal: the built-in types, and the user-defined types. Both scalar types will be described. Let us first examine the four built-in or "standard" scalar types: INTEGER, REAL, CHAR, and BOOLEAN.

THE INTEGER TYPE

Integers, i.e., whole numbers, may be positive or negative. The maximum and the minimum size for integers that may be represented in a given Pascal installation is limited by the precision used. In practice, it is only possible to represent the integers between $-(MAXINT + 1)$ and $+MAXINT$, where MAXINT represents the largest number provided by the installation. MAXINT is a predefined constant that may be used to determine or print out the maximm value for integers that is available.

The following are examples of valid Pascal integers:

```
1234
0
1
- 234
MAXINT
+ 10
```

Here are examples of illegal integers:

```
1,234          (a comma is not allowed)
1.2            (this is not an integer)
```

Operators for Integers

For each data type, Pascal defines valid *operators*. Operators operate on one or two operands (values) and perform a specific operation. Operators are generally represented by mathematical symbols, such as + and −, or by reserved words, such as DIV for integer division.

Let us first define the operators and then look at examples of their use. The standard built-in Pascal operators for integers include arithmetic operators and relational operators. The five arithmetic operators are:

+	addition (plus sign)
−	subtraction (minus sign)
*	multiplication
DIV	division (yields a truncated integer result—truncation is the dropping of any digits to the right of the decimal point).
MOD	modulus (A MOD B yields the remainder of the division of A by B). Thus: A MOD B = A − (A DIV B) * B

The six relational operators are:

>	greater than
>=	greater than or equal to
<	less than
<=	less than or equal to
=	equal to
<>	not equal to

These six relational operators may be used on *any standard scalar data type*. They produce a *Boolean value* that is TRUE or FALSE. Boolean values will be defined later on in this chapter.

Note that the division operator for integers that will give an integer result is DIV. The symbol "/" is used to obtain a real number result. The operator DIV *always* results in an *integer* result. This convention helps to avoid errors.

Examples of arithmetic operators are:

    4 − 3 = 1

    5 + 6 = 11

    2 * 12 = 24

20 DIV 6 is 3	(note that when using decimal (real) numbers, the / would be used, and the result of 20/6 would be 3.333)
(– 20) DIV 6 is – 3	(if a negative operand is allowed by the implementation)
9 MOD 4 is 1	(the result of 9/4 is 2, with a remainder of 1).

If A is exactly divisible by B, then A MOD B is 0.

Standard Functions for Integers

Since only a few symbols are available as part of the character set on most computers, traditional mathematical symbols used to denote a square root, a power or an integral, are not available. Standard identifiers are used instead.

A Pascal identifier that performs an operation on one or more operands and yields a result is called a *function*. User-defined functions will be discussed in Chapter 7. In this chapter, we will simply describe those standard functions that may be used with the four scalar types.

The standard functions are essentially similar to operators, but generally perform more complex operations. Traditionally, in programming languages, the most-often used operations are represented by the special symbols called operators, while the less-often used ones are called functions. In Pascal, functions are always represented by a standard identifier followed by parentheses. The argument(s) on which they operate must be enclosed within the parentheses.

Four standard functions are provided in Pascal that yield an integer result:

ABS(I)	absolute value of the integer I. For example: ABS(– 4) is 4 ABS(3) is 3
SQR(I)	square of the integer I. For example: SQR(2) = 2∗2 = 4 SQR(– 3) = (– 3)∗(– 3) = 9
TRUNC(R)	integer portion of R where R is a real (decimal) number. For example: TRUNC(1.2) is 1 TRUNC(– 2.3) is – 2

ROUND(R)	integer closest to R. It is analogous to TRUNC, except that R is rounded to the nearest integer, either up and down. Whenever the fractional part of R is exactly 0.5, it is rounded up if R is positive, or down if R is negative. For example: ROUND(1.2) is 1 ROUND(1.8) is 2 ROUND(− 2.4) is − 2.

In the following example using Pascal functions, the mathematical expression:

$$AX^2 + BX + C \qquad \text{(where all numbers are integers)}$$

may be expressed as:

A * SQR(X) + B * X + C

and the expression:

$$|I| \times J$$

becomes:

ABS(I)*J

THE REAL TYPE

In Pascal, *real* numbers correspond to the usual decimal (floating point) numbers. The minimum and maximum magnitudes of real numbers depend upon the implementation. In Pascal, a real number must have a decimal point, at least one digit to the left of the decimal point, and at least one digit to the right. The following are examples of legal real values in Pascal:

       + 12.0
       − 12.1
       + 0.1
          3.14159

The following are examples of invalid real values:

.123	(digit missing to the left of the decimal point)
12	(decimal point missing. This is an integer. However, most implementations will convert an integer into a real, i.e., 12 into 12.0)
1.	(digit missing to the right of the decimal point).

The representation of reals with a decimal point is the most common representation. However, another representation of reals, often used in physics, is also allowed in Pascal: it is called the *exponential notation* or *scientific notation*. An example of this notation is:

1.0E+2 which represents $1 \times 10^2 = 100$

In this exmple, 1.0 is called the *mantissa,* and the number following the E is called the *exponent* or *characteristic*. The exponent specifies the power of ten used. It indicates that the decimal point should be moved to the right (or to the left if the exponent is negative) by that many positions. Another example is 1.2E-3, which represents 0.0012 or 1.2×10^{-3}.

This representation is a shorthand notation which is convenient for very small or very large numbers, i.e., whenever there are several zeroes in a number. The plus sign in front of the number following the E may be omitted.

As indicated previously, the range of real numbers that may be represented depends upon the installation. Usually, six digits are allocated to the mantissa and two digits are allocated to the exponent. Let us call MINREAL the smallest positive real that may be represented, and MAXREAL the largest one. As a result of the limited precision, it is only possible to represent positive reals between the installation-dependent MINREAL and MAXREAL, and negative reals between −MINREAL and −MAXREAL. There is a range of numbers between −MINREAL and +MINREAL which cannot be represented, although zero itself can be represented. In short, very small values as well as very large values cannot be represented.This is illustrated in Figure 3.1.

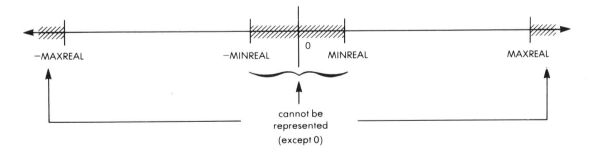

Figure 3.1: *Representation of Reals*

As a result of the limitation on the precision with which a real may be represented, arithmetic operations performed on real numbers will usually not result in an exact value. Using an example in the decimal system, ⅓ may be represented by 0.333333 if only seven decimal digits are available to represent the result. This is an approximation of the exact value of ⅓, since the exact representation of ⅓ requires an infinite number of 3's after the decimal point. This is why it is advisable not to test the value of any real number for equality. For example, ⅓ multiplied by 3 will probably not be equal to 1. If many operations are carried out, the error due to the truncation or to the rounding off of the result will increase with the number of operations, and can become quite large in some cases.

In most simple calculations, the approximation due to the limited precision of the internal representation will be almost invisible. However, in numerical computations which are complex and must be accurate, special care must be exercised and the rules of numerical analysis must be followed in order to obtain results that are as accurate as possible. In particular, the following recommendations apply:

— Do not test a real value for equality. Instead, test that the difference between two real values is less than a specified amount.
— Avoid subtracting two nearly equal real numbers.
— Minimize the number of calculations involved.

Operators for Reals

In addition to the six relational operators, which were introduced in the preceding section and apply to all reals, there are four arithmetic operators available for the real data type. They are:

+ addition
− subtraction
* multiplication
/ division (DIV may not be used for real numbers).

Here are examples of operations:

$$1.2 + 1.3 = 2.5$$
$$1.2 - 1.3 = -0.1$$
$$2.0 * 3.1 = 6.2$$
$$2.2 / 2.0 = 1.1$$

Functions for Reals

The following standard functions will yield a real value:

ABS (R)	absolute value of R.	(These two func-
SQR(R)	square of R, or R × R	tions may operate
		on a real or an in-
		teger argument,
		yielding a result of
		the same type)
SIN(R)	sine of R	(These six func-
COS(R)	cosine of R	tions may operate
ARCTAN(R)	arc tangent of R (in radians)	on a real or
LN(R)	natural logarithm of R	an integer
EXP(R)	exponent of R	argument yielding
SQRT(R)	square root of R	a real result)

Here are examples of the standard functions:

ABS(– 5.21)	=	5.21
ABS(6.789)	=	6.789
SQR(4.0)	=	16.0
SQRT(4.0)	=	2.0

Two standard functions will convert a real into an integer: TRUNC(R) and ROUND(R). These functions were described in the section on integers.

THE CHARACTER TYPE

Characters are any of the symbols available on the installation. For example:

　　A　B　Z　+　/　*　?

Characters are always represented in single quotes or apostrophes in Pascal:

　　'A'　'B'　'Z'　'+'　'/'　'*'　'?'　' ' (a blank)

The single quote must be written twice, in quotes:

　　''''

Characters will be used when processing, reading or printing text. Internally, each character is represented by a numeric code of binary digits (or bits) such as: '10110001'. Generally, 8 bits (one byte) are used for each character.

Therefore, when two characters are compared, it is actually their corresponding codes that are compared. A will be less than B provided that the binary code used to represent A is less than the binary code used to represent B. This rule applies to all characters, including digits and punctuation marks.

Characters, like any other scalar type, are ordered, i.e., they follow each other in a given sequence. However, a practical constraint is introduced on their ordering by the implementation: characters are represented by different codes, depending upon the computer manufacturer. For example, on IBM computers, the EBCDIC code is used. On small computers, the ASCII code is universally used (see Appendix G). The internal ordering of the alphanumeric symbols (the characters) depends upon their internal code, since it is the value of the codes that is compared.

In practice, any code guarantees that the letters of the alphabet are "in the right order." However, a code will not guarantee that they are adjacent. The digits from 0 to 9 are always in the correct order and are contiguous:

$$'A' < 'B' < 'C' < ... < 'Z' \text{ and } '0' < '1' < '2' < ... < '9'$$

Also, the number of characters is code-dependent, and may vary from 64 to 256. The most common number with the ASCII code is 128.
Note: 'AB' is not a *character*, but a *string* of characters, a different type which will be introduced in a later chapter.

Also, when referring to the ASCII code table in Appendix G, remember that a digit declared as a character is represented as an ASCII code (8 bits). In contrast, a digit declared as an integer is represented in a different code that may use 16 or 32 bits. The two internal representations of that digit are different.

OPERATORS AND FUNCTIONS FOR CHARACTERS

There are no arithmetic operators available to perform computations on characters. However, the six standard relational operators are available, as well as four standard functions. These functions are described here for a more complete text, but they will not be used in our simple programs.

ORD(C)   Ordinal function: yields the ordinal value of that character, i.e., the internal integer code that represents it.

CHR(I)   Character function: yields the character C corresponding to the integer I in the internal representation of the character set.

PRED(C)   Predecessor function: yields the previous character in the representation used.

SUCC(C)   Successor function: yields the next character in the representation used.

Here are examples:

PRED('B') is 'A'
SUCC('E') is 'F'

The following relationships hold:

PRED(C) = CHR(ORD(C) − 1)
SUCC(C) = CHR(ORD(C) + 1)
CHR(ORD(C)) = C
ORD(CHR(I)) = I

They also hold with the ASCII code:

ORD('G') = ORD('H') − 1
ORD('Y') = ORD('Z') − 1
ORD('Z') = ORD('Y') + 1

Note: the PRED and the SUCC functions have been introduced for characters, as this is the way in which they are ordinarily used. However, these functions also apply to integers and Booleans. They do not, however, apply to real numbers.

Remember when using the relational operators on characters that the ordering of the characters is implementation-dependent. In general, the ordering of the upper-case letters and the digits will be the "normal" (or common) one. However, do not compare other characters unless you know the internal ordering used in your particular system. If the ASCII code is used, for example, refer to Appendix G to establish the internal ordering of the characters. It is important to know the ordering of characters when processing text.

THE BOOLEAN TYPE

The word "Boolean" is derived from the algebra theory developed by Boole. The type BOOLEAN may take two values: TRUE or FALSE. It is called a *logical* type. Combinations of Boolean values are called Boolean expressions, and are used to make logical decisions. A Boolean data type may only take one of the logical values TRUE or FALSE. Such Boolean values are usually obtained as the result of a comparison.

For example: I = 4 will be FALSE if I has the value 5. Here are other examples:

2 = 3	is	FALSE
10 = 10	is	TRUE
11 > 9	is	TRUE
1.2 <= 2.1	is	TRUE

The use of Boolean expressions to control the execution of a program
will be discussed in Chapter 6.

Operators for Booleans

In addition to the six usual relational operators, three special Boolean
operators are also available:

AND	logical AND
OR	logical OR
NOT	logical negation

These three Boolean operators are traditionally defined by *truth tables*,
as shown in Figure 3.2.

A	B	A **AND** B
F	F	F
F	T	F
T	F	F
T	T	T

A	B	A **OR** B
F	F	F
F	T	T
T	F	T
T	T	T

A	**NOT** A
F	T
T	F

Figure 3.2:   Truth Tables

In Figure 3.2:

— (A AND B) is TRUE only if both A and B are TRUE. It is FALSE in all other cases.
— (A OR B) is TRUE if either A or B or both are TRUE. It is FALSE only if A and B are both FALSE.
— (NOT A) is the opposite of A: if A is TRUE, NOT A is FALSE.

Additional logical operators can be defined using the relational operators:

A = B   (denotes equivalence)
A <> B   (denotes an exclusive OR)
A <= B   (denotes an implication)

The truth table for these three types is shown in Figure 3.3.

A	B	A = B	A < > B	A <= B
F	F	T	F	T
F	T	F	T	T
T	F	F	T	F
T	T	T	F	T

Figure 3.3:   Additional Truth Tables

In Figure 3.3:

— (A = B) is TRUE if A and B are both TRUE or FALSE, i.e., have the same Boolean value.
— (A <> B) is TRUE if A and B have different Boolean values.
— (A <= B) is TRUE if A<B or A = B. (F<T by definition.)

Functions for Booleans

A few Boolean functions are available in Pascal that will yield a Boolean value of TRUE or FALSE. They are called *predicates*. For clarity, only one example of this type of function, ODD(I), will be presented here.

ODD(I) is TRUE if integer I is odd, and FALSE if I is even.

The other two Boolean functions available in Pascal that will yield a Boolean value are EOF and EOLN. They will be described in Chapter 11.

USER-DEFINED TYPES

Additional types may be defined by the programmer with the TYPE declaration. This declaration will be introduced later on in this chapter, after the VAR declaration has been presented.

TYPE DEFINITIONS

The type of each variable must always be described before the variable is used. Three mechanisms are provided to define the type of an identifier: the built-in variable declaration (VAR), the implicit TYPE declaration of constants, and the explicit TYPE definition. They will be examined in turn.

The VAR Declaration

We have already used the VAR declaration. Here is an example:

VAR   X,Y : REAL;

This statement declares X and Y as REAL variables. Similarly:

VAR   I,J,K : INTEGER;

defines I, J and K as INTEGER variables.

Here are other examples of variable declarations:

VAR   A : REAL;
         B : REAL;
         M,N : CHAR;
         TEST : BOOLEAN;

or:

VAR   A,B : REAL;
         K,L : INTEGER;

Note that A,B may be declared together or separately, and that VAR may be used only once at the beginning of the list of variables to be declared.

Here is another example where several variables are declared at the same time:

VAR   DAY,MONTH,WEEK : INTEGER;

These examples show the syntax of a VAR declaration very clearly. However, the symbolic syntax diagrams are often used to provide a formal definition. We will introduce this concept here. Use it if you feel comfortable with it. Do not use it if you do not readily understand it. Other diagrams will be presented throughout the book. However, they are more useful as concise references than as learning tools. The formal syntax diagram for a VAR definition is shown in Figure 3.4.

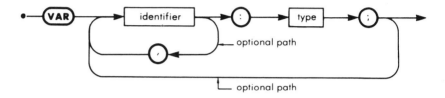

Figure 3.4:   VAR Declaration Syntax

In such diagrams, a box with rounded edges is used to represent predefined words, i.e., reserved words and standard identifiers, such as 'VAR'. A circle is used to represent reserved symbols such as ',', ':', or ';'. A rectangle is used for syntax elements that are defined elsewhere in their own diagram. In the example in Figure 3.4, there are two such rectangles: 'identifier' and 'type'. Finally, the lines and the arrows are used to indicate authorized paths. For example, let us use the diagram of Figure 3.4 to verify the syntax of:

VAR   A,B,C : INTEGER;

The corresponding path is shown in Figure 3.5.

This diagram shows how the VAR declaration is constructed step-by-step by following the rules of the syntax. We can thus verify that the VAR declaration is indeed legal.

Once you become familiar with such diagrams, they provide a concise and convenient way to verify the syntax in a specific case. The complete syntax diagrams are shown in Appendix F.

The VAR declaration serves two syntactic purposes:

1. It tells the compiler that the identifiers in the VAR declaration are VARiables, and not another kind of identifier, such as function or procedure names.
2. It defines the type of each of these variables as REAL, INTEGER, BOOLEAN, or CHAR.

The use of VAR has three resulting advantages:

1. It simplifies the compiler design.
2. It enforces greater programming discipline by requiring the programmer to declare all of the variables explicitly before they are used.
3. It allows the compiler to check the validity of operations performed on specific data types.

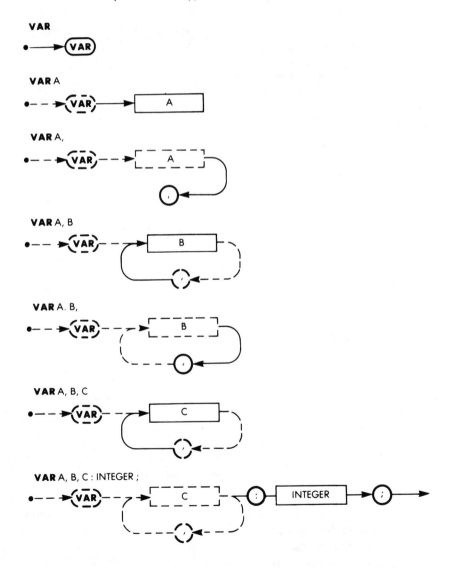

VAR

VAR A

VAR A,

VAR A, B

VAR A. B,

VAR A, B, C

VAR A, B, C : INTEGER ;

Figure 3.5:   Following the Syntax Diagram

Implicit Type Declaration (Constants)

A *constant* is an actual value of a given data type. In the case of integers, the following are constants: 22, 3, 15. In the case of characters, examples of constants are: 'S' or 'T'. Symbolic constants are used whenever it is convenient to represent a value by a name. For example, the following symbolic constants could be useful:

        PI = 3.14159
        SALESTAX = 6.5

The CONST declaration is used to define a symbolic constant. It defines the type of the constant identifier *implicitly*; i.e., the symbolic constant is given the type of the value assigned to it. For example:

        CONST I = 2;

defines I as an integer constant (and assigns I the value 2).

        CONST NAME = 'ABC25?';

defines NAME as a *character string* constant (a sequence of characters). Here is another example:

        CONST TWO = 2;
        VAR A : INTEGER;
        BEGIN
            A := TWO;

The first line in this program defines the constant named TWO as an INTEGER, and assigns it the value 2. The symbol TWO may now be used in the program as a constant with the value 2.

As a typical example, it may be desirable to define PI = 3.14159 as a constant. In general, if a number or a string of characters is used more than once in a program, or if this number or string might be changed throughout the program in a later version, it is advantageous to declare this number or string of characters as a constant at the beginning of the program. In this way, if the value of the constant has to be changed throughout the program, then only one statement has to be changed. This technique leads to what is called a "cleaner program," i.e., a program less prone to errors in the event of future changes.

In summary, constant values may be used freely within the statements as long as the constants are expressed as *literals*, i.e., as values or characters. However, if a name is used for a constant, this name must be explicitly declared in a CONST declaration.

As another example of a syntax diagram, the formal syntax of a constant is shown in Figure 3.6.

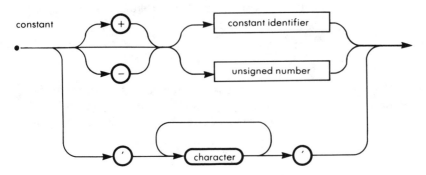

Figure 3.6:   Syntax of a Constant

User-Defined TYPE

Pascal provides standard type identifiers such as INTEGER, REAL, BOOLEAN, and CHAR. However, it is often convenient to use different names for these standard types, or even to create names for new types that the programmer may construct.

The TYPE definition allows the programmer to define an identifier as being the name of a new type. For example:

TYPE   SCORE = INTEGER;

This definition defines the new type SCORE (an INTEGER type). SCORE may at first appear to be of little value if it is used only to relabel the existing type designator INTEGER; however, its value will become apparent after we have described the mechanisms used for constructing new data types in Pascal in Chapter 8.

Here is an additional example that demonstrates the convenience of renaming a type:

TYPE   DAYOFWEEK, MONTH = INTEGER;

The following variable declaration then becomes legal:

VAR   PAYDAY : DAYOFWEEK;
         BIRTHMONTH : MONTH;

This is not just a mnemonic convenience, but a syntactic one. We will later see that DAYOFWEEK can be restricted to the values 1 through 7. Then, whenever a variable of type PAYDAY is used, the compiler will automatically check that the value of the variable is an integer between 1 and 7.

The TYPE definition is, therefore, a powerful facility for defining new types, especially when the new type is associated with a set of values. Many examples will be provided in the following chapters.

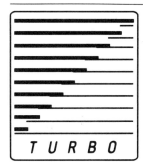

TURBO PASCAL STANDARD TYPES

In addition to the four standard data types in Standard Pascal, Turbo Pascal provides the BYTE scalar type. The BYTE type is a subrange of the INTEGER type, and can be assigned values between 0 and 255. It can be used where ever the INTEGER type is legal.

TURBO PASCAL STANDARD FUNCTIONS

Turbo Pascal includes a number of standard functions additional to those in Standard Pascal.

Standard Functions for Integers

These three functions operate on integer arguments and return integer results.

HI(I)   Shifts high order byte of I to low order byte in result (same as I shr 8)

LO(I)   Isolates low order byte of I (same as I and $00FF)

SWAP(I)   Exchanges high and low order bytes of I

Standard Functions for Real Numbers

These two functions operate on real or integer arguments and return the results as real numbers.

FRAC(R)   Fractional portion of R

INT(R)   Integer portion of R

Other Standard Functions

RANDOM   Returns a random real number in the range $0 <= num < 1$

RANDOM(I)   Returns a random integer in the range $0 <= num < I$

SIZEOF(Name)   Returns the space used in memory in bytes for variable or type (Name)

UPCASE(ch)   Returns the uppercase letter corresponding to (ch) if (ch) is a lowercase letter, otherwise returns (ch)

TURBO PASCAL BOOLEAN OPERATORS

Turbo Pascal includes the Boolean operator XOR in addition to the three Standard Pascal Boolean operators discussed earlier in the chapter. The truth table for the XOR operator is shown in Figure 3.7. (A XOR B) is TRUE if either A or B is TRUE. It is FALSE if A and B are either both TRUE or both FALSE.

TURBO PASCAL CONSTANTS

PI is a predefined real constant in Turbo Pascal which is equal to 3.1415926536E+00, and need not be declared.

MAXINT is a predefined integer constant in Turbo Pascal equal to 32767.

INTEGER OVERFLOW

Integer overflow occurs when the intermediate or final result of an integer operation or expression exceeds the maximum integer value (MAXINT) available on a particular system. When an overflow occurs, a part of the result is either lost or is shifted into the sign bit of the integer value.

A	B	A XOR B
F	F	F
T	F	T
F	T	T
T	T	F

Figure 3.7: XOR Truth Table

As was mentioned above, MAXINT for Turbo Pascal is 32767. In Turbo Pascal, an integer overflow condition does not generate an error. For example, one way to calculate the number of yards in a mile is:

yards = feet per mile * inches per foot / inches per yard

or:

yards : = (5280 * 12) div 36

The result should be 1760 yards per mile. However, in Turbo Pascal the result is −60. This is because the intermediate result of (5280 * 12) is 63360, which exceeds MAXINT. Turbo Pascal returns a value of −2176 for the expression (5280 * 12). The solution is either to revise the expression to prevent overflows, or to use real variables and constants instead of integers. The above expression can be rewritten as:

yards : = 5280 div 3

or as a real expression:

yards : = 5280.0 * (12.0 / 36.0)

and can be converted back to integer if required with the TRUNC or ROUND real to integer transfer functions.

It is the programmer's responsibility to insure than intermediate and final results in integer expressions will not cause an overflow condition.

Note also that when converting between real and integer, intermediate expression values should be kept as small as possible by careful arrangement of the order of evaluation of the expression's parameters (as in the real expression above). This approach will reduce the possibility of rounding and precision errors in the final integer result.

SPECIAL VERSIONS OF TURBO PASCAL

Two special versions of Turbo Pascal are available for those who have special computational requirements.

8087 Math Coprocessor

Turbo 8087 is a 16-bit version of the compiler for use on computers equipped with the 8087 numeric coprocessor. It performs real math several times faster than the standard version and has an increased numeric range and precision for scientific and other number-crunching applications.

BCD Real Arithmetic

Turbo BCD is a 16-bit version of the compiler for use in business and financial applications where increased precision is required. This version eliminates the cumulative rounding errors that can occur in the standard Turbo Pascal when performing most types of binary arithmetic operations, by using BCD real arithmetic.

SUMMARY

The four fundamental data types in Pascal are called the scalar types: integer, real, character and Boolean. Specific operators and functions are defined for each data type.

In Pascal, the type of a variable must always be defined before it is used. The basic declaration is the VAR declaration, which assigns a type to a variable.

The way in which additional type names may be created with TYPE and how constants are declared with CONST was also shown.

Knowledge of the four scalar types is fundamental to using Pascal. All four types will be used extensively in the chapters that follow. If you do not feel sufficiently familiar with the definitions, read this chapter once again. Once you feel that you understand the material presented, move on to the next chapter, where we will construct expressions and statements, and begin writing actual programs.

EXERCISES

3-1: Define the term variable.

3-2: Is an identifier always a variable?

3-3: Are the following legal integers?

   1: 24   2: − 32   3: − 200,000   4: 1.24

3-4: What is the result of:
   1: TRUNC(32.12)   2: ROUND(0.5)   3: ROUND(32.12)

3-5: Are the following legal reals?

   1: 1234   2: 24,232.00   3: 1.234   4: .12

3-6: Assuming that characters are internally represented in ASCII code (as per Appendix G) compute:

   1: ORD('f')   2: CHR(8)   3: PRED('z')   4: SUCC('a')

3-7: Assume that A is TRUE and B is FALSE. What is the value of:

   1: A AND B   2: A OR B   3: NOT B

3-8: When is it legal to write:

A := TWENTYFOUR

3-9: What operations can be done on characters (excluding the relational operators and the reserved functions)?

3-10: What is the type of the result of the following expressions:

1: A < B   2: 3.0/1.5
3: (1 + 6) = (6 + 1)   4: 5 * 6 DIV 3

3-11: Compute the result of:

1: TRUNC(1.75)   2: ROUND(1.75)
3: TRUNC(2.3)   4: ROUND(2.3)

3-12: Give examples for each of the four scalar types.

CHAPTER 4

EXPRESSIONS
AND STATEMENTS

INTRODUCTION

The four types of scalar variables available in Pascal, as well as the operators and standard functions that may be used with each type, have been presented. In this chapter, we will show how combinations of variables and operators may be used to build expressions to perform calculations. Expressions will be used in the programs presented throughout the text and should be studied carefully. Next, we will introduce our first statement: the assignment statement. We will then be able to write simple programs.

EXPRESSIONS

Loosely defined, an *expression* consists of a sequence of terms separated by operators. The following are examples of expressions:

```
10 + 6
6 * 21
A + 16
A – B + 6
```

Note that when writing expressions, all the operators used in an expression must be valid for the type of data that they operate upon. The formal syntax for an expression is shown in Appendix F. Because the formal definition is complex, we will not present the complete definition here, but rather a simplified one. In this chapter, we will define typical expressions that will be used in subsequent chapters. Then, as we become more knowledgeable about Pascal, we will complete this definition by indicating other possibilities that can be used to specify valid expressions.

So far, the informal definition given for an expression is a sequence of constants or variables separated by valid operators. Let us now refine this definition by listing the four basic rules that must be used when constructing expressions.

1. A single constant or variable is a valid expression. It may be preceded by a plus or a minus sign. Examples are: 22, ALPHA, – 2.5.

2. A sequence of terms (variables, constants, functions) separated by operators is a valid expression. Examples are: 1.1 + 2.25 – 3.2 or A + B * 6.

3. Two operators adjacent to each other are not valid. Parentheses must be used. For example, to multiply 2 by − 3, we may not write: 2 * − 3, as this would be confusing. Instead, we must write 2 * (− 3).

4. Finally, any variable or constant may be replaced by a function call. In the case of Boolean (logical) expressions we will see that any expression may also be preceded by "NOT" and be valid.

We will now examine in detail the two most important types of expressions: arithmetic expressions and Boolean expressions.

ARITHMETIC EXPRESSIONS

Recall that the basic rule in an arithmetic expression is that all types must be consistent. In an *integer expression,* all variables, constants and results of functions must be integers. In a *real expression*, all variables, constants and results of functions must be real.

However, there is an exception: integers may be used in a real expression. Integer values will be converted automatically into a real type. For example, if N is a real, writing N + 1 will result in 1 being internally converted to 1.0. However, when learning how to program, this practice is not encouraged as it may lead to errors.

Let us present examples of simple expressions using a binary operator and two operands. A *binary operator*, also called a *dyadic* operator, is an operator that requires two operands. Multiply and divide are binary operators. A *unary*, or *monadic* operator requires only a single operand. For example, the monadic plus and minus signs are unary operators. If we assume that I and J are of type integer, the following are valid integer expressions:

        J + 1
        I + J
        I * J
        I DIV 2

And the following are invalid integer expressions:

        I + 1.0   (1.0 is not an integer)
        .01 * J   (.01 is not an integer)

Let us now examine examples of *valid real expressions*. A and B are assumed to be of type real.

        A + 10   (the integer 10 is automatically converted to real)
        A * B
        B / 1.5

Here are examples of *invalid real expressions:*

A * * B	(two multiplication symbols in sequence)
A DIV 2	(DIV is *integer* division)

Operator Precedence

An ambiguity may arise when specifying a sequence of operations. For example:

A := 2 + 3 * 2

The above instruction probably means A := 2 + (3 * 2) = 2 + 6 = 8. However, it might mean (using the rules of many pocket calculators):

A := (2 + 3) * 2 = 5 * 2 = 10

"2 + 3 * 2"is an *arithmetic expression.* In any programming language, it is important to specify the order in which expressions are evaluated. In Pascal, a *precedence* technique is used. In the case of our example, * is said to have a higher precedence than + . As a result, the multiplication will be performed first:

3 * 2 (= 6)

Then the addition will be performed:

2 + 6

Each Pascal operator has a precedence level. When two operators are adjacent, the one with the higher precedence is executed first. Whenever an ambiguity remains, the expression is evaluated from left to right. The following list shows the various operators and their priority level:

— The relational operators (=, <, >, <=, >=, < >) have the lowest precedence.

— Next come: +, −, OR

— Then: *, /, DIV, MOD, AND

— At a higher priority is: NOT

— At the highest precedence level is: ( )

For example:

The expression:	Means:	The result is:
2 * 3 + 2	(2 * 3) + 2	8
2 * 3 + 2 * 4	(2 * 3) + (2 * 4)	14
6 * 2 DIV 3	(6 * 2) DIV 3	4
3 + 4 − (5 * 2 − 1)	(3 + 4) − ((5 * 2) − 1)	−2
4.0/3.0 * 2.0	(4.0/3.0) * 2.0	2.6666

In summary, remember that parentheses have the highest precedence, followed by multiplication and division, and then addition and subtraction.

USING STANDARD FUNCTIONS

We have indicated that an expression consists of variables, constants, or functions separated by operators. Thus far, in our examples, we have used only variables or constants. However, we have seen in the previous chapter that a number of standard functions are predefined in Pascal. These functions may also be used in expressions. A function is called (used) by writing the name of the function followed by an argument enclosed in parentheses. For example, the mathematical expression for a quadratic equation is:

$$AX^2 + BX + C$$

where A and X are assumed to be real variables, may be expressed as:

$$A * SQR(X) + B * X + C$$

where SQR() is the square function. The computer looks at the argument within the parentheses, obtains its value, then computes the value of the function.

Similarly, the root of a quadratic equation will depend upon the determinant. The value of this determinant is:

$$B^2 - 4AC$$

and the square root of the determinant will be expressed as:

$$SQRT(SQR(B) - 4.0 * A * C)$$

where SQRT( ) denotes the square root function. The standard functions provided by Pascal are listed in Figure 4.1.

A function may be placed in an expression anywhere we might place a variable or a constant of the same type.

When using a standard function, do not forget to watch for the data type of the arguments of the function as well as the data type of the result. The argument type must be valid for the function. The result type must be valid for the type of expression considered. These two types (argument and result) are not necessarily the same. For example, the ROUND function requires a real argument and will yield an integer result. The rules relating to data types must always be strictly respected. A summary of the legal data types for each Pascal function is shown in Figure 4.1.

FUNCTION	OPERAND(S)	RESULT
ABS	integer, real	same as operand
ARCTAN	integer, real	real
CHR	integer	character
COS	integer, real	real
EOF	text file	Boolean
EOLN	text file	Boolean
EXP	integer, real	real
LN	integer, real	real
ODD	integer	Boolean
ORD	scalar except real	integer
PRED	scalar except real	same as operand
ROUND	real	integer
SIN	integer, real	real
SQR	integer, real	same as operand
SQRT	integer, real	real
SUCC	scalar except real	same as operand
TRUNC	real	integer

Figure 4.1:   Standard Functions

SUMMARY OF ARITHMETIC EXPRESSIONS

An arithmetic expression may be loosely defined as a succession of operators and operands. Standard Pascal functions may be used instead of variables. User-defined functions may also be used. They will be examined in Chapter 7.

Finally, in order to eliminate any ambiguity when evaluating an expression, each operator has a precedence level.

BOOLEAN EXPRESSIONS

We learned in the previous chapter that the three logical operators AND, OR, and NOT operate only on Boolean values (TRUE or FALSE). They may be used to create a Boolean expression. In addition, the relational operators may be used to compare any two real variables and will result in a Boolean value TRUE or FALSE as well. They may also be used within a Boolean expression.

In the case of Boolean expressions, Pascal imposes an additional requirement. All subexpressions must be enclosed in parentheses unless they start with a NOT.

Let us assume that K, L, M, and N have been defined as Boolean variables. The following are examples of Boolean expressions:

> K AND L   (a Boolean operator is used)
> NOT K
> M = N   (a relational operator is used)

More complex examples of Boolean expressions are:

> K AND M = NOT N   (three operators are used)
> I * J = 2   (an arithmetic expression is compared to 2)
> K AND M OR NOT N
> (A = B) OR (C = D) AND (A – C = 0) (subexpressions are parenthesized)

The rules of precedence also apply. For example:

> B > C + 5 will be evaluated as B > (C + 5).

In this last example, the expression on the right of the relational operator is an arithmetic expression and therefore does not have to be enclosed in parentheses. The + operation has a higher precedence than the relational operator and will be evaluated first. However, when in doubt, do not hesitate to use parentheses. They will improve the readability of the program and avoid errors.

THE BASIC RULES OF BOOLEAN ALGEBRA

When using Boolean variables, it is useful to know some of the basic rules of Boolean algebra that may be used to simplify Boolean expressions. For example:

> NOT(NOT K) is equivalent to K
>
> NOT(J OR K) is equivalent to (NOT J) AND (NOT K)
>
> NOT(J AND K) is equivalent to (NOT J) OR (NOT K).

Similarly,

> NOT(J < K) is equivalent to J >= K
>
> NOT(J <> K) is equivalent to J = K, and vice versa.

When testing the equality of numbers, do not test a real number for strict equality if this number was the result of a computation. This is because the computer uses a fixed number of bits internally to represent any number, which means that the computer will represent any real number with a limited precision. It may happen that a real number should be equal, for example, to 1.0. However, internally, this number might be stored as 0.999999. Equality is defined only within the limits of the precision of the representation being used. If you must test for equality, the correct way of doing it is to verify that the difference between the two numbers is less than 10^{-n} where n specifies the precision of the comparison. For example, using n = 3 insures that the two numbers are within $10^{-3} = 1/1000$ of each other. In other words, the difference between two computed numbers will almost never be exactly zero.

STATEMENTS

We have indicated that each Pascal program must include *at least one statement* and usually includes many statements. The formal syntax for a statement in Pascal is shown in Appendix F. It is rather complex. We will, therefore, introduce the various types of statements in turn as we go along. We have already encountered two types of statements in our first two program examples. In our first example, we encountered the statement:

WRITELN('HELLO');

This is an *output statement*. Input and output statements will be described in the next chapter.

The next example we encountered was:

TOTAL := A + B;

This is an *assignment statement*. The assignment statement is probably the most important type of statement. The formal syntax of an assignment statement is shown in Figure 4.2.

Figure 4.2: Syntax of the Assignment Statement

The statement consists of a variable identifier followed by the symbol ':=', followed by a valid expression. The symbol ':=' is called the *assignment operator*. The assignment means that the expression on the right will be evaluated and that the resulting value will be assigned (given) to the variable on the left. In other words, the computed value of the expression will become the value of the variable from now on. In order for this statement to be meaningful, the expression must naturally evaluate to a correct value. This implies in particular that any variables contained within the expression already have a value assigned to them. For example, the following are valid assignments:

```
A : = 2.0;
B : = A + 4.0;        (* A has been defined above *)
C : = 2.0 * 3.0 + 4.0;
```

The assignment may be performed on any data type. For example, if the variable LETTER has been declared as type CHAR, the following is a valid assignment:

```
LETTER : = 'A';
```

Similarly, if I and J are integers, the following are valid assignments:

```
I : = 2;
J : = 2 + 2;
```

It is legal, but not recommended, to assign an integer value to a real variable. In that case, the integer value will be automatically converted to a real number.

As another example, assuming that I and J are of type integer and that Z is of type Boolean, the following is a valid assignment:

```
Z : = I < J;
```

The assignment operator ':=' must be distinguished from the relational operator '=' ('=' tests for equality). This is important to remember if you have programmed in BASIC, where both operators are represented by the same symbol (=).

The Empty Statement

The empty statement is only explained here in order to cover the subject completely, and will not be used in this book. A non-existent statement may generally be used wherever a statement is legal. It is called the *empty statement* and includes no symbols and has no effect.

For example:

```
A : = 2; ;
```

includes two statements:

        A := 2;
        The empty statement (terminated by ;)

One of the effects of the empty statement is to allow the use of spurious ';' where they are not required, without causing a syntax error. For example:

        A := 2;
    END.

is legal, even though the semi-colon is not necessary. The semi-colon is interpreted as an empty statement.

The Compound Statement

   Generally, a group of statements may be used wherever a single statement is legal. Such a group of statements is called a *compound statement*. A compound statement must be bracketed by BEGIN and END. Here is an example:

    BEGIN
        I := 3;
        J := 4;
        WRITELN(I,J)
    END;

Such compound statements will be used in Chapter 6 as we use control structures. A semi-colon is not necessary after BEGIN or before END. The semi-colon is used only to separate statements, not to terminate them.

TURBO PASCAL STANDARD ARITHMETIC FUNCTIONS

   In addition to the Standard Pascal functions listed in Figure 4.1, Turbo Pascal supports several other standard functions. They are listed in Figure 4.3.

TURBO PASCAL BOOLEAN EXPRESSIONS

   As was mentioned in the previous chapter, Turbo Pascal also includes the XOR Boolean operator.

FUNCTION	OPERAND(S)	RESULT
FRAC	integer, real	real
INT	integer, real	real
HI	integer	integer
LO	integer	integer
RANDOM	integer	integer
SIZEOF	var or type	integer
SWAP	integer	integer

Figure 4.3: ***Additional Turbo Pascal Functions***

SUMMARY

We have now learned how to combine variables, constants, operators and functions into valid expressions. We have seen that types may not be mixed freely and that consistency of types must be used in any expression. We have learned to resolve possible ambiguities in complex expressions by using the precedence of operators or parentheses. And finally, we have learned to use one of the most important types of statements, the assignment. In order to receive and display data, we will need to study another important type of statement: the Input and Output statements, which will allow us to communicate with the user of the program. This will be the topic of the next chapter.

EXERCISES

4-1: *Evaluate the following expressions:*

*1. 1 * 4 * 2 − 4 * 2 + 3*
*2. 1.1 * 2.2 / 1.1 * 3.3 / 2.2 − 5.5*
*3. SQR(2 + 3 * 4)*

4-2: *Evaluate the following expressions:*

*1. 1 + 2 * 3 + 10 DIV 5*
*2. (6 DIV 3 − 2) * 8*
*3. 12.0 / 4.0 − 3.0 * 3.0*
*4. 16 * 2 − 8 * 2 + 4 * 4*

4-3: *Are the following assignments legal?*

1. A := 2 + 3.0;
2. A + 2 := B;
3. 3 := 2 + 1;
4. A :− 2 − (−(−1 + 2) − 3) − 2 * 4;

4-4: *Are the following assignments legal?*

1. A := 2 * −3;
2. B := (−6.73) 2;
3. Q := 2 + B = 7 * 12;
4. R := 6.4 DIV 8;
5. Q := 2 + B := 8;

4-5: *Translate the following mathematical expressions into Pascal expressions, using appropriate functions.*

1. $3x^2 + 2x − 2$
2. $|4a|$
3. $\sqrt{6a − 2x^2}$

4-6: *What is the effect of the following program?*

```
PROGRAM BOOLEANTEST(OUTPUT);
VAR P,Q,R,S,RESULT : BOOLEAN;
BEGIN (* BOOLEANTEST *)
     P := TRUE;
     Q := P;
     R := FALSE;
     S := R;
     WRITELN;WRITELN; (* SKIP TWO LINES *)
     RESULT := NOT(P);
     WRITELN(RESULT);
     RESULT := NOT(NOT(Q));
     WRITELN(RESULT);
     RESULT := Q OR S;
     WRITELN(RESULT);
     RESULT := P AND S;
     WRITELN(RESULT);
     RESULT := P AND Q AND R;
     WRITELN(RESULT);
     RESULT := (P OR R) AND Q;
     WRITELN(RESULT
END (* BOOLEANTEST *)
```

CHAPTER 5

INPUT
AND OUTPUT

INTRODUCTION

Input and output statements are used in nearly every program in Pascal so that values may be entered and displayed or printed. In the first program example in Chapter 1, a WRITELN statement was used to display a message ("HELLO"). This is an output statement. Similarly, a READ(A,B) statement was later used to read the values of two variables A and B typed at the keyboard.

From a hardware standpoint, input statements and output statements allow the program to communicate with a computer peripheral such as a terminal, a printer or a disk. An *input statement* is used to read characters from the terminal. An *output statement* is used to print or display characters on the terminal.

From a logical standpoint, all of the terminals are considered as *files* by the program. The various types of input/output statements provided by Pascal will be described in this chapter.

COMMUNICATING WITH A FILE OR THE TERMINAL

Input and output statements operate on *files*. For our purposes, a file is defined here as a sequential collection of information that may be referred to by name. Since they fulfill these requirements, the keyboard, the screen and the printer are considered as files. Since we have not yet learned about generalized files, the examples given in this chapter will only communicate with the terminal. The terminal is viewed by the program as two files, named INPUT and OUTPUT. This is the purpose of the (INPUT,OUTPUT) file declaration in the program header. We will use the computer keyboard as our input medium. Our output medium will be the terminal screen or the printer (if a printing terminal is available).

The concept of a file is illustrated by the diagram in Figure 5.1.

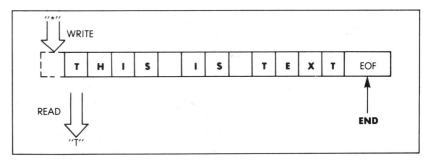

Figure 5.1: The Concept of a File

The diagram in Figure 5.1 shows how a READ operation might copy the value of one element of the file, (here the letter "T"), into a program variable and how a WRITE operation can transfer a value from the program into the file. The file is terminated by a special marker, called EOF (End Of File). Let us now look at some input statements.

READ AND READLN

READ and READLN statements are called *input statements*. These two statements serve to read values from an input file, the keyboard in our case. An example of a READ statement is:

```
PROGRAM SUM(INPUT,OUTPUT);
VAR A,B,TOTAL:INTEGER;
BEGIN
    READ(A,B);
```

In this example the input medium is the keyboard: the values of A and B are read from the keyboard. This choice is communicated to the computer by including the word 'INPUT' in the program definition:

```
PROGRAM SUM(INPUT,OUTPUT);
```

The READ and READLN statements must be written in a specific manner. As shown in the example above, the READ or READLN is normally followed by a left parenthesis, one or more variables separated by commas, and terminated by a right parenthesis. The result of a READ or READLN is to read values from the INPUT and assign them to variables. Here are additional examples of READ and READLN statements:

```
READ(A,B,C);
READLN(TAXRATE,GROSSINCOME);
```

Data typed in at the keyboard may be any type valid for the type of variable that is used. In all cases, except when *characters* are used as input, data may be typed in and separated by one or more spaces, or a new line.

The difference between a READ statement and a READLN statement is that the READ statement allows the next READ to continue to read values on the same line, while the READLN statement will move to a new line after it is executed. The difference between the two types of read instructions evolves from the time when most computer input was accomplished through punched cards and each punched card stored one line of text. These punched cards were usually divided into fields containing values. In many cases, it was desirable for the program to read only (for example) four fields out of the ten fields present on a data card. In such a case, the READLN statement would be used to force the card reader to eject to the next card (the next line). However, READ can also be used in an interactive environment to read characters and respond on the same line. Examples will illustrate the use of READ and READLN.

An example of a READ statement is:

READ(A,B,C,D);

The data will appear on the terminal exactly as we type it in, for example it might appear in the following form:

2.0   3.5   −6.1   2.3

The line is terminated with blanks, or with a "return" (a special key on the keyboard).

The same data read with the following statements:

READ(A,B);
READLN(C);
READ(D);

would appear at the terminal like this:

2.0   3.5   −6.1
2.3

Note how the READLN statement causes the display to "move up" after input, so that "2.3" will automatically appear on the next line.

When reading numerical data, spaces and new lines added between numbers are ignored. When reading a real number, the two usual notations may be used: decimal and scientific.

For example, the real 12.0 may be read as:

12.0

or equivalently, as:

+1.2E+01

or even as:

12

An integer may be read as a real.

When reading character-type data, each character is significant. Once all of the characters on a line have been read, an attempt to read the next character, past the last character on the line will yield a space. That is, reading a "carriage return" yields a space.

As stated, all of the characters on a line do not have to be read. For example, the program may read only the first ten characters of a line with a READ, and proceed on to the next line by specifying a READLN. The remaining characters (past the first ten characters) will then be ignored.

Here is an example program with various types being read:

```
PROGRAM INEXAMPLE(INPUT,OUTPUT);
VAR I,J : INTEGER;
     A,B : REAL;
     M,N : CHAR;
BEGIN
     READ(I,J);
     READ(M,N);
     READLN(A,B)
END.
```

Here is a possible input at the keyboard:

```
4       92SY
1.23  −5.6
```

Here is another example:

```
PROGRAM INEX2(INPUT);
VAR I,J : INTEGER;
     A,B : REAL;
     M,N : CHAR;
BEGIN
     READ(A,M,N,I)
END.
```

Here are four possible inputs and the resulting values of the variables:

INPUT	A	M	N	I
1.25Y2344	1.25	'Y'	'2'	344
+1.2E+05Y2344	1.2E+05	'Y'	'2'	344
1.2E05Y2344	1.2E+05	'Y'	'2'	344
1.25Y 2344	1.25	'Y'	' '	2344

Terminating the Input

Two standard functions are provided to facilitate input: EOLN and EOF. Their role will be briefly described here. However, they will be described in detail in Chapter 11, as they are most often uses with files. with control structures.

It may be necessary to read a sequence of numbers or characters on a line for which we do not know the precise length. The EOLN function is provided for this purpose. The EOLN (End Of Line) function is a standard Boolean function which is TRUE when the end of line is detected; otherwise it is FALSE. Thus, we can keep reading until the end of line function becomes TRUE. When it becomes TRUE, the complete line has been read.

Another standard function, called EOF (End-Of-File), will detect the end-of-file. This function corresponds, for example, to the case where the last card has been read by the card-reader. The function EOF(INPUT) may be used to ensure that all data has in fact been read. EOF by itself means EOF(INPUT). EOF becomes TRUE once all data has been read.

The following is an example using EOF and EOLN. This example is only shown here for completeness and you will better understand this example after you have studied Chapter 6. This program will successively read each character in a file line-by-line, and then process each character. In the example, "process" stands for any valid Pascal statements that may be used to process the character C.

```
PROGRAM  ALLTHEFILE(INPUT,OUTPUT);
VAR C : CHAR;
BEGIN
     WHILE NOT EOF DO
          BEGIN
          WHILE NOT EOLN DO
                    BEGIN
                    READ(C);
                    process(C)
                    END; (* WHILE *)
          READLN
          END (* WHILE *)
END. (* ALLTHEFILE *)
```

WRITE AND WRITELN

We have already encountered several examples of the WRITELN instruction in previous chapters:

```
PROGRAM GREETING(OUTPUT);        (* PROGRAM HEADING *)
(* A SIMPLE PASCAL PROGRAM *)
BEGIN
     WRITELN('HELLO')                  (* STATEMENT *)
END.
```

and:

```
PROGRAM SUM(INPUT,OUTPUT);
VAR A,B,TOTAL : INTEGER;
BEGIN
     WRITELN('ENTER TWO NUMBERS TO BE ADDED...');
     READ(A,B);
     TOTAL := A + B;
     WRITELN('THE SUM OF ',A,' AND ',B,' IS ',TOTAL)
END.
```

Like the READ and READLN statements, the WRITE and WRITELN statements are normally followed by a left parenthesis and a list of strings or values to be printed, separated by commas, and terminated by a right parenthesis. As we can see in the first example above a character string enclosed in single quotes will be printed *as it is stated*, including any blanks that it may contain. In the second example, we can see that variables will be evaluated and that their *values* will be printed. When printing a character string, remember that in order to print out a quote, the quote itself must be enclosed in quotes.

A Boolean value will be printed as either TRUE or FALSE. A *real* value will be printed in *exponential notation*. All items to be printed in the list within the parentheses will be printed on the same line. If several WRITE instructions are used in succession, then all of these items will be printed *on the same line*. Using WRITELN will force the printer to move to the beginning of the following line *after* printing. For example:

```
WRITE('THIS IS AN ');
WRITE('EXAMPLE');
```

will result in:

```
THIS IS AN EXAMPLE
```

and:

```
WRITELN('THIS IS AN')
WRITE('EXAMPLE');
```

will result in:

```
THIS IS AN
EXAMPLE
```

Here are some examples of output with various types of data:

```
VAR I,J,K : INTEGER;
     A,B : REAL;
     C,D : CHAR;
     U,V : BOOLEAN;
(...program statements...)
I := 1;                              (* the value of I will print as 1 *)
J := I + 1;                          (* J will print as 2 *)
K := 5;                              (* K will print as 5 *)
A := 1.1 + 3.5 * 2.0;                (* A will print as 8.1 *)
B := A/2;                            (* B will print as 4.05 *)
C := '?';                            (* C will print as ? *)
D := '=';                            (* D will print as = *)
U := I = J;                          (* U will print as FALSE *)
V := A > B;                          (* V will print as TRUE *)
WRITELN('INTEGERS ARE',I,J,K);
WRITELN('REALS ARE',A,B);
WRITELN('OTHERS ARE',C,' ',D,' ',U,V);
```

The output will be the following three lines:

```
INTEGERS ARE       1      2      5
REALS ARE       8.1000000000E+00       4.0500000000E+00
OTHERS ARE? = FALSE       TRUE
```

Note that spaces have been automatically added to the left of integers, reals, and Booleans. This is called an automatic output formatting feature of the Pascal compiler.

Formatting the Output

When printing a given data type such as INTEGER, REAL, OR BOOLEAN, each Pascal implementation uses a standard number of columns. Unfortunately, the conventions vary with each installation. For example, an implementation might use twelve columns for integers, ten columns for a Boolean, and twenty-four columns for a real number.

It is often desirable to produce neatly tabulated data. In this case, it becomes necessary to override the standard number of columns provided by the particular implementation. Therefore each item to be printed may be followed by a colon and an integer (value or expression). This positive integer specifies the minimum field width for that item. If the item to be printed requires fewer characters, it will be preceded by leading blanks. If the item should require more space, then as many characters as necessary will be used. For example:

```
WRITE('THE TEXT IS RIGHT': 18);
WRITELN('ALIGNED': 8);
```

will produce:

THE TEXT IS RIGHT ALIGNED.

The first field specification allocates eighteen spaces to 'THE TEXT IS RIGHT'. This will be printed as:

bTHE TEXT IS RIGHT

where b denotes a blank.

The second field specification allocates eight spaces to 'ALIGNED' so that is will be printed on the same line as 'bALIGNED', where b denotes a blank.

Note: in some installations, the first character of a line is not printed, as it is interpreted as a command to the printer. In such a case, be careful never to use this first character to represent data.

In the case of REAL items only, a *dual* field specification may be used with a colon followed by an INTEGER, followed by another colon, followed by an INTEGER. The first integer still specifies the minimum field width. If the second field specification is used, the number will be printed in fixed-point notation rather than exponential notation and the integer value specifies the number of digits to be printed after the decimal point. Here is an example:

```
VAR I : INTEGER;
    A : REAL;
    C : CHAR;
BEGIN
    I := 12;
    A := 2.1;
    C := '?';
    WRITE('INDENT': 10 , I : 3 , A : 4 : 1 , C : 2)
END.
```

This will print:

Blanks are inserted to the left where needed. This format may be used to obtain neatly aligned printouts, such as tables.

Other control facilities may be provided depending upon the installation. Most printers will not print more than 132 characters per line. Also, in many cases, the first character in each line is not printed and has a special meaning:

— A space means a line feed (single spacing).
— A + means overprinting (no line feed).
— A 0 means double spacing.
— A 1 means "go to the top of the next page."

However, these conventions depend upon the installation. Generally a PAGE command is available to move to the next page.

In order to skip a line, a standard programming "trick" may be used. For example:

```
WRITELN('ONE');
WRITELN;
WRITELN ('THREE');
```

produces the following output:

ONE

THREE

with a blank line in the middle.

Finally, an expression may be used in an output statement instead of a value. For example:

WRITELN('ONE + TWO = ', 1 + 2);

produces the output:

ONE + TWO =   3

This also applies to the field specifications. For example:

WRITE(A : I + 1 : J + K);

might produce

−12.41

TURBO PASCAL INPUT/OUTPUT

Turbo Pascal input/output facilities are described in detail in Chapter 11. The READ and WRITE statements in Turbo Pascal used for communication with the keyboard and screen are essentially the same as in Standard Pascal, aside from the following exceptions. Some slight differences also occur with respect to the KEYPRESSED function, and the Page statement.

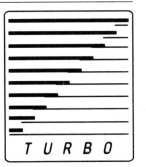

WRITE and WRITELN

Unlike Standard Pascal, Turbo Pascal does not use a preset column size for all unformatted output. Specifically, leading and trailing spaces are not added to output values, except when the output is a real number. Positive reals have two leading spaces and negative reals have one leading space. Reals do not have trailing spaces.

When the WRITE and WRITELN statements are used to output integer and Boolean values without a format specification (also called a *write parameter*) formatting spaces are not included. (See pages 70–72 for more on format specifications.)

Real values without a format specification are displayed in exponential format in a field 18 characters wide, in the following form:

R >= 0.0 bbn.nnnnnnnnnnEsnn

R < 0.0   b−n.nnnnnnnnnnEsnn

where

    b = blank
    n = number (0–9)
    s = sign (+ or −)
    E = letter "E" for exponent

If a format specification is provided for numeric values, it is ignored if it is smaller than that required to display the value. The minimum width for real numbers in exponential format is seven characters for R $>=$ 0.0 and eight for R $<$ 0.0.

A character value with a format specification N will be output in right-justified format in a field N characters wide and preceded by $N-1$ blanks. This form (ch:N) can be used to format output reports and screens. For example,

    WRITELN(' ':20,'TITLE');

displays 20 spaces followed by TITLE.

The KEYPRESSED Function

Turbo Pascal provides a function called KEYPRESSED that tests whether an input character is waiting to be read in the keyboard buffer. It returns a value of TRUE if a key has been pressed on the keyboard since the last READ or READLN statement was executed, otherwise it returns FALSE.

The PAGE Statement

The Standard Pascal PAGE statement is not implemented in Turbo Pascal.

SUMMARY

The input and output instructions are quite easy to use. The formatting of the actual output becomes a little more complex. Practice is strongly recommended to understand the actual formatting of any output.

All of the basic concepts required to write simple programs have now been introduced. The power of the computer does not simply lie in its capability to carry out arithmetic or other operations, but also in its capability to make decisions and execute different actions based upon the results of tests. One of the most important characteristics of a computer program is the ability to change the way in which a program is executed depending upon values which have been read or computed. In the next chapter, we will study the ways to alter the flow of control within a program.

EXERCISES _____

5-1: Write a program to print out the squares of the first ten integers.

5-2: Read ten real numbers, and print them out in reverse order.

5-3: Read the first ten characters in two consecutive lines of text, then write them out.

5-4: Print a neatly formatted table of squares and square-roots. Label it. Use dashes and exclamation points to draw horizontal and vertical lines.

5-5: Compute the sales table that applies to your state. Prices may range from $0.01 to $100.00. Once a price is typed in, the program should print the price, the sales tax, and the total.

5-6: Print a multiplication table.

5-7: Using the following lines of input, what is the output of the program READWRITE?

1.063	27	06.488	2	17.26	58.0	11
2.31	76.523	7	.641	-5	18.3	45.7	-7
8.6	2	5.154	6	.729	628
3.16	8	7.5	-10	4.108	14	6.74

```
PROGRAM READWRITE (INPUT, OUTPUT);
VAR   A, C, E: REAL;
      B, D: INTEGER;
BEGIN (* READWRITE *)
      WRITELN; WRITELN;
      READLN (A, B, C, D, E);
      WRITELN (A:5:1, C:6:2, E:7:3, B:4, D:4);
      WRITELN;
      READLN (A, B);
      READLN (C, D, E);
      WRITELN (A:5:1, C:6:2, E:7:3, B:4, D:4);
      WRITELN;
      READLN (E, D, A, B, C);
      WRITELN (E:5:1, A:6:2, C:7:3, D:4, B:4);
      WRITELN
END. (* READWRITE *)
```

CHAPTER 6

CONTROL
STRUCTURES

SEQUENTIAL EXECUTION

In the previous chapters we learned the rules for writing simple Pascal programs. We also examined several examples of simple programs, which consisted of a small number of statements to be executed in sequence. Executing each statement in turn, in the order that it appears in the program listing, is known as *sequential* execution.

A computer can do more than just execute statements sequentially. If the computer were only capable of sequential execution, it would in a sense be nothing more than a good pocket calculator. A computer can make *decisions* based on specific *tests*. In other words, depending upon the value of a specific variable or variables when the program is executed, decisions can be made that will result in one part of the program or another being executed. Instructions that allow such conditional tests modify the *flow of control* within the program.

A related concept is the capability that computers have to automatically execute a group of instructions over and over again, in a repetitive manner. This is called a *program loop* facility.

In this chapter we will study the facilities provided in Pascal for altering the flow of control within the program, i.e., those instructions that will result in the non-sequential execution of a group of instructions. Three categories of instructions will be distinguished: the repetition statements, the conditional branch statements, and the unconditional branch statements.

REPETITION STATEMENTS

Repetition statements allow the convenient execution of a loop. Let us first clarify the concept of a loop through an example. We will compute the sum of the first twenty-five integers. This can be accomplished by using a formula. Here, however, we will use the following algorithm:

1: SUM = 0
2: NUMBER = 1
3: NEWSUM = SUM + NUMBER
4: NEWNUMBER = NUMBER + 1
5: If NEWNUMBER is greater than 25, then stop.
   Otherwise, go back to step 3.

This algorithm can be represented symbolically by a flowchart as shown in Figure 6.1.

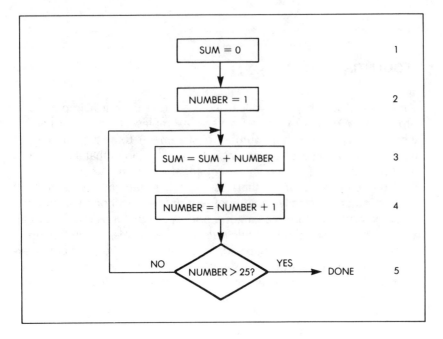

Figure 6.1: Flowchart for Integer Addition

In a flowchart, rectangles are used for simple statements and diamonds or rounded rectangles are used for test decisions. Each step in the algorithm, labeled 1 through 5, is represented by a box in the flowchart in Figure 6.1. Note that the arrow pointing from the bottom diamond-shaped box in the flowchart goes back into the third statement (box). The three statements numbered 3, 4, and 5 in the flowchart will therefore be executed repeatedly until the value of the variable NUMBER becomes greater than 25. This is an example of a *loop*.

In the conventional language of flowcharts, statements such as statement 3 are usually written:

SUM = SUM + NUMBER

This statement means that the new value of SUM is equal to the old value of SUM plus NUMBER. However, the equal sign should not be interpreted in the traditional mathematical sense. Rather, it is meant as an assignment statement. In order to avoid possible confusion, Pascal uses a specific symbol for the assignment ':=', and this is the symbol we will use from now on. The Pascal form of that statement is:

SUM := SUM + NUMBER

Pascal provides three facilities for automatic looping: REPEAT, WHILE, and FOR. Any of these three statements could be used for our integer addition problem. However, each of these statements provides specific convenience features which we will now describe.

REPEAT STATEMENT

The REPEAT statement can be used to repeat a group of statements in a program. The informal syntax of this statement is:

REPEAT statement(s) UNTIL (condition is true)

The formal syntax for this statement is shown in Figure 6.2.

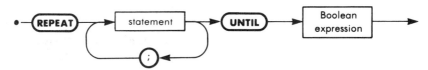

Figure 6.2:   Syntax for REPEAT

One or more statements may appear between the reserved words REPEAT and UNTIL. The condition is specified with a Boolean expression. For example, the Boolean expression may use the six relational operators:

= > < >= <= <>

or any of the legal Boolean operators. Here is a program that will compute the sum of the first 25 integers:

```
PROGRAM SUM25 (INPUT,OUTPUT);
(* SUM OF FIRST 25 INTEGERS *)
VAR SUM,NUMBER : INTEGER;
BEGIN
SUM := 0;
NUMBER := 1;
REPEAT
     SUM := SUM + NUMBER;
     NUMBER := NUMBER + 1
UNTIL NUMBER > 25;
WRITELN ('THE SUM OF THE FIRST 25 INTEGERS IS',SUM)
END.
```

Figure 6.3: INTEGER SUM Program

The program in Figure 6.3 represents one example of translating the algorithm previously described into a Pascal program. Several points are worth noting. For example, the variables SUM and NUMBER are declared as integer.

VAR SUM,NUMBER : INTEGER;

The next two statements in the program are called the *initialization phase.* They assign initial values to the two variables SUM and NUMBER before the loop is entered:

SUM : = 0;
NUMBER : = 1;

Variables that will be used to accumulate a result within a loop must generally be initialized. Usually, each loop is preceded by an initialization phase like the one previously described.

The loop follows:

REPEAT
    SUM : = SUM + NUMBER;
    NUMBER : = NUMBER + 1
UNTIL NUMBER $>$ 25;

This loop will cause the two statements contained within it to be executed until NUMBER becomes greater than 25. Each time that the loop is executed, NUMBER is incremented by one. As a result, the loop will be executed exactly 25 times.

After a program has been written, it should always be checked by hand, before executing it on the computer. We will now check this particular program and verify the correct operation of the loop.

When the program is started, SUM becomes 0, and NUMBER becomes 1. The first time the loop is entered, SUM becomes:

         SUM : = SUM + NUMBER;
or   SUM : = 0 + 1 (=1)
and:
         NUMBER : = NUMBER + 1;
or   NUMBER : = 1 + 1 (=2)

Remember that the expression to the right of the assignment symbol

(:=) is evaluated first. This reads as:

new-value-of-NUMBER is old-value-of-NUMBER + 1

Then UNTIL is reached. NUMBER is 2.

'NUMBER > 25'

evaluates as '2 > 25' which is FALSE. The loop is then repeated. The second time around, NUMBER takes the value 3, and the loop is repeated, etc.

Once NUMBER takes the value 26, the Boolean expression (NUMBER > 25) evaluates as TRUE, and the loop terminates. By examining the program you should be able to verify that SUM is indeed the sum of

1 + 2 + 3 + ... + 25.

Note: It is always important to check the initial and the end value of the loop control variable. Here, the end value of NUMBER is 26.

Even though they are legal, we have not used BEGIN...END within the loop, because they are not necessary. The program finally terminates by printing a message, and the value of the SUM:

WRITELN('THE SUM OF THE FIRST 25 INTEGERS IS', SUM)

Remember, that when using the REPEAT UNTIL statement, the statements placed between REPEAT and UNTIL will be executed *at least once.* The condition that is being tested will be examined only at the end of the loop. We will see that the WHILE statement allows us to do the reverse, i.e., to test for a condition at the beginning of the loop.

WHILE STATEMENT

The informal syntax of the WHILE statement is:

WHILE (Boolean expression is true) DO statement

The formal syntax for this statement is shown in Figure 6.4.

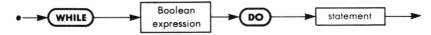

Figure 6.4: Syntax for WHILE

When examining the syntax, by convention, "statement" in a rectangle stands for either an isolated statement or a compound statement delimited by BEGIN and END. As long as the specified expression holds true, the statement or group of statements following the DO will be executed repeatedly. Unlike REPEAT, a group of statements must be made into compound statements by bracketing them with BEGIN and END. For example, let us now rewrite our previous program and compute the sum of the first 25 integers using the WHILE statement. The corresponding program is:

```
PROGRAM SUM25B(INPUT,OUTPUT);
(* SUM OF FIRST 25 INTEGERS *)
VAR SUM,NUMBER : INTEGER;
BEGIN
SUM := 0;
NUMBER := 1;
WHILE NUMBER < 26 DO
    BEGIN
        SUM := SUM + NUMBER;
        NUMBER := NUMBER + 1
    END;
WRITELN ('THE SUM OF THE FIRST 25 INTEGERS IS',SUM)
END.
```

Figure 6.5:   INTEGER SUM Program—Version 2

This program contains the same number of statements as the program in Figure 6.3. The difference between the two programs is that with the program in Figure 6.5, the test is performed *before* the group of statements is executed. As a result, in some cases the group of statements may not be executed at all, whereas in the case of REPEAT, the group of statements will always be executed at *least once*.

Notice that the test is reversed when compared to the REPEAT: the test is performed for NUMBER < 26 instead of NUMBER > 25 (i.e., NUMBER >= 26). This is because the WHILE statement is executed as long as the condition remains TRUE. It stops being executed when the condition is no longer TRUE. By contrast, the REPEAT statement is executed as long as the condition is FALSE. It stops whenever the condition becomes TRUE.

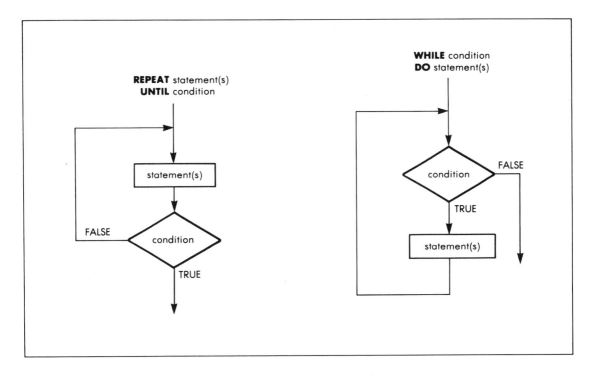

Figure 6.6:   WHILE vs. REPEAT

Using the symbolic representation of a flowchart (see Figure 6.6), the difference between the two types of repetition statements is illustrated in this figure.

Figure 6.7 shows another example of the use of the WHILE statement. We will compute the average of the first n integers, where the value of n will be supplied at the keyboard. In this program, NUMBER will successively take the values 0, 1, 2, up to a maximum value MAX, which is entered at the keyboard.

A loop is used to compute the sum of the first MAX integers (as in the previous example). After the loop is executed, the SUM is divided by the number of integers, i.e., MAX. This is the AVERAGE:

AVERAGE : = SUM / MAX;

Note that SUM and MAX are of type INTEGER, and that AVERAGE is a REAL. This is a legal statement.

Finally, the value of AVERAGE is printed:

        WRITELN ('THE AVERAGE OF THE FIRST', MAX, 'NUMBERS IS', AVERAGE)
    END.

    PROGRAM AVERAGE (INPUT,OUTPUT);
    VAR AVERAGE : REAL;
        SUM,NUMBER,MAX : INTEGER;
    BEGIN
        READLN(MAX);
        SUM : = 0;
        NUMBER : = 0;
        WHILE NUMBER < MAX **DO**
            BEGIN
                NUMBER : = NUMBER + 1;
                SUM : = SUM + NUMBER
            END;
        AVERAGE : = SUM / MAX;
        WRITELN ('THE AVERAGE OF THE FIRST', MAX, 'NUMBERS IS', AVERAGE)
    END.

Figure 6.7: AVERAGE Program

WHILE and REPEAT

Remember that, in the case of a WHILE statement, a group of statements found in a compound statement *must* be bracketed by BEGIN and END. In the case of REPEAT, this format is optional.

As a practical recommendation, on installations where execution time is restricted, the Boolean expression tested by WHILE or REPEAT should be as simple as possible in order to reduce execution time, since it is evaluated every time the loop is executed. This consideration also holds true for the statement(s) within the loop.

For the two repetitive statements we have studied thus far, i.e., the WHILE statement and the REPEAT statement, we have repeatedly executed a statement or group of statements until some condition held true or false. This condition may result from the value of a variable read from the keyboard or an input file, or from a *counter variable* (a frequent occurrence) that is regularly incremented each time that the loop is executed. In the program examples we have presented thus far, the value of NUMBER was incremented by one every time that the loop was executed. NUMBER is called a counter variable.

A special mechanism is provided in Pascal (as well as in nearly all high-level languages) for the automatic execution of the loop coupled with the automatic incrementation of such a counter variable. This mechanism is called the DO or FOR loop in various languages; it is known as the FOR statement in Pascal.

FOR STATEMENT

A simple example of a FOR statement is:

SUM : = 0;
FOR I : = 1 **TO** N **DO** SUM : = SUM + I;

The effect of this statement is to execute the statement following the DO N times. The first time this statement is executed, I has the value 1. The second time it is executed, I has the value 2, etc. Thus, SUM is given the value of the sum of the integers from 1 through N.

The informal syntax of the FOR statement is:

FOR counter variable : = initial value **TO** final value **DO** statement

Optionally, DOWNTO may be used instead of TO.

When using this type of repetition statement, the number of times the loop will be executed becomes fixed at the time that the FOR statement is entered. First, the counter variable (I in our example) is assigned the 'initial value'. Then, before each execution of the statement or compound statement in the loop, the counter variable is tested to see if it is greater than (or less than, with DOWNTO) the final value. If this condition is true, execution of the loop is terminated. After each execution of the loop, the counter variable is incremented by 1, or decremented by 1 if DOWNTO is used.

The syntax diagram for the FOR statement is presented in Figure 6.8.

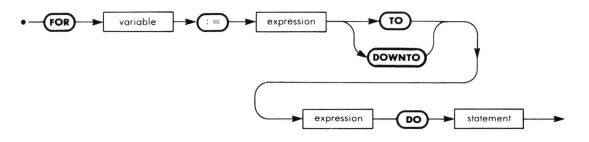

Figure 6.8: FOR Syntax

Here is an example of the FOR statement used in an AVERAGE program:

```
PROGRAM AVERAGE2(INPUT,OUTPUT);
VAR AVERAGE : REAL;
    I,MAX,SUM : INTEGER;
BEGIN  {For typographical reasons, no indentation is used after BEGIN}
READLN(MAX);
SUM := 0;
FOR I := 1 TO MAX DO
    BEGIN
    SUM := SUM + I       {This BEGIN-END pair is optional}
    END;
AVERAGE := SUM / MAX;
WRITELN('THE AVERAGE OF THE FIRST', MAX, 'NUMBERS IS', AVERAGE)
END.  (* AVERAGE2 *)
```

{This BEGIN-END pair is optional} BUT IF OPTIONAL,
HOW DOES IT KNOW WHERE THE END OF THE
STATEMENT IS? IS THE DEFAULT A SINGLE (RATHER
THAN A COMPOUND) STATEMENT? YES

Figure 6.9: AVERAGE Program—Version 2

A comparison of this program to the one in Figure 6.7 shows that this program has been significantly shortened. In the program in Figure 6.9, the FOR statement performs the initialization and automatic incrementing of I (called NUMBER in the program in Figure 6.7), and specifies the end of the loop test (when I reaches the values MAX).

Many program loops are implemented with this type of *counter* or *control variable* (I in the example above). This facility is important and should be thoroughly understood. However, the following restrictions apply to this statement:

1. The control variable (I, in our example) may be used for computations within the loop (as we have done). However, its value may not be modified within the loop. For example, it would be illegal to write I := 4 within the loop itself.

2. Neither the starting value nor the ending value for the control variable may be changed within the loop. Further, the control variable, the start value and the end value must all be of the same type. They are usually integers and may be any scalar type but real.

3. The FOR statement will not have any effect if the start value is greater than the end value (less than in the case of a DOWNTO) because the test for completion is made prior to each execution of the loop.

The value of the control variable (I in our example) is undefined after a normal exit from the loop. For example, one should *not* write:

J := I + 1;

after the loop, since the value of I is undefined.

NESTED LOOPS

It is entirely legal to have a loop appearing as part of a statement within another loop. A loop embedded within another loop is called a *nested loop*. Any number of loops may be embedded within a loop. For example, Figure 6.10 displays a program that will print the multiplication table for the first N integers to be multiplied by integers from 1 to M:

```
PROGRAM MULTABLE(INPUT,OUTPUT);
VAR I,J,K,M,N, : INTEGER;
BEGIN
READLN(M,N);
FOR I := 1 TO M DO
    BEGIN
    WRITELN;
    FOR J := 1 TO N DO
        BEGIN
        K := J * I;
        WRITELN(J,' X ',I,' = ',K)
        END
    END
END.   (* MULTABLE *)
```

Figure 6.10: MULTIPLICATION TABLE Program

Looking at this program in more detail, M and N are read at the keyboard:

READLN(M,N);

The FOR loop is then executed M times:

FOR I := 1 **TO** M **DO**

A blank line is typed:

>   WRITELN;

Then a new loop is executed N times:

>   **FOR** J := 1 **TO** N **DO**

The loop computes the product K of I and J:

>   K := J * I;

and prints it on a new line:

>   WRITELN (J,'×',I,'=',K)

This is done N times, then the control variable I is incremented by 1 (outer loop), a blank line is printed, and the inner loop is started again. Assuming M = 12 and N = 9, the result will be:

```
1 × 1 = 1
2 × 1 = 2
3 × 1 = 3
4 × 1 = 4
5 × 1 = 5
6 × 1 = 6
7 × 1 = 7
8 × 1 = 8
9 × 1 = 9

1 × 2 = 2
2 × 2 = 4
3 × 2 = 6

.   .   .   .   .
```

Note that the inner loop cycles completely before the outer loop can execute again.

THE THREE LOOP STATEMENTS — A SUMMARY

In many cases, any of the three loop statements may be used:

>   **REPEAT**   ...   **UNTIL**
>   **WHILE**   ...   **DO**
>   **FOR**   ...   **DO**

However, each of the three loop statements has restrictions previously described which may make it unsuitable in specific cases. Here are summaries of the three loop statements.

The REPEAT statement always executes the associated statement(s) at least once. This statement should not be used if this action could cause a problem (for example, if a division by zero, or some other meaningless case could occur).

The REPEAT statement tests at the end of the loop, therefore it may be used to test for conditions that have just occurred, such as the value of a variable read or computed within the loop.

The WHILE statement tests for the specified condition before executing the loop. The statement(s) within the loop may not be executed at all. The WHILE statement may also test for conditions that may have just occurred within the loop. However, these conditions will have occurred within the *prior* loop iteration.

The FOR statement executes for a set number of times. The number of times it executes may not be altered within the loop. The FOR statement is efficient, as it results in fewer instructions and it automatically increments or decrements the counter variable. However, the FOR statement does not test for a condition.

CONDITIONAL STATEMENTS

We have now learned how to conveniently execute loops. However, we require more facilities than those already described. In particular, we need the capability to execute one statement if a condition is true, and another statement if the condition is not (in the case of a binary choice). Another useful facility involves a case in which a variable may have more than two values (such as the set of values 1 2 3 4 5 6) and we need to execute only one out of six statements, depending upon the value of the variable. Both of these conditional statements are provided in Pascal. They are called the IF statement and the CASE statement. IF is used for a binary choice. CASE is used for an n-ary choice, when n is greater than 2.

Binary Choice: The IF Statement

A simple example of the IF statement is:

IF NUMBER $>$ 10 **THEN** WRITELN('NUMBER $>$ 10')

The formal syntax for the IF statement is shown in Figure 6.11.

Figure 6.11:   IF Syntax

The IF clause is used in the case of a binary (two-possibilities) choice. The expression tested must be Boolean, i.e., evaluate to either TRUE or FALSE. The IF statement may take two forms:

> **IF** Boolean expression **THEN** statement
>
> **ELSE** statement

or

> **IF** Boolean expression **THEN** statement

The ELSE clause is optional. The IF-THEN-ELSE statement is illustrated in Figure 6.12 by means of a flowchart representation.

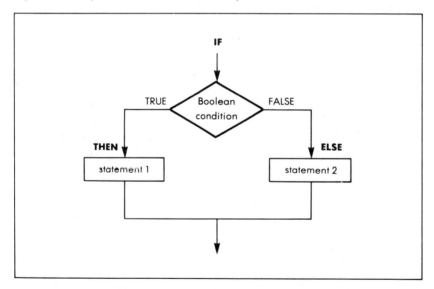

Figure 6.12:   IF-THEN-ELSE Flowchart

Figure 6.12 shows that if the specified Boolean expression after the IF is true, then statement 1 will be executed. If the condition is not true, then statement 2 will be executed. However, the ELSE clause is optional.

To help us better understand the IF statement let us consider another example. We will type numbers at the keyboard and count those numbers greater than 10. This program will stop when we type 0 at the keyboard. Here is the program:

```
PROGRAM COUNT(INPUT,OUTPUT);
VAR COUNT,NUMBER : INTEGER;
BEGIN
        COUNT : = 0;
        REPEAT
            READLN(NUMBER);
            IF NUMBER > 10 THEN COUNT : = COUNT + 1
        UNTIL NUMBER = 0;
        WRITELN('NUMBERS > 10 :', COUNT)
END.
```

Figure 6.13: Program To COUNT NUMBERS

In this simple example, we have omitted the ELSE clause which was not required.

This program reads a NUMBER at the keyboard:

READLN(NUMBER);

If this NUMBER is greater than 10, COUNT is incremented by 1. Otherwise nothing happens.

IF NUMBER > 10 THEN COUNT : = COUNT + 1

This action is REPEATed until a 0 is typed in:

UNTIL NUMBER = 0;

Then the program prints the value of COUNT and stops:

WRITELN('NUMBERS > 10 :',COUNT)

In contrast with the preceding loop statements, the IF statement does not cause execution of a loop. The IF statement simply tests for a condition. If this condition is true, the IF statement causes the execution of the statement that follows THEN; this statement is executed once.

If the condition is false, the statement that follows the ELSE is executed. If there is no ELSE, nothing happens, and the next statement in the program is executed.

In order to specify the test conditions, a complex Boolean expression may be used. For example, let us write a program that will generate a diagnostic whenever we type an integer number smaller than 50 or greater than 60. This is called a filter program. This filter accepts only those integer numbers whose values are between 50 and 60 inclusive.

```
PROGRAM FILTER(INPUT,OUTPUT);
VAR NUMBER : INTEGER;
BEGIN
REPEAT
    READLN(NUMBER);
    IF (NUMBER < 50) OR (NUMBER > 60) THEN
        WRITELN('ILLEGAL NUMBER')
UNTIL NUMBER = 0
END.
```

Figure 6.14: A FILTER Program

This program terminates whenever a 0 is typed at the keyboard.

If we review this program in more detail, we see that the condition specified after the IF is:

$$(NUMBER < 50) \text{ OR } (NUMBER > 60)$$

If NUMBER is equal to 53, then

$$NUMBER < 50 \text{ is FALSE}$$
and $$NUMBER > 60 \text{ is FALSE}$$

The resulting Boolean expression

$$(NUMBER < 50) \text{ OR } (NUMBER > 60)$$

is FALSE and the IF statement has no effect.

Whenever NUMBER is less than 50 or greater than 60, the IF is executed and a message is printed: 'ILLEGAL NUMBER'.

Nested Tests

Any type of statement may be used after a THEN or after an ELSE. In a case in which a sequence of binary choices is required, an IF statement may be used within another IF statement.

For example:

```
IF VOLTAGE > 2 THEN
    IF VOLTAGE > 20 THEN
        IF VOLTAGE > 100 THEN
            WRITELN('VOLTAGE OUT OF RANGE')
        ELSE SCALE : = HIGH
    ELSE SCALE : = NORMAL
ELSE WRITELN('VOLTAGE BELOW 2V');
```

Figure 6.15: VOLTAGE TEST Segment

The program segment above will set the proper SCALE for the VOLTAGE value:

— A voltage greater than 100V will be out of range.
— A voltage between 20V and 100V will set the SCALE to HIGH (a constant).
— A voltage between 2V and 20V will set the SCALE to NORMAL (a constant).
— A voltage less than 2V will also be out of range.

In this example, there are three IF statements that are nested. The use of nested IF statements corresponds to a binary *decision tree*. Such a tree is illustrated in Figure 6.16.

Look at each box in the tree, and see how it corresponds to an IF..THEN..ELSE clause in the program. Whenever more than two alternatives exist, another statement may be considered; this is the CASE statement.

MULTIPLE CHOICE: CASE STATEMENT

The CASE statement is provided in Pascal for situations in which the number of alternatives available is greater than two. Depending upon the value of an expression which may take n different values, one of the n statements will be executed.

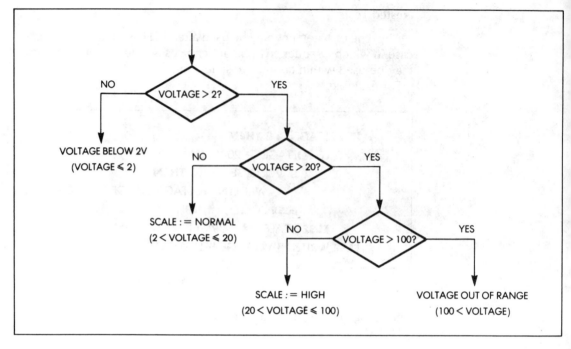

Figure 6.16:   A Binary Decision Tree

Here is an example of a CASE statement:

```
CASE MONTH OF
        1:  WRITELN('JANUARY');
        2:  WRITELN('FEBRUARY');
        3:  WRITELN('MARCH');
        .
        .
        .
       12:  WRITELN('DECEMBER')
END;
```

The formal syntax of the CASE instruction is shown in Figure 6.17.

The expression following the CASE must evaluate to a non-real scalar type. For example, we could not directly test for (VOLTAGE > 2) with this expression, as we did in the previous examples, because we would be testing for a range of numbers.

As long as the expression following the CASE evaluates to a constant listed in the statement (called a CASE label), the corresponding statement will be executed.

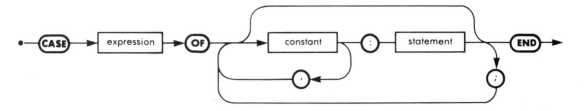

Figure 6.17:   CASE Syntax

If n (constant : statement) pairs are listed, this statement provides an n-ary choice.

Figure 6.18 shows a program example using the CASE statement. It will read a number representing a month, then spell it out.

A number is typed at the keyboard. If this number is greater than 12 or less than 1, it is rejected and a message is printed: ('ERROR - NO SUCH MONTH'), since there is no month less than 1 or greater than 12. Otherwise, if the month number typed was 1, then 'JANUARY' will˙ be printed; if the number typed was 2, then 'FEBRUARY' will be printed, etc.

```
PROGRAM SPELLMONTH(INPUT,OUTPUT);
VAR MONTH : INTEGER;
BEGIN
WRITELN('TYPE MONTH NUMBER');
READLN(MONTH);
IF (MONTH > 12) OR (MONTH < 1) THEN WRITELN('ERROR - NO SUCH MONTH ')
ELSE
     CASE MONTH OF
          1: WRITELN('JANUARY');
          2: WRITELN('FEBRUARY');
          3: WRITELN('MARCH');
               .

               .

               .

          12: WRITELN('DECEMBER')
     END (* CASE *)
END. (* SPELLMONTH *)
```

Figure 6.18:   Program For SPELLING THE MONTH

This example shows that, depending upon the value of the number MONTH, one of 13 events will occur:

— One of the twelve months of the year will be printed;
— A message will be printed if the value of MONTH is incorrect.

This example can be called a 13-way branch. Formally, the CASE statement is a multi-way branch. It allows the selective execution of a statement or group of statements, depending upon the value of the expression following the CASE. If the expression following the CASE ever evaluates to a value not specified in the constants following the CASE, it is an error, and the program fails. Remember that the CASE statement must be terminated by an END. There is no matching BEGIN.

The CASE labels may be any non-real scalar type. More than one label may be associated with a statement. For example, here is a CASE statement where the labels are characters and are grouped:

```
CASE SYMBOL OF
'A': WRITELN('FOUND A');
'B', 'C', 'D': WRITELN('FOUND B,C,D');
'E', 'F', 'G': WRITELN('FOUND E,F,G');
'*': WRITELN('FOUND *')
END;
```

CASE Summary

The CASE statement is an n-way branch. This branch is symbolically illustrated in Figure 6.19.

The CASE statement is generally used when a variable or an expression may evaluate to one of n values. This value may be any legal non-real scalar, such as character, integer, Boolean.

If computer time is restricted, and one particular value has a much higher probability of coming up than the others, it is usually more efficient to use an IF statement first, so that this value is tested for, before other alternatives are considered.

UNCONDITIONAL BRANCH: GOTO

We now know about the IF and CASE statements, and how to use them to perform conditional branching, i.e., to execute selected statements depending upon the value of an expression. This branching does not alter the sequential execution of the program as a whole. There are times in a program, however, when it may be desirable to skip over a portion of the program, jump out of a loop, or go back to a specific point. This action is called an unconditional branch, and is accomplished by using a GOTO statement.

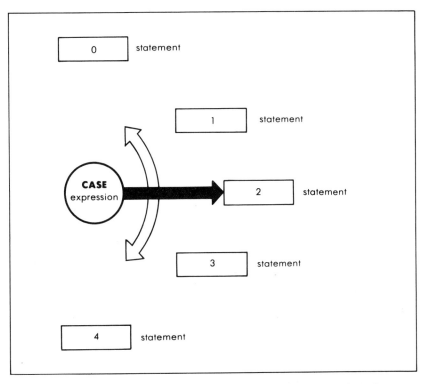

Figure 6.19: *Symbolic Representation of a CASE*

The syntax of a GOTO statement is:

GOTO label

where *label* is a number (up to 4 digits) associated with a statement.

Executing a GOTO statement will cause the labeled statement to be executed next. This statement may appear after or before the GOTO instruction. However, there are some restrictions that apply. We will point them out later in this section, when discussing the concept of scope.

In summary, the GOTO statement specifies which statement will be executed next. A label is used to allow a GOTO statement to specify the statement that should be executed next. A label is an integer number followed by a colon and placed before a statement in a program. A label may not be longer than four digits. For example:

GOTO 100;

. . .

100: statement

GOTO 100 will result in the statement labeled as 100 being executed next. Labels must be declared using a LABEL declaration. The LABEL declaration must appear before the CONSTant or VARiable declarations. Here is an example of a GOTO statement within a program:

PROGRAM TEST(INPUT,OUTPUT);
    LABEL 100;
    VAR A,B,C : INTEGER;
    . . .
    GOTO 100;

The GOTO command is powerful, and may lead to confusion when reading a program. A GOTO statement forces a branch to an arbitrary location within the program, which may make the flow of control difficult to follow. For this reason, GOTO statements are discouraged in Pascal. Whenever possible, the other control constructs such as WHILE, REPEAT, etc. should be used. In fact, many compilers will even generate warning diagnostics whenever a GOTO statement is used. In cases where the programmer feels that a GOTO statement is indispensable, comments should be used within the program to clarify what is happening.

As a general rule, whenever a GOTO statement must jump backwards in a program, the programmer could have used one of the structured statements instead. In the case of a forward jump, the use of the GOTO may be indispensable.

Let us look at an example of a forward jump:

    IF VALUE = N, **THEN GOTO** 100
    . . .
    100: . . .

The concept of *scope* is defined in the next chapter. If you decide to use GOTO statements, you might want to read the next chapter, and then come back to the rest of the section on GOTO statements. (No, this recommendation is not a GOTO NEXT CHAPTER this is a PROCEDURE call — but we have not explained procedures yet!)

A GOTO may only jump within the scope of the label that it uses. As a general rule, if a label is defined in an external (enclosing) block, one may jump to it from within. If a label is defined within a block, one can only jump to it from within that block, but not from outside the block.

Examples of legal and illegal GOTO statements are shown in Figure 6.20.

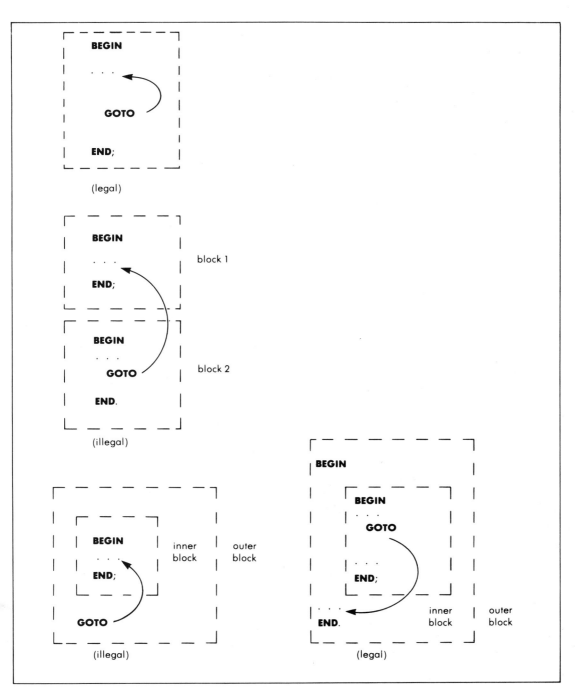

Figure 6.20: GOTO Jumps

TURBO PASCAL FOR LOOP

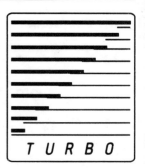

T U R B O

Unlike Standard Pascal, the control variable of a Turbo Pascal FOR statement or loop is defined (i.e. exists) after completion of the loop. After a FOR statement is executed, the control variable contains the last TO or DOWNTO value (unless a GOTO was used to exit the loop before completion). If the FOR loop is not executed because the initial value is greater than the final value (TO) or less than the final value (DOWNTO), no assignment is made to the control variable.

According to the rules of good programming, practice dictates that this feature should not be used as it is highly implementation specific and will result in nonportable programs. Instead, it is a good idea to assign the value of the control variable to another variable within the loop, and use that variable elsewhere in the program.

TURBO PASCAL CASE STATEMENT

In Standard Pascal, the result of a CASE statement is undefined (an error) if there is no case label equal to the value of the selection variable. Turbo Pascal, however, handles this situation differently. It will execute the next statement in the program. For example:

```
PROGRAM CASE1;
VAR SELECTOR : INTEGER;
BEGIN
     SELECTOR : = 4;
     CASE SELECTOR OF
          1: WRITELN('CASE1 EXECUTED');
          2: WRITELN('CASE2 EXECUTED');
          3: WRITELN('CASE3 EXECUTED')
     END; (* CASE *)
     WRITELN('THIS IS ALWAYS PRINTED')
END.
```

The preceding example would not execute properly in Standard Pascal because the *selector* value does not match any of the CASE labels. However, in Turbo Pascal this doesn't cause a problem; the CASE alternatives are ignored and the statement following the CASE structure is executed.

TURBO PASCAL CASE . . . ELSE STATEMENT

Turbo Pascal has one control structure that is not provided in Standard Pascal: the CASE . . . ELSE statement. If none of the case labels contains the value of the case selector expression and an ELSE clause is provided, then the statement(s) following the ELSE are executed. Note that multiple statements are allowed in the ELSE clause. For example:

```
PROGRAM CASE2;
VAR SELECTOR : INTEGER;
BEGIN
      SELECTOR : =  4;
      CASE SELECTOR OF
            1: WRITELN('CASE1 EXECUTED');
            2: WRITELN('CASE2 EXECUTED');
            3: WRITELN('CASE3 EXECUTED');
      ELSE
            WRITELN('NO MATCH');
            WRITELN('ELSE EXECUTED')
      END; (* CASE *)
      WRITELN('THIS IS ALWAYS PRINTED')
END.
```

As the example shows, the CASE . . . ELSE structure allows trapping of any "no-match" conditions in CASE statements.

TURBO PASCAL GOTO STATEMENT

Turbo Pascal's use of the GOTO statement is slightly different from Standard Pascal's use of GOTO statements and labels.

- LABEL declarations need not be the first declaration in a given block, and multiple LABEL declarations are allowed in a single block.

- Labels are not restricted to four digit unsigned integers as in Standard Pascal. They may contain any combination of letters and digits, and unlike identifiers, they may begin with a digit.

- GOTO statements cannot branch outside the procedure or function block in which they are declared.

SUMMARY

All of the Pascal statements available for modifying the sequential execution of a program have been presented in this chapter. These statements included the repetition statements (REPEAT...UNTIL, WHILE...DO, FOR...DO), the conditional statements (IF..THEN..ELSE, CASE..OF), and the unconditional GOTO statement.

The power of computer programs stems on one hand from their capability to test and decide, and on the other hand, to execute loops a number of times.

The repetition and the conditional statements that have been described will be used throughout the rest of this book, in nearly all of the programs. The contents of this chapter are, therefore, essential and should be thoroughly understood before proceeding to the next chapter.

The chapters that follow are not essential to the novice programmer. The information presented up to and including this chapter should enable the beginning programmer to write many interesting programs. It is recommended that you test your comprehension of the material by solving many of the exercises at the end of this chapter.

EXERCISES_____

6-1:   Compute the sum of the first N integers using a FOR statement.

6-2:   Is the following program equivalent to the program presented in Figure 6.3, where the sum of the first 25 integers is computed?

    SUM : = 0;
    NUMBER : = 0;
    REPEAT
            NUMBER : = NUMBER + 1;
            SUM : = SUM + NUMBER
    UNTIL NUMBER > 25;

6-3:   Is the previous program equivalent to the one in Figure 6.3 with:

    UNTIL NUMBER = 26;

6-4:   Modify the program in Figure 6.3 so that it can compute the sum of the first N integers, where N is a positive integer entered at the keyboard.

6-5:   Follow the example of the program shown in Figure 6.3, and write a program that will compute the average of the first 25 integers.

6-6:   If the compound statement in the program in Figure 6.7 is changed as follows:

    SUM : = SUM + NUMBER;
    NUMBER : = NUMBER + 1;

    what other change(s) must be made to the program?

6-7:   Rewrite the AVERAGE program in Figure 6.7 using the REPEAT...UNTIL statement.

6-8:   Compute the average of n numbers which are typed at the keyboard and are not necessarily consecutive integers.

6-9: Do the same exercise as above except change it so the average must be computed until an end-of-file marker is encountered in the input. All numbers are read from the keyboard. You may choose any end-of-file symbol.

6-10: Rewrite the Filter program of Figure 6.14 so that the minimum and maximum legal values are specified at the keyboard. In addition, count the numbers accepted and rejected.

6-11: Using the example of the program in Figure 6.18, write a program that will read a date in the format MM DD YY, where DD is the day, MM is the month, and YY is the year. The program must convert it to a standard date, such as March 15, 1981. The program should continue to convert dates until a 00 is typed as part of any input. In addition, the program should check for input validity and reject unreasonable input.

6-12: Rewrite the program in Figure 6.17 so that the typing of the first three characters of a MONTH at the keyboard causes the program to complete the typing of the name of the month automatically. For example, 'JAN' should result in the printing of 'UARY'.

6-13: Write a program that prints the equivalence table between Celsius and Fahrenheit in both directions between two values specified by the user at the keyboard. For example, it should be capable of printing the Celsius equivalent of Fahrenheit temperatures from 0 to 200 F. The formula is:

$$C = 5/9(F-32)$$

6-14: Write a program that will plot a vertical curve representing a function as a sequence of stars or dots. Choose a simple function such as sine.

Hint: For each line, compute the position where a star should be printed using the ROUND function. Print an appropriate horizontal sequence of blanks, then a star. Do not forget to scale your printout in function of the width of your paper.

For the dedicated programmer: print the x and the y axis, plus graduations.

6-15: **(Secret Code)** Read a sequence of characters typed at the keyboard. Stop whenever the letters STOP have been typed at the keyboard in this order, but not necessarily one after the other. For example, the sequence A B C _S_ A B C _T_ A _O_ A B C _P_ should cause the program to stop.

6-16: What is the effect of the following instructions (look carefully)?

```
IF A > 2 THEN;
    BEGIN
        B := 2;
        C := 3
    END;
```

Hint: Observe the program very carefully.

6-17: Explain the difference between an IF and a CASE.

6-18: When using the following conditional statements, how many times will the loop be executed?

1. REPEAT   2. WHILE

CHAPTER **7**

PROCEDURES AND FUNCTIONS

PROGRAM ORGANIZATION

When developing a program, the programmer often needs to give a name to a group or *block* of statements that accomplish a specific task within the program. This block used within the main program is often referred to as a *subprogram* or a *subroutine*. In Pascal two different methods are provided for giving a name to a block: *procedures* and *functions*.

The essential difference between a procedure and a function is that a function returns a *value* that may be used in an expression, while a procedure has no value associated with its name. In short, a procedure may be used instead of a statement. A function may be used instead of a variable.

Functions are generally used to create new operations (or "functions") that are not provided in standard Pascal. Procedures are generally used to structure a program, and to improve its clarity and generality.

Functions and procedures make a program more readable, and therefore less prone to errors. They also make a program easier to debug. Functions and procedures may often be reused in other programs. Libraries of common functions and procedures are available for most installations.

Like types in Pascal, functions and procedures may be either "built-in" or user-defined. The built-in functions are called *standard functions*. The standard functions that operate on scalar types were previously described in Chapter 3.

In this chapter, the rules for defining and using procedures and functions will be described.

PROCEDURES

A *procedure* is used to identify a subprogram within a program. The procedure name defines a block of statements that will be executed as a program every time the name of the procedure is invoked.

For example, a Pascal program might include the following statements:

```
BEGIN
    GETDATA;
    PRINTHEADER;
    COMPUTE;
    PRINTRESULT
END.
```

where each of the four statements is simply the name of a procedure. Writing the name of a procedure causes the procedure to be executed. This type of structuring makes this program segment very readable. Naturally, this requires that each procedure has previously been defined. Each of these procedures is formally defined at the beginning of the program, and will perform the actions required. For example, Figure 7.1 shows the declaration of the PRINTHEADER procedure.

```
PROCEDURE PRINTHEADER;
    CONST WIDTH = 20;
    VAR I : INTEGER;
    BEGIN
    FOR I := 1 TO WIDTH DO WRITE ('*');
    WRITELN('* THIS IS THE TABLE *');
    FOR I := 1 TO WIDTH DO WRITE('*');
    WRITELN;
    END;   (* PRINTHEADER *)
```

Figure 7.1:   Declaration of PRINTHEADER Procedure

This simple procedure will print:

```
********************
*   THIS IS THE TABLE   *
********************
```

and could be easily modified to print any other header.

Here is a simplified example of a program that defines and uses two procedures:

```
PROGRAM   CHECKBALANCE(INPUT,OUTPUT);
VAR OLDBALANCE,NEWCHECK,NEWBALANCE : INTEGER;
    PROCEDURE READCHECKAMOUNT; (* PROCEDURE DEFINITION *)
    (declarations)
    BEGIN
    (statements)
    END;   (* READCHECKAMOUNT *)

    PROCEDURE COMPUTEBALANCE; (* PROCEDURE DEFINITION *)
    (declarations)
    BEGIN
    (statements)
    END;   (* COMPUTE BALANCE *)
```

BEGIN

(statements)

READCHECKAMOUNT; (* PROCEDURE CALL *)

COMPUTEBALANCE; (* PROCEDURE CALL *)

(statements)

END.   (* CHECKBALANCE *)

Procedures offer two advantages:

1. They improve program readability by giving a name to a task and thereby clarifying its purpose.
2. They shorten the program (if the procedure is used more than once), as they eliminate the need to write out the corresponding statements repeatedly.

For example, assuming that the COMPUTE procedure is used twice in the main program, the resulting flow of execution is illustrated in Figure 7.2.

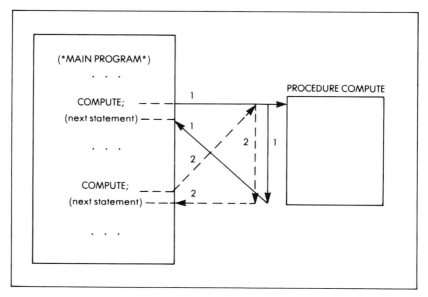

Figure 7.2:   Calling the Procedure

In Figure 7.2, the COMPUTE procedure is *called* (used) for the first time when the statement:

COMPUTE;

is encountered in the main program. The result is to execute the "body" of the procedure, as defined at the beginning of the main program. This *procedure-body* or *procedure-block* is shown conceptually on the right side of the diagram in Figure 7.2. This *procedure call* results in a *transfer of control* to the procedure, shown by the arrows labeled "1." Once the procedure has been executed, the next statement (following 'COMPUTE') in the main program is then executed.

In the Figure 7.2, the procedure COMPUTE is invoked a second time in the main program:

COMPUTE;

This results in the second procedure call illustrated by the arrows labeled "2." The body of the procedure is executed once again. Note how this procedure, or any other procedure can be used any number of times in the program. The procedure is called by merely writing its name.

In summary, a procedure may be *called* from different points in the main program. All of the statements in the procedure definition, however, only have to be written out once, at the beginning of the program. A procedure may then be executed as many times as desired within the rest of the program. Conceptually, everything happens as if the body of the procedure were inserted into the program at every point where it is called.

A procedure is written in essentially the same way as a program. For example, the PRINTHEADER procedure is declared with:

PROCEDURE   PRINTHEADER;

It is followed by the usual declarations, and a BEGIN...END block of statements.

At the end of a procedure, it is good programming practice to write the name of the procedure in brackets as a comment on the same line as the END, in order to improve program readability.

For example:

PROCEDURE PRINTHEADER;
(declarations)
BEGIN   (* PRINTHEADER *)
   (statements)
END;   (* PRINTHEADER *)

Note: the rule in Pascal is that the PROCEDURE and FUNCTION declarations must appear immediately after any VAR declarations in the main program.

For example:

PROGRAM SAMPLE(INPUT,OUTPUT);
VAR A,B,C : REAL;
PROCEDURE ALPHABETIZE; (* PROCEDURE DECLARATION *)
BEGIN
   (statements)
END;(* ALPHABETIZE *)

Unlike a PROGRAM, one may not declare (INPUT,OUTPUT) for a procedure. These declarations are not needed because the procedure block is defined within the PROGRAM block. INPUT and OUTPUT must be declared for the PROGRAM and are therefore accessible to the procedure. (*Block structure* and the *scope of identifiers* will be discussed later in this chapter.)

Figure 7.3: Syntax of a Procedure

The formal definition of a procedure is shown in Figure 7.3. This definition must always include the word PROCEDURE, followed by a name and one or more statements that define the effect of the procedure (the "block"). The definition of a procedure may also include one or more *parameters*. Parameters will now be explained.

Parameters

Thus far, we have only shown an example of a procedure that accomplishes a "stand-alone" action ("print a header"). This procedure does not receive information from the main program nor does it transmit information back to it. For example, the PRINTHEADER procedure may be used to conveniently print a variety of headers throughout the program. Ideally, we would simply specify the message to be printed and say something like:

PRINTHEADER ('LIST OF SQUARES');

or perhaps:

PRINTHEADER ('RESULTS');

In other words we would like to pass information to the procedure. An item of information formally passed to or from a procedure is called a *parameter*.

Parameters may be used to transmit information to a procedure as well as to receive values the procedure may have computed or obtained. A parameter is a mechanism used for formal communication with a procedure. All parameters must be listed in parentheses in the procedure definition statement. This is the "parameter list" shown in Figure 7.3. Each parameter is followed by its type.

The parameters in the parameter list are called *formal parameters*. A formal parameter declared in the procedure definition statement may be viewed as a "place marker." An actual value or variable will be substituted for this parameter at the time the procedure is called. This substitution occurs throughout the procedure body. The parameters in the procedure call are called *actual parameters*.

Let us illustrate this concept by going back to the procedure in Figure 7.1 and modifying it to print a variable number of asterisks. The revised procedure takes the following form:

```
PROCEDURE PRINTHEADER(WIDTH : INTEGER);
VAR I : INTEGER;
BEGIN
     (modified statements)
END; (* PRINTHEADER *)
```

In this procedure WIDTH is a *parameter*. Note that each parameter must be followed by its type (in this case INTEGER). In order to print twenty asterisks, we would simply say:

```
PRINTHEADER(20);
```

Similarly, in order to print thirty asterisks, we would say:

```
PRINTHEADER(30);
```

Of course, we would also modify the program to center the text within the header.

So far we have only used parameters to pass information to a procedure. When a procedure must pass a result(s) back to the calling program, the parameter(s) used to that effect must be declared as *variable parameters*, i.e., preceded with VAR.

Let us look at an example:

```
PROCEDURE COMPUTER(VAR A,B : INTEGER; VAR RESULT : REAL);
```

where A,B are used to supply values to the procedure, and RESULT will hold the value of the result computed by the procedure.

When calling procedures, four kinds of parameters may be used: *values* (fixed numbers), *variables* (identifiers), *functions*, and *procedures*. When a *value* is specified as a parameter, this parameter is said to be *passed by value*. When a *variable* is specified as a parameter, the parameter is said to be *passed* (or called) *by reference*. Parameters are passed by value or by reference for essentially the same reasons that constants and variables are used in the main program: a value is fixed, a variable may take various values.

In the PRINTHEADER example above, the parameter WIDTH is passed by value. Generally, whenever information must only be passed *to* a procedure, it is passed by value. Whenever information must be passed to a procedure and a new value obtained from it after processing, it is passed *by reference*, so that the main program may use the resulting values later. In short, passing by reference is used when an assignment will be done to the named variables and the new values will be used later on in the main program. Functions and procedure parameters are described in a separate section in this chapter.

Now, let us look at an example of a simple procedure that replaces two numbers by their squares:

```
PROCEDURE  SQUARE(VAR A,B : REAL);
    BEGIN
        A := A * A;
        B := B * B
    END; (* SQUARE *)
```

The effect of this procedure is to assign to A the value of its square, and then do the same to B. The identifiers appearing within the definition are called formal parameters. In this procedure definition, A and B are the *formal parameters*. The identifiers used in the call are called the *actual parameters*. To use the procedure, we will write, for example:

```
SQUARE(X,Y);
WRITELN(X,Y);
```

X and Y are two variables defined within the main program, that must have a value at the time the SQUARE procedure is called. These variables are called the *actual parameters*. The statements shown above will result in printing the squares of the values of X and Y. Note that, in this example, the two parameters are called by name since the variables A and B represent X and Y throughout the procedure.

Let us now look at the VAR parameter declaration. An abbreviated VAR parameter declaration was used in the parameter definition:

PROCEDURE   SQUARE(**VAR** A,B : REAL);

The declaration:

VAR A,B : REAL

accomplishes three purposes:

1.   It defines A and B as REAL.
2.   It declares A and B as variables within SQUARE.
3.   It allows the values of the actual parameters to be changed.

In this case, the actual parameters *must be variables*.

Note that each *actual parameter* must correspond to a *formal parameter*. In the above example, X corresponds to A, and Y corresponds to B. In addition, in Pascal, the actual variables must be distinct from one another.

The Four Parameter Types

We have discussed two types of parameters so far: value and variable. To be complete, Pascal defines two more types of parameters: *procedure parameters*, and *function parameters* in which the names of functions and procedures may also be used as parameters. These two additional types of parameters will be described later in this chapter once functions have been explained.

Passing a Parameter by Reference and by Value—A Summary

When passing a parameter by reference, VAR must be used in the procedure definition. However, when passing a parameter by value, VAR is *not* used.

In the procedure call, when passing by reference, a variable name *must* be used for the actual parameter. When passing by value, any expression may be used, including a constant or a variable.

In the case in which a variable is passed by value, the variable's value is substituted for the formal parameter at the time of the call. The corresponding formal parameter in the procedure might receive a new value as the result of an assignment when the procedure is executed. However, contrary to passing by reference, this will have no effect on the variable that was used for the parameter in the call.

A variable passed by value can only be used to pass information into a procedure; it may not be used to receive information from the procedure.

Recursion

A procedure name may be invoked within the procedure definition; that is a procedure may call itself. This is known as a *recursion*, and will be explained later in the chapter.

Standard Procedures

Standard procedures are provided in Pascal. They are listed in Appendix C. Most implementations provie additional built-in procedures. Examples of standard procedures will be provided for Turbo Pascal.

FUNCTIONS

A *function* is a name given to one or more statements that perform a specific task. A function results in a value being assigned to its name upon execution of that function. A call to a function is always used in an expression. Unlike a procedure, a function identifier has a value. For example, here is a simple function that computes the mean of A and B:

```
FUNCTION  MEAN(A,B : REAL) : REAL;
  BEGIN
        MEAN := (A + B) / 2.0
  END;   (* MEAN *)
```

This function declaration defines a function called MEAN with two parameters of type REAL called A and B. The value of the result of the function will be of type REAL. The *body* of the function follows the declaration. Here, it includes only a single statement, bracketed by BEGIN and END.

The formal definition of a function in Pascal syntax is shown in Figure 7.4.

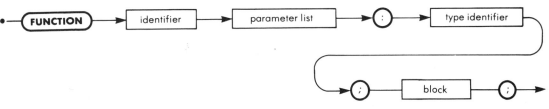

Figure 7.4: Syntax of a Function

A function is defined in the same way as a procedure, except that with a function a result is returned and the type of the result must always be specified. Parameters are optional. For completeness, let us indicate that the result must be either a scalar, a subrange type, or a pointer. (The subrange data type will be studied in the next chapter; pointers will be described in Chapter 13.)

A special requirement exists in the case of a function: the function identifier must be assigned a value within the function block. This value is the value taken by the function once it is executed. For example, the function MEAN that we have just defined includes the assignment:

        MEAN := (A + B) / 2.0

The function identifier may not be used like a variable. It may only be assigned a value and cannot be tested or accessed.

A function is used in much the same way that a variable is used, i.e., by placing it in an expression. However, unlike a variable, a function may have one or more parameters.

Generally, a function is used to give a name to a group of statements which perform a computation that must be done several times in the program. Different values for the parameters may be used each time. This way, it is only necessary to define the computation process once; it can then be used repeatedly by the various program parts when needed. For example, the SQRT is a (built-in) function and may be used many times within a program.

Recall again that the essential difference between a function and a procedure is that a function takes a value and is used within an expression. For example, we could write:

        VALUE := MEAN(X,Y);

where X and Y are actual parameters; and later write:

        NEWVAL := MEAN(M,N);

where M and N are new parameter values.

Like procedures, functions may be called *recursively*. Also, standard functions are provided by Pascal. Standard functions are listed in Appendix C.

We have now defined functions, procedures and parameters. In the process, we have indicated that variables may be declared within a function or within a procedure.

We must now examine the possible conflicts this may create with names of variables that already exist. We will discuss the concept of block structure, and define the scope of identifiers.

BLOCK STRUCTURE AND SCOPE OF IDENTIFIERS

When a function or a procedure is called, the function or the procedure may need to perform internal computations. Thus, variables (e.g., A, B, C) may be defined and used within the function or procedure for this purpose.

For example, assuming that the values of A and B must be exchanged, a variable TEMP is required. We write:

```
TEMP : = A;
 A : = B;
 B : = TEMP;
```

You should verify that:

```
A : = B;
B : = A;
```

does not work. TEMP is needed.

Or, more formally:

```
PROCEDURE EXCHANGE(VAR A,B : REAL);
VAR TEMP : REAL;
BEGIN
    TEMP : = A;
     A : = B;
     B : = TEMP
END; (* EXCHANGE *)
```

To be able to use standard or library functions or procedures without encountering problems, internal variable names such as A, B, and C should not interfere with other variables also named A, B, and C which might be declared and used in the main program. For example, if there is a variable A in the main program, an assignment to A within a function might change the value of A in the main program. This fact would make functions unsafe to use.

In Pascal, and in several other programming languages, this problem is solved by defining the *scope* of each variable. The scope of a variable is its domain of accessibility which will be defined in this section. For example, a variable defined within a procedure or a function is said to be *local* to that procedure or function. A *local* variable will have no effect outside the procedure or function, and will disappear once the procedure or function has been executed.

Conversely, a variable defined in the main program header is said to be *global* and may be used, referenced, or changed anywhere in the program, including any functions or procedures.

Now, let us consider the case where A, B, and C are defined in the main program, and A, B, and C are also defined as (local) variables for a FUNCTION. In this case, there are six variables all together. Within the function, A, B, and C are *local variables,* and they will have no effect on the *global* variables A, B, C in the main program, even though they have the same name. A local name is said to supersede a global one. By using local variables, one may safely define any variable that a function or a procedure will use. Any name may be used, even if it is already used elsewhere. A variable defined within a function is *local* to that function and cannot be used outside the function.

The *scope* of a variable is limited to only the block for which it is defined. An example is shown below:

```
PROGRAM DEMO(INPUT,OUTPUT);
CONST ONE = 1;
VAR I,J,K, : INTEGER;
    A,B,C : REAL;
PROCEDURE GETDATA(VAR X : REAL);
    VAR L,M : INTEGER;
        Y : REAL;
    BEGIN
        ...
    END; (* GETDATA *)
FUNCTION COMPUTE (P,Q : INTEGER) : INTEGER;
    VAR J,K : INTEGER;
    BEGIN
    ...
    END; (* COMPUTE *)
BEGIN
...
END. (* DEMO *)
```

Figure 7.5: Block Structures

This program (DEMO) defines one constant (ONE) and six variables (I,J,K,A,B,C). These identifiers belong to the main program and, as such, are said to be *global variables*. Global variables are accessible to any procedure or function within the program that does not use the same identifiers.

Let us examine the procedure GETDATA in Figure 7.5. The procedure GETDATA defines a formal variable parameter X, and three identifiers (L, M, Y). These four new identifiers are said to be *local* to the procedure. They have a meaning only within the block of the GETDATA procedure and their definition will 'die' as soon as the procedure exits. In other words, within the procedure, it is legal to use the identifiers ONE,I,J,K,A,B,C of the main program as well as X,L,M,Y. Once the procedure exits, the seven identifiers ONE,I,J,K,A,B,C will still have a meaning, as they are *global identifiers*. The other four will be undefined.

Let us now look at the function COMPUTE in Figure 7.5. This function may use all of the global identifiers defined in the main program, such as ONE,I,J,K,A,B,C, GETDATA, COMPUTE. In addition, it has two formal parameters, P and Q, and defines two local variables, J and K whose meaning will "die" upon function exit. However, this time, we may have a problem! Notice that the variables J and K are defined within the function COMPUTE, however, they have *already been defined* within the main program.

Will this have an effect on the main program? You already know that the answer is no: within each block such as a function or a procedure, variables may be redefined as being *local* by listing them in the definition of the function. The J and K appearing within the function COMPUTE will have a different meaning within that function, and no effect whatsoever on the global variables named J and K in the main program. Recall that this allows the programmer to use or create a library of system functions, without having to worry about the fact that a function might accidentally modify or erase some of the variables in the main program.

Within the body of the main program in Figure 7.5, the only user-defined identifiers that have a meaning are: ONE, I,J,K,A,B,C, GETDATA and COMPUTE.

The scope of the identifiers used in the DEMO program in Figure 7.5 is illustrated in Figure 7.6.

In summary, using an identifier within the block where it is defined is a legal use of a local reference. Using (anywhere in a program) an identifier defined in an (enclosing) outer block, is a legal use of a non-local reference. Using an identifier defined in an inner block outside that block is illegal unless the same identifier has also been defined in the outer block. (An example of such a case would be if the identifier would simply happen to have the same spelling as the one in the inner block, but is otherwise unrelated.)

In principle, with the scope mechanism, the programmer no longer has to worry about the fact that a procedure or a function might inadvertently change or destroy the values of some variables in the main program. Well, that is almost the case. In fact, a procedure or a function may change the value of a global identifier in two ways:

1. Through an explicit parameter
2. By assigning a value to a global identifier.

This mechanism is called a *side-effect*.

block: identifiers	PROGRAM DEMO (global identifiers)	PROCEDURE GETDATA	FUNCTION COMPUTE
ONE	✔	✔	✔
I	✔	✔	✔
J	✔	✔	(superseded below)
K	✔	✔	(superseded below)
A	✔	✔	✔
B	✔	✔	✔
C	✔	✔	✔
GET DATA	✔	✔	✔
X		✔	
L		✔	
M		✔	
Y		✔	
COMPUTE	✔		✔
P			✔
Q			✔
J			✔
K			✔

(PROCEDURE GETDATA column, rows X–Y bracketed: LOCAL TO GETDATA)

(FUNCTION COMPUTE column, rows COMPUTE–K bracketed: LOCAL TO COMPUTE)

Figure 7.6: Scope of Identifiers

Side-Effects

When the name of a parameter called by reference, or the name of a global variable (defined within the main program) is used to the left of an assignment statement within a procedure, or a function, the value of that variable will be altered by the procedure or the function.

Here is an example:

```
PROGRAM DEMO(INPUT,OUTPUT);
VAR A,B,C : REAL;
PROCEDURE RESET(VAR M,N : REAL);
    BEGIN
        A := 0; M := 0; N := 0
    END; (* RESET *)
```

BEGIN
   READ(A,B,C);
   RESET(B,C);
   WRITELN(A,B,C)
END. (* DEMO *)

Let us examine the procedure RESET. This procedure sets the two parameters M and N to zero. However, it also sets the global variable A to zero. When the DEMO program is executed, values will be typed in for A, B, C. When RESET is called, B and C are substituted for M and N and they are zeroed. In addition, A is also zeroed.

When the values of A, B, C are printed, A, B and C are 0. This may be what was intended. The danger, however is the following: the procedure RESET only lists M and N as parameters.

When a variable has been declared as a parameter, it is expected and normal that its value might be changed. However, when the variable belongs to the main program and is not listed as a parameter, this technique may result in unwanted accidents.

For example, if RESET were used at a later date, or by someone else, we might forget that RESET also changes A. This would result in an error. Whenever possible, all variables affected by a procedure should be listed as parameters.

To summarize the example above, a procedure may be used that modifies a variable named A which belongs to the main program and is not a parameter. Since often one does not look at the complete listing of a procedure, this "side-effect" of calling the procedure could be catastrophic.

The parameter mechanism is provided to prevent such catastrophes. The recommended procedure is to always list as formal parameters all the identifiers that one wishes to make available to an inner block, such as a procedure or a function.

It is possible to legally modify global identifiers with a procedure or a function, but this is a dangerous and error-prone technique and should be avoided if possible. Furthermore, when writing your own functions and procedures, avoid using the names of identifiers that have already been used in an outer block. Even though it is legal to use identifiers having names identical to global identifiers, this should be avoided as it creates a situation in which errors could cause disastrous results.

FUNCTIONS AND PROCEDURES AS PARAMETERS

Thus far, we have only discussed two types of parameters: constants and variables. We have however, indicated that functions and procedures may also be passed as parameters. The complete syntax for the parameter list is shown in Figure 7.7.

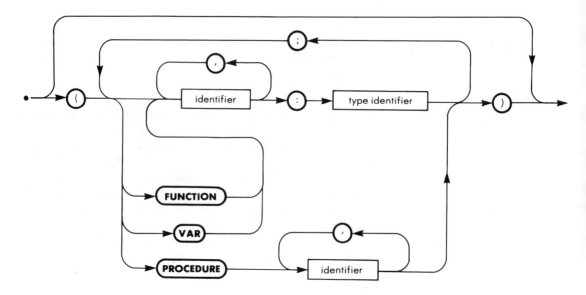

Figure 7.7: *Syntax of a Parameter List*

The syntax shows that variables, functions and procedures may be used as parameters. Here are examples of declarations:

PROCEDURE COMPUTEIT(**FUNCTION** SHMOO : REAL; A,B : REAL);
PROCEDURE ALPHA(**PROCEDURE** BETA);
FUNCTION GAMMA(**FUNCTION** DELTA : INTEGER) : REAL;

Here is a specific example:

PROCEDURE PRINTIT(**FUNCTION** F1, F2 : REAL; A, B, C : REAL);
BEGIN
   ...
X := F1(C) − A;
Y := F2(C) + B;
   ...
END (* PRINTIT *)

The PRINTIT parameter list includes:

— Two real functions: F1 and F2
— Three real variables: A, B, C

This allows PRINTIT to use the two functions F1 and F2 within the procedure:

$$X := F1(C) - A;$$
$$Y := F2(C) + B;$$

Because F1 and F2 are formal parameters, the PRINTIT procedure may be called with any actual functions passed as parameters. This way, a repetitive procedure may be written only once, using symbolic names for the functions F1, F2 and F3. The actual names of the functions are then provided at the time of the procedure call. For example, the procedure call for the above procedure might be:

PRINTIT(SQUARE,COMPUTE,1,10,8)

where SQUARE is a function that will be substituted for F1, and COMPUTE a function that will be substituted for F2. This procedure may be executed any number of times using different functions as parameters. However, some implementations forbid the use of the Standard Pascal functions as parameters.

Standard Pascal imposes one restriction: when passing procedures or functions as parameters, these procedures or functions may only use *value parameters*. Thus, if a procedure or a function is used as a parameter within another one, the only way it can bring results back with it is by using assignments to global variables.

Caution: Passing functions and procedures as parameters is a powerful facility, especially if your implementation allows passing them as variable parameters.

Two problems may occur:

1. It is the programmer's responsibility to always use the correct number of parameters during calls. Most compilers do not check this and may execute the call incorrectly.
2. Assignments to global variables (not declared as parameters) within a function or procedure may cause catastrophic side effects.

SCOPE REVISITED

The concept of scope has already been defined: variables are accessible only within the block where they are defined.

This concept also applies to functions and procedures passed as parameters. For example, when a function is passed as a parameter in a procedure, all of its variables become accessible within the block where it is used. Conversely, the local variables of the procedure that uses this function become global to the function. Here is an example:

```
PROGRAM MAIN(INPUT,OUTPUT);
FUNCTION ALFA(X : REAL): REAL;
    BEGIN
    ...
    END;        (* ALFA *)
PROCEDURE BETA (FUNCTION F : REAL; M,N, : REAL);
    VAR A,B,C : REAL;
    BEGIN

        ...
    END;        (* BETA *)
BEGIN           (* PROGRAM MAIN *)
...
END.            (* MAIN *)
```

In this example, the function F is a parameter to the procedure BETA.

The local variables A, B and C of BETA become global to the function F. If F ever assigns values to variables A, B and C that are not local to F, side-effects will occur as the values of A, B, C within BETA will be modified.

In summary, remember that when a function or a procedure is used, its block becomes imbedded within the block where it is used. Thus, those variables that are global to a function or a procedure will be different if that function is used within different blocks. Similarly, a procedure may be defined *within* a procedure. For example:

```
PROCEDURE P (X,Y : REAL);
VAR A,B,C : REAL;
PROCEDURE Q (I : INTEGER);
    BEGIN
    ...
    END;     (* Q *)
BEGIN
...
END;     (* P *)
```

In this example, Q is defined within P. Q is then always within the block of P. All declarations made in P may be used in Q, and the procedure Q may be used within P.

RECURSION REVISITED

We have already indicated that the scope of a function or a procedure declaration includes (only) its own block. The name of the function or a procedure may therefore be used within the function or the procedure. For example, a function may call itself within that function. This is called the recursion facility. For example, we could compute the *factorial* of N, defined as:

$$N! = 1 * 2 * 3 * \ldots * N$$

with:

$$0! = 1 \text{ by convention}$$

by using the formula:

$$FAC(N) = FAC(N - 1) * N$$

where FAC is an integer function. This is legal and it works. This formula is applied in the following way:

$$\text{Assume } N = 1 \text{ and } FAC(1) = 1$$

Then FAC(2) is computed as:

$$
\begin{aligned}
FAC(2) &= FAC(1) * 2; \\
&= 1 * 2 \\
&= 2
\end{aligned}
$$

And FAC(3) is computed as:

$$FAC(3) = FAC(2) * 3;$$

Automatically, FAC(2) is computed as defined by the formula:

$$
\begin{aligned}
FAC(3) &= (FAC(1) * 2) * 3 \\
&= 1 * 2 * 3 \\
&= 6
\end{aligned}
$$

And generally FAC(N) is computed as

$$
\begin{aligned}
FAC(N) &= FAC(N - 1) * N \\
&= (FAC(N - 2) * (N - 1)) * N \\
&= ((FAC(N - 3) * (N - 2)) * (N - 1)) * N \\
&= \ldots \\
&= 1 * 2 * 3 * \ldots * (N - 2) * (N - 1) * N
\end{aligned}
$$

However, recursion uses a large amount of memory inside the computer, and usually consumes more time than if a simpler computation had been used. If time and memory space are not important, then recursion can be used indiscriminately. However, since computer time is usually valuable, and memory space limited, a mathematical formula or algorithm should be used rather than recursion wherever possible. Recursion is, however, a powerful facility, and should be considered, especially when performing logical decisions or logical analysis. For example, functions or procedures are often called recursively when traversing a *decision tree*.

In summary, recursion is an extremely valuable facility, if no other convenient alternative exists. Recall that recursion is less desirable when computing a mathematical result that could also be obtained with a simpler formula.

RECURSION EXAMPLE

The Fibonacci sequence is defined in the following way. It is a sequence of numbers such that each consecutive number is equal to the sum of the two preceding numbers. The beginning of the sequence appears as:

0,1,1,2,3,5,8,13,21,34

And we can easily verify that:

$$0 + 1 = 1 \quad \text{(element 2)}$$
$$1 + 1 = 2 \quad \text{(element 3)}$$
$$1 + 2 = 3 \quad \text{(element 4)}$$
$$2 + 3 = 5 \quad \text{(element 5)}$$
etc.

A program is presented in Figure 7.8 that calculates the value of the nth element in the Fibonacci sequence. The equation used to compute the nth element is:

$$FIB(N) = FIB(N-1) + FIB(N-2)$$

This formulation lends itself well to the use of a recursive function call. For example, FIB(4) would be effectively computed as:

$$
\begin{aligned}
FIB(4) &= FIB(3) &&+ FIB(2) \\
&= FIB(2) &&+ FIB(1) + FIB(1) + FIB(0) \\
&= FIB(1) + FIB(0) &&+ 1 \quad + 1 \quad + 0 \\
&= \quad 1 \quad + \quad 0 &&+ 2 \\
&= \quad 3
\end{aligned}
$$

Figure 7.8 presents the corresponding program and a typical run.

```
PROGRAM FIBONACCI(INPUT,OUTPUT);
(* PROGRAM TO CALCULATE FIBONACCI NUMBER GIVEN *)
(* ITS PLACE IN THE SERIES *)
VAR FIBNUM: INTEGER;
FUNCTION FIB(COUNT: INTEGER): INTEGER;
BEGIN (* FIB *)
     IF COUNT > 1 THEN FIB := FIB(COUNT-1) + FIB(COUNT-2)
     ELSE IF COUNT=1 THEN FIB := 1
          ELSE FIB := 0
END; (* FIB *)
BEGIN (* FIBONACCI *)
     REPEAT
          WRITE ('ENTER NUMBER :');
          READLN (FIBNUM);
     UNTIL FIBNUM >= 0;
     WRITELN('THE FIBONACCI NUMBER IS ',FIB(FIBNUM))
END. (*FIBONACCI*)
```

Figure 7.8: FIBONACCI Program

Here is a typical run:

ENTER NUMBER : **14**

THE FIBONACCI NUMBER IS   377

Note: in the run, boldface type is used to indicate characters that were typed by the user.

Let us examine the program in Figure 7.8. First a single global variable is declared:

VAR FIBNUM: INTEGER;

This variable will hold the value typed at the keyboard by the user indicating the number of the Fibonacci element to be computed. This value must be an integer $> = 0$. A specific check to verify this fact will be made later in the program.

Then, the function FIB is defined to compute the value of the Fibonacci element:

FUNCTION FIB(COUNT: INTEGER): INTEGER;

This function has one parameter called COUNT. The result will be stored in FIB. The compound statement appearing within the function implements the formula that was presented, and two special cases:

— When the argument is 0,   FIB(0) is defined as 0
— When the argument is 1,   FIB(1) is defined as 1

This statement is accomplished with two IF clauses:

```
BEGIN (* FIB *)
    IF COUNT > 1 THEN FIB := FIB(COUNT−1) + FIB(COUNT−2)
    ELSE IF COUNT=1 THEN FIB := 1
        ELSE FIB := 0
END; (* FIB *)
```

The use of the two IF clauses in this program is illustrated in Figure 7.9. This statement assumes that COUNT $> = 0$. Also note the use of recursion to compute the value of FIB: the function FIB is used (called) within the IF clause.

Finally, the main program body reads a FIBNUM that rejects any negative value, and prints the result.

```
BEGIN (* FIBONACCI *)
    REPEAT
        WRITE ('ENTER NUMBER :');
        READLN (FIBNUM);
    UNTIL FIBNUM > = 0;
        WRITELN ('THE FIBONACCI NUMBER IS ', FIB(FIBNUM))
END. (* FIBONACCI *)
```

Note how this program keeps reading until it gets a non-negative number. This simple example illustrates the use of a recursive function call, and the use of proper input techniques (e.g., the rejection of invalid numbers).

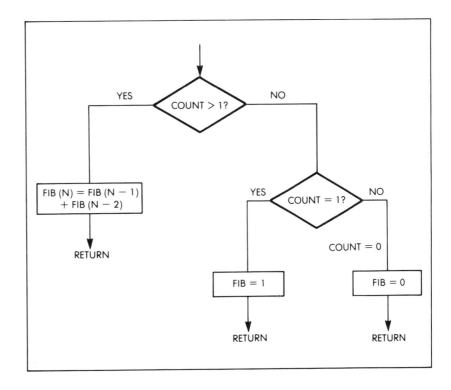

Figure 7.9: The Two IF Clauses

FORWARD REFERENCES

Normally, a function or a procedure may be called by another function or procedure only if the function or procedure being called has been defined before the function or procedure calling it. There are cases where this is undesirable, or even impossible, if many different functions and procedures must call each other. The *forward reference* is provided in Pascal to overcome this problem.

A forward reference is accomplished by declaring the function or procedure as *FORWARD* at the beginning of the program before the actual function or procedure definitions are given. An example is shown in Figure 7.10

```
PROGRAM SOLVE(INPUT,OUTPUT);
PROCEDURE DRAW(I : INTEGER); FORWARD;
FUNCTION QUADRATIC(X : REAL) : REAL; FORWARD;
PROCEDURE COMPUTE (Y,Z : REAL);
    VAR P : REAL;
    BEGIN
    ...
    END; (* COMPUTE *)
PROCEDURE DRAW;
    BEGIN
    ...
    END; (* DRAW *)
FUNCTION QUADRATIC;
    BEGIN
    ...
    END; (* QUADRATIC *)
BEGIN
...
END. (* SOLVE *)
```

Figure 7.10:   SOLVE Program

In this example, DRAW and QUADRATIC are declared as FOR-WARD. Now let us examine the order of the actual declarations. It is:

COMPUTE

DRAW

QUADRATIC

Without the FORWARD declarations, COMPUTE would not be allowed to use DRAW or QUADRATIC which are declared afterwards. However, both DRAW and QUADRATIC could use COMPUTE. Using the two FORWARD declarations, DRAW and QUADRATIC may be used within COMPUTE.

Note that the FORWARD declaration is identical to any subprogram declaration; however, the body is replaced by the word FORWARD. When the full declaration appears further on in the program, the heading is reduced to the name of the specified procedure or function.

EXTERNAL PROCEDURES

On many computer installations, library procedures or functions are provided which are written in Pascal, FORTRAN or other languages. They are already compiled (i.e., translated into executable code), and may be executed directly. Using the EXTERNAL declaration, such library procedures or functions can be used in a Pascal program in essentially the same way that a FORWARD reference is used. The word FORWARD is replaced by EXTERN or FORTRAN, depending upon the installation. The procedure or the function being used is not listed within the body of the program, but may still be called. For example:

PROCEDURE : FINDCHARACTER(X:REAL) : FORTRAN;

would be called from the main program by writing:

FINDCHARACTER(2.5);

No procedure body appears in the program in the case of an external declaration. The system will automatically find the external program within the library and execute it. Only formal parameters may be used when communicating with an external function or procedure. Global variables are not accessible.

RESTRICTIONS ON PARAMETERS

To make our definition of parameter more complete, two additional restrictions on parameters should be mentioned:

1. File parameters must always be variable parameters, i.e., passed by reference.
2. An element of a packed structure may not be listed as an actual variable parameter. (Packed structures will be defined in a later chapter.)

Additional restrictions or extensions may exist for each version of Pascal as well.

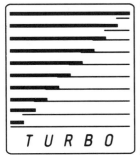

TURBO PASCAL PROCEDURES AND FUNCTIONS AS PARAMETERS

Turbo Pascal does not support the Standard Pascal feature of passing procedures and functions as parameters. Procedures and functions may not be declared as formal parameters to a procedure or a function.

TURBO PASCAL AND PACKED STRUCTURED TYPES

Turbo Pascal does not support the Standard Pascal feature of packed structured types, because all Turbo data structures are automatically packed and unpacked. The reserved word PACKED is allowed in declarations, but is ignored and has no effect. The Standard Pascal PACK and UNPACK procedures are not implemented.

TURBO PASCAL PARAMETER TYPE CHECKING

The V compiler directive in Turbo Pascal can be used to relax parameter-type checking. If this directive is active, the type of the formal and actual parameters passed must match exactly and string types must be exactly the same declared length or an error will be flagged. This directive is normally active ({$V+}) enabling strict type-checking. However, you can disable it ({$V-}) to allow strings of different declared lengths to be passed.

UNTYPED PARAMETERS

Turbo Pascal allows *untyped* formal parameters in procedures and functions. This facility is useful for passing the address of a variable to a procedure for absolute memory location calculations.

TURBO PASCAL EXTERNAL SUBPROGRAMS

External procedures and functions are declared in Turbo Pascal in the following form:

> **PROCEDURE** DRAW(A,B,C : REAL); **EXTERNAL** 'FILENAME';
> **FUNCTION** COMPUTE(A,B,C : INTEGER) : REAL; **EXTERNAL** 'FILENAME';

External subprograms are specially written assembly language programs that must manipulate the computer's hardware registers and stack.

TURBO PASCAL INLINE PROCEDURES

Turbo Pascal provides a unique facility for including machine language instructions within Turbo Pascal programs to perform operations not normally allowed in Turbo. This feature is the INLINE statement. The form of the INLINE statement is

> **INLINE** ($90/$2345/sum + 1/list + */02);

Each parameter in the INLINE statement is separated by a slash (/) and generates either a byte or word value. The value of a variable is its address or offset. The asterisk (*) is equal to the current value of the location counter.

TURBO PASCAL EXIT AND HALT PROCEDURES

EXIT and HALT are special Turbo Pascal 3.0 statements that can be used to exit from a procedure, function, or program.

EXIT causes an immediate exit from the current subprogram or program block. It is similar to a GOTO label placed just before the END statement of the block. If it is called in the main program block, it terminates the program.

HALT causes immediate termination of the program and a return to the operating system (in compiled programs). If an integer parameter is specified it will be returned to the operating system as an ERRORLEVEL value, otherwise 0 will be returned.

SUMMARY

Functions and procedures provide a convenient way to treat a block of statements as a module. Functions take a value and must be part of an expression. Procedures may be used instead of a statement.

Communication with a function or a procedure is performed by means of parameters. A function or a procedure may define its own local variables, which have no effect on the outside program.

The functions and procedures used with parameters significantly enhance the power and flexibility of Pascal. Therefore, functions and procedures are used extensively throughout Pascal.

In practice, large programs are normally designed to include a collection of functions and procedures that perform specific actions. Each function or procedure may then be designed, refined and debugged separately.

EXERCISES

7-1: *Read a character and a number typed at the keyboard. Design a procedure that will draw a line including N times that character, where N is the number that was read at the keyboard. For example, after typing '*' and '3', the procedure might print '***'. Your program should check the reasonableness of the number typed at the keyboard.*

7-2: *As a variation of the previous exercise, write a program that will read ten characters from the keyboard, then print a line of ten times each character. Each successive line should be offset by one character to the right of the previous one. Use a procedure or a function wherever possible.*

7-3: *Write a procedure that converts a length expressed in inches into miles, yards, feet, and inches. Read LENGTH at the keyboard.*

7-4: Write a function that computes the maximum value of X,Y,Z where X,Y,Z are REAL.

7-5: In the program PARAMTEST below, what are the global variables? Can they be used in both VARVAL and SHOWSCOPE? What is the output of the program?

```
PROGRAM PARAMTEST (INPUT, OUTPUT);
VAR G1, G2: INTEGER;
     PROCEDURE VARVAL (PM1: INTEGER; VAR PM2: INTEGER);
     VAR PR1, PR2 : INTEGER;
     BEGIN (* VARVAL *)
         PR1 := 1;
         PR2 := 2;
         PM1 := PM1 + PR1 + PR2;
         PM2 := PM2 + PR1 + PR2
     END;  (* VARVAL *)
     FUNCTION SHOWSCOPE (PM1: INTEGER): INTEGER;
     VAR G1, FN: INTEGER;
     BEGIN (* SHOWSCOPE *)
         G1 := 0;
         FN := 2;
         PM1 := PM1 + FN;
         WRITELN (PM1);
         WRITELN (G1);
         SHOWSCOPE := G1
     END; (* SHOWSCOPE *)
BEGIN (* PARAMTEST *)
     WRITELN; WRITELN;
     G1 := 1;
     G2 := 2;
     VARVAL(G1,G2);
     WRITELN(G1);
     WRITELN(G2);
     G2 := SHOWSCOPE(G1);
     WRITELN(G1);
     WRITELN(G2);
     WRITELN; WRITELN
END. (* PARAMTEST *)
```

7-6: *Which numbers will the PARAMTEST program (defined above) print?*

7-7: *In the following statements, explain which variables are actual parameters, and which are formal parameters:*

PROCEDURE TEST 1 (VAR A,B,C : INTEGER);

TEST 1 (X,Y,Z);

7-8: *Examine the program RECURSE below. What does this program do to the input? What is the output?*

```
PROGRAM RECURSE (INPUT,OUTPUT);
    PROCEDURE READWRITE;
    VAR CH: CHAR;
    BEGIN (* READWRITE *)
        READ(CH);
        IF CH <>  ' ' THEN READWRITE;
        WRITE(CH)
    END; (* READWRITE *)
BEGIN (* RECURSE *)
    WRITELN; WRITELN;
    WRITELN ('TYPE A WORD IN RESPONSE TO THE PROMPT ');
    WRITELN ('TO STOP TYPE A BLANK.');
    WRITE('  ');
    READWRITE;
    WRITELN; WRITELN; WRITELN
END. (* RECURSE *)
```

CHAPTER **8**

DATA TYPES

TYPES

In this chapter, we will present a complete overview of the data types available in Pascal and the rules that apply to them. But first, let us consider the reasons for distinguishing one data type from another. Thus far, we have encountered four examples of data types: integers, reals, Booleans, and characters. These types are logically or mathematically distinct, and specific operators are used with each type. For example, adding two *characters* together does not have an obvious result! The addition operation is unavailable for characters in Pascal. Formally, addition is not defined for the data type 'characters'. From this example, therefore, we can conclude that each data type will have a set of operators that can be reasonably used with that particular type.

Data types are distinguished for two purposes:

1. So that the compiler may use the proper internal representation for each type.

2. So that the programmer will use the proper operators for each type.

The type definition is used for distinguishing data types.

In this chapter, we will review the reasons for distinguishing data types, then we will present an overview of all the types available in Pascal, and finally examine the mechanisms for defining data types.

WHY DATA TYPES?

We have just stated two purposes for data types. Let us examine them. Recall that throughout the book we have always declared the data type of each variable before using it:

```
VAR  I,J    : INTEGER;
     A,B    : REAL;
     LETTER : CHAR;
```

The first advantage of declaring a data type prior to its use is so that the compiler (the computer program that translates our Pascal program into machine-executable code) will be able to detect erroneous operators applied to the wrong type. This is very useful if the programmer is careless or if the program is long. The second advantage resulting from the formal declaration of data types is to facilitate the design of the compiler.

Each data type is represented inside the computer's memory in a specific format. If identifier types could change dynamically, i.e., as the program is being executed, this would complicate the proper allocation of the computer's memory. This dynamic change would also slow down the execution of the program.

Since the easy implementation of Pascal on a computer (i.e., designing a Pascal compiler with reasonable ease) was one of the considerations when the Pascal language was created, Pascal requires that all data types be formally declared before they are used. As such, when the compiler translates the program prior to execution, it can make all of the correct decisions relative to space allocation for each type of variable. A resulting advantage, which has just been mentioned, is that the compiler can verify the syntactic correctness of expressions at the time that they are being translated, rather than when they are actually executed. This process speeds up execution.

Some programmers feel that formal data type declarations such as those required by Pascal are a disadvantage: "the computer should know." However, bear in mind that every programming language is the result of many compromises between ease of use by the programmer and ease in compiler construction for the implementer. Languages exist that do not require formal type declarations and that allow data types to be modified dynamically as execution proceeds. However, compilers or interpreters for these languages tend to be much more difficult to implement. This is the case, for example, with the APL language.

Let us summarize the main requirements of data types in Pascal.

GENERAL RULES FOR DATA TYPES

The main rules that apply to data types in Pascal are:

— Every variable may have only one type. Naturally this applies only to the block where the identifier is declared.
— The type of each variable must be declared before the variable is used in an executable statement.
— The formal rules of Pascal declarations are specified by the syntax in Appendix F. In particular, declarations must be made in a specified order. This order is summarized in Figure 8.1.
— Finally, only specific operators may be applied to each data type.

Additional user-defined operators may be created using the PROCEDURE and the FUNCTION facilities provided by the language. In general, at least five standard operators should be logically available for all scalar data types: the assignment $:=$, and the tests for not equal $(<>)$, equal $(=)$, greater than $(>)$, and less than $(<)$. However, additional restrictions are placed by Pascal upon these operators. These

```
PROGRAM

LABEL

CONST

TYPE

VAR

PROCEDURE

FUNCTION
```

Figure 8.1:   Order of Pascal Declarations

restrictions will be explained later. It is important therefore to read this chapter carefully in order to efficiently and correctly use the data types provided by Pascal.

Note that Pascal provides many valuable facilities for defining and using additional data types. In this chapter, we will study the rules for creating new data types that are defined by the user. We will study in detail the many structured types defined by Pascal in the following chapters.

The various data types that are allowed by the language are an important and powerful facility in Pascal and should be thoroughly understood. Designing a program involves the design of a suitable algorithm (a step-by-step specification of the solution to a problem) and the use of effective data structures. Thus far, we have presented only simple programming examples using simple algorithms and a few variables. In the following chapters, we will present more complex programs requiring more complex data structures.

Having understood why data types are necessary, let us learn the various types and their correct uses.

SCALAR TYPES

Scalar types are the basic data types available in Pascal. Each scalar data type is composed of a set of distinct, ordered values. This means that for any two values A and B, one of the following relationships holds true:

$$A > B$$
$$A = B$$
$$A < B$$

As a result, all of the relational operators may be applied to all of the scalar types, as long as the two operands A and B are of the same type. Recall that the six relational operators are:

$$> \quad >= \quad < \quad <= \quad = \quad <>$$

In addition, three standard functions operate on scalar types (excluding REAL):

SUCC(N)	the successor of N
PRED(N)	the predecessor of N
ORD(N)	the ordinal number of N

The number of elements contained in a given data type is called the *cardinality* of that type. The ordinal number of the first value in a set is 0.

The two basic kinds of types are unstructured types which are scalars and *structured* types which are constructed from unstructured types. The unstructured types will be reviewed in this chapter. We have already learned about and used most of the unstructured data types. Let us review them systematically for clarity.

Two kinds of unstructured data types may be distinguished: standard (built-in), and user-defined. Let us examine the standard types first.

Standard Scalar Types

Four standard data types are automatically provided by Pascal. They are: INTEGER, REAL, CHAR, and BOOLEAN. They were descibed in Chapter 3 and have been used in all of the program examples thus far.

User-Defined Scalar Types

The TYPE statement was introduced in Chapter 3 to create new names for the four standard data types. For example:

TYPE DAY = INTEGER;

Thus far however, this facility has not been used as it has not offered any significant advantage.

The value of the TYPE declaration will now become apparent after we define the other possibilities.

Enumeration

Thus far, when we have used TYPE or VAR we have only listed identifiers. For example:

VAR A,B : REAL;

However, there are three possibilities to choose from. Following a TYPE or a VAR, one may either:

1. List type identifiers of previously defined types such as REAL, INTEGER, CHAR, etc.
2. List a sequence of identifiers such as (RED,GREEN,BLUE). This is called an *enumeration*.
3. List two constants separated by '..' such as '0..1000'. This is called a *subrange*.

When a type is defined by enumeration, a list of constants must be given which establishes the values contained in the data type and their order with respect to one another.

Enumerated types are defined in TYPE or VAR statements as follows:

TYPE type name   = (constant,constant,...)
VAR variable name   = (constant,constant,...)

The syntax diagram for enumerated type declarations is shown in Figure 8.2.

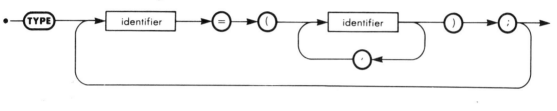

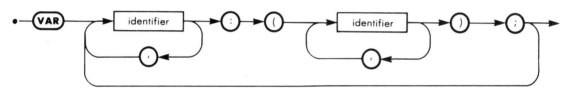

Figure 8.2: Enumerated Type Syntax

Let us consider some examples:

TYPE BASICOLOR = (RED,GREEN,BLUE); {enumeration}
DAY = (SUNDAY,MONDAY,TUESDAY,WEDNESDAY,THURSDAY,FRIDAY,SATURDAY);
COOKED = (RARE,MEDRARE,MEDIUM,MEDWELL,WELLDONE);

With the above definitions, the following relationships hold:

RED < GREEN < BLUE
SUNDAY < MONDAY < ... < SATURDAY
RARE < MEDRARE < MEDIUM < MEDWELL < WELLDONE

This is a powerful facility for giving a name to an ordered sequence composed of known elements.
An advantage that results from using this facility is that the compiler

will automatically verify that a variable of the type BASICOLOR may only take the values RED, GREEN or BLUE. Here are additional examples:

TYPE MONTH = (JAN,FEB,MAR,APR,MAY,JUN,JUL,AUG,SEP,OCT,NOV,DEC);
          RANK = (LIEUTENANT,CAPTAIN,GENERAL);
          NAMES = (ALBERT,CHARLES,DANIEL,FRANK);

Then, variables can be declared as belonging to this user-defined type:

VAR MEETINGDAY : WORKDAY;
        FISCAL : MONTH;
        OFFICER : RANK;
        PERSON : NAMES;

An abbreviated declaration may also be used. For example, we could write:

VAR WORKDAY : (MON,TUES,WED,THUR,FRI);
        SUMMER : (JUNE,JULY,AUGUST);

In this case, the variable SUMMER is assigned an unnamed type which can take on the values JUNE, JULY, and AUGUST. The only drawback to the above notation is that the new data type does not have a specific name. Therefore, other variables cannot be defined as belonging to that type.

Let us now examine the subrange type.

Subrange

Pascal permits the definition of types that are a subsequence of any scalar type (except REAL) that has been previously defined. This type is called a scalar subrange data type. The following are examples of subrange types:

TYPE WORKDAY = MONDAY .. FRIDAY;   {SUBRANGE OF DAY}
          SUMMER = JUN .. AUG;   {SUBRANGE OF MONTH}
          MONTHDIGITS = 1 .. 12;   {SUBRANGE OF INTEGERS}
          PASSINGSCORE = 6 .. 10;
          GOODVOLTAGE = 100 .. 120;
TYPE EARLYWEEK = MONDAY .. WEDNESDAY; {SUBRANGE OF WORKDAY}
          BESTSCORES = 8 .. 10;   {SUBRANGE OF PASSINGSCORE}
          FIRSTHALF = 'A' .. 'L';   {SUBRANGE OF ALPHABET}

In these examples, when assigning types to variables, TYPE can be legally replaced by VAR, as in the previous section.

The formal definition for this type is:

TYPE typename = lowerlimit..upperlimit

VAR variable name(s) : lowerlimit..upperlimit

The traditional Pascal diagram is shown in Figure 8.3.

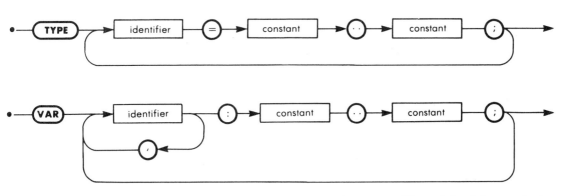

Figure 8.3:   Subrange Syntax

Restrictions

In the definition of an enumerated type or a subrange type, three restrictions apply:

1. The lower limit must be less than the upper limit.
2. There must be at least one element.
3. There may not be a partial overlap between two subranges.

Operations on User-Defined Scalars

The six relational operators, as well as SUCC, PRED, and ORD, may all be applied to user-defined scalar types. The other arithmetic and Boolean operators may not be applied to these types. When using PRED and SUCC, the ordinal value of the first constant in the definition of the type is 0. There is clearly no predecessor to the first constant, and no successor to the last one. The ordering of the data type is as shown in the data definition.

DATA TYPES IN TURBO PASCAL

As was mentioned earlier, the requirement that declarations be made in a specific order (see Figure 8.1) and that they occur either not at all or only once in a block is relaxed in Turbo Pascal. Declarations may appear in any order and any number of times as long as they appear before the statement section of the block.

RETYPING IN TURBO PASCAL

Turbo Pascal allows any scalar type (except real) to be *retyped*. Retyping is the reverse of the ORD( ) function and allows one scalar type to be translated to another. It is similar in operation to the CHR( ) function that converts integer values to character values.

Retyping works by using the scalar type identifier as a conversion function. For example:

```
CHAR(65) = 'A'
INTEGER('A') = 65
```

Retyping works for any defined scalar type.

SUMMARY

All user-defined Pascal types must be declared with a TYPE definition or a VAR declaration before they are used. There are two fundamental types: unstructured (scalar and subranges) and structured (non-scalar).

The unstructured types have been defined in this chapter: INTEGER, REAL, BOOLEAN, CHAR, and user-defined.

The structured types such as arrays, sets, records, and files are built from these unstructured types.

EXERCISES

8-1: *Find the declarations that are illegal:*

1. **CONST**	ONE = 1;	
2.	RANGE = 1..5;	
3.	DOT = '.';	
4. **TYPE**	GAME = (POKER,BRIDGE,BLACKJACK,ROULETTE);	
5.	MUSIC = (PIANO,HARP,GUITAR);	
6.	POSINT = 0..1000;	
7.	WEEK = (MON,TUES,WED,THUR,FRI,SAT,SUN);	

```
 8. VAR      'A' : CHAR;
 9.          BRIGHT : (YELLOW,ORANGE);
10.          LASVEGAS : (BLACKJACK,ROULETTE);
11.          INSTRUMENT : PIANO..GUITAR;
12.          EARLYWEEK : MON..WED;
13.          DAY : 1..31;
14.          MONTH : 1..12;
15.          WEEK : 1..52;
16.          LARGE : 100..MAXINT;
17.          INSTRUMENT : MUSIC;
```

8-2: *Give five examples of an enumerated data type and five examples of a subrange type.*

8-3: *Is the TYPE statement indispensable?*

8-4: *What is the advantage of an enumerated and a subrange data type?*

CHAPTER 9

ARRAYS

DATA STRUCTURES

Designing a computer program involves the solution of two problems:

1. Devising an efficient algorithm.
2. Designing or specifying appropriate data structures.

Converting the algorithm into a programming language is called *coding*. *Programming* also involves the design of suitable data structures.

Examples of simple data structures are lists and tables. The ability to use or create complex data structures is an important characteristic of any programming language. Pascal offers excellent facilities for specifying complex data structures. They are: arrays, records, files, sets, and lists. Each will now be described in this and the following chapters.

Data structures are collections of data elements. These structures will now be constructed from the primary data types defined in the previous chapter. Then, more complex structures will be created by using these primary data types as well as the new structured types as building blocks. The structuring method of each new type will be studied.

THE ARRAY

The array type is the simplest structured type in Pascal. Let us first introduce the concept of an array by looking at the example in Figure 9.1.

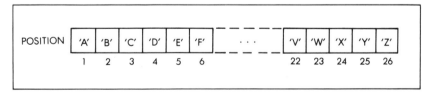

Figure 9.1: A Simple Array

The array in Figure 9.1 has 26 components, the letters of the alphabet. We will refer to the first element of the array POSITION as:

POSITION[1]

Its value is 'A'. 1 is called the *index* that refers to the first entry.

This simple example is called a simple array. It is a one-dimensional structure. More complex examples will be presented later.

In Pascal, the basic array type is a one-dimensional list of elements. More complex array types will be constructed from this simple type.

Let us now introduce the formal type ARRAY. An ARRAY, like any Pascal type, must be declared before it is used. The formal definition is shown in Figure 9.2.

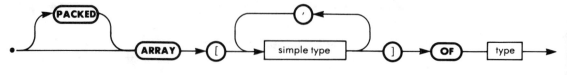

Figure 9.2: *Array Syntax*

Here is a formal array type definition:

       TYPE RANK = **ARRAY**[1..26] **OF** CHAR;

that defines the new type RANK. It is followed by:

       VAR POSITION : RANK;

This definition could also be abbreviated as:

       VAR POSITION : **ARRAY** [1..26] **OF** CHAR;

Remember from the previous chapter that [1..26] represents the numbers 1,2,3,4,5,...,25,26, and that CHAR is the type "character."

Here is another simple example, defining the array GRADE:

       TYPE GRADE = **ARRAY**[1..10] **OF** INTEGER;

This definition is followed by a variable definition such as:

       VAR SCORE : GRADE;

GRADE is a new (array) type. This new type contains 10 *components*. They must all be of the same type. Their type here is INTEGER, and it is called the *base type*.

The specification [1..10] is called the *index type*, and must be enclosed in square brackets. The *index* is used to refer to a specific component of an array. For example, the ten components of the array SCORE are:

SCORE[1]
SCORE[2]
SCORE[3]
SCORE[4]
SCORE[5]
SCORE[6]
SCORE[7]
SCORE[8]
SCORE[9]
SCORE[10]

In order to give a value to SCORE[1], we may write:

SCORE[1] : = 124;

Remember from the definition of GRADE that each component of this array must be of the type INTEGER.

Each component of an array may be used like any other variable of the same type. For example, the following is legal:

SCORE[1] : = 124;
SCORE[2] : = 100;
WRITELN('TOTAL SCORE 1 + 2 =', SCORE[1] + SCORE[2]);

Refer to the formal syntax in Figure 9.2. Note that an ARRAY may also be specified as PACKED. This feature will be explained at the end of this chapter.

Here is a second simple example:

TYPE MONTHNBR = **ARRAY**[MONTH] **OF** INTEGER;
VAR MM : MONTHNBR;

In this second example, we assume that MONTH has been defined as a subrange data type as in the previous chapter; the values of MONTH are JAN, FEB, up to DEC. Here, MM is a twelve-element integer array. Its elements are referenced as MM[JAN], MM[FEB], etc. This array definition enables us to refer to the MM value as JAN, FEB, etc., instead of having to use an integer between 1 and 12.

Note that in the formal definition of Figure 9.2, any unstructured scalar or subrange type may be used for the index type except REAL.

REFERENCING THE ELEMENTS OF AN ARRAY

Elements of an array are referenced by using the name of the array variable, followed by a left bracket and a legal expression, and terminated by a right bracket. Here are some examples:

```
SCORE[1]
SCORE[9]
SCORE[2 * 5 − 2]
```

OPERATING ON AN ARRAY

Components of an array may be used in any manner that is legal for their type. For example, assuming that the elements of SCORE are of type INTEGER, the following statements are legal:

```
TOTAL3 := SCORE[1] + SCORE[2] + SCORE[3];
AVERAGE56 := (SCORE[5] + SCORE[6])/2;
SCORE[7] := SCORE[1];
```

In addition, two operators may be used on an array as a whole: assignment (:=) and equality (=). For example, assuming that A and B are arrays of the same size and type, we may write:

```
A := B;
```

It is important to remember that these two operations concern *entire* arrays. It should also be noted that some Pascal compilers may not provide the equality operation.

MULTI-DIMENSIONAL ARRAYS

The examples we have given so far are lists or one-dimensional arrays. However, more complex arrays may be defined in PASCAL: they are called multi-dimensional arrays.

We will first introduce the concept of a two-dimensional array by looking at an example, as shown in Figure 9.3. This example shows the keys of a standard touch-tone telephone. This arrangement is called a two-dimensional array or a *matrix*. The elements of this array are: 0, 1, 2, 3, 4, 5, 6, 7, 8, 9, *, #. The array is organized in four rows and three columns.

Let us call this array 'K'. The usual convention is to designate each element of the array K by the notation K[I,J], where I is the row number and J is the column number that the key belongs to. For example, the key '*'

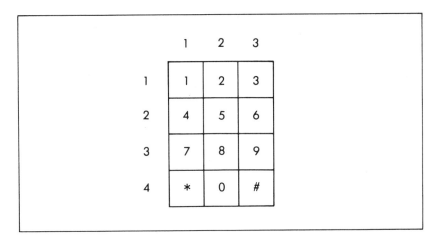

Figure 9.3:   A Two-dimensional Array

belongs to row 4 in column 1. In array notation, the value of K[4,1] is '*'.

This example illustrates a two-dimensional data structure. An array can also have additional dimensions. An array with n dimensions is called an *n-dimensional* array.

Formally, looking at the syntax of an array in Figure 9.2, note that the components of an array may be other arrays. A multi-dimensional array can be defined in the following way:

VAR   MULTIDIM : **ARRAY**[N1..N2] **OF ARRAY**[N3..N4] **OF** type;

As another example, a 4-by-4 keyboard can be defined as a 4-by-4 array in the following manner:

TYPE   KEYBOARD = **ARRAY**[1..4] **OF ARRAY**[1..4] **OF** KEY;
VAR   POSITION : KEYBOARD;

or like this:

TYPE   ROW = **ARRAY**[1..4] **OF** KEY;
        KEYBOARD = **ARRAY**[1..4] **OF** ROW;

which may also be abbreviated as:

TYPE   KEYBOARD = **ARRAY**[1..4, 1..4] **OF** KEY;

This abbreviated notation is convenient, as it resembles the usual mathematical convention.

Using this abbreviation, the definition of MULTIDIM above may be written as:

VAR MULTIDIM : **ARRAY**[N1..N2, N3..N4) **OF** type;

An element of MULTIDIM is referred to as:

MULTIDIM[I][J]

or, using the abbreviated notation, as:

MULTIDIM[I,J]

For example, assuming the statement:

VAR LAYOUT : KEYBOARD;

the key on the second row and the third column of a KEYBOARD matrix is referred to as:

LAYOUT[2,3]

or equivalently as:

LAYOUT[2][3]

It is, of course, possible to use any valid operators on elements of multi-dimensional arrays. For example, assuming that A is a two-dimensional array of reals, and that B is a mono-dimensional array, we can write:

B[I] := A[I,J] + 2.1;

or even:

M := N[I];

As a result of this last statement, M will become equal to the Ith row of N where N is a two-dimensional array. This statement is valid only if the col dimension of N is equal to the row dimension of M.
We can also write:

A[2,3] := A[1,2] + A[2,3];

Arrays are not limited to two dimensions, and more dimensions may be used, following the same rules for declaration and use.

ARRAY OF CHARACTERS

An array of characters may be used to store a *string*, i.e., a sequence of characters. However, any array of characters must have a *finite dimension*. Such an array requires that the maximum length of the string be known in advance. For example, assume that we are designing a mailing list program. Twenty characters may be used to represent the name, and thirty characters for each of the following two lines (company name, or profession or address), etc. The complete format for the proposed mailing list program is shown in Figure 9.4.

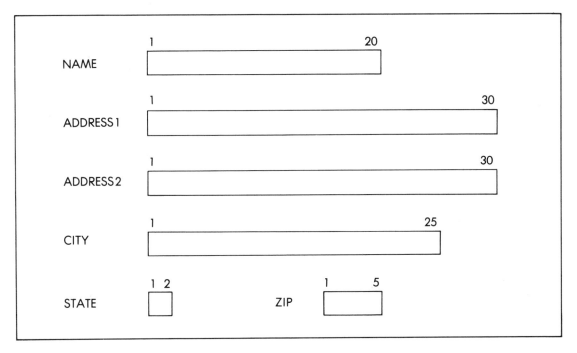

Figure 9.4:   A Mailing List Format

When an array of characters is used, the individual components of the array are characters. Whenever the relational operators >, <, <= and >= are used, the internal code used to represent the character set determines the ordering of the characters.

When comparing strings, the usual "lexicographic" (alphabetical) ordering rules are used so that: "Roger" is greater than "Peter."

Only strings of equal length may be compared. Whenever a string contains characters other than letters of the alphabet and digits, care must be exercised when comparing them: remember that the result of the comparison will depend on the internal code used to represent those characters.

CASE STUDY 1: MATRIX ADDITION

Theory

A matrix is generally defined as a two-dimensional array, although more dimensions can be used. A telephone keyboard is a visual example of a matrix.

Matrix addition is performed by adding the corresponding elements of two matrices of identical dimensions. For example:

$$\begin{bmatrix} 1 & 2 & 3 \\ 0 & 1 & 2 \\ 0 & 0 & 1 \end{bmatrix} + \begin{bmatrix} 0 & 1 & 2 \\ 3 & 4 & 5 \\ 1 & 0 & 0 \end{bmatrix} = \begin{bmatrix} 1 & 3 & 5 \\ 3 & 5 & 7 \\ 1 & 0 & 1 \end{bmatrix}$$
$$\quad\;\; A \qquad\qquad\quad B \qquad\qquad\; R$$

If R is the result, and A and B are the two matrices to be added, the equation is:

$$R[I,J] = A[I,J] + B[I,J] \text{ for each valid pair } [I,J]$$

Figure 9.5 presents a Pascal program that prints the sum of several matrices.

Three constants are used in the program in Figure 9.5:

ROWSIZE and COLSIZE specify the dimensions of each matrix.
ADDNUM specifies the number of matrices to be added together.
ADDNUM is set to 2 in this example.

In this program, the first matrix, MATX, is read at the keyboard. Then, each matrix that is to be added to the first matrix is typed element by element into HOLDIN, and then immediately added to MATX.

The row and column positions of the element being entered are in ROWIN and COLIN. ADDIN is a dummy variable used in the addition loop. The corresponding program declarations are:

```
PROGRAM ADDMATX (INPUT,OUTPUT);
CONST   ROWSIZE  = 5;
        COLSIZE  = 5;
        ADDNUM   = 2;
VAR     MATX : ARRAY[1..ROWSIZE, 1..COLSIZE]OF INTEGER;
        ADDIN,HOLDIN,ROWIN,COLIN: INTEGER;
```

```
PROGRAM ADDMATX (INPUT, OUTPUT);
CONST    ROWSIZE = 5;  (* ROW SIZE OF MATRIX *)
         COLSIZE = 5;   (* COLUMN SIZE OF MATRIX *)
         ADDNUM = 2;(* NUMBER OF MATRICES TO BE ADDED *)
VAR      MATX:          (* ADDEND MATRIX *)
              ARRAY [1..ROWSIZE, 1..COLSIZE] OF INTEGER;
         ADDIN,         (* SUMMATION INDEX *)
         HOLDIN,        (* HOLDS MATRIX ELEMENT AS IT IS INPUT *)
         ROWIN,         (* ROW INDEX *)
         COLIN:         (* COLUMN INDEX *)
              INTEGER;
BEGIN (* ADDMATX *)
    (* INPUT FIRST MATRIX *)
      FOR ROWIN := 1 TO ROWSIZE DO
        FOR COLIN := 1 TO COLSIZE DO
          READ(MATX[ROWIN,COLIN]);
    (* THIS LOOP IS ADDED SO THAT THE NUMBER OF MATRICES TO BE ADDED *)
    (* CAN BE CHANGED BY SIMPLY CHANGING THE CONSTANT ADDNUM. *)
      FOR ADDIN := 1 TO (ADDNUM - 1) DO
        FOR ROWIN := 1 TO ROWSIZE DO
          FOR COLIN := 1 TO COLSIZE DO
              BEGIN (* READ, ADD *)
                  READ(HOLDIN);
                  MATX[ROWIN,COLIN] := MATX[ROWIN,COLIN] + HOLDIN
              END; (* READ, ADD *)
    (* PRINT MATRIX *)
      FOR ROWIN := 1 TO ROWSIZE DO
        BEGIN (* PRINT ONE ROW *)
              FOR COLIN := 1 TO COLSIZE DO
                  WRITE(MATX[ROWIN,COLIN]:3);
              WRITELN
        END (* PRINT ONE ROW *)
END. (* ADDMATX *)
```

Figure 9.5: MATRIX ADDITION Program

The first matrix is read:

```
BEGIN
    FOR ROWIN := 1 TO ROWSIZE DO
        FOR COLIN := 1 TO COLSIZE DO
            READ (MATX[ROWIN,COLIN]);
```

Note that the elements are read a *row* at a time:

```
MATX[1,1]     MATX[1,2]     MATX[1,3] . . .
```

until all rows have been read.
The next matrix is read in the same way:

```
FOR ADDIN := 1 TO (ADDNUM − 1) DO
    FOR ROWIN := 1 TO ROWSIZE DO
        FOR COLIN := 1 TO COLSIZE DO
            BEGIN
                READ (HOLDIN);
```

and the current element is immediately added to the proper element of
MATX:

```
                MATX[ROWIN,COLIN] := MATX[ROWIN,COLIN] + HOLDIN
    END;
```

The result is then printed:

```
FOR ROWIN := 1 TO ROWSIZE DO
    BEGIN
        FOR COLIN := 1 TO COLSIZE DO
            WRITE(MATX[ROWIN,COLIN]:3);
        WRITELN
    END
END.
```

A typical input is shown below:

```
1  1  1  1  1
2  2  2  2  2
3  3  3  3  3
4  4  4  4  4
5  5  5  5  5
5  5  5  5  5
4  4  4  4  4
3  3  3  3  3
2  2  2  2  2
1  1  1  1  1
```

Followed by a typical output:

```
6  6  6  6  6
6  6  6  6  6
6  6  6  6  6
6  6  6  6  6
6  6  6  6  6
```

Matrix Addition Summary

This program demonstrates the input and output of array elements in "row-major order" (row by row), along with the use of multiple indices and nested DO loops.

CASE STUDY 2: QUICKSORT

Sorting

A frequent task that arises with arrays is to sort elements in ascending or descending order. The task seems simple, but the solution is not. A simple algorithm can be designed that will sort elements of an array. However, such an algorithm is usually very inefficient when sorting a large array: it may require minutes or even hours. The real problem lies in designing an efficient algorithm that will sort a large array within a short period of time.

This latter problem is complex, and many solutions have been devised. For a discussion of the merits of various techniques, see reference [18].

One of the simplest sorting techniques is the "bubble sort" technique which can be implemented using a short program. This technique requires approximately $\frac{1}{2} N^2$ operations, where N is the number of items to be sorted.

The "Quicksort" technique is a fast algorithm that divides the search interval into sections to achieve higher speed, and requires only N $\times$ Log_2 N operations to sort N items. For example, if N = 1000 items, Quicksort is about 50 times faster than a bubble sort or similar algorithm. The speed of Quicksort is even more noticeable as N becomes larger.

Quicksort Algorithm

The Quicksort algorithm will be described here, along with its Pascal implementation. The implementation of Quicksort uses a bubble sort procedure, so that both sorting techniques will have been presented. The bubble sort algorithm will be described within the context of the bubble sort procedure, when we describe the Pascal implementation.

Quicksort operates as follows:

1. Quicksort selects an approximate median value for the elements to be sorted.
2. The array is scanned, and elements are exchanged until the resulting array contains two sections: elements greater than the median element, and elements less than or equal to the median element.
3. The two steps above are repeated on each section that has more than P elements (P will be equal to 6 in our program).
4. Once the sections have become small enough, each section is then sorted with a bubble sort (an efficient algorithm for a small number of elements). The result is a sorted array.

Quicksort Example

An example of Quicksort is shown in Figure 9.6. The eleven array elements are shown on the first horizontal line. They include:

> 91, 4, 27, 63, 32, 55, 87, 43, 16, 74, 9

Let us look at the steps listed in Figure 9.6 in detail.

Step 1 — A median value is selected by comparing the first, middle and last elements, i.e.; the elements in positions 0, 5 and 10. Their values are:

> 91 (position 0)
>
> 55 (position 5)
>
> 9 (position 10)

The median value is 55.

Step 2 — The median value is placed in position 0 of the array by exchanging it with the element that is there. This is illustrated on line 2 of Figure 9.6, where the values 55 and 91 have been exchanged.

Step 3 — The elements of the array are examined from right to left and compared to the median until a value is found that is less than the median. This value is then exchanged with the median. In our example, the value of the last element (position 10) is compared to the value of the median (now in position 0). These values are:

9 (position 10)   : element examined
55 (position 0)   : median

9 is less than the median, and the exchange is performed, as shown in line 3 of Figure 9.6.

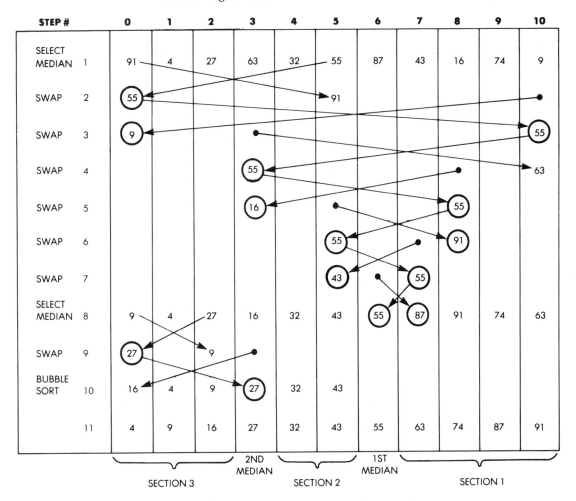

Figure 9.6: *Quicksort Example*

Step 4 — Location 0 now contains a value smaller than the median. Location 10 contains the median. In this step, the array is scanned from left to right until a value larger than the median is found. This value is exchanged with the median.

In our example the situation is the following:

Position 10 : 55 (median)

Position 0 : 9 ("small element")

Position 1 : 4 : less than median

Position 2 : 27 : less than median

Position 3 : 63 : greater than median.

63 is, therefore, exchanged with the median, resulting in the situation shown in line 4 of Figure 9.6.

Steps 5 to 8 — The array is scanned alternately in each direction until it contains two sections, as shown in line 8 of Figure 9.6. The leftmost section of the array, containing elements in positions 0 to 5, contains elements with values that are less than the median. The median is in position 6.

The rightmost section of the array, containing elements in positions 7 to 10, contains values that are greater than the median.

The rightmost section (called section 1 in the illustration) contains only four elements. The leftmost section contains six elements.

Steps 9 — 10 — The Quicksort algorithm is applied to the leftmost section, resulting in the situation shown in line 10 of Figure 9.6. At this point, the two new resulting sections (called sections 2 and 3 in the illustration) contain three elements and two elements, respectively.

Step 11 — A bubble sort is now applied to each of the three sections, resulting in a completely sorted array, as shown in line 11 of Figure 9.6.

Quicksort Program

The Quicksort program for this algorithm is shown in Figure 9.7.

A sample run of the program is shown in Figure 9.8. Twelve values are entered at the keyboard, and the result of the Quicksort is typed underneath.

The program in Figure 9.7 uses one array and six procedures:

SWAP exchanges two elements

GETARRAY reads the elements of the array to be sorted, as typed at the keyboard

PRINTARRAY prints the sorted values in four-column format

BSORT performs a bubble sort

FINDMEDIAN finds a median value

SORTSECTION quicksorts an array section.

```
PROGRAM QSORT(INPUT,OUTPUT);
(* PROGRAM TO SORT A NUMERIC ARRAY USING 'QUICKSORT' ALGORITHM *)
(* ADAPTED FROM VOLUME 3, 'ART OF COMPUTER PROGRAMMING' BY KNUTH *)
(* GLOBAL IDENTIFIERS *)
CONST MAX=100; (* MAXIMUM ARRAY SIZE *)
TYPE STANDARDARRAY = ARRAY[0..MAX] OF REAL;
VAR NUMBERS: STANDARDARRAY; (* NUMERIC ARRAY *)
    LAST: INTEGER;
PROCEDURE SWAP(VAR A,B: REAL);
VAR T: REAL;
BEGIN
    T := A;
    A := B;
    B := T
END;
PROCEDURE GETARRAY(VAR TOP: INTEGER); (* FILL ARRAY FROM INPUT *)
VAR INDEX: INTEGER;
    TEMP : REAL;
BEGIN (* GETARRAY *)
    INDEX := 0;
    WHILE NOT EOF(INPUT) DO
        BEGIN
            WRITE('INPUT ARRAY(',INDEX:4,')  :');
            READLN(TEMP);
            (* VALIDATION TEST WOULD GO HERE *)
            NUMBERS[INDEX] := TEMP;
            INDEX := SUCC(INDEX)
        END;
    WRITELN;
    WRITELN(INDEX-1:4,' VALUES ENTERED');
    TOP := INDEX-2
END; (* GETARRAY *)
PROCEDURE PRINTARRAY(TOP: INTEGER); (* OUTPUT ARRAY *)
VAR INDEX: INTEGER;
BEGIN (* PRINTARRAY *)
```

Figure 9.7: QUICKSORT Program

```
        FOR INDEX := 0 TO TOP DO
            BEGIN
                IF INDEX/4 = TRUNC(INDEX/4) THEN WRITELN;
                WRITE(NUMBERS[INDEX]:8:2)
            END
END;
PROCEDURE BSORT(START,TOP: INTEGER; VAR ARRY: STANDARDARRAY);
(* BUBBLE SORT PROCEDURE, SORTS ARRAY FROM START TO TOP, INCLUSIVE *)
VAR INDEX: INTEGER;
    SWITCHED: BOOLEAN;
BEGIN (* BSORT *)
    REPEAT
        SWITCHED := FALSE;
        FOR INDEX := START TO TOP−1 DO
            BEGIN
                IF ARRY[INDEX] > ARRY[INDEX+1] THEN
                    BEGIN
                        SWAP(ARRY[INDEX],ARRY[INDEX+1]);
                        SWITCHED := TRUE
                    END
            END;
    UNTIL SWITCHED = FALSE
END
PROCEDURE FINDMEDIAN(START,TOP: INTEGER; VAR ARRY: STANDARDARRAY);
(* PROCEDURE TO FIND A GOOD MEDIAN VALUE IN ARRAY AND PLACE IT *)
(* AT BEGINNING OF SECTION TO BE SORTED *)
VAR MIDDLE: INTEGER;
    SORTED: STANDARDARRAY;
BEGIN (* FINDMEDIAN *)
    MIDDLE := (START+TOP) DIV 2;
    SORTED[1] := ARRY[START];
    SORTED[2] := ARRY[TOP];
    SORTED[3] := ARRY[MIDDLE];
    BSORT(1,3,SORTED);
    IF SORTED [2] = ARRY[MIDDLE] THEN
        SWAP(ARRY[START],ARRY[MIDDLE])
```

Figure 9.7: QUICKSORT Program (continued)

```
        ELSE IF SORTED[2] = ARRY[TOP] THEN
              SWAP(ARRY[START],ARRY[TOP])
END; (* FINDMEDIAN *)
PROCEDURE SORTSECTION(START,TOP: INTEGER);
(* PROCEDURE TO SORT A SECTION OF THE MAIN ARRAY, AND *)
(* THEN DIVIDE IT INTO TWO PARTITIONS TO BE SORTED *)
VAR SWAPUP: BOOLEAN;
    S,E,M: INTEGER;
BEGIN (* SORTSECTION *)
    IF TOP-START < 6 THEN (* SORT SMALL SECTIONS WITH BSORT *)
        BSORT(START,TOP,NUMBERS)
    ELSE
        BEGIN
            FINDMEDIAN(START,TOP,NUMBERS);
            SWAPUP := TRUE;
          (* START SCANNING FROM ARRAY TOP *)
            S := START; (* LOWER COMPARISON LIMIT *)
            E := TOP; (* UPPER COMPARISON LIMIT *)
            M := START; (* LOCATION OF COMPARISON VALUE *)
            WHILE E > S DO
                BEGIN
                    IF SWAPUP = TRUE THEN
                        (* SCAN DOWNWARD FROM PARTITION TOP *)
                        (* AND EXCHANGE IF SMALLER THAN MEDIAN *)
                        BEGIN
                            WHILE (NUMBERS[E] >= NUMBERS[M])AND(E>M) DO
                                E := E-1;
                            IF E > M THEN
                                BEGIN
                                    SWAP(NUMBERS[E],NUMBERS[M]);
                                    M := E
                                END;
                            SWAPUP := FALSE
                        END
```

Figure 9.7: *QUICKSORT Program (continued)*

```
                                ELSE
                                    (* SCAN UPWARD FROM PARTITION START *)
                                    (* AND EXCHANGE IF LARGER THAN MEDIAN *)
                                    BEGIN
                                        WHILE (NUMBERS[S] <= NUMBERS[M])AND(S<M) DO
                                            S := S+1;
                                        IF S < M THEN
                                            BEGIN
                                                SWAP(NUMBERS[S],NUMBERS[M]);
                                                M := S
                                            END;
                                        SWAPUP := TRUE
                                    END
                                END;
                            SORTSECTION(START,M-1); (* SORT LOWER HALF OF PARTITION *)
                            SORTSECTION(M+1,TOP) (* SORT UPPER HALF OF PARTITION *)
                        END
                END; (* SORTSECTION *)
                BEGIN (* QSORT - MAIN PROGRAM *)
                    GETARRAY(LAST);
                    SORTSECTION(0,LAST);
                    PRINTARRAY(LAST)
                END. (* QSORT *)
```

Figure 9.7   QUICKSORT Program (continued)

The program body includes only three executable statements and is self-explanatory:

```
    BEGIN
        GETARRAY (LAST);
        SORTSECTION (0,LAST);
        PRINTARRAY (LAST)
    END.
```

Each procedure will be explained in turn.

Program Variables

This program declares one constant, MAX (the maximum array size)

```
INPUT ARRAY(     0)    :12.5
INPUT ARRAY(     1)    :22
INPUT ARRAY(     2)    :3.3
INPUT ARRAY(     3)    :92.67
INPUT ARRAY(     4)    :400
INPUT ARRAY(     5)    :606.1
INPUT ARRAY(     6)    :−4
INPUT ARRAY(     7)    :56
INPUT ARRAY(     8)    :44
INPUT ARRAY(     9)    :0
INPUT ARRAY(    10)    :22
INPUT ARRAY(    11)    :78
INPUT ARRAY(    12)    :
12 VALUES ENTERED
−4.00    0.00     3.30    12.50
 22.00   22.00   44.00    56.00
 78.00   92.67  400.00   606.10
```

Figure 9.8: Sample Quicksort Run

and two variables: NUMBERS (the array) and LAST (the position of the last element in the array):

```
PROGRAM      QSORT(INPUT,OUTPUT);
CONST        MAX = 100;
TYPE         STANDARDARRAY = ARRAY[0..MAX] OF REAL;
VAR          NUMBERS: STANDARDARRAY;
             LAST: INTEGER;
```

Procedure SWAP

The procedure SWAP exchanges the values of A and B, using a temporary variable T. The need for T has already been indicated earlier in this chapter.

```
PROCEDURE SWAP(VAR A,B: REAL);
VAR T: REAL;
BEGIN
    T := A;
    A := B;
    B := T
END;
```

A and B are variable parameters. T is a local variable. A, B and T are local identifiers.

Procedure GETARRAY

The procedure GETARRAY reads values typed at the keyboard until an EOF character is typed. These values are placed in the global array called NUMBERS. The position of the last element is returned via the parameter TOP.

This procedure uses two local variables: INDEX and TEMP. INDEX is the position of the current element within the array, and TEMP stores the last value typed:

```
PROCEDURE GETARRAY(VAR TOP: INTEGER);
VAR      INDEX  : INTEGER;
         TEMP   : REAL;
BEGIN (* GETARRAY *)
     INDEX : = 0;
```

Values are read with a WHILE loop until an EOF is found:

```
WHILE NOT EOF(INPUT) DO
    BEGIN
         WRITE('INPUT ARRAY(',INDEX:4,')    :');
         READLN(TEMP);
         NUMBERS[INDEX] : = TEMP;
         INDEX : = SUCC(INDEX)
    END;
    WRITELN;
    WRITELN(INDEX −1 : 4,' VALUES ENTERED');
    TOP : = INDEX −2
END; (* GETARRAY *)
```

Note that this procedure (like others in this program) modifies the value of the global variable NUMBERS. This is a (voluntary) side-effect.

Procedure PRINTARRAY

The procedure PRINTARRAY prints the array NUMBERS up to position TOP in a four-column format. This procedure uses the local variable INDEX. Since INDEX is local to PRINTARRAY, this variable has no relationship with the INDEX used in the previous GETARRAY procedure. INDEX is used again simply because it is convenient to use the name INDEX and legal to do so. The values are printed with a FOR...DO statement:

```
PROCEDURE PRINTARRAY(TOP: INTEGER);
VAR INDEX: INTEGER; (* THIS IS ANOTHER LOCAL VARIABLE *)
BEGIN
    FOR INDEX : = 0 TO TOP DO
        BEGIN
            IF INDEX MOD 4 THEN WRITELIN;
            WRITE(NUMBERS[INDEX]:8:2)
        END
END;
```

Note the "programming trick" used to print in a 4-column format:

IF INDEX MOD 4 **THEN** WRITELIN;

The output is moved to the next line after every fourth number output, since the equality specified in the IF-clause is TRUE only when INDEX is a multiple of 4.

Procedure BSORT

Procedure BSORT is a bubble sort procedure. This procedure accepts three parameters: the array ARRY to be sorted, and the beginning and end positions: START and TOP.

The bubble sort algorithm operates by letting the "lightest" element "bubble up" to the top, just like air bubbles in a tall container of liquid. This algorithm operates as follows:

Step 1 — The first element is compared to the second element. If the second element is smaller, the two are exchanged.

Step 2 —1 The second and third elements are compared. If the third element is smaller than the second, the two are exchanged.

Step 3 — The process continues with the third and fourth element, etc., until the end of the array is reached.

Step 4 — If no exchange has occurred, the algorithm terminates. If any exchange has occurred during this "pass," the process is repeated. Eventually, all elements are ordered, no exchange occurs, and the algorithm terminates. An example is shown in Figure 9.9.

The BSORT procedure uses two local variables:

— INDEX points to the current array element. (INDEX + 1 will point to the following one.)
— SWITCHED indicates whether or not an exchange has taken place during the current pass.

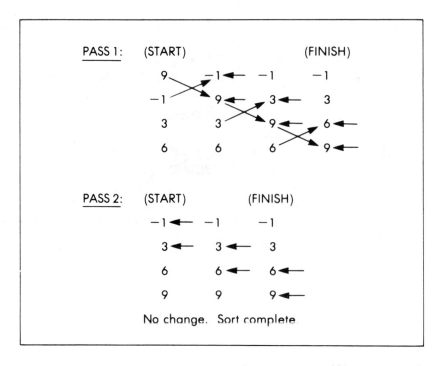

Figure 9.9: A Bubble Sort Example

SWITCHED is set to FALSE at the beginning of each pass, and tested at the end of each pass. If SWITCHED is still FALSE at the end of the pass, the sort is complete. Otherwise, the pass is repeated.

A REPEAT...UNTIL loop is used since the value of SWITCHED must be tested at the *end* of the loop.

This procedure uses the SWAP procedure (described in a previous section) to exchange the elements

    ARRY[INDEX]

and   ARRY[INDEX + 1]

whenever the second element is less than the first:

```
        PROCEDURE BSORT(START,TOP: INTEGER; VAR ARRY: STANDARDARRAY);
        VAR     INDEX: INTEGER;
                SWITCHED: BOOLEAN;
        BEGIN
            REPEAT
                SWITCHED := FALSE;
                FOR INDEX := START TO TOP −1 DO
```

```
        BEGIN
          IF ARRY[INDEX] > ARRY[INDEX + 1] THEN
            BEGIN
                SWAP(ARRY[INDEX],ARRY[INDEX + 1]);
                SWITCHED := TRUE
            END
        END;
      UNTIL SWITCHED = FALSE
END;
```

Notice the two nested loops used in this procedure. The outer loop is created by the REPEAT...UNTIL and causes successive passes. The inner loop is created by the FOR...DO and compares the values of all successive element pairs in ARRY in sequence. A SWAP occurs whenever the IF is satisfied and the "flag variable" SWITCHED is turned on accordingly to memorize the event.

Procedure FINDMEDIAN

The procedure FINDMEDIAN finds an approximation of the median value in a specified section of the array and places it at the beginning of that section. The procedure uses three parameters:

— ARRY for the array to be examined, and,
— START, TOP to specify the positions of the first and last elements to be examined.

The procedure FINDMEDIAN uses two local variables:

— MIDDLE points to the middle element.
— SORTED is used to store the values of the first array element, middle element, and last element.

In the case where the array section has an odd number of elements (such as 5), the middle element is the element residing in position 2 (the third position, starting at 0).

```
PROCEDURE FINDMEDIAN(START,TOP: INTEGER; VAR ARRY: STANDARDARRAY);
VAR     MIDDLE: INTEGER;
        SORTED: STANDARDARRAY;
BEGIN
    MIDDLE := (START + TOP) DIV 2;
```

Note the use of the integer divide DIV in order to obtain an integer result (the position of the "middle" element).

Once the value of the middle element has been read, this value is then compared to the values of the first and last element. Three possibilities can exist:

1. The value of the middle element is the middle value, i.e., it is between the other two values.
2. The first element contains the middle value.
3. The last element contains the middle value.

A test is, therefore, performed to determine which element of the array, if any, should be exchanged with the first element. This test is accomplished by writing the values of the three elements into the array SORTED:

```
SORTED[1] : = ARRY[START];
SORTED[2] : = ARRY[TOP];
SORTED[3] : = ARRY[MIDDLE];
```

Then these three values are sorted with a bubble sort:

```
BSORT(1,3,SORTED);
```

The value of the "true middle" is contained in SORTED[2]. This value is, therefore, compared to the middle and the last elements of the array to determine which values to exchange:

```
IF    SORTED[2] = ARRY[MIDDLE] THEN
      SWAP(ARRY[START],ARRY[MIDDLE])
ELSE IF SORTED[2] = ARRY[TOP] THEN
      SWAP(ARRY[START],ARRY[TOP])
END;
```

Procedure SORTSECTION

The procedure SORTSECTION sorts the elements of the array into two groups:

1. Less than the middle value
2. Greater than the middle value.

The corresponding flowchart is shown in Figure 9.10. In this procedure, four local variables are used:

— SWAPUP is used to remember which direction the array section is to be scanned.
— S, E, and M are used to represent the positions of the start element, the end element, and the median value, respectively.

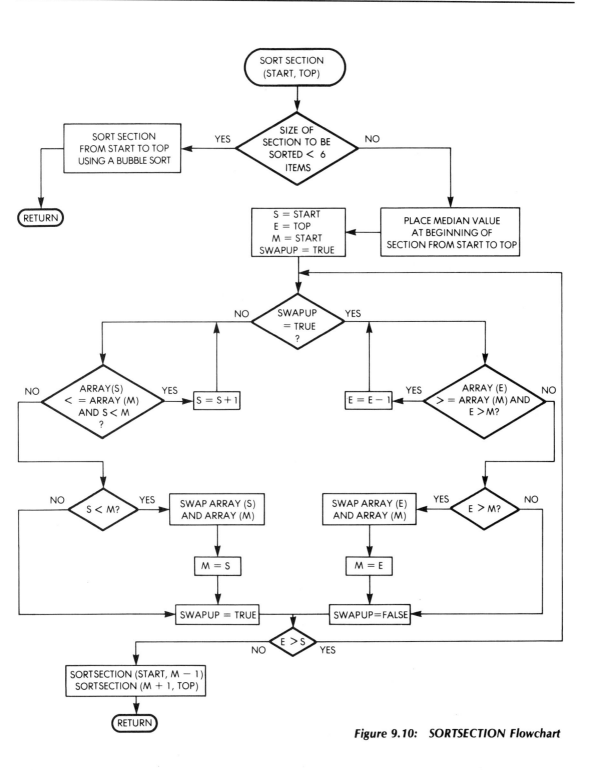

Figure 9.10: SORTSECTION Flowchart

The procedure SORTSECTION sorts sections of the main array as long as there are 6 elements (or more) in a section. When groups have less than 6 elements, they are sorted with a bubble sort.

The first scan starts at the 'top' of the array section, i.e., with the last element (at position E). SWAPUP is initially set to TRUE:

```
PROCEDURE SORTSECTION(START,TOP:INTEGER);
VAR SWAPUP: BOOLEAN;
    S,E,M : INTEGER;
BEGIN
    IF TOP—START < 6 THEN BSORT(START,TOP,NUMBERS)
    ELSE
        BEGIN
            FINDMEDIAN(START,TOP,NUMBERS);
            SWAPUP := TRUE;
            S        := START;
            E        := TOP;
            M        := START;
```

E initially points to the last element. The value of that element is compared to the value of the middle element. If the value of the last element is greater, that element does not need to be moved (as long as E > M) and the pointer E is decremented:

```
WHILE E > S DO
    BEGIN
        IF SWAPUP = TRUE THEN
            BEGIN
                WHILE (NUMBERS[E] >= NUMBERS[M]) AND (E > M)
                DO E := E — 1;
```

This WHILE loop is repeated until E becomes equal to M. However, if the value of the last element is less than the value of the middle element, a swap must be performed (as long as E > M):

```
IF E > M THEN
    BEGIN
        SWAP(NUMBERS[E],NUMBERS[M]);
        M := E
    END;
    SWAPUP := FALSE
END
```

The swap is recorded by setting SWAPUP to FALSE. With SWAPUP set to FALSE, the array will next be scanned from the bottom up, as long as S < M, or until a swap is made.

The ELSE clause will be executed next. This alternate pass operates essentially in reverse of the earlier IF clause.

```
ELSE (* UPWARD SCAN *)
    BEGIN
        WHILE (NUMBERS[S] <= NUMBERS[M])AND
            (S < M) DO S := S + 1;
        IF S < M THEN
        BEGIN
            SWAP(NUMBERS[S],NUMBERS[M]);
            M := S
        END;
        SWAPUP := TRUE
    END
END;
```

Once the two sections have been created, the process is repeated on each section:

```
SORTSECTION(START,M − 1);
SORTSECTION(M + 1,TOP)
END
END;
```

Quicksort Summary

This program illustrates many practical programming techniques: use of nested loops, global and local variables, decision flags, use of procedures and parameters, and use of arrays. The Quicksort program should be studied carefully.

PACKED ARRAYS

Often, one byte (8 binary bits) is used internally to represent a character. Most microcomputers store all data in bytes, and are well suited to the representation of characters.

However, Pascal was originally implemented on large computers that use a smaller number of bits per character (6), and a much larger number of bits per data element (32 or 60 bits, for example). In such a case, storing a 6-bit character in a 60-bit word wastes a substantial amount of memory space.

To remedy this problem, the PACKED form of type is provided in Pascal. The effect of this statement is to compact an array so that each element occupies a minimum amount of storage. For example, a character would occupy only one byte. The formal definition is:

PACKED ARRAY[TYPE1] **OF** TYPE2;

The usual operations are available on the components of a packed array:

$$:=, \ =, \ <> \ , \ < \ , \ > \ , \ \ <=, \ \ >=$$

For example, the following is legal:

> **VAR** TITLE : **PACKED ARRAY**[1..16] **OF** CHAR;
> HEADING : **PACKED ARRAY**[1..5] **OF** CHAR;

followed in the program by:

> TITLE := 'TABLE OF SQUARES';
> HEADING := '10−50';

In this example, the string variables TITLE and HEADING are assigned the value of string constants. This requires that the index type for the string variable be [1..N], where N is greater than or equal to the length of the string constant.

However, using a packed array also generally results in slower access to individual array elements. As a result, two built-in procedures are provided: PACK( ) and UNPACK( ) that perform the obvious function.

For example, assume:

> **VAR** A : **ARRAY**[M..N] **OF** X;
> B : **PACKED ARRAY**[U..V] **OF** X;

with N−M >= V−U. The unpacking procedure is performed by executing:

> **FOR** I := U **TO** V **DO** A[I − U + J] := B[I];

where J is the starting position in A into which the unpacked array should be copied. This is accomplished automatically by the built-in procedure:

> **UNPACK** (B,A,J);

Conversely, the procedure:

PACK (A,J,B);

automatically performs:

FOR I := U **TO** V **DO** B[I] := A[I − U + J];

where J is the position in A where the string that is to be packed into B begins.

In summary, packed arrays normally result in a savings of memory space. However, for computers using 16 bit words or more that do not have built-in byte access, the use of packed arrays results in a loss of execution speed if characters have to be accessed frequently: several characters are packed in a single word so that the retrieval of any specific character takes a longer time. In order to improve the execution speed, it may be advantageous to use the UNPACK procedure before performing complex or multiple selections on the elements of an array. After performing these selections, the array can be repacked again with the PACK procedure.

TABLES OF FUNCTION VALUES

It is often convenient to store a set of values for a function in a table. If the value of the function cannot be computed exactly, or if the computation requires a long time, it is often advantageous to look up a table value rather than to compute it. If precision is required, table values can be used together with an interpolation method between two successive entries in the table. This technique can be implemented in Pascal by using arrays to store the values. The following is an example of a straightforward application of an array where the function Y = F(X) is stored as:

VAR F : **ARRAY**[X] **OF** Y;

For example, the TRANSCEND function could be defined as:

VAR TRANSCEND : **ARRAY** (0..N) **OF** 0.. MAXINT;

where we assume that 0 is the value of TRANSCEND[0] and N is the largest integer such that TRANSCEND[N] <= MAXINT.

Of course, the table must be filled in order to be usable. It can be filled by explicitly assigning the values of the table with constants, or by computing the values of all the elements of the table once. This way, a complex computation is executed only once, resulting in improved program efficiency.

Using this array technique, any reasonable function may be implemented, i.e., any reasonable correspondence may be applied between the array value and its index. For example, the usual numbers can be spelled out as 'ONE', 'TWO', etc. An array function will establish a correspondence between '5' and 'FIVE', '6' and 'SIX', etc. However, note that it is unfortunately not possible to go back from 'FIVE' to '5', since a string may not be directly used as an index.

TURBO PASCAL ARRAYS

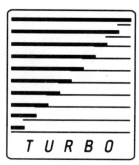

The main extensions to Standard Pascal arrays in Turbo Pascal are the additional facilities provided for STRINGs and character arrays. These added reserved functions and procedures provided by Turbo Pascal are called *intrinsics*.

Turbo Pascal allows an entire array or string to be copied to another variable of the same type with one assignment statement.

Turbo Pascal does not support PACKED ARRAYS of any kind. This is because all data types are automatically packed and unpacked as they are accessed.

Memory Usage

Turbo Pascal variable arrays reside in the program's DATA segment (in 16-bit versions) and must share the maximum available variable area of 64K bytes with other program variables and the stack. Large data structures should use the heap to conserve variable space.

Range Checking

The Turbo Pascal compiler can provide range checking of index values, depending on the state of the R compiler directive. The Range directive is normally passive ({$R−}), but can be activated during program testing ({$R+}). The use of range checking slows program execution significantly.

TURBO STRING TYPE

Turbo Pascal includes the predeclared type STRING. A STRING is stored as an ARRAY OF CHARs and has a *length*. The Turbo function LENGTH returns the length of the string (e.g. the number of characters currently assigned to it).

The maximum number of characters a particular string can contain is indicated by the length specified in square brackets in the string's TYPE or VAR declaration:

        CITY : STRING[12];
        STATE : STRING[2];

The absolute maximum length of any STRING type variable is 255 characters.

A string value can be assigned or modified with an assignment, a READ, or the STRING operators, procedures, and functions described in this section.

For example:

        STATE : = 'CA';
        READLN(CITY); (* READS UP TO EOLN OR EOF *)

When using a READ or READLN on a STRING type, all characters are read, up to and excluding the end-of-line character (or end-of-file). Thus, only one STRING may be read with READ or READLN at a time.

An attempt to read:

        READLN(STRING1,STRING2,STRING3);

will result in STRING2 and STRING3 being empty or *null* strings with a length of 0.

String characters or *elements* are accessed in much the same way as array elements. The first character of a STRING is element 1. Using the above example:

        STATE[1] contains 'C'
        STATE[2] contains 'A'

A STRING[N] may be considered an ARRAY [0 . . N] OF CHAR, with the current string length stored as a character value in element 0. Thus, if:

        CITY : = 'FRESNO';

then the following statements are true:

        LENGTH(CITY) = 6;
        ORD(CITY[0]) = 6; (* THE ORD() FUNCTION CONVERTS A *)
                          (* CHAR TYPE TO AN INTEGER VALUE *)

The memory space used by a string is the declared size plus one byte.

Therefore, using the above examples, the following statements are true:

        SIZEOF(CITY) = 13;
        SIZEOF(STATE) = 3;

String variables are commonly used to read a file name entered at the keyboard:

    VAR
            FILENAME : STRING[20];
            F : FILE;
    BEGIN
            WRITE('SPECIFY FILENAME. . .');
            READLN(FILENAME);
            ASSIGN(F,FILENAME);
            RESET(F);

            . . .

String Operators

Strings can be assigned by using the assignment operator := in Turbo Pascal. The Turbo Pascal STRING type can be used with the standard Pascal CHAR types (variable and constant) and ARRAYs OF CHAR (of the same length).

String variables and constants can be compared with other strings regardless of length by using the six relational operators: =, <>, <, >, <=, and >=. The result of the comparison is based on ASCII character values and lexicographical (i.e. dictionary) ordering. This is an important feature when processing text or sorting. Shorter strings are "less than" longer strings because they have a smaller ASCII character value. Leading and trailing spaces are included in the comparison. Uppercase is "less than" lowercase. (See the ASCII chart in Appendix G.)

For example:

        'A' < 'B' is TRUE
        'A' < 'a' is TRUE
        'A' > 'b' is FALSE
        'ABC' < 'ABCDEF' is TRUE
        'ABD' > 'ABC' is TRUE

You can use the UPCASE function described below to simplify mixed case comparisons.

The concatenation operator (+) is the only string operator provided in Turbo Pascal. (Relational operators are not string specific.) It may be used to combine character and string type constants and variables. It acts the same as the CONCAT function (described below), but is not compatible with some other Pascals that support strings, like UCSD Pascal.

For example:

```
STRING1 : = 'THIS IS ';
CH : = 'A';
STRING2 : = ' TEST';
WRITELN(STRING1 + CH + STRING2);
```

prints

```
THIS IS A TEST
```

Note that if the resulting string is over 255 characters in length a run-time error will occur causing the program to stop running.

String Procedures

Turbo Pascal provides four STRING procedures and two general procedures that manipulate strings and convert them to and from numeric types. They are DELETE, INSERT, FILLCHAR, MOVE, STR, and VAL.

DELETE(string, index, n)   This procedure deletes *n* characters from *string* beginning at character *index*.

For example:

```
TEST_STRING : = 'THIS IS A STRING';
DELETE(TEST_STRING,6,5);
WRITELN(TEST_STRING);
```

prints

```
THIS STRING
```

Because this procedure modifies the source string, it is sometimes necessary to use a dummy variable to save the original value for later use.

INSERT(source_string, destination_string, index)   This procedure inserts *source_string* into *destination_string* beginning at character *index* in the *destination_string*.

For example:

```
SOURCE_STRING : = 'LONG ';
DESTINATION_STRING : = 'THIS IS A STRING';
INSERT(SOURCE_STRING,DESTINATION_STRING,11);
WRITELN(DESTINATION_STRING);
```

prints

THIS IS A LONG STRING

Because this procedure modifies the source string, it is sometimes necessary to use a dummy variable to save the original value for later use.

STR(value, string)   The STR procedure transforms a numeric value into a string. *Value* is a *write parameter* that can be either type INTEGER or type REAL. Write parameters are expressions with special formatting commands (see WRITE and WRITELN), and can include a format suffix in the form (R:X:Y) for real values and (I:X) for integer values.
For example, if you type

INTNBR : = 23456;
STR(INTNBR,NUM_STRING);

you will be able to manipulate the number 23456 like a string. Now if you type

WRITELN(NUM_STRING + 'FF');

the computer will return

23456FF

Note: This procedure must never be used in WRITE or WRITELN statements in 8-bit versions of Turbo Pascal because it will generate an infinite recursive call.

VAL(string, variable, error_code)   The VAL procedure transforms a string into a numeric value. *String* is a properly formatted string representing a numeric value. Leading and trailing spaces are not allowed. *Variable* is a variable of type INTEGER or type REAL, and its type determines the type of conversion done. *Error_code* returns an integer value of 0 if the conversion was successful, otherwise it returns the position of the character in *string* that caused the error.
For example:

VAR
INTVAL : = INTEGER;
ERR : = INTEGER;
NUM_STRING : = STRING[20];

> **BEGIN**
>> NUM_STRING : = '456';
>> VAL(NUM_STRING, INTVAL, ERR);
>> WRITELN(INTVAL,' ',ERR);

prints

> 456 0

NOTE: This procedure must never be used in WRITE or WRITELN statements in 8-bit versions of Turbo Pascal because it will generate an infinite recursive call.

FILLCHAR(variable, n, value)   This procedure fills *n* bytes of memory with *value* beginning at the location of the first byte of *variable*. It can be used to quickly initialize arrays and strings with a value, or to make them equal to zero.

When used with strings, remember that the first byte of a string *must* contain the current length of the string as a CHAR value. This creates no problems when filling with 0 (ASCII NUL), but when presetting a string to another value, you must assign the new length of the string to element 0 as the final step.

MOVE(variable1, variable2, n)   This procedure copies *n* bytes of memory beginning at the first location of *variable1* to *n* bytes of memory beginning at *variable2*. It can be used to quickly copy large arrays and strings.

String Functions

Turbo Pascal provides five functions that are useful for manipulating strings: COPY, CONCAT, LENGTH, POS, and UPCASE.

COPY(string, index, n) : STRING   This function copies *n* characters from the string starting at character *index* and returns the resulting string as its value. For example:

> TEST_STRING : = 'THIS IS A STRING';
> RESULT_STRING : = COPY(TEST_STRING,6,8);
> WRITELN(RESULT_STRING);

prints

> IS A STR

CONCAT(string1, string2,... stringn) : STRING This function concatenates *n* strings and returns the resulting string as its value. For example, if

>   STRING1 : = 'THIS';
>   STRING2 : = ' IS';
>   STRING3 : = ' AN';

Then the function

>   CONCAT(STRING1,STRING2,STRING3,' EXAMPLE');

returns the string

>   THIS IS AN EXAMPLE

This function acts the same as the concatenation operator (+), but is more compatible with other Pascals that support strings, like UCSD Pascal.

   Note that if the resulting string is over 255 characters in length a run-time error will occur.

LENGTH(string) : INTEGER This function returns an integer representing the current length (in characters) of the string.
   For example:

>   STRING1 : = '0123456';
>   WRITELN(LENGTH(STRING1));

prints

>   7

POS(object, string) : INTEGER This function returns an integer representing the position of the first character of *object* within *string*. If *object* occurs several times within *string*, POS returns the location of the first occurrence. If *object* does not occur within the *string*, POS returns 0.
   For example:

>   STRING1 : = 'AN';
>   STRING2 : = 'THIS IS AN EXAMPLE';
>   WRITELN(POS(STRING1,STRING2));

prints

>   9

This function can be combined with other string operators to facilitate certain operations. For example:

```
STRING1 : = 'A LONG AND COMPLEX TEXT.';
STRING2 : = 'RATHER ';
INSERT(STRING2,STRING1,POS('C',STRING1));
WRITELN(STRING1);
```

prints

A LONG AND RATHER COMPLEX TEXT.

UPCASE(character) : CHAR This function converts lowercase characters to uppercase characters and returns the resulting character. If *character* is a lowercase alphabetic letter, it is converted to the uppercase equivalent, otherwise it is returned unchanged.

For example

```
CH : = 'j';
WRITELN(UPCASE(CH));
```

returns

J

This function can also be used to convert strings from lowercase to uppercase. For example, the following function:

```
TYPE
     DATSTR = STRING[255];

FUNCTION UPPERCASE (STR1 : DATSTR) : DATSTR;

VAR
     INDEX, LEN : INTEGER;

BEGIN
     LEN : = LENGTH(STR1);
     FOR INDEX : = 1 TO LEN DO
          STR[INDEX] : = UPCASE(STR1[INDEX]);
     UPPERCASE : = STR1
END;
```

or procedure:

```
TYPE
        DATSTR  =  STRING[255];

PROCEDURE UPPERCASE (VAR STR1 : DATSTR);

VAR
        INDEX, LEN : INTEGER;

BEGIN
        LEN : =  LENGTH(STR1);
        FOR INDEX : =  1 TO LEN DO
                STR[INDEX] : =  UPCASE(STR1[INDEX])
END;
```

transforms the string

'A very useful string function.'

to the string

'A VERY USEFUL STRING FUNCTION.'

SUMMARY

The array is traditionally one of the most widely used data structures in programming. Arrays are widely used in mathematical computations, logical representations, and in any application where large amounts of similar data must be processed. Tables, implemented as single or multidimensional arrays, can be filled with data and used to determine the behavior of a program. This technique, called table-driven software, can lead to easily customized programs.

Pascal allows the definition of simple one-dimensional arrays as well as multi-dimensional arrays (arrays of arrays). Arrays may also be optionally packed to conserve memory.

Arrays can often be used to advantage to represent values of a frequently-used function, resulting in improved execution speed of a program.

EXERCISES

9-1: *Define an array-valued function that gives 'ONE' the value 1, 'TWO' the value 2, etc., up to 'TEN'.*

9-2: *Design a suitable array and program whereby the program can spell out any digit between 1 and 10.*

9-3: *Same as exercise 9-2 but for:*

  1. The days of the week (1 to 7)
  2. The months of the year (1 to 12)

9-4: *Write a program that spells out a dollar and cents amount ("checkwriter").*

9-5: *Given ten names, sort them in alphabetical order.*

9-6: *Type in a sentence. Output the words in alphabetical order. Assume a maximum word size of twenty characters and the maximum number of words to be thirty.*

9-7: *Read a sentence. Print out the number of times each letter is used in the sentence.*

9-8: *Read a sequence of integers. Print out the largest and the smallest integer. Indicate the number of times the largest integer was input.*

9-9: *Store 20 words of a language dictionary as word-pairs. Type in a word —output the translation. For example, the program starts in dictionary mode. You type:*

BLUE	BLEU
YELLOW	JAUNE
TREE	ARBRE
HOUSE	MAISON
IS	EST
SEE	VOIR
MAN	HOMME
WOMAN	FEMME

(etc. — up to 20 words)

Now, go into translation mode. You type:

TREE

and the answer must be:

ARBRE

9-10: *Same as Exercise 9-9, but translate an entire sentence of words. For example, you type:*

MAN SEE BLUE HOUSE

and you obtain:

HOMME VOIR BLEU MAISON

9-11: *Read a word. Spell it backwards.*

9-12: *Write a program to read in and multiply two five by five matrices, printing the result. (Matrix multiplication is defined A * B = C where element c[i,j] is the sum of a[i,k] times b[k,j] as k ranges from 1 to the size of the matrix.)*

9-13: *(Spelling) Type in a set of ten words. Then, type any word. The program must detect misspellings. Any word typed that does not match one in the set of ten words is considered a misspelling.*

9-14: *Write a program that prints giant headlines. Each character is stored as a 7 by 9 matrix of asterisks. Print each character 'sideways' so that a complete word may be printed on paper. For example, the letter I may be represented as:*

```
          *         *

          ********

          *         *
```

9-15: *Write a program to read from the keyboard a series of ten names. Then read ten social security numbers. The names and numbers are assumed to be in corresponding order. The output should consist of a list of the names, each followed by the corresponding social security number.*

CHAPTER 10

RECORDS
AND VARIANTS

INTRODUCTION

Each programming language provides facilities for specifying algorithms and representing data structures. An important limitation of many languages is the representation of suitable data structures. Most programming languages, especially scientific languages such as FORTRAN, do not supply any facility for defining or constructing data structures more complex than simple arrays. Pascal provides an unusually large variety of constructs for defining complex structures. These structures include arrays, records, files, and sets. The facilities for defining records will be described in this chapter.

RECORD

The record type in Pascal is probably the most convenient data structure available. It is well-suited for business-oriented applications, but may also be used for scientific calculations. It is therefore important to understand what records are, and how they can be used.

A record is conceptually analogous to the information contained in a business file. For example, a school record might include:

1. Name
2. Address
3. Telephone number
4. Birthdate
5. Reference number
6. Courses taken
7. Grades

Let us consider the possible Pascal data types that can be used to represent each element of the above record:

1. Name: array of characters
2. Address: array of characters
3. Telephone number: integer (or array of characters)
4. Birthdate: array of characters
5. Reference number: integer
6. Courses taken: array of strings
7. Grades: array of integers

This record is a collection of diverse data types. It could easily be represented by a Pascal record.

A record in Pascal is a collection of data of various types. Each item in a record is called a *field*. Each of the lines in the school record above is a field of that record. In other words, a record is a collection of fields that may be of different types.

As another example, let us consider a sales record. This record may combine the name of the customer, the address, the telephone number, the internal customer number, and the total sales to date. A Pascal record can also be easily constructed to represent this information. It is declared as follows:

```
TYPE SALESLIST =
    RECORD
        NAME : PACKED ARRAY[1..30] OF CHAR;
        ADDRESS : PACKED ARRAY[1..80] OF CHAR;
        TELNBR : PACKED ARRAY[1..15] OF CHAR;
        CUSTOMERNBR : 1..999;
        TOTALSALESTODATE : REAL
    END;
```

This record type is called a SALESLIST.

— The first field in the record is NAME. It is of type string and represents the customer name. It uses 30 characters.
— The second and the third fields are respectively called ADDRESS and TELNBR and are also arrays of characters. The address has 80 characters. The telephone number has 15 characters.
— The fourth field is called CUSTOMERNBR and is of type INTEGER. Its value must be between 1 and 999.
— The fifth field is called TOTALSALESTODATE and is of type REAL.

Note that the RECORD definition is terminated by an END. Each field in a record may be of any type, including the type RECORD.

We have informally defined a record and provided an example. We will now present the formal definition.

FORMAL DEFINITION

The formal syntax of a record is shown in Figure 10.1.

We can see by examining the 'field list' in Figure 10.1 that a record declaration may have a *fixed part* and/or a *variant part*. The variant part will be described later in this chapter. The fixed part consists of one or more identifiers followed by a colon and the type specification.

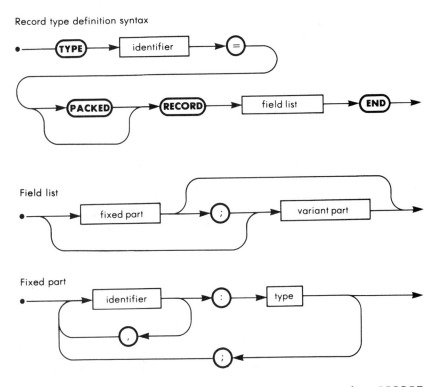

Figure 10.1: Syntax for a RECORD

Here is an example:

TYPE DATE = **RECORD**
      MONTH : 1..12;
      DAY : 1..31;
      YEAR : 1900..2000

END;

Note that each element of the record is declared separately. The RECORD definition is terminated by an END.

In this simple example, an ARRAY could also have been used. We could also define an LDATE record as:

TYPE LDATE = **RECORD**
      DAY : 1..31;
      MONTH : (JAN,FEB,MAR,APR,MAY,JUN,JUL,AUG,
             SEP,OCT,NOV,DEC);
      YEAR : 1900..2000
END;

A simplified definition of a record type at this point is:

    identifier = **RECORD** fixed part **END**

As usual, we may use TYPE or VAR to declare a record. The fields defined within the record may have any type, including the type record. As an example, here is a record that uses the previous record LDATE within two of its fields:

```
TYPE EMPLOYEERECORD =
  RECORD
          NAME : PACKED ARRAY[1..12] OF CHAR;
          POSITION : PACKED ARRAY[1..20] OF CHAR;
          EMPLOYEENBR : INTEGER;
          BIRTHDATE : LDATE;
          SEX : (M,F);
          SALARYRATE : REAL;
          EXEMPTIONS : REAL;
          DATEHIRED : LDATE;
          VACATIONTIME : REAL;
          SICKLEAVE : REAL
  END;
```

OPERATIONS ON RECORDS

In order to reference an element of a record, a special notation is used. A record element is designated by:

    record name.field identifier

For example, let us define:

    VAR FULLTIMER : EMPLOYEERECORD;

Elements of EMPLOYEERECORD above are referenced as follows:

    FULLTIMER.NAME := 'JOHN HIGGINS';
    FULLTIMER.EXEMPTIONS := 2.5;

Here is a more complicated example, still referring to the same record:

    FULLTIMER.BIRTHDATE.YEAR := 1938;

The formal definition of a record component is shown in Figure 10.2.

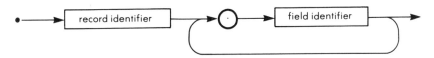

Figure 10.2: Record Component Syntax

To reference a field within a record, the name of the record must be specified, followed by a period, and then the name of the field.

The following example shows the way in which values can be assigned to all of the fields of FULLTIMER.

We first define:

VAR FULLTIMER : EMPLOYEERECORD;

We now assign values to the components of FULLTIMER:

FULLTIMER.NAME : = 'ALFRED GREEN';
FULLTIMER.POSITION : = 'SENIOR PROGRAMMER---';
FULLTIMER.EMPLOYEENBR : = 241;
FULLTIMER.BIRTHDATE.DAY : = 10;
FULLTIMER.BIRTHDATE.MONTH : = MAR;
FULLTIMER.BIRTHDATE.YEAR : = 1948;
FULLTIMER.SEX : = M;
FULLTIMER.SALARYRATE : = 8.50;
FULLTIMER.EXEMPTIONS : = 3.5;
FULLTIMER.DATEHIRED.DAY : = 25;
FULLTIMER.DATEHIRED.MONTH : = JAN;
FULLTIMER.DATEHIRED.YEAR : = 1980;
FULLTIMER.VACATIONTIME : = 45.5;
FULLTIMER.SICKLEAVE : = 39.5;

Note that no quotes are required (or allowed) around JAN and MAR. These identifiers have been defined as values of an enumeration type. They are not strings.

Here is another example. We first define three variables of type SALESLIST:

VAR INDIVIDUALS,RETAILERS,DISTRIBUTORS : SALESLIST;

where SALESLIST is the record previously defined. The customer number

123 may then be assigned to an individual by the following statement:

INDIVIDUALS.CUSTOMERNBR : = 123;

Similarly, the name of the ABC Company may be entered in the appropriate sales list by writing:

RETAILERS.NAME : = 'ABC COMPANY------------------';

Note: blank spaces are indicated by----. You must supply enough blanks to fill the string, although some versions of Pascal will pad with blanks automatically.

When operating on elements of a record, any operator compatible with the element's type may be used. However, no operator may be used on a complete record except the assignment operator (: =).

When assigning one record variable to another record variable, one record is copied into another that has a different name. Of course, both must be of the same type.

For example, using the following variable definitions:

VAR TODAYSDATE,DATEHIRED,DATEOFCHANGE : DATE;

we can write:

DATEOFCHANGE : = TODAYSDATE;

Provided that TODAYSDATE had a value, this will result in assigning this value to DATEOFCHANGE. The day, the month, and the year fields of DATEOFCHANGE will be updated simultaneously.

Records may also be used as parameters in functions and procedures. When used as parameters, records may be referred to by value or by variable. Records may also be declared as part of other structures such as arrays.

THE WITH STATEMENT

When operating on fields within a record, one must use the record identifier, followed by a period, and then one or more field identifiers. This is required in order to avoid any ambiguity, since any identifier used in the field of a record may also legally appear in other places within a Pascal program. However, if there are many identifiers, this requirement may become cumbersome.

Here is an example using the EMPLOYEERECORD that we have already defined:

```
TYPE DATE =
    RECORD
            DAY : 1..31;
            MONTH : (JAN,FEB,MAR,APR,MAY,JUN,JUL,AUG,SEP,OCT,NOV,DEC);
            YEAR : 1900..2000
    END;{DATE}
    EMPLOYEERECORD =
    RECORD
            NAME : PACKED ARRAY[1..12] OF CHAR;
            POSITION : PACKED ARRAY[1..20] OF CHAR;
            EMPLOYEENBR : INTEGER;
            BIRTHDATE : DATE;
            SEX : (M,F);
            SALARYRATE : REAL;
            EXEMPTIONS : REAL;
            DATEHIRED : DATE;
            VACATIONTIME : REAL;
            SICKLEAVE : REAL
    END; (EMPLOYEERECORD)
```

We could complicate the program further by redefining NAME within EMPLOYEERECORD as:

NAME : **RECORD** FIRSTNAME,SECONDNAME,LASTNAME : NSTRING **END**;

with the prior definition:

TYPE NSTRING = **PACKED ARRAY**[1..15] **OF** CHAR;

A value is assigned to NAME as follows:

```
                FULLTIMER.NAME.FIRSTNAME : = 'ALFRED---------';
                                            {15 characters}
                FULLTIMER.NAME.SECONDNAME : = 'JOHN----------'
                FULLTIMER.NAME.LASTNAME : = 'GREEN----------';
```

This example demonstrates how cumbersome this notation can be. Ideally, we should avoid repeating record names so many times.

The WITH statement is provided to alleviate this problem. The WITH statement allows the record identifier to be specified only once and to have one or more statements operate on the field identifiers, thus eliminating the need to specify the record identifier every time. For example:

FULLTIMER

```
WITH EMPLOYEERECORD DO
    BEGIN
            NAME := 'JOHN BROWN';
            POSITION := 'SUPERVISOR';
            EMPLOYEENBR := 24
    END;    (* EMPLOYEERECORD *)
```

FULLTIMER

The effect of the WITH statement is to insert implicitly the required 'EMPLOYEERECORD' before the name of the fields within the WITH block.

The above WITH statement is equivalent to:

FULLTIMER

```
EMPLOYEERECORD.NAME := 'JOHN BROWN';
EMPLOYEERECORD.POSITION := 'SUPERVISOR';
EMPLOYEERECORD.EMPLOYEENBR := 24;
```

The formal syntax of the WITH statement is shown in Figure 10.3.

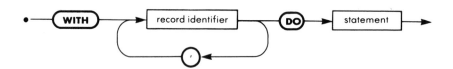

Figure 10.3:   WITH Statement Syntax

The record identifier in Figure 10.3 must be an actual record *variable*, not an identifier used to define a record type.

The WITH statement may also be used with multiple variables in order to extend the scope of field identifiers. For example, assume that A is a variable of type RECORD, that B and C are fields of type RECORD, and that X, Y, Z are field identifiers within these records. Assume that we need to specify:

```
A.B.X := 3;
A.B.Y := 'ALPHA';
A.C.Z := 1;
```

We can simplify these specifications by writing:

WITH A,B,C, **DO**
    BEGIN
        X := 3;
        Y := 'ALPHA';
        Z := 1;
    END;

The notation:

WITH A,B,C, **DO**

is equivalent to:

WITH A **DO**
    WITH B **DO**
        WITH C **DO**

Note that the WITH statement automatically defines a *scope* for the identifiers (or fields) within its block.

In the formal definition in Figure 10.3, DO may be followed by any statement. For example, an IF...THEN clause may be used to advantage:

VAR CALLDATE : DATE;
    ...{ASSUME CURRENTMONTH = JAN}
    WITH CALLDATE **DO**
        IF MO = CURRENTMONTH **THEN** MO := SUCC(CURRENTMONTH);
    ...

The above program moves the CALLDATE ahead by one month. When run once a month, this program would be used to schedule an automatic call or letter. (Note: this does not work when MO = DEC.)

Without the WITH statement, this program becomes:

VAR CALLDATE : DATE;
    IF CALLDATE.MO = CURRENTMONTH **THEN**
        CALLDATE.MO := SUCC(CURRENTMONTH);

SCOPE OF IDENTIFIERS

The scope of an identifier used within a record is that particular record. This means that, for example, if DAY is used as a field within the record DATE, the variable DAY may appear in any other program segment, including other records. Any possible confusion is eliminated by the requirement that every field name must be preceded by the name of the record in which it appears. In order to refer to DAY within the record LASTDATE, one must write:

LASTDATE.DAY

If DAY also appeared in the record called ALFA, we would refer to it by writing:

ALFA.DAY

Naturally, within a given RECORD, all field names must be distinct.

Remember that the statement following the WITH behaves as a block, for the purpose of defining the scope of the variables that appear within that statement.

CASE STUDY 1: INVENTORY MANAGEMENT

The Problem

Managing an inventory is a common business problem. Typically, the items that make up an inventory are kept in stock and the total number of available parts must be updated each time a part is sold or purchased.

The Inventory Management program will read a series of values into records containing four fields:

> Field A: part identification number
> Field B: number of parts in stock
> Field C: number of parts purchased
> Field D: number of parts sold

The end of input is indicated by all-zero fields.

Field B, containing the number of parts in stock, will be updated automatically, using the information in Fields C and D. The two fields C and D, containing the number of parts purchased and the number of parts sold, will be reset to zero. The program then prints the list of parts, along with the number of items in stock and a message indicating whether or not the stock has been increased or decreased.

A sample input is shown in Figure 10.4.

```
05763 18 20 16          A = part #
84502 25 15 30          B = in stock
23476 63 50 42          C = purchased
52873 12 10 18          D = sold
62481 14 15 12
21965 82 60 71
17248 10 05 07
00000 00 00 00
 A   B  C  D
  _____/
    Fields
```

Figure 10.4: Sample Input for Inventory Program

A sample output is shown in Figure 10.5.

PART	AMOUNT IN STOCK	
5763	22	INCREASED
84502	10	DECREASED
23476	71	INCREASED
52873	4	DECREASED
62481	17	INCREASED
21965	71	DECREASED
17248	8	DECREASED

Figure 10.5: Sample Output for Inventory Program

The program listing is shown in Figure 10.6.

```
PROGRAM UPDATE (INPUT, OUTPUT);
TYPE PARTREC = RECORD
                    NUMBER : INTEGER;     (* PART NUMBER *)
                    INSTOCK : INTEGER;    (* NUMBER IN STOCK *)
                    PURCH   : INTEGER;    (* NUMBER PURCHASED *)
                    SOLD    : INTEGER     (* NUMBER SOLD *)
               END; (* RECORD *)



VAR PART:  PARTREC;              (* PART BEING UPDATED *)
    INC:   BOOLEAN;              (* FLAG FOR INCREASED OR DECREASED *)
                                 (* NUMBER IN STOCK *)


BEGIN (* UPDATE *)
   (* PRINT HEADINGS *)
    WRITELN; WRITELN;
    WRITELN('                                AMOUNT');
    WRITELN('                                IN');
    WRITELN('                    PART        STOCK');
    WRITELN('                    ====  ======');
    WRITELN;
    WITH PART DO
       BEGIN (* WITH PART RECORD *)
            READLN(NUMBER, INSTOCK, PURCH, SOLD);
            WHILE NUMBER < > 0 DO
                BEGIN (* FOR EACH RECORD *)
                   (* UPDATE RECORD *)
                    IF PURCH > SOLD THEN INC : = TRUE
                    ELSE INC : = FALSE;
                    INSTOCK : = INSTOCK + PURCH − SOLD;
                    PURCH : = 0;
```

Figure 10.6: INVENTORY MANAGEMENT Program

```
                    SOLD := 0;

            (* OUTPUT RECORD *)
                WRITE ('              ',NUMBER:5,'      ',INSTOCK:3);
                IF INC = TRUE THEN WRITELN ('  INCREASED')
                ELSE WRITELN ('  DECREASED');
            (* READ NEXT RECORD *)
                READLN( NUMBER, INSTOCK, PURCH, SOLD)
        END   (* FOR EACH RECORD *)
    END   (* WITH PART RECORD *)
END.  (* UPDATE *)
```

Figure 10.6: INVENTORY MANAGEMENT Program (cont.)

The Program

A four-field record is used to store the four numbers that characterize a part:

```
PROGRAM UPDATE(INPUT,OUTPUT);
TYPE PARTREC = RECORD
                NUMBER  : INTEGER;   (* PART NUMBER *)
                INSTOCK : INTEGER;   (* FIELD B *)
                PURCH   : INTEGER;   (* FIELD C *)
                SOLD    : INTEGER    (* FIELD D *)
                END; (* RECORD *)
```

Two variables are used:

```
VAR PART : PARTREC;
    INC : BOOLEAN;
```

PART denotes the part record being updated. INC is a Boolean flag used to remember if the stock has been increased or decreased.

In order to reference the four fields of PART, the correct notation is:

> PART.NUMBER
> PART.INSTOCK
> PART.PURCH
> PART.SOLD

However, a shorthand notation may be used with the WITH facility. This approach is the solution used in this program:

```
WITH PART DO
    BEGIN
        READLN(NUMBER,INSTOCK,PURCH,SOLD);
```

A part number of zero terminates the input. Otherwise, a processing loop is executed:

```
WHILE NUMBER <> 0 DO
    BEGIN
        IF PURCH > SOLD THEN INC : = TRUE
        ELSE INC : = FALSE;
        INSTOCK : = INSTOCK + PURCH − SOLD;
        PURCH : = 0;
        SOLD : = 0;
```

The record is immediately updated and a negative number of parts in stock would correspond to a back order situation. The updated contents of the record are then displayed, and a special message is generated, depending upon the value of the flag variable INC:

```
WRITE('----------',NUMBER:5,
        '-----',INSTOCK:3);
IF INC = TRUE THEN WRITELN('--INCREASED')
ELSE WRITELN('--DECREASED');
```

and the next record is read:

```
                READLN(NUMBER,INSTOCK,PURCH,SOLD)
            END
        END
END.
```

CASE STUDY 2: CREDIT CARD NUMBER VALIDATION

The Problem

Most numbers used as identification codes, such as credit card account numbers, contain a validation or "check digit." The value of this digit is computed as a function of the other digits in the number. Thus, if one digit is changed in the number (by accident or otherwise) or is read incorrectly, the check digit will reflect this change. When the number is read into the computer, the actual validation digit is computed from the digits read, and then it is compared to the check digit stored with the number. Both check digits should match.

This Validation program (shown in Figure 10.9) will read a series of records containing the following fields:

— Field A: credit card number (10 individual digits)
— Field B: purchase amount
— Field C: store or dealer number (8 individual digits)

The program will verify the validity of the numbers in Fields A and C, using a check digit technique. The last digit of each number must be the sum of the preceding digits modulo 9 (i.e., the remainder when the sum of all the digits is divided by nine). The program must print all entries that have an erroneous identification number or an erroneous dealer number.

A typical input is shown in Figure 10.7.

Credit Card #	Purchase Amount	Dealer #
4 5 7 6 3 1 8 2 0 0	684.50	2 2 5 1 5 3 0 0
2 3 4 7 6 6 3 5 0 4	252.87	3 1 2 1 0 1 8 7
2 4 8 1 1 4 1 5 1 0	219.65	8 2 6 0 7 1 5 6
1 7 2 4 8 1 0 0 5 0	723.70	3 8 6 4 2 9 6 4
2 6 4 1 8 0 7 7 9 8	642.89	9 7 1 3 7 9 0 0
3 1 7 4 0 6 4 3 6 2	123.87	9 5 2 1 5 6 7 8
2 5 6 7 4 5 6 8 6 4	368.86	3 4 6 7 8 9 0 7
4 1 2 4 6 8 8 5 4 3	754.84	5 6 7 8 8 5 4 3
0 0 0 0 0 0 0 0 0 0	000.00	0 0 0 0 0 0 0 0

Figure 10.7: **Input to VALIDATION Program**

The corresponding output is shown in Figure 10.8.

BAD CREDIT CARD NUMBER
credit card number: 2347663504
amount: 252.87
dealer number: 31210187

BAD DEALER NUMBER
credit card number: 2481141510
amount: 219.65
dealer number: 82607156

BAD CREDIT CARD NUMBER
BAD DEALER NUMBER
credit card number: 1724810050
amount: 723.70
dealer number: 38642964

BAD CREDIT CARD NUMBER
credit card number: 3174064362
amount: 1123.87
dealer number: 95215678

BAD DEALER NUMBER
credit card number: 2567456864
amount: 368.86
dealer number: 34678907

BAD CREDIT CARD NUMBER
BAD DEALER NUMBER
credit card number: 4124688543
amount: 754.84
dealer number: 56788543

Figure 10.8:   Output from Validation Program

```
PROGRAM VERIFY (INPUT, OUTPUT);
TYPE      CHECKNUM = ARRAY [1..10] OF 0..9;
          CREDITREC = RECORD
                          CCNUM: CHECKNUM; (* CREDIT CARD NUMBER *)
                          AMT: REAL;
                          DLRNUM: CHECKNUM(* DEALER NUMBER *)
                      END;  (* RECORD *)
VAR PURCHASE:      CREDITREC;
    CCOK, DLROK:        BOOLEAN;
FUNCTION NUMOK(LN:INTEGER; NUMBER: CHECKNUM): BOOLEAN;
    VAR INDX, CHKDIGIT: INTEGER;

    BEGIN (* NUMOK *)
        CHKDIGIT := 0;
        FOR INDX := 1 TO LN - 1 DO
            CHKDIGIT := CHKDIGIT + NUMBER[INDX];
        CHKDIGIT := CHKDIGIT MOD 9;
        IF CHKDIGIT < > NUMBER[LN] THEN
            NUMOK := FALSE
        ELSE NUMOK := TRUE
    END;  (* NUMOK *)

PROCEDURE READREC;
    VAR INDX: INTEGER;
    BEGIN (* READREC *)
        FOR INDX := 1 TO 10 DO
            READ(PURCHASE.CCNUM[INDX]);
        READ(PURCHASE.AMT);
        FOR INDX := 1 TO 8 DO
            READ(PURCHASE.DLRNUM[INDX]);
        READLN
    END; (* READREC *)

PROCEDURE PRINTREC;
    VAR INDX: INTEGER;
```

Figure 10.9: VALIDATION Program

```
        BEGIN (* PRINTREC *)
             WRITE('    CREDIT CARD NUMBER: ');
             FOR INDX := 1 TO 10 DO
                 WRITE(PURCHASE.CCNUM[INDX]:1);
             WRITELN;
             WRITELN('    AMOUNT:          ',PURCHASE.AMT:5:2);
             WRITE('    DEALER NUMBER:      ');
             FOR INDX := 1 TO 8 DO
                 WRITE(PURCHASE.DLRNUM[INDX]:1);
             WRITELN; WRITELN
        END;  (* PRINTREC *)

BEGIN (* VERIFY *)
     READREC;
     WHILE PURCHASE.AMT < > 0 DO
         BEGIN (* CHECK RECORD *)
             IF    NUMOK(10, PURCHASE.CCNUM) THEN
                   CCOK := TRUE
             ELSE CCOK := FALSE;
             IF NUMOK(8,PURCHASE.DLRNUM) THEN
                   DLROK := TRUE
             ELSE DLROK := FALSE;
             IF (NOT CCOK) OR (NOT DLROK) THEN
                   BEGIN (* BAD RECORD *)
                       IF NOT CCOK THEN
                           WRITELN('    BAD CREDIT CARD NUMBER');
                       IF NOT DLROK THEN
                           WRITELN('    BAD DEALER NUMBER');
                       PRINTREC;
                   END; (* BAD RECORD *)
             READREC
         END   (* CHECK RECORD *)
END. (* VERIFY *)
```

Figure 10.9: VALIDATION Program (cont.)

The Program

The program listing is shown in Figure 10.9. This program uses a three-field record type called CREDITREC, where each account number is stored as an array of integers:

```
PROGRAM  VERIFY(INPUT,OUTPUT);
TYPE CHECKNUM = ARRAY[1..10] OF 0..9;
     CREDITREC = RECORD
                     CCNUM   : CHECKNUM;
                     AMT     : REAL;
                     DLRNUM  : CHECKNUM
                 END;
VAR PURCHASE : CREDITREC;
    CCOK,DLROK : BOOLEAN;
```

The two variables CCOK and DLROK are used to remember whether or not the credit card number is okay, and if the dealer code is okay.

One function and two procedures are used. The Boolean function NUMOK is used to determine the validity of the check digit in an account number. The algorithm is straightforward. If the account number has LN digits, the first (LN − 1) digits are added together, and the modulo 9 is obtained. This computation yields a computed check digit. This computed digit is then compared to the check digit stored in position LN. If both digits match, NUMOK is set to TRUE; otherwise, it is set to FALSE.

```
FUNCTION  NUMOK(LN: INTEGER; NUMBER: CHECKNUM): BOOLEAN;
    VAR INDX,CHKDIGIT : INTEGER;
    BEGIN (* NUMOK *)
        CHKDIGIT := 0;
        FOR INDX := 1 TO LN − 1 DO
            CHKDIGIT := CHKDIGIT + NUMBER[INDX];
        CHKDIGIT := CHKDIGIT MOD 9;
        IF CHKDIGIT <> NUMBER[LN] THEN
            NUMOK := FALSE
        ELSE NUMOK := TRUE
    END; (* NUMOK *)
```

The procedure READREC is used to read a record, a field at a time, in the appropriate format:

```
PROCEDURE READREC;
    VAR INDX : INTEGER;
    BEGIN (* READREC *)
        FOR INDX := 1 TO 10 DO
            READ(PURCHASE.CCNUM[INDX]);
        READ(PURCHASE.AMT);
        FOR INDX := 1 TO 8 DO
            READ(PURCHASE.DLRNUM[INDX]);
        READLN
    END; (* READREC *)
```

The procedure PRINTREC is used to print a record in a clear format, including field names:

```
PROCEDURE PRINTREC;
    VAR INDX : INTEGER;
    BEGIN (* PRINTREC *)
        WRITE('   CREDIT CARD NUMBER:   ');
        FOR INDX := 1 TO 10 DO
            WRITE(PURCHASE.CCNUM[INDX]:1);
        WRITELN;
        WRITELN('   AMOUNT:   ',PURCHASE.AMT:5:2);
        WRITE('   DEALER NUMBER:   ');
        FOR INDX := 1 TO 8 DO
            WRITE(PURCHASE.DLRNUM[INDX]:1);
        WRITELN; WRITELN
    END; (* PRINTREC *)
```

The program reads the first record:

```
BEGIN
    READREC;
```

Then, as long as the purchase amount is not 0, the program executes repeatedly:

WHILE PURCHASE.AMT $<>$ 0 **DO**
    BEGIN

The program uses the NUMOK function to verify the value of the check digit in the two relevant fields, and remembers the logical result in CCOK and DLROK:

IF NUMOK(10,PURCHASE.CCNUM) **THEN**
    CCOK : = TRUE
ELSE CCOK : = FALSE;
IF NUMOK(8,PURCHASE.DLRNUM) **THEN**
    DLROK : = TRUE
ELSE DLROK : = FALSE;

Once these checks have been performed, any erroneous record must be printed along with a diagnostic:

IF (**NOT** CCOK) **OR** (**NOT** DLROK) **THEN**
    BEGIN (* BAD RECORD *)
        IF NOT CCOK **THEN** WRITELN('---BAD CREDIT CARD NUMBER');
        IF NOT DLROK **THEN** WRITELN('---BAD DEALER NUMBER');
        PRINTREC;
    END;
    READREC
  END
END.

VARIANTS

The records we have defined thus far are rigid structures that cannot be changed. Often when defining a data structure such as a record, it would be convenient to have two or three sub-types of the record, depending upon the value of a field in the record. For example, in a personnel file an extra field might be required to store the maiden name of a married woman. This specific field would not be required for a man.

Such a facility is provided in Pascal. It is called the *variant* record facility. Variant records can be specified conveniently by using a version of the CASE statement. For example:

```
TYPE CATEGORIES = (INDIVIDUAL,COMPANY);
     INVOICE = RECORD
               INVOICENBR : 0..99999;
               TODAYSDATE : DATE;
               ITEMCODE : 0..9999;
               DESCRIPTION : ARRAY[1..40] OF CHAR;
               QUANTITY : 0..99999;
               PRICE : REAL;
               NAME : ARRAY[1..32] OF CHAR;
               ADDRESS : ARRAY[80] OF CHAR;
               TOTALDUE : REAL
               CASE CUSTOMERTYPE : CATEGORIES OF
                   INDIVIDUAL: ();
                   COMPANY:
                       (CREDITRATING : BOOLEAN;
                       CUSTOMERNBR : 0..9999;
                       MINDISCOUNT : REAL)
               END;
```

In this example, if the CUSTOMERTYPE is an INDIVIDUAL, no new fields are added to the basic record. This is shown as: (). However, if the CUSTOMERTYPE is a COMPANY, three additional fields are added to the record: CREDITRATING, CUSTOMERNBR, and MINDISCOUNT.

This optional record field specification is called a variant. Using the *variant* facility, a single record type may be constructed that will include one or more fields, depending upon the type of the specific variable. This is a powerful facility which significantly improves program readability and provides convenience. However, variants also increase the risk of error. For example, when referring to an INDIVIDUAL in the example above, one must never try to access the CREDITRATING or the CUSTOMERNBR, as these fields are not defined in the case of an INDIVIDUAL.

The special field following the CASE, i.e. CUSTOMERTYPE, is called the tag field. This tag field is defined as being of type CATEGORIES and belongs to the record INVOICE. It is the value of the tag field which determines which fields of the variant are valid. The formal definition for a variant part is shown in Figure 10.10.

Looking at the syntax for a variant in Figure 10.10, it is apparent that the tag field identifier following the CASE may be omitted. Such a record

Variant part

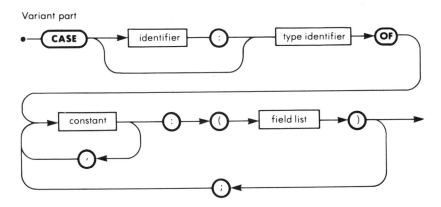

Figure 10.10:   Variant Syntax

variant with no tag field is called a *free union*. Free unions are used infrequently, and may not be provided by some implementations. They should not be used by an inexperienced programmer, as the probability of error is very high.

Only one variant may be used in a list of fields and it must occur last. However, this does not prevent variants from being nested.

In summary, a variant allows a single record type to be used in two or more cases. This concept is illustrated in Figure 10.11. Note that the fields allocated to CASE 1 and CASE 2 in Figure 10.11 may also be subdivided.

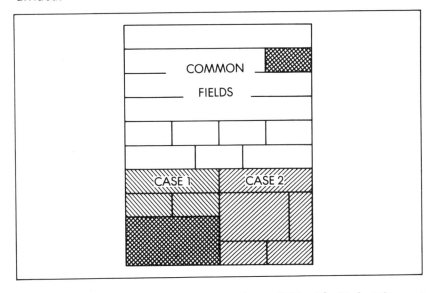

Figure 10.11:   The Variant Concept

TURBO PACAL VARIANT RECORDS

Unlike Standard Pascal, Turbo Pascal allows only one variant part in a record, and it must be the last field in the record.

SUMMARY

Records provide an important facility for structuring data in complex ways. They are generally used for business or text-oriented applications, but may be used for any other application. A record is basically a collection of values of various data types that has a name and may be conveniently manipulated as a unit. Special rules apply to records that allow references to an element and the specification of variants.

EXERCISES

10-1: *Design a record structure that will contain a sequence of names and birth dates typed in the format NAME-mm/dd/yy, where mm is the month, dd is the day, and yy is the year. Print this list by chronological age.*

10-2: *Improve the previous exercise by checking for illegal birth dates. For example, February 30 should be rejected.*

10-3: *Write a program that reads a student's name followed by a sequence of grades. Sort and print the list of students in order, highest to lowest, according to the total of each one's scores.*

10-4: *Examine the section of the program in Figure 10.9 after*

      BEGIN (* CHECK RECORD *)

Can you shorten it by using

      CCOK := NUMOK (...) *and* DLROK := NUMOK (...)

rather than the **IF...ELSE** *clauses?*

CHAPTER **11**

FILES

BASIC DEFINITIONS

A *file* is the basic module of information handled by the *operating system*. The operating system is the program in charge of managing the computer system's resources for the user. For example, a program is stored as a file. First it is typed in with an editor program, then it is stored as a text file. Once compiled by the compiler, the translated program becomes a *binary file*.

Informally, a file can be defined as an information module that has a name. Also, all data within the file is homogeneous, i.e., of the same type. For example, a file may be either binary or text.

The format and the properties of files are generally defined by the operating system of the computer on which they reside. Each operating system stores and organizes files differently. In addition, the operating system may provide a number of file attributes such as Read/Write, Read Only, Owner Number, and others.

Pascal provides facilities for accessing, creating and manipulating files. However, files created by a Pascal program obey specific rules and are subject to a number of restrictions.

PASCAL FILES

The essential property of a file in the Pascal language is that it may be read or written one element at a time. In theory, files of information may be accessed in a number of ways. Two examples are random access and sequential access. In practice, specific access mechanisms are provided to examine, read, or write each element of a file. Pascal restricts the access to files to a sequential access mode. This can be contrasted to the direct, or random access mode, which is often used by the operating system. Thus a Pascal file is generally accessed as if it were stored on a magnetic tape (a sequential device), rather than on a disk (a random access device).

A Pascal file is a collection of units or blocks having the same structure. For example, a file may consist of characters, arrays, or records. Each Pascal file is terminated by a special End-Of-File marker, called EOF. All Pascal files are sequential files: elements of a file must be accessed one after the other. It is not possible to jump ahead or backwards in a file. In Pascal, a file may be empty. For example, an empty file is usually created at the time a file is originally defined. The operations that create and manipulate files will now be described.

FORMAL DEFINITION

The syntax for a file type definition is shown in Figure 11.1.

Figure 11.1: Syntax of a File Declaration

For example:

> **TYPE** VALUES = **FILE OF** INTEGER;

In principle, any legal data type may be used to specify the elements of the file. However, in practice, a file of files is usually not allowed by most systems even though it is legal. Since files of characters occur frequently, a standard file type called TEXT is provided in Pascal. It is defined as:

> **TYPE** TEXT = **FILE OF** CHAR;

The type TEXT will be studied separately in the following section.

In order to use a file, the file itself must be declared as a variable. If the file is permanent, i.e., exists prior to program execution, the file must:

1. Be declared as a variable.
2. Appear in the program header.

For example, the file SPEED is declared by:

> **VAR** SPEED : **FILE OF** INTEGER;

and in the program header as:

> **PROGRAM** COMPUTE (INPUT,OUTPUT,SPEED);

It is important to remember that the TYPE or the VAR definition assigns a type to a file, but not a length. The file is the only data structure in Pascal with a length that may vary dynamically at execution time. A file is empty when created. Elements are then added or examined. In Standard Pascal, elements may not be removed or modified.

Here is an example showing how elements are accessed. The file 'SENTENCE' is defined:

> **VAR** SENTENCE : **FILE OF** CHAR;

An empty file will be created by a REWRITE:

SENTENCE

(empty)

An element is then added to it (the command will be described below):

SENTENCE

And then another:

At this point, SENTENCE is a file of length 2.

STANDARD FILES

Two standard files are provided in Pascal: INPUT and OUTPUT, and a standard type: TEXT. The standard files INPUT and OUTPUT must not be declared as variables, and do not need to be included in the program header, unless a READ or a WRITE appears within the program without a corresponding file name. However, in order to avoid the risk of an error, it is usually a good precaution to include INPUT and OUTPUT in the program header. In fact, many implementations insist that this be done in any case. The standard type TEXT was mentioned earlier and will be described in more detail later on in this chapter.

WRITING ON A FILE

A file is a sequence of elements that have the same type or structure. For example, a file may be a sequence of characters, numbers, or records. A file may be logically represented as a sequence of identical modules, as shown in Figure 11.2.

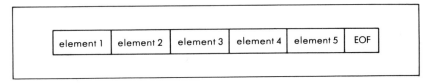

Figure 11.2: Representation of a File

In Figure 11.2, the file contains five elements. In order to refer to an element within a file, we must know the numeric position of the element we want to access or examine.

In Pascal, only one element of a file may be accessed at any time. A *pointer* points to the current element at all times. Every time that an element is added to a file, the pointer is moved to point to the end of the file. Here is an example:

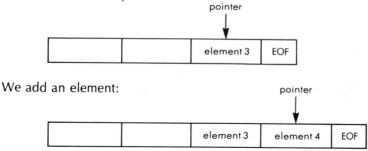

We add an element:

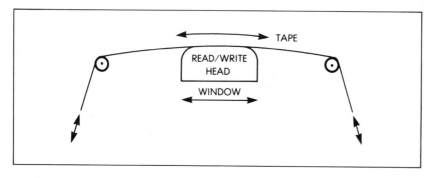

This is called a *window* system. The process is analogous to a magnetic tape moving in front of a read/write head (see Figure 11.3).

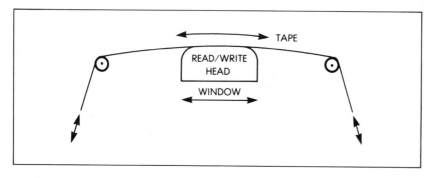

Figure 11.3: **Magnetic Tape Moving in Front of a Read/Write Head**

The window is called the *buffer variable,* and is represented as F↑ where F is the name of a file. By definition F↑ always contains the current element that may be accessed within the file.

For example, the *buffer variable,* or access window for the file called SPEED at a given time is shown in Figure 11.4.

Writing a new value in a file F is accomplished by assigning the new value to F↑, then PUTting it in the file. A new value is always added at the end of a file. This requires that the window be correctly positioned.

Recall that when a file is initially defined, it is empty. A non-empty file will be created by writing an element into the file. We will now study the appropriate commands.

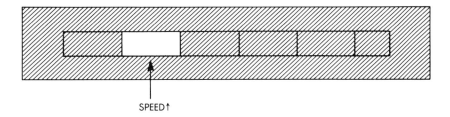

Figure 11.4:   The Access Window

A file does not exist before writing into it. If a new file has already been declared, the file must formally be created with a special command called REWRITE before it is used. Thus, to actually create the (empty) file SPEED, we will execute the statement:

REWRITE(SPEED);

If the file SPEED has already been used, and contains any values or elements, they are erased by this command. The location pointer or *access window* is set at the first possible position within the file, which is the empty file (see Figure 11.5).

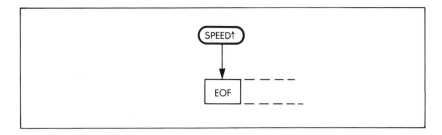

Figure 11.5:   Creating a File

Next, the value NUMBER is assigned to SPEED↑, and written into the file. This is accomplished with the special built-in procedure PUT:

SPEED↑ : = NUMBER;
PUT(SPEED);

The result of these two statements is shown in Figure 11.6. One element has been added to the file, and the access window has been automatically moved to the right by one position.

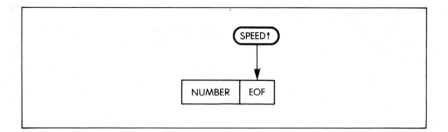

Figure 11.6:   Writing into a File

Since this sequence of two Pascal instructions is very common, a standard command has been provided to abbreviate it in the case of a text file. It is called WRITE. The two instructions in our example may be abbreviated as:

WRITE(SPEED, NUMBER);

This applies to text files only. When using WRITE or PUT, the buffer variable is undefined at the end of the instruction, as illustrated in Figure 11.6. The file name may be omitted from the WRITE command. It will then be assumed to be OUTPUT.

In summary, when the buffer variable is pointing to the end of the file, the WRITE command appends a new element to the end of the file, as illustrated in Figure 11.7. This requires that the file was opened for writing and that the end-of-file was reached by successive writing. The pointer is generally advanced with the standard procedure PUT.

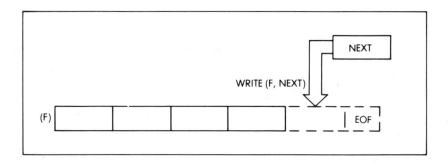

Figure 11.7:   Appending an Element to a File

WRITE Summary

Two procedures may be used to write into a file:

Put(F) appends the value of F↑ to the file F. The value of F↑ is undefined afterwards. PUT *must* always write at the end of a file. (EOF(file), described below, must be TRUE before using PUT.)

WRITE(F,ELEMENT) assign ELEMENT to F↑, then performs a PUT(F). This function works only on a TEXT file.

In addition, a file is opened or erased with:

REWRITE(F) the file becomes the empty file and is opened for writing.

READING A FILE

Once a file has been created, and values have been entered into it, the file may then be read. Four procedures are provided for reading or examining a file: EOF, RESET, GET, and READ. Each will be described in turn.

The EOF Function

The standard Boolean function EOF(F) tests to see whether or not the current window F↑ points to the End-Of-File, i.e., past the last element of a file. If it does, EOF(F) is TRUE. Otherwise, it is FALSE. For example, PUT(F) may only be used when EOF(F) = TRUE and the file is open for writing.

The RESET Procedure

The RESET procedure positions the window to the first element of the file. Thus executing

RESET(SPEED);

produces the results shown in Figure 11.8.

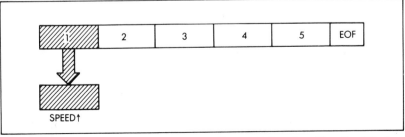

Figure 11.8: Resetting the Window

In this example, the file SPEED contained five elements. After executing the RESET procedure, the buffer variable contains the first element of the file. If the file had been empty, the buffer variable would be undefined. This condition may be tested with an EOF. EOF(SPEED) is TRUE whenever the end of the file has been reached or the file is empty.

The GET Procedure

In order to read a specific element of a file, usually the file pointer must be reset to the first element, then moved to the appropriate element. The file pointer may be advanced by one element at a time, using the GET procedure. The EOF function is normally used before a GET, to test whether or not the file is empty, because a GET on an empty file results in an error condition.

The READ Procedure

A standard READ procedure, similar to the WRITE procedure, is also available in Pascal, for use on text files only. Thus:

>   READ(SPEED,ELEMENT);

is equivalent to:

>   ELEMENT : = SPEED↑;

>   GET(SPEED);

READ Summary

EOF(F)	is a function used to test if F↑ is the EOF. In that case, EOF(F) is TRUE.
RESET(F)	moves the window back to the first element of the file (F↑ is set to the first element of F) and opens it for reading only.
GET(F)	moves the window to the next element of F: F↑ is set to the next element of F. EOF(F) must be FALSE prior to the GET.
READ(F,ELEMENT)	is equivalent to: ELEMENT := F↑ ;GET(F).

Important Notes

In Standard Pascal, the READ and WRITE procedures were originally supplied only for TEXT files. However, in most implementations, they are generally available for any type of file. Of course, when reading or writing a file, the element being read or written must be compatible with the type of the file. Also, whenever there is no file specification given as part of a READ or EOF, it is automatically assumed to be an INPUT. Similarly with a WRITE, the file is assumed to be OUTPUT.

It is important to remember that Pascal files are organized sequentially. They must be *opened* for input or output. In practice this means that a READ may not be followed by a WRITE, and that a WRITE may not be followed by a READ. The file must be RESET before any READs, and a REWRITE must be executed before any WRITEs.

CASE STUDY 1: FILEMERGE

The program in Figure 11.9 merges two files (A and B) containing integers. Each file is ordered in ascending order so that:

— In file A, $A(I) >= A(I-1)$
— In file B, $B(I) >= B(I-1)$

The resulting file C is obtained by merging the elements of A and B in such a way that:

$$C(I) >= C(I-1)$$

This program includes three WHILE loops. The first loop will extract elements from A or B (the smaller element first), until either A or B is empty. The loop will test whether the current element of A is smaller than the current element of B. If it is smaller, then this element of A goes into C.

```
PROGRAM MERGEAB(INPUT, OUTPUT, FILEA, FILEB, FILEC);
(* PROGRAM TO MERGE TWO INTEGER FILES *)
VAR FILEA,FILEB,FILEC : FILE OF INTEGER;
        LASTELEMENT : BOOLEAN;
BEGIN
        RESET(FILEA);
        RESET(FILEB);
        REWRITE(FILEC);
        LASTELEMENT := EOF(FILEA) OR EOF(FILEB);
        WHILE NOT LASTELEMENT DO BEGIN
                IF FILEA↑ <= FILEB↑ THEN
                        BEGIN
                                FILEC↑ := FILEA↑ ;
                                GET(FILEA);
                                LASTELEMENT := EOF(FILEA)
                        END
                ELSE
                        BEGIN
                                FILEC↑ := FILEB↑ ;
                                GET(FILEB);
                                LASTELEMENT := EOF(FILEB)
                        END;
```

Figure 11.9: FILEMERGE Program

```
                    PUT(FILEC);
            END;
            WHILE NOT EOF(FILEB) DO
                BEGIN
                    FILEC↑ := FILEB↑ ;
                    PUT(FILEC);
                    GET(FILEB)
                END;
            WHILE NOT EOF(FILEA) DO
                BEGIN
                    FILEC↑ := FILEA↑ ;
                    PUT(FILEC);
                    GET(FILEA)
                END
        END.
```

Figure 11.9: FILEMERGE Program (continued)

After files A, B, and C have been defined, they are initialized. A and B will be read:

```
    RESET(FILEA);
    RESET(FILEB);
```

C will be written:

```
    REWRITE(FILEC);
```

A logical variable called LASTELEMENT is defined. It will be TRUE whenever either the EOF for A or the EOF for B is reached.

```
    LASTELEMENT := EOF(FILEA) OR EOF(FILEB);
```

Then, the buffer variables for files A and B are compared within a WHILE loop:

```
    WHILE NOT LASTELEMENT DO BEGIN
        IF FILEA↑ < = FILEB↑  THEN
```

The lowest value is assigned to the buffer variable for file C. For example, if the buffer variable for file B is less than that for file A, then the following block of code is executed:

```
ELSE
    BEGIN
        FILEC↑ := FILEB↑ ;
        GET(FILEB);
        LASTELEMENT := EOF(FILEB)
    END;
```

The element is now written into file C, and the window is advanced:

PUT(FILEC);

The WHILE loop terminates:

```
END;
```

This loop will continue until LASTELEMENT becomes TRUE, i.e., until either EOF(FILEA) or EOF(FILEB) becomes TRUE.
Note: when examining this statement remember that LASTELEMENT is a BOOLEAN value.

At the end of this loop, the entire contents of one of the files has been transferred to C, along with (possibly) some elements of the other file (B or A).

Now, the remaining elements of the file which have not been completely copied into C must be transferred. Two loops are provided for this purpose: one, in case the file is B, and another, in case the file is A.

Note that using REPEAT...UNTIL is not practical in either of the cases, since it is guaranteed that either EOF(A) or EOF(B) is TRUE. Therefore, one of the loops will not be executed at all. REPEAT would execute a loop at least once.

Here is a numerical example:

A contains:

FILEA:	1	4	6	EOF

B contains:

FILEB:	2	5	7	21	50	EOF

After execution of the WHILE loop terminates, FILEC contains:

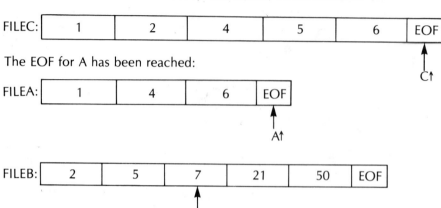

The body of the third loop is not executed because EOF(FILEA) is TRUE.

PERMANENT AND TEMPORARY FILES

Files may be permanent or temporary. A file becomes permanent when it is written on a permanent storage device such as a disk or a tape. Each installation provides specific commands for storing permanent files. For example, text may be typed in as input to an editor program written in Pascal. Obviously, the resulting file should be preserved for future use.

In case text must be added to the file, the editor program will need to access this existing text file. This is an example of an *external* file. Files that may already exist at the time a program is run are called external files. Their names must be included in the program heading, in the same way that parameters are passed to a procedure or a function.

Whenever a file is used within the program and then discarded, the file is called a local file.

TEXT FILES

The file type TEXT is a special built-in type within Pascal. It is defined as:

TYPE TEXT = **FILE OF** CHAR;

Because text files are so common and important, three special operators are provided in Pascal for processing text files. These three procedures are: EOLN, READLN, and WRITELN. They will be described in this section.

Text files are composed of lines, separated by end of line (EOLN) markers. The actual end of line marker depends upon the code used. In the case of the ASCII code, the combination carriage-return/linefeed is used. However, this is made transparent in Pascal. Each line is composed of characters. The three special operators automatically recognize or generate the end of line markers, thus respecting the text structure:

EOLN(F) is a Boolean function that tests for the end of line marker. It is true if the end of line will be the next character to be read. In this case, F↑ will be a blank after a READ or a GET, regardless of the actual control characters used internally to denote an end of line.

READLN(F,variable list) reads as many lines as necessary to fulfill the variable list, then skips to the next line of text from the file F. READLN(INPUT) is equivalent to READLN. If no variable list is given, READLN will skip to the beginning of the next line in the text file.

WRITELN(F,variable list) writes a complete line of text, up to the end of line marker, plus a carriage return and a linefeed. WRITELN(OUTPUT) is equivalent to WRITELN. If no variable list is given, WRITELN will terminate the current line of the text file.

In addition, the READ and WRITE procedures offer other facilities when operating on text files. For example, they will automatically convert any integer, real or Boolean (for a WRITE operation), into a string of CHARs on writing to a file. A series of parameters may also be used to read or write a sequence of characters simultaneously. For example:

        READ(LETTER,C1,C2,C3);

is equivalent to:

        READ(LETTER,C1);
        READ(LETTER,C2);
        READ(LETTER,C3);

Note that READ(C1,C2,C3) means:

        READ(INPUT,C1,C2,C3)

The parameters C1, C2, C3 must be CHAR, INTEGER or REAL variables. The same rule applies to READLN, WRITE, and WRITELN. However, in the case of a WRITE, C1, C2, C3 may be expressions.

Additional facilities are available on most Pascal implementations which facilitate the processing of text files. However, they are generally specific to the implementation, and should be handled accordingly.

TEXT FILE PROCESSING

The following are examples of typical text-processing *program blocks*:

Line Transfer:

```
VAR C : CHAR;
      A,B : TEXT;
{TRANSFER A LINE FROM FILE A TO FILE B}
RESET(A); REWRITE(B);
WHILE NOT EOLN(A) DO
    BEGIN
          READ(A,C);
          WRITE(B,C)
    END; {WHILE}
```

File Copying:

```
{TRANSFER FILE ALONG WITH EOLNs}
RESET(A); REWRITE(B);
WHILE NOT EOF(A) DO
    BEGIN
        WHILE NOT EOLN(A) DO
            BEGIN
                  READ(A,C);
                  WRITE(B,C)
            END; {WHILE}
      READLN(A);
      WRITELN(B)
    END; {WHILE}
```

These examples can be easily modified. In particular, the character read from A may be processed instead of written into B. For example, the frequency of occurrences of a given letter could be tallied, or, the message in A could be encrypted (see the section of this chapter on exercises).

THE INPUT AND OUTPUT FILES

INPUT and OUTPUT are pre-defined Pascal text files. They normally refer to the input medium (usually a keyboard) and the output medium (CRT screen or printer). When no text file type is indicated, either IN-PUT or OUTPUT is automatically assumed.

In other words, the following pairs of expressions are equivalent:

Expression:	Means:
EOF	EOF(INPUT)
EOLN	EOLN(INPUT)
READ(CH)	READ(INPUT,CH)
READLN	READLN(INPUT)
WRITE(CH)	WRITE(OUTPUT,CH)
WRITELN	WRITELN(OUTPUT)

where CH represents a character.

When using INPUT or OUTPUT, RESET or REWRITE may not be used for these two files.

CASE STUDY 2: CIPHER PROGRAM

The Problem

In order to protect the contents of a file from unauthorized reading, the contents of the file are sometimes enciphered. The principle of a simple cipher is to replace each letter in the text by another symbol in such a way that no two letters are enciphered into the same symbol, or so that the result cannot be deciphered anymore. One of the simplest algorithms is to replace each letter by the nth one following it in the alphabet. Here, n is set to 3, but this could be easily changed. In this case, an A will be a D, an E will be an H, etc.

The program must work both ways in order to encipher and decipher a file. The first digit typed at the keyboard will specify the function to be performed:

'0' means encipher.
'1' means decipher.

Input to the program is shown in Figure 11.10.

> The Ecology Center is expanding its curbside recycling program. In addition to newspapers, we now pick up your recyclable glass containers, aluminum, and cans from right in front of your home.
>
> This latest program should more than triple the amount of materials we collect. Besides drastically reducing the quantity of materials destined for landfill, we will be saving valuable natural resources and lessening the need for imported fuels.

Figure 11.10: Input for a Cipher Program

The corresponding output is shown in Figure 11.11.

```
1
#####WKH#HFRORJ ¦ #FHGWHU#LV#SDGGLAJ#LWV#FXUEVLGH#UHF ¦ FOLGJ
SURJUDP1##LG#DGGLWLRG#WR#GHZVSDSHUV/#ZH#ARZ#SLFN#XS# ¦ RXU
UHF ¦ FODEOH#JODVV#FRGWDLGHUV/#DOXPLGXP/#DDG#FDGV#JURP#ULJKW
LG#JURQW#RJ# ¦ RXU#KRPH1
#####WKLV#ODWHVW#SURJUDP#VKRXOG#PRUH#WKDG#WULSOH#WKH#DPRXGW#RI
PDWHULDOV#ZH#FROOHFW1##EHVLGHV#GUDVW1FDOO ¦ #UHGXFLGJ#WKH#TXDGWLW
RI#PDWHULDOV#GHVWLGHG#JRU#ODDGILOO/#ZH#ZLOO#EH#VDYLGJ#YDOXDEOH#
ADWXUDO#UHVRXUFHV#DGG#OHVVHGLGJ#WKH#CHHG#IRU#LPSRUWHG#IXHOV1
```

Figure 11.11:   Output of Cipher Program

Once enciphered, the file contains a '1' in the first line.
Note: this output of this program can now be used as input to decipher
the file.

The Program

The Cipher program listing is shown in Figure 11.12. Two files are used:

> INFILE holds the text typed in at the keyboard.
> OUTFILE holds the modified text after enciphering or decipher-
> ing.

Two variables are used:

> CH holds the character read.
> ENCIPH is a flag indicating whether or not the enciphering
> mode is TRUE.

The corresponding declarations are:

```
PROGRAM ENDECIPHER(INPUT,OUTPUT,INFILE,OUTFILE);
VAR     CH: CHAR;
        ENCIPH: BOOLEAN;
        INFILE,OUTFILE: TEXT;
```

The two files must be opened for input and output respectively:

```
BEGIN
     RESET(INFILE);
     REWRITE(OUTFILE);
```

```
PROGRAM ENDECIPHER(INPUT, OUTPUT, INFILE, OUTFILE);
VAR CH:         CHAR;                (* HOLDS CHARACTER READ *)
    ENCIPH:     BOOLEAN;             (* FLAG FOR ENCIPHERING *)
    INFILE, OUTFILE:   TEXT;
BEGIN (* ENDECIPHER *)
    RESET(INFILE);
    REWRITE(OUTFILE);
    READLN(INFILE, CH);
  (* SET FLAG AND WRITE THE KEY LINE *)
    IF CH = '0' THEN
        BEGIN (* ENCIPHER FLAG *)
            ENCIPH : = TRUE;
            WRITELN(OUTFILE, '1')
        END    (* ENCIPHER FLAG *)
    ELSE   (* CH = '1' *)
        BEGIN (* DECIPHER FLAG *)
            ENCIPH : = FALSE;
            WRITELN(OUTFILE, '0')
        END; (* DECIPHER FLAG *)
    WHILE NOT EOF(INFILE) DO
        BEGIN (* READ FILE *)
            WHILE NOT EOLN(INFILE) DO
                BEGIN (* READ LINE *)
                    READ(INFILE, CH);
                    IF ENCIPH THEN
                        CH : = SUCC(SUCC(SUCC(CH)))
                    ELSE
                        CH : = PRED(PRED(PRED(CH)));
                    WRITE(OUTFILE, CH)
                END; (* READ LINE *)
            WRITELN(OUTFILE);
            READLN(INFILE)
        END (* READ FILE *)
END. (* ENDECIPHER *)
```

Figure 11.12: CIPHER Program

The first character typed in specifies encipher ('0') or decipher ('1'):

```
READLN(INFILE,CH);
```

The ENCIPH flag is set accordingly, and the "opposite" character is written on the output file:

```
IF CH = '0' THEN
    BEGIN
        ENCIPH : = TRUE;
        WRITELN(OUTFILE,'1')
    END
ELSE
    BEGIN
        ENCIPH : = FALSE;
        WRITELN(OUTFILE,'0')
    END;
```

The text from the input file will be read until an end-of-file character is found:

```
WHILE NOT EOF(INFILE) DO
```

A line is read:

```
BEGIN
    WHILE NOT EOLN(INFILE) DO
```

A character is read in and either enciphered or deciphered, depending on the value of the ENCIPH flag, and then it is saved in OUTFILE:

```
BEGIN
    READ(INFILE,CH);
    IF ENCIPH THEN CH : = SUCC(SUCC(SUCC(CH)));
    ELSE CH : = PRED(PRED(PRED(CH)));
    WRITE(OUTFILE,CH)
END;
```

The program moves to the next line:

```
        WRITELN(OUTFILE);
        READLN(INFILE)
    END
END.
```

Cipher Summary

This program illustrates the use of an input and an output file, and shows how text is read a character at a time, line by line, until the end of the input. Each character is processed as it is read and the contents of INFILE and OUTFILE are printed separately.

CASE STUDY 3: FIND OCCURRENCES OF A STRING

The Problem

The goal of this exercise is to design a program that will search a file of text for a given string and display each occurrence of the string, counting the total number of times the string has been found in the text. This is a common task when processing text files.

The corresponding program will illustrate the use of arrays of characters, files, and text-processing.

A typical input file is shown in Figure 11.13.

```
NOW IS THE TIME FOR ALL GOOD MEN TO ⎫
COME TO THE AID OF THEIR COUNTRY.    ⎬ INPUT FILE
THIS IS THE END.                     ⎭
```

Figure 11.13: Input File for MATCHCOUNT

A run with the input given above results in the output shown in Figure 11.14.

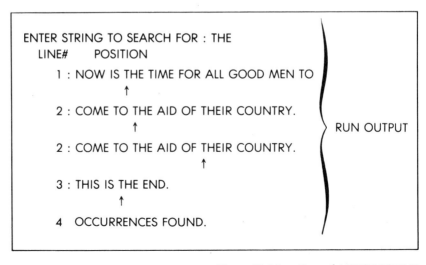

Figure 11.14: Run of MATCHCOUNT

```
PROGRAM MATCHCOUNT(INPUT,OUTPUT,SRCFIL);
(* PROGRAM TO COUNT NUMBER OF OCCURRENCES OF A GIVEN STRING *)
(* IN A FILE AND PRINT THE LINES CONTAINING THE STRING *)
TYPE STRING = ARRAY[1..120] OF CHAR;
VAR WDCOUNT,LINECOUNT,WDLEN,LINELEN,WDPOS,INDEX: INTEGER;
     LINE,WORD: STRING;
     SRCFIL: TEXT;
PROCEDURE PRINT(VAR STRNG: STRING; LENGTH: INTEGER);
VAR INDEX: INTEGER;
BEGIN
     FOR INDEX := 1 TO LENGTH DO WRITE(STRNG[INDEX]);
     WRITELN
END;
PROCEDURE FIND(VAR STR1,STR2: STRING; LEN1,LEN2: INTEGER;
                 VAR POSITION: INTEGER):
(* PROCEDURE TO FIND LOCATION OF STR1 IN STR2 *)
(* STARTS LOOKING AT POSITION, RETURNS LOCATION IN POSITION *)
(* RETURNS POSITION > LEN2−LEN1+1 IF NO MATCH *)
VAR CNT1,CNT2,CMPVAL: INTEGER;
BEGIN
     CNT1 := 1; CMPVAL := LEN2 − LEN1 + 1; (* SPEEDS UP LOOP *)
     REPEAT
          POSITION := POSITION+1;
          IF STR2[POSITION] = STR1[1] THEN  (* CHK IF 1ST CHRS MATCH *)
               BEGIN  (* CHECK IF REST OF STRING MATCHES *)
                    CNT1 := 1;
                    CNT2 := POSITION;
                    REPEAT
                         CNT1 := CNT1+1;
                         CNT2 := CNT2+1
                    UNTIL (STR2[CNT2] <> STR1[CNT1]) OR (CNT1 > LEN1)
               END;
     UNTIL (POSITION>CMPVAL) OR (CNT1>LEN1) (* EOLN OR WORD FOUND *)
END;
BEGIN (* MATCHCOUNT *)
     WDCOUNT := 0;
```

Figure 11.15: MATCHCOUNT Program

```
        LINECOUNT :=0;
        WDLEN := 0;
        WRITE('ENTER STRING TO SEARCH FOR :');
        REPEAT  (* GET STRING TO MATCH *)
            WDLEN := WDLEN+1;
            READ(WORD[WDLEN])
        UNTIL EOLN;
        WDLEN := WDLEN-1;
        WRITELN;
        RESET(SRCFIL);
        WRITELN('LINE#  POSITION');
        WHILE NOT EOF(SRCFIL) DO
            BEGIN
                LINELEN := 0;
                REPEAT  (* GET LINE TO CHECK *)
                    LINELEN := LINELEN+1;
                    READ(SRCFIL,LINE[LINELEN])
                UNTIL EOLN(SRCFIL);
                LINECOUNT := LINECOUNT+1;
                WDPOS := 0;
                REPEAT  (* LOOP TO CHECK FOR MULTIPLE MATCHES *)
                    FIND(WORD,LINE,WDLEN,LINELEN,WDPOS);
                    IF (WDPOS > 0) AND (WDPOS < = LINELEN-WDLEN+1) THEN
                        BEGIN  (* MATCH FOUND - SHOW IT *)
                            WDCOUNT := WDCOUNT+1;
                            WRITE(LINECOUNT:5,' :');
                            PRINT(LINE,LINELEN);
                            FOR INDEX := 1 TO WDPOS+6 DO
                                WRITE(' ');
                            WRITELN('↑')
                        END
                UNTIL WDPOS > LINELEN - WDLEN + 1
            END;
        WRITELN;
        WRITELN(WDCOUNT:6,'  OCCURRENCES FOUND.')
    END. (* MATCHCOUNT *)
```

Figure 11.15: **MATCHCOUNT Program (continued)**

The Program

The program listing is shown in Figure 11.15. The program uses a file called SRCFIL, of type TEXT, to store the text to be searched:

PROGRAM MATCHCOUNT(INPUT,OUTPUT,SRCFIL);

The type STRING is defined as an array of 120 characters, the maximum width of a line on most printers. The two variables LINE and WORD are declared as STRINGs:

TYPE   STRING = **ARRAY**[1..120] **OF** CHAR;
VAR   WDCOUNT,LINECOUNT,WDLEN,LINELEN,WDPOS,INDEX: INTEGER;
         LINE,WORD: STRING;
         SRCFIL: TEXT;

This program uses two procedures: PRINT and FIND. The PRINT procedure displays or types a string, STRING, up to a given position within the string called LENGTH:

PROCEDURE PRINT (**VAR** STRNG: STRING; LENGTH: INTEGER);
VAR INDEX : INTEGER;
BEGIN
        FOR INDEX := 1 **TO** LENGTH **DO** WRITE(STRNG[INDEX]);
        WRITELN (* MOVE TO NEXT LINE *)
    END;

The procedure FIND searches the string STR2 for the occurrence of the string STR1. The search starts at the location following POSITION. If a match is found, POSITION returns the location of the match. Otherwise, POSITION returns a value greater than LEN2-LEN1, indicating a no-match situation. LEN2 is the length of STR2. LEN1 is the length of STR1.

The procedure declares three local variables. CNT1 and CNT2 are counter variables used in the search loop. CMPVAL is the last position of STR2 that should be examined. When the POSITION counter exceeds CMPVAL, the search has failed.

PROCEDURE FIND (**VAR** STR1,STR2: STRING; LEN1,LEN2: INTEGER;
                       VAR POSITION: INTEGER);
VAR CNT1,CNT2,CMPVAL: INTEGER;
BEGIN
        CNT1 := 1; CMPVAL := LEN2 − LEN1 + 1;

A REPEAT loop is used to implement the search. The variable POSI-TION points to the first letter within STR2 that is tested for a match with the first letter of STR1. The first letters of STR1 and STR2 are compared:

REPEAT
POSITION : = POSITION + 1;
IF STR2[POSITION] = STR1[1] **THEN**

If the first letters of each string match, the remaining ones are compared. CNT1 points to the next letter of STR1. CNT2 points to the next letter of STR2.

BEGIN
CNT1 : = 1;
CNT2 : = POSITION;
REPEAT
CNT1 : = CNT1 + 1;
CNT2 : = CNT2 + 1

The characters respectively pointed to by CNT1 and CNT2 are compared:

UNTIL (STR2[CNT2] <> STR1[CNT1])
OR (CNT1 > LEN1)
END;

This REPEAT loop stops in either of two cases:

1. STR2[CNT2] <> STR1[CNT1] : the characters do not match, i.e., no string match was found.
2. CNT1 > LEN1 : all LEN1 characters of STR1 matched those starting at location POSITION of STR2, i.e., a match was found.

The external REPEAT loop is repeated:

UNTIL (POSITION > CMPVAL) **OR** (CNT1 > LEN1)
END;

This loop stops in two cases:

1. CNT1 > LEN1 : a match had been found within the inner REPEAT loop.
2. POSITION > CMPVAL : the end of STR2 has been reached without a match.

Note that, in either case, POSITION holds the information relative to the match when the FIND procedure terminates.

The program itself is straightforward:

WDCOUNT	is used to hold the number of successful matches.
LINECOUNT	is used to count and display the lines of text.
WORD	holds the string to be looked up in the text.
LINE	holds a line of text.
WDLEN	holds the number of characters within the WORD.
LINELEN	holds the number of characters within the LINE.
WDPOS	holds the position just before the one at which the search will start.

Counter variables are initialized to 0 and the WORD is read from the keyboard, a character at a time, until an EOLN is found:

```
BEGIN
      WDCOUNT := 0;
      LINECOUNT := 0;
      WDLEN := 0;
      WRITE ('ENTER STRING TO SEARCH FOR: ');
      REPEAT
            WDLEN := WDLEN+1;
            READ(WORD[WDLEN])
      UNTIL EOLN;
```

The REPEAT loop executes until an EOLN is read, i.e., "one too many" characters are read. The actual length of WORD is therefore:

```
      WDLEN := WDLEN-1;
```

The program now reads the text from the SRCFIL, a line at a time.

```
      WRITELN;
      RESET(SRCFIL);
      WRITELN('LINE #    POSITION');
      WHILE NOT EOF(SRCFIL) DO
          BEGIN
                LINELEN := 0;
                REPEAT
                      LINELEN := LINELEN+1;
                      READ(SRCFIL,LINE[LINELEN])
                UNTIL EOLN(SRCFIL);
```

A line has now been read and is contained in LINE. This line of text is now examined for occurrences of the specified WORD; using the FIND procedure:

```
LINECOUNT := LINECOUNT+1;
WDPOS := 0;
REPEAT
    FIND(WORD,LINE,WDLEN,LINELEN,WDPOS);
    IF(WDPOS > 0) AND (WDPOS < = LINELEN−WDLEN+1) THEN
```

Once FIND has executed, the resulting value of WDPOS is examined to determine whether or not a match has been found. If so, the match is displayed, using the PRINT procedure:

```
BEGIN
    WDCOUNT := WDCOUNT+1;
    WRITE(LINECOUNT:5,'   :');
    PRINT(LINE,LINELEN);
    FOR INDEX := 1 TO WDPOS+6 DO
        WRITE('  ');
        WRITELN(' ↑ ')
END
```

This process is repeated for possible multiple occurrences of WORD within LINE, until no more characters remain to be tested in LINE:

```
UNTIL WDPOS > LINELEN−WDLEN+1
```

The outer WHILE loop is executed until an EOF character is encountered in one input file and the number of matches is displayed:

```
    END;
    WRITELN;
    WRITELN(WDCOUNT : 6,'   OCCURRENCES FOUND.')
END. (* MATCHCOUNT *)
```

TURBO PASCAL FILES

Turbo Pascal differs significantly from Standard Pascal in the way it handles files. These differences are large enough to make it necessary to modify any Standard Pascal program that uses files before running it in Turbo Pascal.

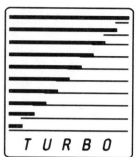

In Standard Pascal, files are formally defined independently of the medium on which they reside. This method of definition was inspired by punched cards and magnetic tape files, which were the commonly used storage media when Pascal was first defined. As a result, all access to files in Standard Pascal is sequential (item by item) as it is in punched cards and magnetic tapes.

In Turbo Pascal, however, files are defined as disk files. Disks are now the most prevalent storage device for microcomputers. As a result, the sequential-access mechanisms provided in Standard Pascal are often insufficient and inconvenient for these random-access disk-based files. New structures and access mechanisms for file access are provided in Turbo Pascal.

File Variables

The first major difference between Turbo Pascal and Standard Pascal is the way in which files are linked to a program. In Standard Pascal, you open files by referencing their file name in the program heading and they close when the program terminates. In Turbo Pascal, disk files must be linked to a particular file variable with the ASSIGN(filevar, filename) procedure and prepared for processing or "opened" with RESET or REWRITE before they are used. Also, files must be explicitly closed with the CLOSE(filevar) procedure after they have been used or data will be lost.

In Turbo Pascal, the file name is linked to a file variable with the ASSIGN procedure before the file is opened for processing. RESET (filevar) opens an existing file for processing and sets the record pointer to the first record (0). REWRITE(filevar) creates a new file (or overwrites an existing file) and opens it for processing with the record pointer set to record 0. When used with TEXT files, files opened with RESET can only be used for input operations and those opened with REWRITE can only be used for output operations.

External File Names

Valid file names are string literals or variables consisting of one to eight characters followed by an optional file type of a period and up to three characters. The following are examples of valid file names in

Turbo Pascal:

'FILENAME.TYP'
'INFILE.DAT'
'MAY.DAT'
'DATAFILE'
'DATA1'

Linking Files

The process of linking a data file to the program, and opening it for input looks like this:

```
VAR INFILE : FILE OF DATATYPE;
    DATA : DATATYPE;
BEGIN
    ASSIGN(INFILE,'FILENAME.TYP'); {LINK FILENAME.TYP TO
                                                   INFILE}

    RESET(INFILE);  {OPEN FOR INPUT}
    . . .
    READ(INFILE, DATA);
    . . .
    CLOSE(INFILE);
END.
```

A similar technique is used to link, open, and access an output file in Turbo Pascal:

```
VAR OUTFILE : FILE OF DATATYPE;
    DATA : DATATYPE;
BEGIN
    ASSIGN(OUTFILE,'FILENAME.TYP'); {LINK FILENAME.TYP TO
                                                    OUTFILE}

    REWRITE(OUTFILE);  {OPEN FILE FOR OUTPUT}
    . . .
    WRITE(OUTFILE, DATA);
    . . .
    CLOSE(OUTFILE);
END.
```

When file names are specified interactively (i.e. by a user), it is important to test for the existence of the named file before it is opened. After each I/O operation, the standard function IORESULT returns the result or error code of the operation. (See below for codes.) The following technique provides a method for testing for the existence of files:

```
VAR DATAFILE : FILE OF DATATYPE;
    DATA : DATATYPE;
    EXIST : BOOLEAN;
BEGIN
    ASSIGN(DATAFILE,'FILENAME.TYP');
    {$I-} RESET(DATAFILE) {$I+};
    EXIST := IORESULT = 0; {CHECK IF FILENAME.TYP EXISTS}
    . . .
```

The Boolean variable EXIST in the above example can be used to check that a file name actually exists before opening the file for input, or that it doesn't exist before overwriting it with the REWRITE procedure. The {$I-} and {$I+} are compiler directives that disable and enable I/O error checking, so the program doesn't stop if an error condition is detected during the RESET operation.

Data Files

Another major difference between Turbo Pascal files and Standard Pascal files is the way in which they access the elements of data files. As was discussed earlier in this chapter, Pascal supports two kinds of files: TEXT and data. TEXT files are made up of text (characters representing the data elements), while data files store numeric values in binary form.

Standard Pascal accesses a data element by using the file identifier to point to the data, and the PUT and GET procedures to actually transfer the element to or from the file.

Turbo Pascal accesses data elements in one step with the READ and WRITE procedures, similar to the method it uses for TEXT files. Because the PUT and GET method used by Standard Pascal is a two-step process, some of these programs cannot be easily translated into Turbo Pascal.

TEXT Files

In Turbo Pascal, the READ, READLN, WRITE, and WRITELN procedures are used with TEXT type files to perform input/output operations. As in Standard Pascal, if no file name is specified, the standard file INPUT or OUTPUT is the default value. These procedures are restricted to text files, standard files, and logical devices.

READ Procedures   There are two READ procedures.

> READ(filevar,var1,var2,. . .,varN)
> READLN(filevar,var1,var2,. . .,varN)

The input data can be a single character, a STRING, or an ARRAY OF CHARacters. Turbo Pascal also allows numeric variables to be used as READ and READLN parameters, but the input data must be converted to the numeric type, otherwise an error is generated. If several numeric type variables are specified in the parameter list, they must be separated by spaces or tabs in the input line. Only one STRING type can be read per line, because a STRING is terminated by a carriage return.

Unlike Standard Pascal, in Turbo Pascal READ can read a complete string or only one character. When reading a STRING, the line will be read until the carriage return (the end of line). At this point, EOLN(filevar) becomes TRUE.

A Boolean value cannot be read. When reading integer or real values, leading blanks and the end of line are eliminated automatically.

WRITE Procedures   There are two WRITE procedures:

> WRITE(filevar,var1,var2,. . .,varN)
> WRITELN(filevar,var1,var2,. . .,varN)

In Turbo Pascal, WRITE and WRITELN do operate on Boolean variables and will print TRUE or FALSE. In addition, they can print an entire STRING with a single statement. For example:

```
VAR COUNTRY : STRING[5];
BEGIN
      COUNTRY : = 'USA'
      WRITELN(OUTPUT,COUNTRY);
END.
```

Field width specifications can be used with Turbo Pascal strings. If the specified field width is longer than the length of the string being written, leading blanks are inserted. If the field width is smaller, the whole string is printed. For example:

```
VAR S : STRING[10];
BEGIN
      S := 'ABCDEF ETC';
      WRITELN(S);
```

```
        WRITELN(S:3);
    WRITELN(S:12)
    END.
```

will produce:

```
    ABCDEF ETC
    ABCDEF ETC
        ABCDEF ETC
```

Standard Files and Logical Devices   Text input/output operations in Turbo Pascal can use several predefined logical devices in addition to disk file names. These devices are treated as TEXT files. They include

CON:, TRM:, KBD:, LST:, AUX:, and USR:

— CON: is the system console I/O device accessed through the operating system, usually the display screen and keyboard. It is normally linked to the system standard files INPUT and OUTPUT.

— TRM: is the system console I/O device accessed in "raw" form, that is, without input editing provided by the operating system.

— KBD: is the system keyboard input device. When used for input, no echo to the system screen is provided. This feature can be used for typing a secret password, for echoing a different character, or for input verification.

— LST: is the system printer list output device.

— AUX: is the system auxiliary punch/reader device, usually the serial I/O modem port.

— USR: is a user definable I/O function as described in the *Turbo Pascal Reference Manual*.

In Turbo Pascal, several "standard" predeclared file variables of type TEXT are automatically available when a program is executed. They include

INPUT, OUTPUT, CON, TRM, KBD, LST, AUX, USR

Two of these, INPUT and OUTPUT, are defaults assumed if a file variable is not listed in READ or READLN, and WRITE or WRITELN procedures respectively. Any additional files used by the program must be declared in the usual way. Standard files need not be linked, opened, or closed.

Untyped Files

Turbo Pascal distinguishes between typed files and untyped files. Typed files are those of Standard Pascal, and untyped files are specific to Turbo Pascal. A Standard Pascal file is defined by:

FILEVAR : **FILE OF** type;

Whereas an untyped file is declared with a type specification:

VAR filevar1, filevar2, . . ., filevarx: **FILE**;

Turbo Pascal untyped files can be used to transfer large blocks of data between two untyped files or to load or save large data buffers (like the video buffer) very quickly from disk because no intermediate disk buffer is used.

Such files are accessed in 128-byte blocks, and data is transferred directly between the disk and the selected variable without the use of internal buffers. All input/output using an untyped file must be performed with the two special functions BLOCKREAD and BLOCKWRITE. The files are linked, opened, and closed with the usual procedures (e.g., ASSIGN, RESET or REWRITE, and CLOSE).

The functions EOF, FILEPOS, FILESIZE, and the procedure SEEK can also be used with BLOCKREAD and BLOCKWRITE.

BLOCKREAD and BLOCKWRITE   BLOCKREAD and BLOCKWRITE are used to transfer blocks between untyped files and large data structures. They have the following syntax:

BLOCKREAD(filevar,var,recs[,result]);
BLOCKWRITE(filevar,var,recs[,result]);

The variable "var" is generally a buffer. A single block is transferred by using 1 as the specification for 'recs' in the parameter list.

After the transfer, BLOCKREAD and BLOCKWRITE return the number of blocks actually transferred. Returning a 0 indicates EOF or an error. The parameters used are the following:

filevar	Must be declared an untyped file
var	Any variable; the transfer will begin at the first byte of variable
recs	The number of blocks of data to be transferred; one block has 128 bytes
result	Returns the actual number of blocks transferred as an integer value (optional) (Turbo 3.0)

Random Access Files

In Standard Pascal, all access to a file is sequential. In Turbo Pascal, specific records can be randomly accessed within a data file using the SEEK procedure. The syntax is

    SEEK(filevar,record-number);

The first record number in a file is record 0. SEEK can be used to access any record. Then READ(filevar,data) can be used to get the record and advance the record pointer. In case the record must be written, WRITE(filevar,data) can be used. For example, record 3 of file SAMPLE stored as 'DEMO.DAT' is accessed by:

```
VAR
        SAMPLE : FILE OF DATATYPE;
        DATA0,
        DATA1 : DATATYPE;
BEGIN
        ASSIGN(SAMPLE,'DEMO.DAT');
        RESET(SAMPLE);
        . . .
        SEEK(SAMPLE,3); {SET CURRENT RECORD POINTER}
        READ(SAMPLE, DATA0);
        . . .
        SEEK(SAMPLE,3); {MOVE BACK RECORD POINTER}
        WRITE(SAMPLE, DATA1);
        . . .
    END;
```

When expanding a random file, the (lastrec + 1) component of any file can be located with the following method:

    SEEK(filevar, FILESIZE(filevar));

because the first record of a file is 0, and FILESIZE returns the number of records in a file (or lastrec + 1).

To recap, the SEEK procedure moves the file pointer to the specified position. The first position in a file is 0. The pointer can be moved to the last record + 1 position so the file can be expanded. This procedure operates only on data files (not TEXT files).

TURBO PASCAL I/O FUNCTIONS AND PROCEDURES

Turbo Pascal includes a number of standard functions and procedures for manipulating TEXT and data files.

ASSIGN(filevar,filename)

The ASSIGN procedure links a FILE type variable to the external file name or logical device specified by the string *file name*.

RESET(filevar)

The RESET procedure opens the file *filename* linked to *filevar* for processing. If the file is a TEXT file, only input (READ) access is allowed.

REWRITE(filevar)

The REWRITE procedure opens a new file (or overwrites an existing file) called *filename* linked to *filevar* for processing. If the file is a TEXT file, only output (WRITE) access is allowed.

CLOSE(filevar)

All open disk files must be closed with the CLOSE(filevar) procedure before the program terminates or any data remaining in the internal file buffers will be lost and the directory entry(s) for the file(s) will not be written properly to the disk. After a CLOSE(filevar) operation, *filevar* is undefined.

In MS/PC-DOS Turbo Pascal, if a file is not properly closed (as when the program is interrupted), all or part of the data will be in a group of "lost clusters" on the disk. This disk space (and the data) can be reclaimed with the DOS CHKDSK program using the /F option.

FILESIZE(filevar)

The FILESIZE function returns the number of components or records currently in the file specified by *filevar*. If FILESIZE(filevar) = 0, the file is currently empty.

FILEPOS(filevar)

The FILEPOS function returns the current position of the record pointer in the file specified by *filevar*. The first component is 0.

EOF(filevar)

When typing text at the console, EOF remains FALSE. You can set EOF to TRUE by typing the EOF character (Ctrl-Z) at the keyboard.

EOF(filevar) is also TRUE if the file is closed. EOF(filevar) is FALSE after a RESET(filevar). If EOF ever becomes TRUE during a file read such as READ(filevar,. . .) it means that the data is undefined (the end of the file has been passed). Note that this can only occur if error checking is disabled with {$I-}. If no *filevar* is specified, the standard file INPUT is assumed.

EOLN(filevar)

The EOLN function is defined only for a TEXT file. The end of line character is a carriage return. EOLN is TRUE on logical devices or standard files if the *current* character is a carriage return or Ctrl-Z. EOLN is TRUE on disk files if the *next* character is a carriage return or Ctrl-Z. Note that whenever EOF(filevar) is TRUE for a TEXT file, EOLN(filevar) is also TRUE. If no *filevar* is specified, the standard file INPUT is assumed.

IORESULT

This function returns the result of an I/O operation as an integer. The result is 0 if there is no error, and has a value between 1 and 255 if an error has occurred. The error numbers are listed below:

0	No error
1	File does not exist
2	File not open for input
3	File not open for output
4	File not open
16	Error in numeric format (text files to numeric variables)
32	Operation not allowed on a logical device
33	Not allowed in direct mode
34	Assign to standard files not allowed
144	Record length mismatch
145	Seek beyond end-of-file
153	Unexpected end-of-file
240	Disk write error
241	Directory is full
242	File size overflow
243	Too many open files (MS/PC-DOS)
255	File disappeared

TURBO PASCAL INPUT/OUTPUT SUMMARY

Turbo Pascal differs considerably from Standard Pascal in the way it handles file I/O. This section summarizes the major differences.

The following Standard Pascal procedures are not provided in Turbo Pascal:

GET, PUT

and the following functions or procedures differ slightly between Turbo Pascal and Standard Pascal:

EOF, EOLN*, READ, WRITE, READLN*, WRITELN*, RESET, REWRITE

(* For use with TEXT files only.)

The following additional functions or procedures are provided in all versions of Turbo Pascal:

BLOCKREAD, BLOCKWRITE, ASSIGN, CLOSE, IORESULT, SEEK,
FLUSH, ERASE, RENAME, FILEPOS, FILESIZE

A few additional functions or procedures are provided only in Turbo Pascal version 3.0 and later:

SEEKEOF, SEEKEOLN*, APPEND*   (* For use with TEXT files only.)

and some functions or procedures are provided only in MS/PC-DOS versions of Turbo Pascal (3.0 and later):

LONGFILESIZE, LONGFILEPOSITION, LONGSEEK
CHDIR, MKDIR, RMDIR, GETDIR

These additional functions or procedures facilitate writing system level programs or control programs.

Turbo Pascal also provides a number of standard *predeclared* files and logical devices that allow direct access to a number of microcomputer system I/O features such as the keyboard and system printer.

SUMMARY

The files are the only data structure that may vary in size. In Standard Pascal, all access to files is sequential. Special operators are provided to read and write files one element at a time, as well as to position the window over the proper file element.

A special predefined type, the TEXT file, is supplied by Pascal along with special operators, to facilitate text processing.

EXERCISES_____

11-1: Write a program that prints the number of times each letter of the alphabet occurs in a given text file.

11-2: Write a program that reads a file and prints it in double or triple space, depending upon the user specifications.

11-3: Write another program like that in Exercise 11-2 but number all of the lines on the output.

11-4: Write a procedure to skip blanks in a line of text being read.

11-5: Sort a file of integers in ascending order. Can this be done with one file? Is it faster to use two?

11-6: Write a text editor program with commands to delete, append, insert, display and change lines in a text file.

11-7: Read a file of records containing the following fields: name, customer number, amount, a field containing a 0 or a 1 (1 if the amount is a credit, 0 if the amount is a debit), address, city, state, and Zip Code. Divide the file into two files, one file of names of people with credit, the other file of names of people with debits. Write only the name and complete address on the output files, not any other information.

CHAPTER 12

SETS

SETS IN PASCAL

A set in Pascal is a collection of objects of the same type. The maximum number of elements in the set is defined by the specific implementation. This number is generally small, and may be on the order of 64 to 256. The type of the objects belonging to the set is called the "base type" of the set. They may be of any scalar type, but not of a structured type. The formal definition of a set is shown in Figure 12.1.

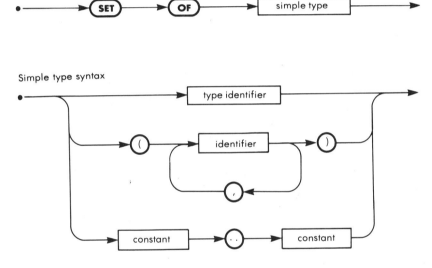

Figure 12.1:   Formal Syntax of the Set Type

For example, let us look at a set declaration:

TYPE CARS = (DODGE, FORD, GM, VOLVO, VW, JEEP, HONDA, TOYOTA, PEUGOT, MERCEDES, RENAULT);

FLEET = **SET OF** CARS;

CARS is an enumeration, and FLEET is a set type. Variables of type FLEET are declared as:

VAR   AVIS, HERTZ, NATIONAL, FUTURECO : FLEET;

The *base type* of FLEET (a set) is CARS. We could write the following assignments in the program:

        AVIS := [FORD, GM];
        HERTZ := [FORD, DODGE];
        NATIONAL := [GM];
        FUTURECO := [ ];

Variables of the type FLEET are sets with 0 to 11 members which were listed in the declaration for the type CARS. If a set has no value, it is called an empty set and is denoted by [ ].

Sets are given values by specifying set constants as a list of constants enclosed in square brackets. (See the previous examples of AVIS, HERTZ, NATIONAL and FUTURECO.) The usual "<i>..</i>" abbreviation may be used for an ordered enumeration, and may, for example, be written:

        RENTACAR := [DODGE .. JEEP];

This is equivalent to:

        RENTACAR := [DODGE, FORD, GM, VOLVO, VW, JEEP];

In general, if a base type has n values (n is called the *cardinality* of the base type), then the cardinality of the corresponding set type is 2^n (the number of different combinations of values).

CONSTRUCTING A SET

Sets may be constructed by enumerating their elements. For example:

        [1, 2, 8, 10]
        ['T', 'M', 'I', 'S']
        [ALPHA, BETA+2, DELTA]
        [1..10]
        ['A' .. 'L']
        ['A' .. 'L', '+', '−', '0' .. '9']

Note that an expression may be used to specify an element. The enumeration symbol "<i>..</i>" may also be used.

The syntax for set construction is shown in Figure 12.2.

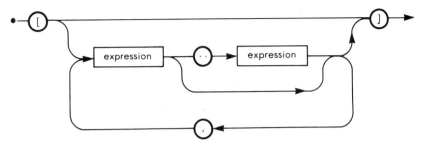

Figure 12.2:   Set Elements

OPERATIONS ON SETS

The three main operations on sets are the union, intersection, and difference (or complement). All three of these operations are provided in Pascal.

The *union* of two sets is a set that contains the elements of both sets. This operation is denoted by a "+". For example:

['A', 'B'] + ['C', 'D', 'E']

results in:

['A' .. 'E']

Symbolically, the union of two sets, S1 and S2, is shown in Figure 12.3.

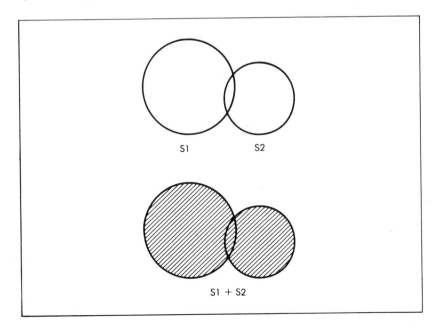

Figure 12.3:   Union of Two Sets (S1∪S2)

The *intersection* of two sets is the set that contains elements common to both sets. The intersection operator is "*". For example:

['A', 'B', 'D', 'F'] * ['B', 'G', 'K']

results in:

['B']

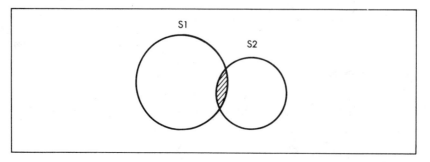

Figure 12.4:   Intersection of Two Sets (S1 ∩ S2)

The intersection of two sets is illustrated in Figure 12.4.

The *difference* of two sets, or the *complement,* is the set of elements of the first set which are not included in the second set. The corresponding operator is" – ". For example:

['A', 'B', 'D', 'F'] – ['B', 'G', 'K']

results in:

['A', 'D', 'F']

The difference of two sets is illustrated in Figure 12.5.

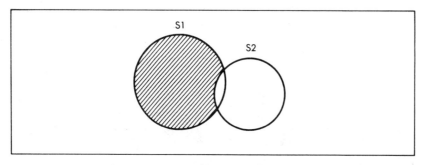

Figure 12.5: Difference of Two Sets (S1—S2)

Relational Operators

The assignment instruction may be used on sets as well as four of the relational operators: = , < >, <=, >=, and a special operator, 'IN'.

The relational operators have the following meanings:

=	Set equality
< >	Set inequality
<=	Inclusion (contained in)
>=	Inclusion (contains)

To be more specific, the set A is contained in the set B if all of the elements of A are in B. For example:

[FORD .. VOLVO] <= [DODGE .. JEEP]   is TRUE

An example of inequality is:

AVIS < > HERTZ   which is TRUE

Set Membership

A special operator, represented by IN, provides the *set membership* function. This function tests if a value is a member of a set. IN is preceded by an expression which must yield a value, and is followed by an expression of the set type. The syntax is:

expression IN set

This operator results in a TRUE or FALSE value. For example, if we must determine whether a character is a digit between 0 and 9, we can write:

CH **IN** ['0'..'9']

The membership function can be used to advantage when testing characters or values against permissible sets.

Here is an example where GRADE must be between 5 and 10:

GRADE **IN** [5..10]

Sets are often combined with the CASE statement. For example:

```
IF LETTER IN ['.', ',', '?', ':', ';']
    THEN
        CASE  LETTER OF
            '.', ',' : WRITELN('DOT OR COMMA');
            '?'     : WRITELN('QUESTIONMARK');
            ':', ';' : WRITELN('COLON OR SEMICOLON')
        END  {CASE}
    ELSE   WRITELN ('NO SPECIAL SYMBOL');
```

CASE STUDY: IDENTIFYING CHARACTERS

The Problem

A common problem when processing text is that of identifying characters or strings as belonging to a specific category. In this program, the characters typed at the keyboard will be classified in one of five categories:

— Upper case letters
— Lower case letters
— Digits from 0 to 9
— Punctuation marks
— Special symbols

A typical input is shown in Figure 12.6.

```
ENTER LINES TO BE EVALUATED:
TO SEE is to BELIEVE.
This one weighs 11.27 lbs!
Testing, testing 1 2 3 ...
```

Figure 12.6:   Input to CATEGORIZECHARS

A typical output is shown in Figure 12.7.

```
FOUND:
    14 UPPERCASE CHARACTERS
    32 LOWERCASE CHARACTERS
     7 NUMERIC CHARACTERS
     7 PUNCTUATION CHARACTERS
     0 SPECIAL CHARACTERS
    13 UNDEFINED CHARACTERS
    ──
    73 TOTAL
```

Figure 12.7:   Output Generated by CATEGORIZECHARS

```
PROGRAM CATEGORIZECHARS(INPUT,OUTPUT);
(* READS LINES AND FINDS CHARACTERS OF THE FOLLOWING CATEGORIES: *)
VAR UPPERALPHA: SET OF CHAR;
      LOWERALPHA: SET OF CHAR;
      NUMERIC: SET OF CHAR;
      PUNCTUATION: SET OF CHAR;
      SPECIAL: SET OF CHAR;
      U,L,N,P,S,UNDEFINED: INTEGER;
      CHR: CHAR;
BEGIN (* CATEGORIZE CHARS *)
      UPPERALPHA := ['A'..'Z'];
      LOWERALPHA := ['a'..'z'];
      NUMERIC := ['0'..'9'];
      PUNCTUATION := ['.',',',':',';','-','!',' " ',';','(',')',' — ','''','?'];
      SPECIAL := ['#','$','%','&','~','=','[',']','+','*','>','<','/', '↑','@'];
      U := 0;
      L := 0;
      N := 0;
      P := 0;
      S := 0;
      UNDEFINED := 0;
      WRITELN('ENTER LINES TO BE EVALUATED:');
      WHILE NOT EOF DO                        {I/O MODULE STARTS}
          BEGIN
              WHILE NOT EOLN DO BEGIN
                  READ(CHR);
                  IF NOT(CHR IN UPPERALPHA + LOWERALPHA + NUMERIC +
                          PUNCTUATION + SPECIAL)
                  THEN UNDEFINED := SUCC(UNDEFINED)
                  ELSE IF CHR IN UPPERALPHA THEN U := SUCC(U)
                      ELSE IF CHR IN LOWERALPHA THEN L := SUCC(L)
                          ELSE IF CHR IN NUMERIC THEN N := SUCC(N)
                              ELSE IF CHR IN PUNCTUATION
                                  THEN P := SUCC(P)
                                  ELSE S := SUCC(S)
```

Figure 12.8: CATEGORIZECHARS Program

```
                END;
                READLN
          END;                                    {I/O MODULE ENDS}
       WRITELN;
       WRITELN('FOUND :');
       WRITELN(U:5,  '  UPPERCASE CHARACTERS');
       WRITELN(L:5,  '  LOWERCASE CHARACTERS');
       WRITELN(N:5,  '  NUMERIC CHARACTERS');
       WRITELN(P:5,  '  PUNCTUATION CHARACTERS');
       WRITELN(S:5,  '  SPECIAL CHARACTERS');
       WRITELN(UNDEFINED:5,  '  UNDEFINED CHARACTERS');
       WRITELN('------');
       WRITELN(U + L + N + P + S + UNDEFINED:5,'TOTAL.')
   END. (* CATEGORIZECHARS *)
```

Figure 12.8:   CATEGORIZECHARS Program (cont.)

The Program

Looking at the program presented in Figure 12.8 we see that each of the five categories of characters is declared as a set, and the proper values are assigned to each set.

```
PROGRAM CATEGORIZECHARS(INPUT,OUTPUT);
(* READS LINES AND FINDS CHARACTERS OF THE FOLLOWING CATEGORIES: *)
VAR UPPERALPHA:.SET OF CHAR;
        LOWERALPHA: SET OF CHAR;
        NUMERIC: SET OF CHAR;
        PUNCTUATION: SET OF CHAR;
        SPECIAL: SET OF CHAR;
        U,L,N,P,S,UNDEFINED: INTEGER;
        CHR: CHAR;
BEGIN (* CATEGORIZE CHARS *)
        UPPERALPHA := ['A'..'Z'];
        LOWERALPHA := ['a'..'z'];
        NUMERIC := ['0'..'9'];
        PUNCTUATION := ['.',',',':',';','-','!',' " ',',','(',')','_','''','?'];
        SPECIAL := ['#','$','%','&','~','=','[',']','+','*',' ','<','/',' ↑ ','@'];
```

Five counter variables named U, L, N, P, S are used to count the number of characters found in the text that belong to each of the five groups. These counter variables are initialized to 0:

U := 0;
L := 0;
N := 0;
P := 0;
S := 0;

A variable called UNDEFINED is used to count the number of characters that do not belong to any of the five groups. This variable is also initialized to 0:

UNDEFINED := 0;

A prompt is generated:

WRITELN('ENTER LINES TO BE EVALUATED:');

and a WHILE loop is executed to capture the text being typed in:

WHILE NOT EOF **DO**

The text is read line by line, as explained in the previous chapter:

BEGIN
    WHILE NOT EOLN **DO BEGIN**
        (statements)
    END;

Within the WHILE loop, each character is read in turn, and tested:

READ(CHR);

If the character does not belong to the union of the five sets, it is undefined:

IF NOT   (CHR **IN** UPPERALPHA + LOWERALPHA + NUMERIC +
              PUNCTUATION + SPECIAL)
THEN UNDEFINED := SUCC(UNDEFINED)

If the character belongs to one of the five sets, the corresponding counter is incremented:

```
    ELSE IF CHR IN UPPERALPHA THEN U := SUCC(U)
      ELSE IF CHR IN LOWERALPHA THEN L := SUCC(L)
        ELSE IF CHR IN NUMERIC THEN N := SUCC(N)
          ELSE IF CHR IN PUNCTUATION
            THEN P := SUCC(P)
            ELSE S := SUCC(S)
          END;
```

Once the WHILE NOT EOLN has been satisfied, the next line is read, until an EOF is found:

```
        READLN
    END;
```

The values of the occurrence counters are then printed out:

```
        WRITELN;
        WRITELN('FOUND :');
        WRITELN(U:5,' UPPERCASE CHARACTERS');
        WRITELN(L:5,' LOWERCASE CHARACTERS');
        WRITELN(N:5,' NUMERIC CHARACTERS');
        WRITELN(P:5,' PUNCTUATION CHARACTERS');
        WRITELN(S:5,' SPECIAL CHARACTERS');
        WRITELN(UNDEFINED:5,' UNDEFINED CHARACTERS');
        WRITELN('------');
        WRITELN(U+L+N+P+S+UNDEFINED:5,' TOTAL.')
    END. (* CATEGORIZECHARS *)
```

TURBO PASCAL SETS

Sets can have (at most) 256 elements and ordinal values of the base type must be in the range 0 . . 255. Set comparisons and assignment operations on two sets are valid, provided that the type of both sets is identical (same base type) or both sets are subranges of the same base type.

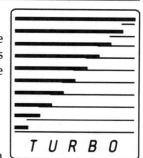

TURBO PASCAL CATAGORIZE EXAMPLE

Because EOLN and EOF of console input are handled differently in Turbo Pascal than they are in Standard Pascal, the code in Figure 12.8

must be changed to run the example program with Turbo Pascal. Define variable CH instead of CHR (because Turbo Pascal uses CHR as a built-in function) and replace the code in Figure 12.8 between the comments {I/O Module Starts} and {I/O Module Ends} with the following code:

```
CH : = CHR(0); { SET CH TO NULL }    {I/O MODULE STARTS }
WHILE NOT (CH  =  CHR(26)) DO
    {TEST FOR CTRL-Z (EOF) }
BEGIN
    READ(KBD,CH);
    WHILE NOT (CH  =  CHR(13)) AND NOT (CH  =  CHR(26)) DO
{TEST FOR CR (EOLN)}
    BEGIN
        WRITE (CH);
        IF NOT (CH IN UPPERALPHA + LOWERALPHA +
                NUMERIC + PUNCTUATION + SPECIAL) THEN
                UNDEFINED : = SUCC(UNDEFINED)
            ELSE IF CH IN UPPERALPHA THEN U : = SUCC(U)
            ELSE IF CH IN LOWERALPHA THEN L : = SUCC(L)
            ELSE IF CH IN NUMERIC THEN N : = SUCC(N)
            ELSE IF CH IN PUNCTUATION THEN P : = SUCC(P)
            ELSE S : = SUCC(S);
        READ(KBD,CH);
    END;
    WRITELN
END;                                        {I/O MODULE ENDS}
```

Enter CTRL-Z to terminate input.

SUMMARY

The set is a convenient data structure provided by Pascal when a variable can only take a small number of values. Note, however, that Pascal sets are not as general as the definition of sets in mathematics. Many implementations impose specific restrictions on the way in which sets may be used or operated on. The set type is, therefore, one of the available alternatives that should be considered when devising an appropriate data structure. Often, other data structures such as files or records can be used to advantage instead of a set. It is important to be familiar with all of the data structures available.

EXERCISES

12-1: *Specify all of the items in your refrigerator as a set. Specify the ingredients required to make five dishes as sets. Determine whether or not each dish can be prepared by checking whether you have the required ingredients.*

12-2: *Write a program to read text and count all the words in that text that contain both the vowels A and E.*

12-3: *Write a program to read a list of names followed by three numbers indicating sex, age and hair color. List all persons of a given sex and hair color within a given age bracket.*

12-4: *Convert the above program into a program for a computerized dating service.*

12-5: *Use sets to determine whether or not a given animal is a member of the set of herbivores, carnivores, or omnivores.*

CHAPTER 13

POINTERS
AND LISTS

INTRODUCTION

This chapter describes another complex data structure that can be easily implemented in Pascal, the list. Strictly speaking, Pascal defines not a list structure, but a pointer type, which may be used to construct list structures. Most programmers will not use lists in simple programs. However, lists are the most flexible data structure available when developing complex programs. Lists are used in many sophisticated programs, including "systems software," such as interpreters, assemblers and compilers.

The basic concepts of lists will be introduced first, then the particular facilities provided in Pascal will be described. This chapter should be read by those readers who intend to make full use of Pascal resources.

DYNAMIC DATA STRUCTURES

All of the data structures that have been defined thus far (with the exception of the file) are static, i.e., they do not change in size as the program executes. In fact, the very purpose of the type definitions is to facilitate the allocation of space by the compiler in the memory of the computer by defining (ahead of time) the maximum amount of space that a structure or a variable is going to require.

When the ordering of elements as well as the number may fluctuate dynamically during program execution, more flexible data structures are required. A list provides this flexibility. An element may be removed or added anywhere in the list without altering the rest of the list. For example, if an extra element were added in the middle of an array, all of the components of the array would have to be moved up or down. Similarly, if one element of the array were removed, all of the remaining elements would have to be moved over the empty position. If one element were added to or removed from a file, the entire file would have to be copied.

Building and manipulating lists requires one fundamental facility, the *pointer*. Pointers and lists will now be defined.

LISTS

A *list* is a collection of elements of the same type, arranged in an arbitrary, yet definite order. For each element of a list, there is a predecessor and a successor element. The predecessor of the first element is the *empty* element. The successor of the last element is also empty. Lists are characterized by several essential properties:

— The way in which the elements are chained together, (i.e., the way in which the predecessor or the successor of a given element can be identified). *Pointers* are usually used for this purpose.

— How and where the elements may be inserted or removed in the list. Usually, this may be done anywhere in the list. However, some lists, such as a *stack,* permit access to only the last element.

— The number of successors or predecessors an element may have. For most lists, there is only one. However, a binary tree allows two *siblings* for each element: a left and a right sibling, in addition to one *parent.*

The file, the array, the set and the record are special lists where all elements are contiguous (stored next to each other). This space is allocated by the compiler prior to program execution, and cannot be expanded, except for a file.

At times, it is desirable to define a more general list structure in which elements may be added or removed freely during program execution. In this case, the size of the list is not known in advance, and a block of contiguous memory locations cannot be allocated by the compiler. Each list entry must reside at whatever location is available in the memory. The problem then becomes one of locating the successor or the predecessor of a given element. Pointers are used for this task.

POINTERS

Here is an example in which the elements of a list are: 'T', 'H', 'E'. They are stored at memory locations 1000, 2222, and 4123, as shown in Figure 13.1.

In order to find the successor of T when examining T, it is necessary to know the address of H. The solution is obvious: the address of H should be stored with T. The same case applies to E. This type of organization of elements in memory is illustrated in Figure 13.2.

Note in Figure 13.2 that the successor of E is 'NIL' as E is the last element in the list. We have created a simple list. The value "2222" associated with the T is the address of the next entry. It is called a *pointer.* The role of each pointer is illustrated symbolically in Figure 13.3.

Note that in Figure 13.3, one additional pointer is necessary to access the list: the FIRST ENTRY pointer. This pointer must be stored at a known memory location of type ↑LIST (read "pointer to the list").

A pointer may be thought of as a position designator, or, graphically, as an arrow pointing to an element of a list. The FIRST ENTRY pointer in Figure 13.3 points to the first element. By moving a pointer up or down

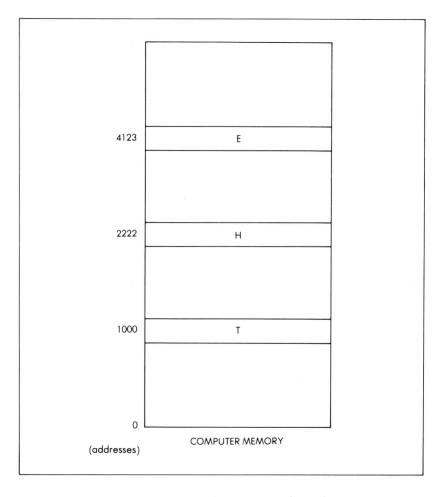

Figure 13.1: *Three Elements in Memory*

a list, it becomes possible to access any element. In our example, elements of the list are singly-linked together, i.e., they contain a single pointer to the next element. As a result, a pointer may only move up. Elements of a list may also contain two or more pointers so that they may point up, down, left or right. A number of list structures may be constructed with pointers. The most important list structures – simple lists, doubly linked lists, and trees – are presented in this chapter.

A pointer is represented in Pascal as:

TYPE NEXT = ↑ELEMENT;

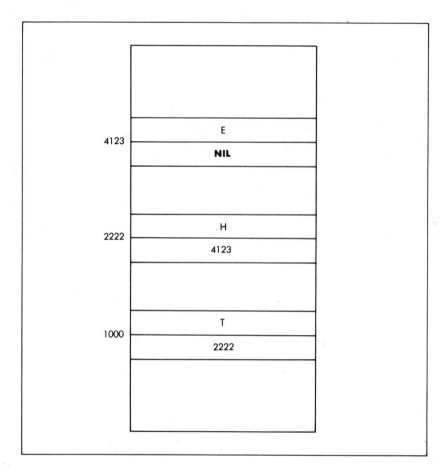

Figure 13.2:   Creating Links

This statement is read as "a variable of type NEXT is a pointer to an object of type ELEMENT." ELEMENT is called a dynamic data type.

The formal syntax of a pointer type is shown in Figure 13.4.

One may write:

VAR PTR : ↑ELEMENT

where PTR is a pointer and PTR↑ has a value of type ELEMENT. The notation PTR↑ refers to the actual value of the element towards which PTR is pointing. This will be clarified by examples in the next section.

Generally, a pointer that does not point to an element, i.e., which is

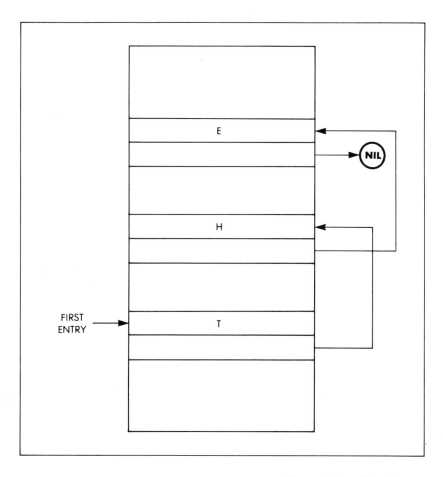

Figure 13.3: The Pointers

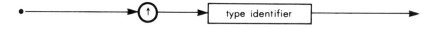

Figure 13.4: Formal Syntax of a Pointer Type

not associated with any element, is given the predefined value NIL:

    PTR := **NIL**;

The value NIL is usually used to indicate the value of a pointer at the end of a list or sublist.

Assignment

Pointers may be assigned. For example, one might write:

P1 : = P2;

where P1 and P2 are two pointers. Observe the situation shown in Figure 13.5.

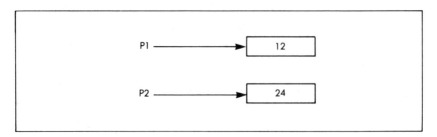

Figure 13.5:   Pointer Assignments

The result of the assignment is shown in Figure 13.6. It is important to remember that the element "12" is not destroyed. Rather, P1 no longer points to it. However another pointer may exist elsewhere (such as P4), which points to it. In this case, the value of 12 would still be accessible through P4.

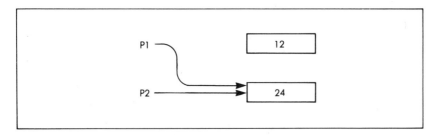

Figure 13.6:   Results of Pointer Assignment

If we had written:

P1↑ : = P2↑

the situation would be similar to the one shown in Figure 13.7.

In this case, the first element has taken the value '24'. If there were no other pointers pointing to these two elements, then the effect is apparently the same as obtained by P1 := P2. However, if there were

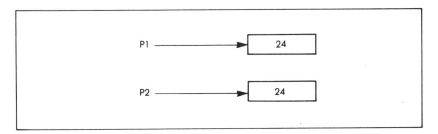

Figure 13.7:   A Similar Situation

other pointers pointing to the elements, it is important to remember that these two assignments are two different operations: P1 := P2 is different from P1↑ := P2↑. One operation refers to the pointers, the other refers to the values that are being pointed to.

CREATING A DYNAMIC VARIABLE

In this section, we will create an actual list structure. Elements will be added to it, and pointers will be created in order to link the elements.

To create a dynamic data structure, one or more pointers need to be associated with one or more values. The resulting object, therefore, contains at least one pointer and one value, which are generally of different types. As a result, the list element is best represented as a *record*.

Let us look at an example:

```
TYPE PTR = ↑OBJECT;
     OBJECT = RECORD
                NEXT : PTR;
                VALUE : VALTYPE
              END;
 VAR P,LLINK,RLINK,LISTBASE : PTR;
```

Note that, as an exception to the general rule, the type used in the definition of a pointer may be *defined after it is used*. Such is the case for OBJECT in the above example. This is called a *forward reference* and is the only instance in which this may occur in Pascal. (A FORWARD declaration must be used for functions or procedures.)

In order to create a structure, we may define a pointer called LISTBASE, which points to the first element of the list. Initially, this pointer will not be pointing to any element and we will write:

```
LISTBASE := NIL;
```

This is called *initializing* the list, which is originally empty. Next, we must create one or more elements that will be inserted into the list. A standard procedure called NEW performs this task in Pascal. The procedure NEW operates on a pointer argument, and "creates" a *dynamic variable* of the type to which the pointer points. This variable is known as a dynamic variable because it is created dynamically during execution, rather than statically, like other variables. For example:

NEW(P);

will create an OBJECT. The name (i.e., the address of this OBJECT) is stored in the pointer P. In fact, NEW(P) creates storage for the OBJECT P↑ within the memory. P is set to point to the new storage.

Once the dynamic variable has been created, both its value and the next pointer fields (as defined in the RECORD) must receive a value. This can be accomplished, for example, by writing:

NEW(P);
P↑.VALUE : = 24;
P↑.NEXT : = LISTBASE;
LISTBASE : = P;

P points to an OBJECT, i.e., a record. The record associated with P is P↑. Recall that the VALUE field of the record P↑ is designated as P↑. VALUE.

The two fields of P↑ are assigned a value:

P↑.VALUE : = 24 ;
P↑.NEXT : = LISTBASE;

Then the LISTBASE pointer is updated from the value NIL to the value of P:

LISTBASE : = P;

The corresponding sequence is shown in Figure 13.8.

Another form of NEW is available which will not be described in detail here, as it is beyond the scope of an introductory book. It is:

NEW(P,T1, ..., Tn)

where T1, ..., Tn are constants representing 'tag' field values. The constants Ti, where i = 1..n, are used to designate variants in a record. This other form of NEW is generally used for space optimization. It is prone

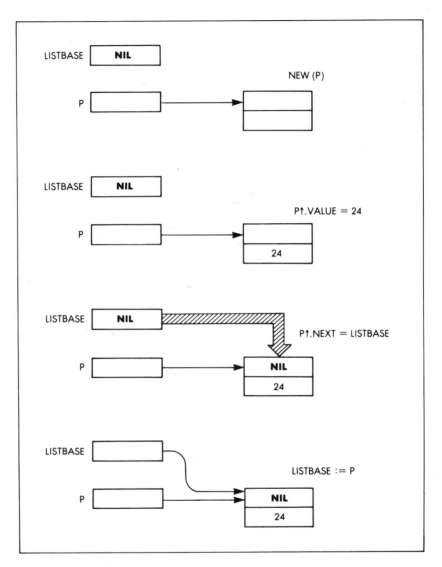

Figure 13.8: *Corresponding Sequence*

to errors, and may also be restricted in various ways by the specific implementation.

Note that when removing an element from a list, the pointers are simply changed, and the element remains untouched. If elements are large, or removed frequently, a considerable amount of storage space may be lost. One solution to this problem is to place all of the removed elements on a *free-list,* and then allocate new element storage from it. Another solution is to use the built-in function DISPOSE to erase a variable, and then reclaim the storage that it was using. The syntax of DISPOSE corresponds to the syntax of NEW:

>DISPOSE(PTR) releases the storage of PTR↑.
>
>DISPOSE(PTR,T1,T2, ...,Tn) should be used if the form
>>NEW(PTR,T1,T2, ...,Tn) had been used.

Unfortunately, the DISPOSE procedure is seldom implemented, so you will usually have to recover storage yourself. Other procedures may be provided by specific implementations.

ACCESSING AN ELEMENT OF A LIST

In order to access an element of a list, we will usually access the first component, then move down the chain of pointers until we have identified the element that we are looking for. The end of the list is detected by finding NIL as the value of a pointer.

For example, we could write:

```
P := LISTBASE;
WHILE P <> NIL DO
    BEGIN
    EXAMINE (P↑.VALUE);
    P := P↑.NEXT
    END;
```

In this example, P is used as a *running pointer*. It is first set to LISTBASE (i.e., to the first element). If no match is found, P is set to P↑.NEXT (i.e., to the pointer field of the element it is pointing to). P now points to the second element, and the loop is repeated until each element has been processed (which is informally denoted by the procedure EXAMINE in the program), and the end of the list is detected (i.e., a NIL is found).

The same program could be used to print all of the elements of the list by using the function WRITE instead of 'EXAMINE'.

ADDING AND REMOVING AN ELEMENT

An element may be added to a list by simply updating two pointers. Let us add a new element (pointed to by P) at the beginning of a list:

```
P↑.NEXT := LISTBASE;
LISTBASE := P;
```

This is illustrated in Figure 13.9.

The process of inserting an element in the middle of a list is slightly more complicated. First, the location in the list where the new element

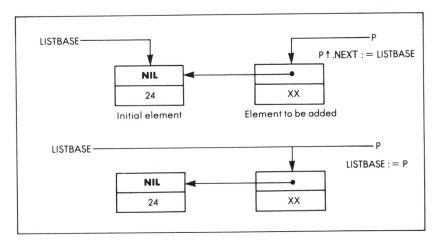

Figure 13.9:   Adding an Element at the Beginning of a List

is to be inserted must be found. This can be accomplished with a program segment that searches the list (like the one given above). Then, the pointer of the new element is set equal to its predecessor, and the pointer of its predecessor is given the value of the pointer to the new element:

P↑.NEXT : = RUNNINGPOINTER↑.NEXT;
RUNNINGPOINTER↑.NEXT : = P;

The process is shown in Figure 13.10:

Inserting an element requires that two pointers be updated (assuming that a simple list with single pointers or a *singly-linked list* is used). Similarly, an element may be removed from the middle of a list by merely modifying the pointers of the element preceding it. This is illustrated in Figure 13.11.

A typical property of the list structure is that no element is physically moved; one or two pointers are simply modified. List structures facilitate sorting: items can be sorted by merely inserting them into the proper place in a list.

OTHER LIST STRUCTURES

Thus far we have used a simple linked list as an example of a list structure. Pointers make it possible to build a larger variety of list structures, which may be used for the efficient representation of structured information. For example, a list that is only accessed through its first element

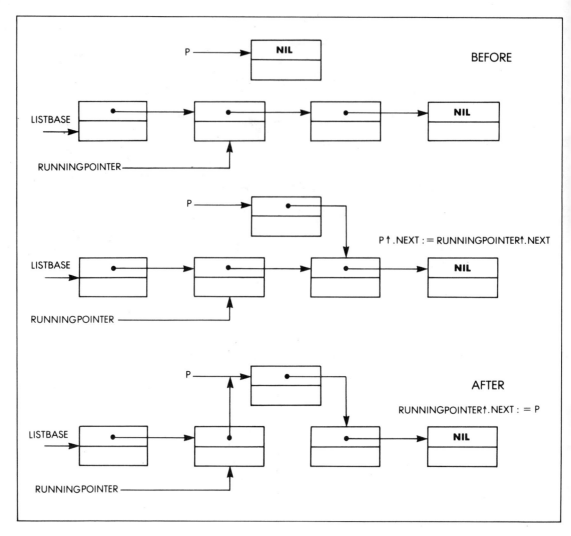

Figure 13.10:   Inserting an Element in the Middle of a List

every time (i.e., a list to which an element is added or removed in the first position), represents a "stack," and is called a "last in first out" (LIFO) list. A list to which elements are added at one end and are removed at the other is called an FIFO list ("first in, first out") or queue. Both of these structures may be implemented with a linked list (see Figure 13.12).

A doubly-linked list may be used whenever elements need to be quickly and efficiently retrieved to the left or right of the current position. An example of a doubly-linked list is shown in Figure 13.13.

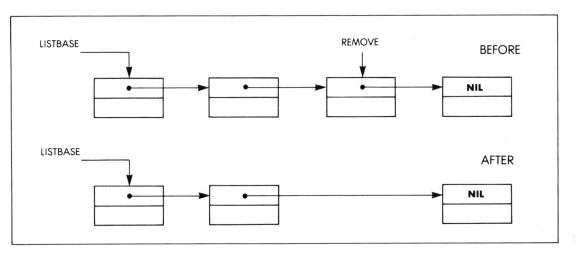

Figure 13.11:   Removing an Element from a List

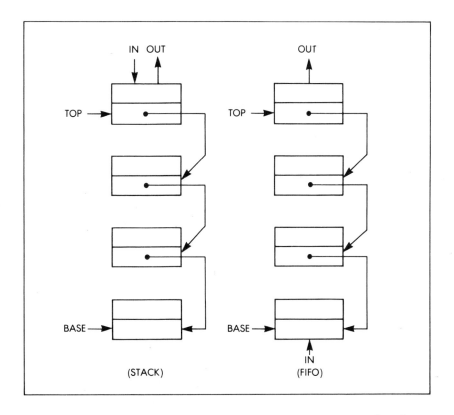

Figure 13.12:   A Stack and FIFO

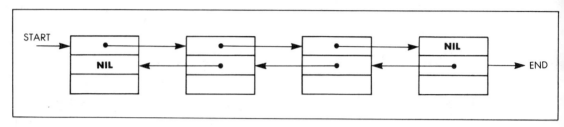

Figure 13.13:   A Double-Linked List Facilitates Two-Way Movement

Note that each element has two pointer fields or links. They are usually called the right link and the left link.

For fast access, a *circular list* may be used, in which the last element points back to the first one. A doubly-linked circular list is shown in Figure 13.14.

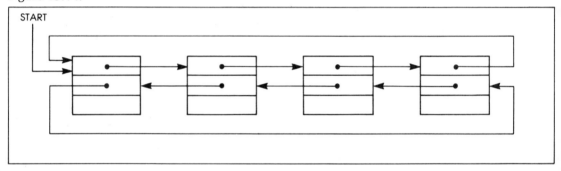

Figure 13.14:   A Circular List Facilitates Access

Binary or other structures may also be built. A binary tree is shown in Figure 13.15.

Note that the items in the tree presented in Figure 13.15 are sorted. The left sibling is always of lower value than the parent, while the right sibling is always of greater value.

Another example of a tree is a genealogical tree. This is not a binary tree but a general tree in which each element may have a large number of siblings.

For each type of data structure, various methods have been devised for accessing the elements, i.e., *traversing* the structure. Entire books are dedicated to this topic; therefore, it will not be addressed here.

CASE STUDY 1: A LIBRARIAN

The Problem

A list of books must be read into a library file. Each record contains the book title, author name and call number. The file should be sorted

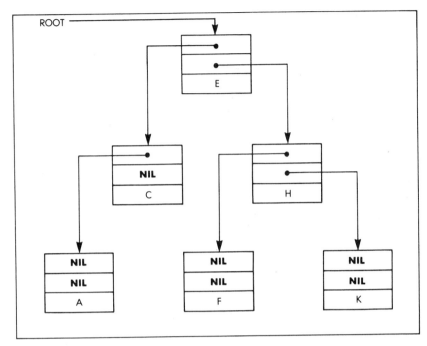

Figure 13.15:   A Binary Tree

by call number, and books may be added or deleted from the file.

This problem is similar to the one encountered in managing most business files, from mailing lists to personnel records. A typical input list to the LIBRARIAN program is shown in Figure 13.16.

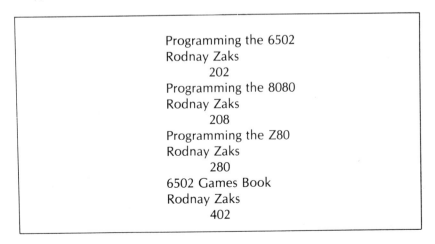

Programming the 6502
Rodnay Zaks
202
Programming the 8080
Rodnay Zaks
208
Programming the Z80
Rodnay Zaks
280
6502 Games Book
Rodnay Zaks
402

Figure 13.16:   LIBRARIAN Input

A typical interactive dialogue is shown in Figure 13.17.

Would you like to INSERT or DELETE a book?
Type I or D: I

Type the name of the book:
6502 Applications

Type the name of the author:
Rodnay Zaks

Type the call number of the book:
302

Type I to insert, D to delete, or F to finish: D

Type the call number of the book: 202

Type I to insert, D to delete, or F to finish: D

Type the call number of the book: 100

No Such Book

Type I to insert, D to delete, or F to finish: F

Library file is now updated

Figure 13.17:   Conversing with the LIBRARIAN

The final library file is shown in Figure 13.18. Notice that book 202 has been deleted.

The Program

A file in Pascal cannot be directly updated. A copy of it must be made to another structure, which is then updated, and copied back to the file. To do this, the structure must possess the following characteristics:

— Easy insertion or deletion of any element
— Sequential ordering of the elements

A simple structure that meets these requirements is a linked list. We will use a linked list in this example. The corresponding program listing is shown in Figure 13.19.

```
                    Programming the 8080
                    Rodnay Zaks
                         208
                    Programming the Z80
                    Rodnay Zaks
                         280
                    6502 Applications
                    Rodnay Zaks
                         302
                    6502 Games Book
                    Rodnay Zaks
                         402
```

Figure 13.18:   Final Library File

In the program, each entry in the library list is defined as a four-field record of type LIBLIST:

TYPE CHARARR = **ARRAY** [1..20] **OF** CHAR;
LIBPTR = ↑LIBLIST;
LIBLIST =
RECORD
NEXT: LIBPTR;
NAME: CHARARR;
AUTHOR: CHARARR;
CALLNO: INTEGER
END; (* RECORD *)

The list structure is shown in Figure 13.20.

Note that the pointer to LIBLIST is defined before the element it will point to:

LIBPTR = ↑LIBLIST;

Six global variables are used:

VAR   FRONT,
BOOK: LIBPTR;
INCALLNO,
INDX: INTEGER;
SELECTION: CHAR;
LIBFILE: TEXT;

```
PROGRAM LIBLIST(INPUT, OUTPUT, LIBFILE);
TYPE CHARARR= ARRAY [1..20] OF CHAR;
      LIBPTR= ↑LIBLIST;
      LIBLIST =
          RECORD
                      NEXT:    LIBPTR;
                      NAME:    CHARARR;
                    AUTHOR:    CHARARR;
                    CALLNO:    INTEGER
          END;  (* RECORD *)
VAR    FRONT,
        BOOK:  LIBPTR;
      INCALLNO,
         INDX:  INTEGER;
    SELECTION:  CHAR;
      LIBFILE:  TEXT;
PROCEDURE INSERT(BOOK: LIBPTR);
     VAR P,Q: LIBPTR;
       BEGIN (* INSERT *)
       IF FRONT = NIL THEN
          FRONT := BOOK
       ELSE
           IF FRONT↑.CALLNO > BOOK↑.CALLNO THEN
               BEGIN (* INSERT AT FRONT *)
                   BOOK↑.NEXT := FRONT;
                   FRONT := BOOK
               END      (* INSERT AT FRONT *)
           ELSE
               BEGIN    (* INSERT IN MIDDLE *)
                   P := FRONT;
                   Q := FRONT;
                   WHILE (P↑.NEXT < > NIL) AND (P = Q) DO
                       BEGIN (* TRAVERSE *)
                           P := P↑.NEXT;
                           IF P↑.CALLNO > BOOK↑.CALLNO THEN
                               BEGIN (* ATTACH *)
```

Figure 13.19: LIBRARIAN Program

```
                                        Q↑.NEXT := BOOK;
                                        BOOK↑.NEXT := P
                            END   (* ATTACH *)
                    ELSE
                            Q := P
                    END;  (* TRAVERSE *)
                IF (P↑.NEXT = NIL) AND (P↑.CALLNO < BOOK↑.CALLNO) THEN
                            (* ATTACH AT END *)
                            P↑.NEXT := BOOK
                END   (* INSERT IN MIDDLE *)
        END;  (* INSERT *)
PROCEDURE DELETE(CALLNO: INTEGER);
    VAR     P,Q: LIBPTR;
            DELETED: BOOLEAN;
    BEGIN (* DELETE *)
        DELETED := FALSE;
        IF FRONT = NIL THEN
            WRITELN('NOTHING TO DELETE.')
        ELSE
            IF FRONT↑.CALLNO = CALLNO THEN
                BEGIN (* DELETE FIRST ELEMENT *)
                    FRONT := FRONT↑.NEXT;
                    DELETED := TRUE
                END   (* DELETE FIRST ELEMENT *)
            ELSE
                BEGIN (* SEARCH LIST *)
                    P := FRONT;
                    Q := FRONT;
                    WHILE   (P↑.NEXT < > NIL) AND (P = Q) AND
                            (P↑.CALLNO < CALLNO) AND (DELETED = FALSE) DO
                        BEGIN (* TRAVERSE AND DELETE *)
                            P := P↑.NEXT;
                            IF P↑.CALLNO = CALLNO THEN
                                BEGIN (* DELETE BOOK *)
```

Figure 13.19: LIBRARIAN Program (cont.)

```
                                                    Q↑.NEXT := P↑.NEXT;
                                                    DELETED := TRUE
                                          END   (* DELETE BOOK *)
                                    ELSE
                                          Q := P
                              END;   (* TRAVERSE AND DELETE *)
                        IF DELETED = FALSE THEN
                              WRITELN (' NO SUCH BOOK ');
                              WRITELN
                        END  (* SEARCH LIST *)
              END;  (* DELETE *)
PROCEDURE READFILE;
        VAR INDX: INTEGER;
             BOOK: LIBPTR;
        BEGIN (* READFILE *)
              RESET(LIBFILE);
              WHILE NOT EOF(LIBFILE) DO
                    BEGIN (* READ BOOK *)
                          NEW(BOOK);
                          FOR INDX := 1 TO 20 DO
                                READ(LIBFILE, BOOK↑.NAME[INDX]);
                          READLN(LIBFILE);
                          FOR INDX := 1 TO 20 DO
                                READ(LIBFILE, BOOK↑.AUTHOR[INDX]);
                          READLN(LIBFILE);
                          READLN(LIBFILE, BOOK↑.CALLNO);
                          INSERT(BOOK)
                    END   (* READ BOOK *)
        END;  (* READFILE *)
PROCEDURE WRITEFILE;
        VAR    P:  LIBPTR;
               INDX:   INTEGER;
        BEGIN (* WRITEFILE *)
              REWRITE(LIBFILE);
              P := FRONT;
```

Figure 13.19: LIBRARIAN Program (cont.)

```
                    WHILE P < > NIL DO
                        BEGIN (* WRITE BOOK *)
                            FOR INDX := 1 TO 20 DO
                                WRITE(LIBFILE, P↑.NAME[INDX]);
                            WRITELN(LIBFILE);
                            FOR INDX := 1 TO 20 DO
                                WRITE(LIBFILE, P↑.AUTHOR[INDX]);
                            WRITELN(LIBFILE);
                            WRITELN(LIBFILE, P↑.CALLNO);
                            P := P↑.NEXT
                        END   (* WRITE BOOK *)
                END; (* WRITEFILE *)
        BEGIN  (* LIBLIST *)
            FRONT := NIL
            READFILE;
            WRITELN ('WOULD YOU LIKE TO INSERT OR DELETE A BOOK?');
            WRITE ('TYPE I OR D:  ');
            READLN(SELECTION);
            WRITELN;
            WHILE SELECTION < > 'F' DO
                BEGIN (* UPDATE LIST *)
                    IF SELECTION = 'I' THEN
                        BEGIN (* READ, INSERT BOOK *)
                            NEW(BOOK);
                            WRITELN('TYPE THE NAME OF THE BOOK:  ');
                            FOR INDX := 1 TO 20 DO
                                IF NOT EOLN THEN
                                    READ(BOOK↑.NAME[INDX])
                                ELSE
                                    BOOK↑.NAME[INDX] := '  ';
                            READLN;
                            WRITELN;
                            WRITELN('TYPE THE NAME OF THE AUTHOR: ');
                            FOR INDX := 1 TO 20 DO
                                IF NOT EOLN THEN
```

Figure 13.19: LIBRARIAN Program (cont.)

```
                                        READ(BOOK↑.AUTHOR[INDX])
                                ELSE
                                        BOOK↑.AUTHOR[INDX] := ' ';
                                READLN;
                                WRITELN;
                                WRITELN('TYPE THE CALL NUMBER OF THE BOOK: ');
                                READLN(BOOK↑.CALLNO);
                                WRITELN;
                                INSERT(BOOK)
                        END;  (* READ, INSERT BOOK *)
                IF SELECTION = 'D' THEN
                        BEGIN  (* GET NUMBER, DELETE BOOK *)
                                WRITE('TYPE THE CALL NUMBER OF THE BOOK: ');
                                READLN(INCALLNO);
                                WRITELN;
                                DELETE(INCALLNO)
                        END;  (* GET NUMBER, DELETE BOOK *)
                WRITE('TYPE I TO INSERT, D TO DELETE, OR F TO FINISH: ');
                READLN(SELECTION);
                WRITELN
            END;  (* UPDATE LIST *)
        WRITEFILE;
        WRITELN(' LIBRARY FILE IS NOW UPDATED ' );
        WRITELN; WRITELN
    END.  (* LIBLIST *)
```

Figure 13.19:   LIBRARIAN Program (cont.)

This program uses four procedures:

INSERT   to insert a new book in the list
DELETE   to remove a book from the list
READFILE   to read the library file and create the corresponding list structure
WRITEFILE   to copy the list structure to the library file.

Each of these procedures will now be examined in turn.

The INSERT procedure inserts a new book at its proper place in the

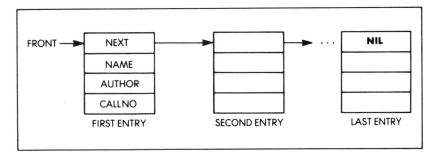

Figure 13.20:   Librarylist Structure

list. The proper place for the book is such that all call numbers in the list are sequential.

If the list is empty, the book is inserted at the beginning of the list:

PROCEDURE INSERT(BOOK: LIBPTR);
    VAR P,Q: LIBPTR;
    BEGIN
      IF FRONT = **NIL THEN** FRONT : = BOOK

If the call number of the book to be inserted is smaller than the call number of the first element of the list, the new book is inserted at the beginning of the list:

    ELSE
      IF FRONT↑.CALLNO > BOOK↑.CALLNO **THEN**
        BEGIN
          BOOK.NEXT : = FRONT;
          FRONT : = BOOK
        END

Otherwise, the list is scanned element by element until the correct position is found, i.e., the call number of each book is read and examined.

Two pointers Q and P are used to point to two consecutive elements. Q points to element n, and P points to element n + 1. Once the CALLNO of the book to be inserted is found to be less than the CALLNO of the element pointed to by P, the new book is inserted between the two elements pointed to by Q and P, as illustrated in Figure 13.21. The new pointers are shown by dashed lines.

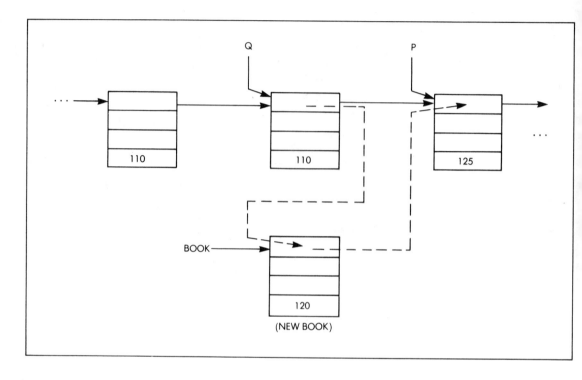

Figure 13.21: *Inserting a New Book in the List*

```
        ELSE
              BEGIN (* INSERT IN MIDDLE *)
                 P : = FRONT;
                 Q : = FRONT;
                 WHILE (P↑.NEXT < > NIL) AND (P = Q) DO
                    BEGIN (* TRAVERSE *)
                       P := P↑.NEXT;
                    IF P↑.CALLNO > BOOK↑..CALLNO THEN
```

The insertion is performed by simply updating two pointers, as shown in Figure 13.21:

```
                    BEGIN
                       Q↑.NEXT : = BOOK;
                       BOOK↑.NEXT : = P
                    END
```

If the proper place has not been found, the pointers are moved to the right:

```
                    ELSE Q := P
        END;
```

If the last element is found, and the new call number is still too large, then the new book is inserted at the end of the list.

```
        IF (P↑.NEXT = NIL) AND (P↑.CALLNO < BOOK↑.CALLNO) THEN
            (* ATTACH AT END *)
            P↑.NEXT := BOOK
        END (* INSERT IN MIDDLE *)
END; (* INSERT *)
```

The DELETE procedure performs the opposite function and operates in the same manner.

A check is made for an empty list:

```
PROCEDURE DELETE(CALLNO: INTEGER);
    VAR P,Q: LIBPTR;
        DELETED: BOOLEAN;
BEGIN
    DELETED := FALSE;
    IF FRONT = NIL THEN
        WRITELN('NOTHING TO DELETE.')
```

Then, a check is made to determine if the book to be removed is the first element:

```
ELSE
    IF FRONT↑.CALLNO = CALLNO THEN
        BEGIN
            FRONT := FRONT ↑.NEXT;
            DELETED := TRUE
        END
```

Otherwise, the list is scanned to the end:

```
ELSE
    BEGIN
        P := FRONT;
```

```
                        Q := FRONT;
               WHILE (P↑.NEXT < > NIL) AND (P = Q) AND
                     (P↑.CALLNO < CALLNO) AND (DELETED = FALSE) DO

                       BEGIN (* TRAVERSE AND DELETE *)
                         P := P↑.NEXT;
                         IF P↑.CALLNO = CALLNO THEN
                            BEGIN
                                 Q↑.NEXT := P↑.NEXT;
                                 DELETED := TRUE
                            END (* DELETE BOOK *)
                         ELSE
                            Q := P
                       END; (* TRAVERSE AND DELETE *)
```

If the end is found with no match, a failure is reported:

```
               IF DELETED = FALSE THEN
                       WRITELN (' NO SUCH BOOK ');
                       WRITELN
            END
         END;
```

The READFILE procedure copies LIBFILE into the appropriate list structure. READFILE reads the file field by field. Each time a new record is found, space must be allocated to the list element, and the NEW procedure is used:

```
       PROCEDURE READFILE;
            VAR INDX: INTEGER;
                BOOK: LIBPTR;
       BEGIN
            RESET(LIBFILE);
            WHILE NOT EOF(LIBFILE) DO
                BEGIN
                    NEW(BOOK);
```

Each line of the record is then read and stored within the new BOOK record:

```
FOR INDX := TO 20 DO
    READ(LIBFILE, BOOK↑.NAME[INDX]);
READLN(LIBFILE);
FOR INDX := 1 TO 20 DO
    READ(LIBFILE, BOOK↑.AUTHOR[INDX]);
READLN(LIBFILE);
READLN(LIBFILE, BOOK↑.CALLNO);
INSERT(BOOK)
        END
    END;
```

The reading proceeds until the end of the file is found.

The WRITEFILE procedure operates in reverse of the procedure READFILE. Each list element is written into LIBFILE one field at a time:

```
PROCEDURE WRITEFILE;
    VAR P: LIBPTR;
        INDX: INTEGER;
BEGIN
    REWRITE(LIBFILE);
    P := FRONT;
    WHILE P <> NIL DO
        BEGIN
            FOR INDX := 1 TO 20 DO
                WRITE(LIBFILE, P↑.NAME[INDX]);
            WRITELN(LIBFILE);
            FOR INDX := 1 TO 20 DO
                WRITE(LIBFILE, P↑.AUTHOR[INDX]);
            WRITELN(LIBFILE);
            WRITELN(LIBFILE, P↑.CALLNO);
            P := P↑.NEXT
        END
END;
```

The main program allows the user to insert or delete from the list. First, the program initializes the FRONT pointer:

```
FRONT := NIL;
```

and reads any existing LIBFILE to create the working list:

        READFILE;

The user is then given a choice of two commands:

        WRITELN ('WOULD YOU LIKE TO INSERT OR DELETE A BOOK?');
        WRITE ('TYPE T OR D: ');
        READLN(SELECTION);
        WRITELN;

An F typed by the user causes the program to copy the new list to a file
and exit:

        WHILE SELECTION < > 'F' **DO**

An 'I' specification results in a new entry being added to the list. First,
space is allocated for it:

            BEGIN
                IF SELECTION = 'I' **THEN**
                    BEGIN (* READ, INSERT BOOK *)
                    NEW(BOOK);

The user is then prompted, and each of the three information fields
are filled in:

The name of the book:

                        WRITELN('TYPE THE NAME OF THE BOOK: ');
                        FOR INDX := 1 **TO** 20 **DO**
                            IF NOT EOLN **THEN**
                                READ(BOOK↑.NAME[INDX])
                            ELSE
                                BOOK↑.NAME[INDX] := ' ';
                        READLN;
                        WRITELN;

Then the author's name:

                        WRITELN('TYPE THE NAME OF THE AUTHOR: ');
                        FOR INDX := 1 **TO** 20 **DO**

```
                              IF NOT EOLN THEN
                                      READ(BOOK↑.AUTHOR[INDX])
                              ELSE
                                      BOOK↑.AUTHOR[INDX] : = ' ';
                      READLN;
                      WRITELN;
```

Then the call number:

```
                      WRITELN('TYPE THE CALL NUMBER OF THE BOOK: ');
                      READLN(BOOK↑.CALLNO);
                      WRITELN;
```

The resulting element is then stored in the appropriate position within the list.

```
                      INSERT(BOOK)
              END;
```

In the case of a 'D', i.e., a delete, the process is simpler:

The call number is obtained:

```
      IF SELECTION = 'D' THEN
              BEGIN (* GET NUMBER, DELETE BOOK *)
                      WRITE('TYPE THE CALL NUMBER OF THE BOOK: ');
                      READLN(INCALLNO);
                      WRITELN;
```

And the corresponding book is deleted, using the DELETE procedure:

```
                      DELETE(INCALLNO)
              END;
```

The user is then prompted again, and the process is repeated:

```
                      WRITE('TYPE I TO INSERT, D TO DELETE, OR F TO FINISH: ');
                      READLN(SELECTION);
                      WRITELN
              END;
```

Once an 'F' is typed, the new list is saved in the file, and the program terminates:

```
WRITEFILE;
WRITELN(' LIBRARY FILE IS NOW UPDATED ');
WRITELN; WRITELN
END.
```

CASE STUDY 2: A BINARY TREE

The Problem

A binary tree must be constructed where each node contains an integer. The resulting tree node values must be printed in order, i.e., left subtree, root, right subtree. They will be in order of increasing values.

A typical input is shown in Figure 13.22.

```
              47
              94
              23
              87
              35
              71
              66
              98
              12
              16
               2
              46
              38
```

Figure 13.22:   Input to the Binary Tree

The corresponding tree is shown in Figure 13.23. The traversal of the tree results in the values shown in Figure 13.24. The tree is built in the following way (see Figure 13.23):

— The first element is entered ("47").

— The next element ("94") is compared to "47." Since it is larger, it becomes its *right* sibling.

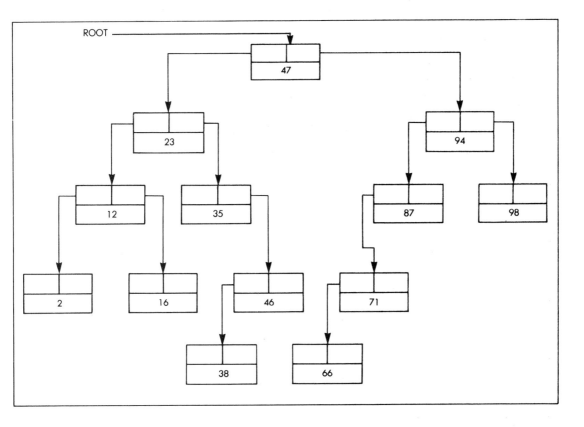

Figure 13.23: The Resulting Binary Tree

— The next element ("23") is compared and it is smaller than "47," thus it becomes its *left* sibling.

— "87" is larger than "47," thus it is compared to the right sibling of "47," i.e., "94." Since "87" is smaller than "94," it becomes its left sibling.

— And so on.

Each new element is compared to the root of the tree. The left branch (down the tree) is examined if the new element is smaller, and the right branch is examined if it is larger. This procedure is repeated, going down the tree, until a NIL pointer is found. Then the new element is inserted and the NIL pointer is altered to point to it.

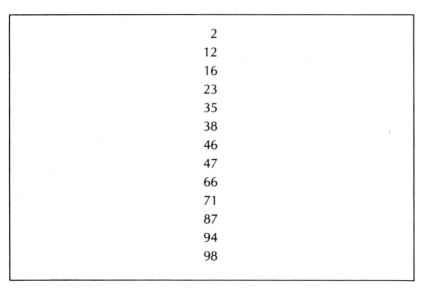

Figure 13.24: Output of Tree Traversal

The traversal of the tree is also quite simple. The left subtree is examined first.

— Starting at the root node of the tree, the leftmost node is found. It is "2." 2
— Then the root of "2" is visited. It is "12." 12
— Then the right subtree of this root is visited. It is "16." 16
— At this point, the subtree 2-12-16 has been visited. The corresponding root node is visited. It is "23." 23
— Then the right subtree of 23 is visited. The leftmost node of that subtree is visited first. "35" does not have any left node. 35
— Then "46" is visited. It has a left node: "38." 38
— Etc.

Binary trees are used for many purposes. They are used in particular when encoding decision algorithms, or analyzing the structure of text or data.

The Program

The program uses a tree structure constructed with pointers. Each node is a three-fold record that includes a value and two pointers, as shown in Figure 13.23. The complete program listing is shown in Figure 13.25.

```
PROGRAM BINARYTREE(INPUT,OUTPUT,INTFILE);
TYPE   TREEPTR = ↑TREE;
       TREE    =
          RECORD
                   DATA:   INTEGER;
                   RIGHT:  TREEPTR;
                    LEFT:  TREEPTR

          END;  (* RECORD *)
       STACKPTR = ↑STACKELEMNT;
       STACKELEMNT=
          RECORD
                 TREELINK: TREEPTR;
                 STACKLINK: STACKPTR
          END; (* RECORD *)
VAR INTFILE:   TEXT;
    ROOT,
    P,
    NODE:   TREEPTR;
    TOP:    STACKPTR;
PROCEDURE INNODE;
(* READS ONE INTEGER FROM INTFILE AND CREATES A NEW NODE, INTIALIZING *)
(* ALL ELEMENTS *)
    BEGIN (* INNODE *)
        NEW(NODE);
        NODE↑.RIGHT := NIL;
        NODE↑.LEFT  := NIL;
        IF EOF(INTFILE) THEN
            NODE↑.DATA := 0
        ELSE
            READLN(INTFILE, NODE↑.DATA)
    END; (* INNODE *)
```

Figure 13.25: BINARY TREE Program

```
PROCEDURE BUILDTREE(PARENT: TREEPTR);
    VAR P,Q: TREEPTR;
    BEGIN (* BUILDTREE *)
        P := PARENT;
        Q := PARENT;
        IF NODE↑.DATA < Q↑.DATA THEN
            BEGIN (* SEARCH LEFT *)
                P := Q↑.LEFT;
                IF P = NIL THEN  (* ATTACH TO EMPTY LEFT *)
                    Q↑.LEFT := NODE
                ELSE
                    BUILDTREE(P)
            END   (* SEARCH LEFT *)
        ELSE
            BEGIN (* SEARCH RIGHT *)
                P := Q↑.RIGHT;
                IF P = NIL THEN  (* ATTACH TO EMPTY RIGHT *)
                    Q↑.RIGHT := NODE
                ELSE
                    BUILDTREE(P)
            END (* SEARCH RIGHT *)
    END; (* BUILDTREE *)
PROCEDURE TRAVERSE;
(* TRAVERSES THE TREE IN ORDER, REWRITING INTFILE IN THE SORTED ORDER *)
    VAR   STACK: STACKPTR;
    BEGIN (* TRAVERSE *)
        WHILE P < > NIL DO
            BEGIN (* GO LEFT AND STACK *)
                NEW(STACK);
```

Figure 13.25:   BINARY TREE Program (cont.

```
                                STACK↑.TREELINK := P;
                                STACK↑.STACKLINK := TOP;
                                TOP := STACK;
                                P := P↑.LEFT
                        END;  (* GO LEFT AND STACK *)
                IF TOP < > NIL THEN
                        BEGIN (* VISIT AND GO RIGHT *)
                                P := TOP↑.TREELINK;
                                TOP := TOP↑.STACKLINK;
                                WRITELN(INTFILE,P↑.DATA);
                                P := P↑.RIGHT;
                                TRAVERSE
                        END   (* VISIT AND GO RIGHT *)
            END;  (* TRAVERSE *)
    BEGIN (* BINARYTREE *)
            RESET(INTFILE);
            INNODE;
            ROOT := NODE;
            INNODE;
            WHILE NODE↑.DATA < > 0 DO   (* EOF MARKER *)
                    BEGIN (* ADD TO TREE *)
                            BUILDTREE(ROOT);
                            INNODE
                    END; (* ADD TO TREE *)
            REWRITE(INTFILE);
            TOP := NIL;
            P:= ROOT;
            TRAVERSE
    END.  (* BINARYTREE *)
```

Figure 13.25: BINARY TREE Program (cont.)

The corresponding declarations for a node are:

PROGRAM BINARY TREE(INPUT,OUTPUT,INTFILE)
TYPE TREEPTR = ↑TREE;
     TREE
        RECORD
            DATA: INTEGER;
            RIGHT: TREEPTR;
            LEFT: TREEPTR
        END; (* RECORD *)

A stack structure will be required by the TRAVERSE procedure. Each element of the stack is a record containing two pointers. Their role will be explained below.

      STACKPTR = ↑STAC.KELEMNT:
      STACKELEMNT =
        RECORD
            TREELINK: TREEPTR;
            STACKLINK: STACKPTR
        END; (* RECORD *)

Five global variables are used:

     VAR INTFILE : TEXT;
         ROOT,P,NODE : TREEPTR;
         TOP : STACKPTR;

This program uses three procedures:

INNODE	reads an integer from INTFILE and creates a new node.
BUILDTREE	attaches the new node at the proper position in the tree.
TRAVERSE	implements the preorder traversal of the tree and writes the values of the nodes into INTFILE.

The INNODE procedure simply allocates space for a new node:

     PROCEDURE INNODE;
       BEGIN
          NEW(NODE);

initializes the two pointer fields to NIL:

<pre>
NODE↑.RIGHT : = **NIL**;
NODE↑.LEFT   : = **NIL**;
</pre>

and reads the integer value of the node from the INTFILE until the EOF is found:

<pre>
IF EOF(INTFILE) **THEN**
        NODE↑.DATA : = 0
ELSE
        READLN(INTFILE, NODE↑.DATA)
END; (* INNODE *)
</pre>

The end of file is indicated to the main program by a zero in the data field.

The BUILDTREE procedure adds a new node to the binary tree. The root of the tree or subtree is called PARENT and is a parameter to the procedure. The tree is examined in a top down fashion until a proper node is found to which the new node can be attached. Two pointers, P and Q, are used. The search starts at the PARENT node:

<pre>
PROCEDURE BUILDTREE(PARENT: TREEPTR);
    VAR P,Q : TREEPTR;
    BEGIN (* BUILDTREE *)
        P : = PARENT;
        Q : = PARENT;
</pre>

If the value field of the new node is less than the value of the current tree node, then we move to the left. The pointer P is set to point to the left sibling of Q↑.

<pre>
IF NODE↑.DATA < Q↑.DATA **THEN**
    BEGIN (* SEARCH LEFT *)
        P : = Q↑.LEFT;
</pre>

Two cases may arise:

— The node pointed to by P is empty. In this case, P = NIL and the new node may be attached there.
— The node is occupied. In this case, the procedure must be repeated:

IF P = **NIL THEN** (* ATTACH TO EMPTY LEFT *)
                Q↑.LEFT := NODE
    ELSE
                BUILDTREE(P)
END (* SEARCH LEFT *)

In this example, BUILDTREE is used recursively. The new point of departure for the search is pointed to by P.

Otherwise, if the DATA field of the new node is greater than or equal to the value of the current node, the search proceeds to the right.

The running pointer P is set to point to the right sibling of Q↑.

  ELSE
        BEGIN (* SEARCH RIGHT *)
             P := Q↑.RIGHT;

Then, the same two cases (as shown above) are considered:

— The node pointed to by P is empty. In this case, P = NIL and the new node may be attached there.
— The node is occupied. In this case, the procedure must be repeated:

              IF P = **NIL THEN** (* ATTACH TO EMPTY RIGHT *)
                         Q↑.RIGHT := NODE
              ELSE
                         BUILDTREE(P)
              END (* SEARCH RIGHT *)
        END; (* BUILDTREE *)

The TRAVERSE procedure uses a stack structure to "remember" its traversal path on the tree. Each stack element stores two pointers:

— A pointer to the next stack entry.
— The value of the tree pointer to be remembered.

The STACKELEMNT type has been declared in the program header:

        STACKELEMNT = **RECORD**
                        TREELINK:TREEPTR;
                        STACKLINK:STACKPTR
                      END;

Two global pointer variables are used:

TOP   points to the top of the stack
P   points to the current element in the tree.

The declarations were made at the beginning of the program:

VAR TOP : STACKPTR;
       P   : TREEPTR;

One local variable called STACK is used which is a pointer to the current element in the stack:

PROCEDURE TRAVERSE;
VAR STACK : STACKPTR;

In order to find the smallest node value in the tree, the search proceeds leftwards until a NIL left link is found. All elements traversed are memorized in the stack, up to the node:

WHILE P < > **NIL DO**
BEGIN

NEW is used to allocate space for each new stack entry:

NEW(STACK);

The new stack entry is created:

STACK↑.TREEELINK := P;
STACK↑.STACKLINK := TOP;

and the two pointers are updated:

TOP := STACK;
P := P↑.LEFT
END;

Looking at the example in Figure 13.23, the initial scan results in the situation shown in Figure 13.26.

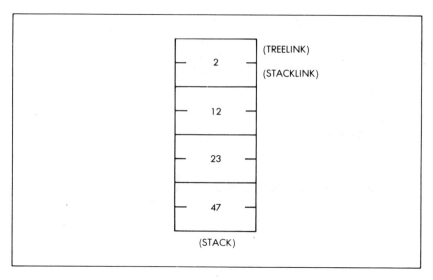

Figure 13.26: Beginning of Traversal

The stack is then examined. If the stack is not empty, the top element is the smallest element, and is written to INTFILE. In our example, this would be "2."

> **IF** TOP < > **NIL THEN**
>   **BEGIN** (* VISIT AND GO RIGHT *)
>   P : = TOP↑.TREELINK;
>   TOP : = TOP↑.STACKLINK;
>   WRITELN(INTFILE,P↑.DATA);

The TOP of the stack has been moved to the next stack entry. Once this is done, the search moves to the right subtree of the node "just removed," and the procedure is repeated (a recursive call).

> P : = P↑.RIGHT;
> TRAVERSE
> **END** (* VISIT AND GO RIGHT *)
> **END**; (* TRAVERSE *)

This time (in our example) the pointer P becomes NIL. The new call of TRAVERSE has the following result:

— The WHILE is not executed since P = NIL
— TOP <> NIL, and one element ("12") is removed from the stack and written to INTFILE. P is reset to point to the right sibling of "12," i.e., to point to "16." The situation is shown in Figure 13.27.

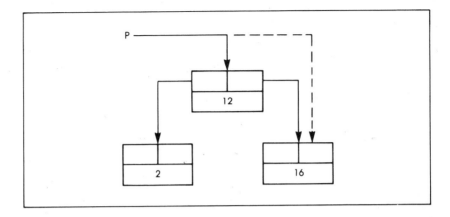

Figure 13.27:   Moving Right

The new call to TRAVERSE will result in "16" being stacked, then written out to INTFILE. At this point, the top element in the stack is "23," and the traversal proceeds until the entire tree has been written out to INTFILE.

The program proper operates quite simply. A first node is obtained:

```
BEGIN (* BINARYTREE *)
    RESET(INTFILE);
    INNODE;
```

This is the root of the tree. The next node is obtained:

```
    ROOT : = NODE;
    INNODE;
```

As long as a node's value is not 0, each new node is read in and added to the tree.

```
    WHILE NODE↑.DATA < > 0 DO (* EOF MARKER *)
        BEGIN (* ADD TO TREE *)
            BUILDTREE(ROOT);
            INNODE
        END; (* ADD TO TREE *)
```

The contents of INTFILE are no longer needed, and the tree will be traversed and written out to INTFILE:

```
        REWRITE(INTFILE);
        TOP := NIL;
        P := ROOT;
        TRAVERSE
    END. (* BINARYTREE *)
```

This program is relatively short, but it implements a complex algorithm in a few statements, using recursion. Study the program carefully, noting the way the tree is constructed and how a stack is designed with a singly-linked list. Notice how, when traversing a complex list such as the one used for the tree, two pointers are kept in order to be able to back up when needed.

TURBO PASCAL DYNAMIC STORAGE MANAGEMENT

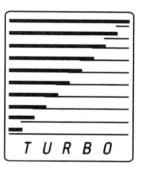

Turbo Pascal supports the use of pointers to dynamic variables located in the unallocated memory or *heap* of the computer. The heap is a stack-like structure in free memory used to store dynamic variables. When the NEW procedure is used to create each variable, space is allocated on the heap for the variable type and the variable's location in the heap is assigned to the pointer used in the NEW statement. The heap grows upward as new variables are created and the heap pointer contains the current address of the top of the heap.

Two Standard Pascal procedures, DISPOSE and MARK/RELEASE, can be used in Turbo Pascal to release heap memory space taken up by dynamic variables. The storage management technique used in a given program cannot be mixed—if DISPOSE is used in a program then MARK and RELEASE must not be used in the same program, and vice versa.

DISPOSE

The Standard Pascal DISPOSE procedure is available in Turbo Pascal version 2.0 and later. DISPOSE(PtrVar) releases the heap space used by individual dynamic variables.

MARK and RELEASE

The MARK and RELEASE procedures are available in all versions of Turbo Pascal. The RELEASE procedure does not work correctly in version 2.0, but Borland has published a replacement procedure. MARK(PtrVar) sets a pointer variable *PtrVar* to the current value of the heap pointer. RELEASE(PtrVar) releases all heap variables from *PtrVar* to the top of the heap. In other words, RELEASE sets the heap pointer to the value of *PtrVar*.

MEMAVAIL and MAXAVAIL

The MEMAVAIL and MAXAVAIL functions return information about the remaining space on the heap. In eight-bit versions of Turbo Pascal, they return the number of bytes free as an integer value. In 16-bit versions, they return the number of paragraphs free as an integer value (a paragraph is 16 bytes). Note that if the value is over 32767, it will be returned as a negative value due to overflow into the sign bit. MAXINT in Turbo Pascal is 32767. To correct this problem, convert the value to a REAL type by using the following code:

```
if val < 0 then
rval := 65536.0 + val
else
rval := val;
```

MEMAVAIL returns an integer value for the amount of free memory remaining in the heap. This function is available in all versions of Turbo Pascal.

MAXAVAIL returns an integer value for the largest contiguous area of free memory remaining in the heap. This function is only available in Turbo Pascal version 2.0 and later.

GETMEM and FREEMEM

The GETMEM and FREEMEM procedures manage heap storage in blocks, rather than using a pointer variable's type to determine the amount of space to allocate or deallocate.

GETMEM(PtrVar,I) allocates *I* bytes of space on the heap and assigns the beginning address to *PtrVar* (much like NEW). GETMEM is available in all versions of Turbo Pascal.

FREEMEM(PtrVar,I) reclaims a block of *I* bytes on the heap originally allocated by GETMEM. *I* must be exactly the same number of bytes as there were originally in GETMEM. FREEMEM is available in Turbo Pascal version 2.0 and later.

Variants

Turbo Pascal does not support records with variant parts as dynamic variables. As a result, the compiler does not allow the following alternate

Standard Pascal forms of the NEW and DISPOSE procedure:

```
NEW(PtrVar,v1,v2, . . . vn);
DISPOSE(PtrVar,v1,v2, . . . vn);
```

SUMMARY

Pointers and lists provide an important facility for creating complex data structures and manipulating them efficiently. Pointers and lists are particularly useful for constructing models or analyzing a given logical structure. They can be of specific value in business-oriented applications and in system software design.

EXERCISES

13-1: *Construct your own genealogical tree and print it. Input in the following format:*

> PARENT1, PARENT2
> = SIBLING1, SIBLING2, ..., SIBLINGN

Terminate input with: "0,0". Make provisions for identical parent names (the program should request additional information), and for the fact that each sibling may marry and become a parent.

13-2: *Write a program with which you can construct a list of appointments or things to do and then modify it by adding or removing entries. Keep entries sorted by date and time.*

13-3: *Modify the program in Exercise 13-2 so that you can record car expenses and maintenance operations. Also, make it so that if you type in the current mileage, the program will alert you to required oil changes and other maintenance operations.*

CHAPTER 14

TURBO PASCAL
AND OTHER PASCALS

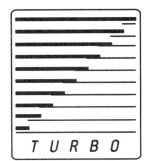

T U R B O

VARIATIONS OF STANDARD PASCAL

Standard Pascal was designed at a time when computers were generally used in a batch mode, that is, programs and data were submitted as decks of cards, and files were stored on magnetic tapes. Many of the Standard Pascal input/output features and file access mechanisms reflect this fact.

With the advent of microprocessors, it became more practical to use low-cost personal computers to execute Pascal programs. However, because the Pascal language was not originally designed to be interactive (i.e., to interact with a user), changes and extensions proved necessary.

Many versions of Pascal as well as an ISO Standard have now been defined (see references [12] and [32]). One of the most popular interactive versions of Pascal is Turbo Pascal, developed in 1983 by Borland International. This version essentially incorporates Standard Pascal, with many extensions, and some differences. Whereas many Standard Pascal implementations are simply language compilers, Turbo Pascal is a complete programming environment and includes features such as:

—Native code Z-80 or 8088 compiler
—WordStar-like editor
—Compilation of programs to memory or file
—Source-code-linked error checking

Only those features of Turbo Pascal that relate to the Pascal compiler have been described in this book. A complete description of the product and its other facilities can be found in reference [8].

TURBO PASCAL OVERVIEW

The main extensions and differences in Turbo Pascal are described in the corresponding Standard Pascal chapters. This chapter summarizes the essential features of Turbo Pascal and presents additional facilities specific to Turbo Pascal. Turbo Pascal's limitations are listed in Appendix I.

Turbo Pascal Files

In order to facilitate user interaction, Turbo Pascal defines several *standard files*. Each time a program is started, several standard files are automatically provided:

INPUT, OUTPUT, CON, TRM, KBD, LST, AUX, and USR

Note the difference between INPUT and KBD. During the usual input, each character is echoed on the screen as it is typed. However, there are instances where typed data should not be displayed, or should be displayed differently. This is the case, for example, when a secret password is typed in. In such a case, KBD can be used instead of INPUT and characters will not be displayed on the screen when they are typed. LST is used to access the system printer or list device. The other standard files are used for special applications and are described in Chapter 11.

Turbo Pascal assumes that files are stored on disk, therefore it supplies random-access mode, not available in Standard Pascal, with the proper functions or intrinsics. (Intrinsics are the additional functions and procedures provided by Turbo Pascal.) Turbo Pascal also defines untyped files that can be transferred block by block.

Modularizing Large Programs

Turbo Pascal generates programs that operate in the 64K bytes or less of memory available on Z-80, 8-bit computers and in a 64K-byte program segment on 16-bit computers like the IBM PC. Large programs must be broken into smaller pieces that can be run in this limited memory space.

In addition to the EXTERNAL declaration described in Chapter 7, Turbo Pascal provides three other methods for breaking a program into separate pieces: include files, chain files, and OVERLAY procedures and functions.

Include Files   Include files are used to break up program source code into manageable blocks that are automatically read from disk by the compiler when the program is compiled. They are often used to build "libraries" of commonly used declarations, procedures, and functions. Include files are specified by the {$I filename.typ } compiler directive placed in the main program module and cannot be nested (that is, include files cannot contain include directives).

Chain Files   The Turbo Pascal compiler allows program modules to be created that can be run successively or "chained" together like a train. The first, or main module, is a regular Turbo Pascal compiled program file. Any number of other modules can be created as chain files and run one after another. Chain files do not include the Turbo Pascal runtime library routines. The library routines consist of about 8K bytes of code at the beginning of a standard compiled program containing subroutines used by all programs. Compiled chain files have the file extension .CHN.

Global variables can be passed between modules as long as they are identically declared at the very beginning of each module. This is necessary because Turbo Pascal does not initialize program variables when a program or module is loaded.

Chained program files must be declared as untyped files and assigned (linked) to a file variable just like any other file. They are activated with the CHAIN(filevar) procedure.

Overlays   Turbo Pascal provides one more method to break up large programs so they will reside in memory successively rather than simultaneously. This is called a memory overlay technique. A group of procedures or functions may be declared as overlays, and they will each reside in the same area of program memory (one at a time) when the program is executed. These OVERLAY subprograms are automatically loaded from disk as they are called by the program.

The OVERLAY declaration allows the programmer to partition a large program into segments that all use the same area of memory. Each consecutive group of overlays in the program uses one block of memory equal to the space required for the largest overlay in the group. For example:

```
          PROGRAM SAMPLE;
              (declarations)
                  OVERLAY PROCEDURE ALPHA;
                  BEGIN
                          . . .
                  END; (*ALPHA*)
                  OVERLAY FUNCTION BETA;
                  BEGIN
                          . . .
                  END; (*BETA*)
              PROCEDURE DELTA;
              BEGIN
                      . . .
              END; (*DELTA*)
          BEGIN
                  . . .
          END. (*SAMPLE*)
```

A procedure or a function can be preceded by a OVERLAY declaration. Each group of overlays is stored in a single disk file with the same file name as the main program and a three digit integer file type representing each overlay group number (i.e. MAIN.000 or MAIN.001).

Overlay procedures and functions must never include calls to other overlays in the same group, however overlays may include overlays. Overlay subprograms cannot be FORWARD declared or recursive.

String Routines

Turbo Pascal also provides a number of useful extensions that process text strings and conduct machine level operations.

As a result of these additional facilities, Turbo Pascal can be used not only to write applications programs but also to write systems software, such as communication routines between two computers.

Machine Level Operations

Turbo Pascal's string intrinsics are discussed in Chapter 9. Some of the more useful machine-level-interface intrinsics are discussed below.

Turbo Pascal allows the use of the logical operators AND, NOT, OR, and XOR as arithmetic operators with integers in bitwise operations. When combined with the SHL (shift left) and SHR (shift right) operators, the HI, LO, SWAP, ADDR, and PTR intrinsics, and where necessary INLINE machine code, many machine level operations are possible. For example, the statement:

ORD(CH) **AND** 127;

can be used to strip the eighth bit from characters in a word-processed file like WordStar.

Turbo Pascal's BDOS and BIOS procedures in CP/M systems and INTR and MSDOS procedures in 16-bit systems provide a direct interface with the microcomputer operating system. Programmers can use these links to access virtually any machine level function.

FILLCHAR(var,num,data)   The FILLCHAR procedure is used to quickly initialize an array or string variable to a single value. The character or byte value specified by *data* is placed in *num* bytes beginning at the first byte of variable *var*.

MOVE(var1,var2,num)   The MOVE procedure copies *num* bytes beginning at the first byte of *var1* to the area beginning at the first byte of *var2*.

SIZEOF(identifier)   This function returns the actual memory space occupied by the specified type or variable. The size is expressed in bytes. SIZEOF is generally used with the FILLCHAR or MOVE procedures.

The SIZEOF intrinsic can be very useful. For example, this program fills a character array with blanks:

```
VAR LINE : ARRAY[1 . . 80] OF CHAR;
BEGIN
      FILLCHAR(LINE[1],SIZEOF(LINE),' ');
END.
```

EXIT   This Turbo Pascal 3.0 procedure terminates execution of the current subprogram block. In the main block, it terminates the whole program.

HALT   This Turbo Pascal 3.0 procedure stops a program at a given point during execution. When HALT is inserted in a program, it causes the program to stop immediately at the indicated point. The operating system is automatically invoked by the compiler.

CLRSCR   This procedure clears the terminal screen and returns the cursor to the home position. It is one of a group of terminal control procedures provided in Turbo Pascal. These procedures require that the compiler be installed for the particular type of terminal used. See Chapter 11 for more details on these routines.

GOTOXY(xcoord, ycoord)   This procedure positions the cursor on the screen at the position specified by xcoord and ycoord. The upper-left corner of the screen is defined as 1,1. A number of other terminal control procedures are also available.

SUMMARY

Turbo Pascal has everything Standard Pascal has, plus some additional features that facilitate interaction, text processing, machine level operations, and disk access, none of which are available in Standard Pascal. All other changes in Turbo Pascal are discussed at the end of each relevant chapter in this book. Turbo Pascal is well-suited for use on CRT terminals such as those used on personal computers, because of its enhancements that support interactive input and output.

CHAPTER 15

PROGRAM DEVELOPMENT

THE PROGRAM DEVELOPMENT PROCESS

Throughout this book, you have learned the rules for developing Pascal programs that perform specific actions. With the skills you have acquired, you should now be able to write simple Pascal programs that automate the process of obtaining solutions to simple problems. However, once a program has been written, it must then be entered and executed on a computer. The complete process required to achieve this result is reviewed in this chapter.

First, the five basic steps required to actually write and execute a Pascal program will be described. Then, the programming phase during which an algorithm is transformed into a program will be analyzed in detail.

THE FIVE STEPS OF PROGRAM DEVELOPMENT

The five steps used to create and use a Pascal program are listed in Figure 15.1.

```
STEP 1.  Designing the program
STEP 2.  Entering the program
STEP 3.  Listing the program
STEP 4.  Compiling and executing the program
STEP 5.  Debugging the program
```

Figure 15.1: The Five Steps of Program Development

Depending upon the circumstance, some steps may be omitted, while other, additional steps may be required. Let us look at each of the five steps.

Step 1. Designing the Program

The word "programming" is used in many ways. It may simply refer to the creation of a program on paper, or it may encompass all of the phases that might be necessary to design a program and get it to work correctly. Because programming usually involves this complete process, the second definition for programming is most often used. We will, therefore, define the action of creating a program on paper as "designing the program." This action is one of the most important phases of the programming process.

Let us look at the program design phase as it is illustrated in Figure 15.2.

Figure 15.2: Program Design Phase

When outlining a solution to a problem, or describing a sequence of actions to be performed, an algorithm should first be specified and data structures (to be manipulated by the algorithm) should be created. Next, the algorithm may be translated into a program, using a programming language such as Pascal.

At this stage, a program is written down on a piece of paper. If possible, each handwritten program should be tested manually in order to verify its validity. In particular, it is highly recommended that the programmer check the validity of the handwritten program in a few typical cases by computing values manually. It is usually the case that in the complete programming sequence the phase requiring the largest amount of time is that of debugging the actual program (i.e., identifying and correcting errors). By using proper design steps and checking the handwritten program, the programmer can often save a significant amount of time during the debugging phase.

After the handwritten program is checked manually for errors, it is entered into the computer system. This is the second phase: entering the program.

Step 2. Entering the Program

The program must now be entered into the computer system as a file. The program that allows the convenient typing of text into a file is called the *editor*. The role of the editor is illustrated in Figure 15.3.

Figure 15.3: The Role of the Editor

The editor is a special program designed to facilitate text entry. It allows the user to erase characters or words, insert or append text, substitute letters or words, and search for given character combinations. The more powerful the editor, the more convenient the program entry phase. A useful feature offered by the editor that is of special value to Pascal users is indented paragraphs. Indented paragraphs are an important aspect of program readability in Pascal.

Once the handwritten program has been typed into the computer system with the assistance of the editor, the program is usually stored on disk as a file. The next step is to examine the file to ascertain that no errors have been introduced by the typing process. The file will need to be listed. This is the third phase: listing the program. (On a small computer, this step may be performed by the compiler.)

Step 3. Listing the Program

The program stored as a file will now be listed on the printer, i.e., typed out. This function is performed by the *file system*, a program which is part of the computer's operating system. The file system allows the transfer of a file from the disk to the printer, as well as the transfer of files from one disk to another. In addition, the file system provides facilities that can be used to change the names of files and specify various attributes. This phase is illustrated in Figure 15.4.

Figure 15.4: The File System

If a printer is not available for listing a file, the file can be shown on the screen of the terminal in order to check it against the handwritten listing. In practice, a *printout* is a significant convenience as it improves program readability and reduces the risk of errors.

The program has now been entered into the computer as a file and is presumed "correct" from all standpoints. It is ready to be executed. In Pascal as well as in most compiled languages, execution proceeds in the two phases described in Step 4.

Step 4. Running the Program

Step 4.1. Compilation A program written in a high-level language cannot be executed directly by the computer since the processor can only understand a limited set of binary instructions. The program must, therefore, be either translated into this binary format, or decoded by an interpreter program. In the case of Pascal, a special "compiler" is generally used. The principle of a compiler is illustrated in Figure 15.5.

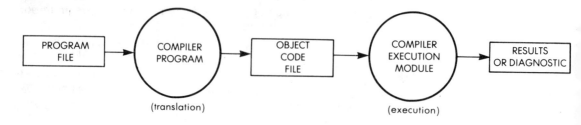

Figure 15.5:   The Principle of a Compiler

Figure 15.5 shows that the program is compiled into *object code*. The high-level instructions (the Pascal statements), are translated into a set of equivalent machine-language instructions. The resulting translated program is called the object code file. If the program contains syntax errors, the compiler will generate *diagnostics*, or error messages which inform the programmer as to the type and location of the errors.

Step 4.2. Execution   Once translated, the object code is ready to be executed. The execution phase is performed by a separate module of the compiler, call the *execution module,* and results in program execution. If the program was correct, results will be displayed or printed. If the program was incorrect, diagnostics will be generated.

The important point here is that most compilers work in at least two phases: a translation phase, followed by an execution phase. In addition, some compilers compact and increase the speed of the object code by optimizing the use of internal computer registers and moving instructions out of loops. Such an optimization pass is important for the speed of execution, but is costly to implement, and therefore seldom provided.

In the case of some Pascal implementations, the approach used is identical in principle, but differs in actual details. Because Pascal was designed to be highly portable, i.e., easy to implement on any computer, the Pascal program is first translated into another standarized representation called P-Code (rather than the binary object code). This process is illustrated in Figure 15.6.

Figure 15.6:   Translating into P-Code

In the second phase, the execution phase, this P-Code is interpreted by a program module, usually part of the 'compiler,' called the P-Code interpreter. This process is illustrated in Figure 15.7.

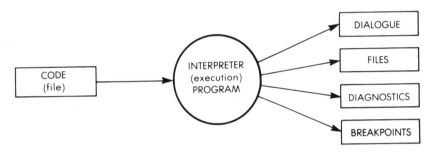

Figure 15.7:   Interpreting the P-Code

The logical effect of using P-Code rather than object code is equivalent to the standard approach but results in lower efficiency. The advantage is that a standard compiler module, written in P-Code, may be designed which translates a Pascal program into its P-Code equivalent. The only remaining problem would then be to design a P-Code interpreter on the host machine. (This is a reasonably simple task.) Compiling to an interpreted P-Code therefore facilitates the implementation of Pascal on a variety of processors. However, the interpreter for the P-Code is less efficient than executing the object code directly and, as a result, execution is slower. Most Pascal implementations use the P-Code approach.

At this point in the programming process, either diagnostics are generated or they are not. If diagnostics are generated as a result of the translation phase or the execution phase, errors have been detected and the programmer must correct them in the original program. The programmer must then go back to step 2 and type in the corrections. In severe cases, it may be necessary to return to step 1 and modify the algorithm, the data structures or the encoding performed earlier. Once corrections have been made, the program (hopefully) works. However, if the program runs and no diagnostics are generated, it does not necessarily mean that the program works correctly in all cases.

In order to test a program, the program must be executed as many times as possible with different data, so that its correct operation can be verified in all cases. In order to facilitate program debugging, a debugger program may be available.

Step 5. Debugging the Program

The function of a debugger program is to facilitate program debugging. The main feature provided by a debugger is the use of *break-points*. A breakpoint is a special command that may be used to force a program to stop at a given location. By being able to stop the program, the programmer may examine values of variables as well as the contents of memory. Thus, it is possible to verify the correct operation of the program at selected breakpoints. In addition, sophisticated debuggers may allow the programmer to keep a "picture" or "snapshot" of the program by recording key values that can be examined at selected break-points. When a breakpoint is reached the debuggers will automatically display the value of specified variables and memory locations. The use of a debugger is illustrated in Figure 15.8.

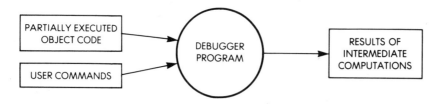

Figure 15.8:   The Debugger

If a debugger is not an available facility, and it generally is not available in most Pascal implementations, other techniques must be used. Let us now look at two of the more common techniques.

The first technique is to debug each program module separately. Each function and each procedure is then tested separately in "typical cases" until each one proves to work satisfactorily. At this stage it is important to remember that even perfectly operational procedures may not work satisfactorily together because of incompatibilities in their shared parameters or unexpected side-effects.

The second technique consists of inserting a number of WRITE statements throughout the program, so that a *trace* of program execution is automatically printed. The trace is the sequence of values printed as execution proceeds. For example, the values of crucial variables and data structures may be printed every time that a loop is entered, or every time that a procedure or a function is invoked. In this way, whenever something goes wrong, it is usually possible to determine the exact group of instructions that caused the error to occur. The most difficult problem, once an error has been found, is to identify the instruction or the group of instructions that caused it. Because Pascal is a block-structured language, a well-designed program facilitates debugging by allowing the programmer to determine which block is at fault. In the case of programs that use advanced techniques, additional steps may be required.

Additional Steps

Many Pascal implementations allow the programmer to use assembly-level language routines within a Pascal program, or to invoke programs written in another language such as FORTRAN. In these cases, such program elements must be linked to the main Pascal program by means of a linker program. The actual details are specific to each implementation.

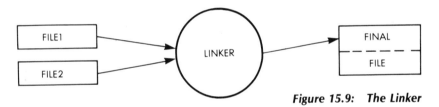

Figure 15.9: The Linker

Summary of Program Development

The programming process involves many steps. The most crucial step is the program design phase. The rules for constructing Pascal programs have already been presented in this book.

After constructing a program, the next step is to enter the program on the computer, and execute it. The details of the editor program as well as the specific commands required to execute the editor program or the compiler are specific to each installation, and are described in the supplier's manual. These commands are generally not standardized.

After constructing a program, the next step is to enter the program on the computer, and execute it. The details of the editor program as well as the specific commands required to execute the editor program or the compiler are specific to each installation, and are described in the supplier's manual. These commands are generally not standardized. One exception is Turbo Pascal, a package that provides a complete programming environment including compiler, editor, debugger, and native-code-executable program generator. This integrated programmer interface makes it easy to develop Pascal programs. The compiler is described throughout this book and there is additional information in reference [8].

WRITING A PASCAL PROGRAM

Programming is generally considered an art rather than an exact science. This is because there is almost never a unique way in which to devise a program solution for a given problem. Many equivalent programs may be constructed for any one problem, using different algorithms, data structures or coding techniques. As a result, programming refers to a great number of techniques that may be used by the program designer. Because there is no single solution, many choices must be made by the programmer in an attempt to optimize his or her time, the program's efficiency, and the size of the program.

A number of theories have been proposed as to the best approach to programming. In practice, it is often claimed that a small number of individuals, perhaps 10% of the programming population, have a natural gift for programming, and will be capable of designing correct programs quickly, and without effort. Such exceptional people tend to have their own theories as to the best approach to programming, and regardless of the theory, they usually achieve their programming objectives.

The bulk of the programming population, however, does not have this natural gift. Unfortunately, most programmers within the remaining 90% of the programming population are convinced that they have this unique programming talent. As a result, they have a tendency to avoid the rules proposed, and they usually fail repeatedly. Experience will eventually correct this.

The purpose of most programming theories is therefore to facilitate the design of programs by those individuals who will benefit from being guided by a set of rules. Almost any set of rules relating to programming is probably better than no rules at all, as rules encourage disciplined programming.

Discipline is the key to success in the design of any program. An important technique used for the disciplined design of computer programs is called the Structured Programming approach. In this approach, the overall problem is expressed as a series of simpler steps. Then each step is broken down into simpler steps, and so on. It is also called a *step-wise refinement* approach or a *top-down approach*.

The Pascal language has been designed to facilitate programming using this approach. In particular, a Pascal program can generally be written as a set of procedures and functions that correspond exactly to the sub-steps of the algorithm. It is good practice to keep these procedures and functions under one page (usually 66 lines) or even one screen (24 lines) in length. This insures that the program is assembled from individually comprehensible pieces. Structured Programming is described in several publications, such as references [13] and [14].

PROGRAMMING STYLE

A structured approach to programming in Pascal generally results in a clear and well-organized program that is both easy to read and debug. A program should be clearly documented and well-formatted. Descriptive comments should be included wherever possible. The operation of each program module should be thoroughly explained by comments embedded in the proper place in the program. This aspect is crucial to the debugging of a program, as well as to the reuse of that program by another person or by the designer later on, in case any changes should be required. In Pascal it is also important to use the formatting opportunities provided by logical blocks such as functions and procedures, as well as the indentation of subelements in a statement within the program, in order to facilitate readability.

Several different indenting and spacing methods have been used in the programming examples throughout this book. This was done so that the reader can become familiar with the different styles.

In summary, there are three essential objectives when designing a program. They are:

1. Correctness. The program must work.
2. Clarity. The organization, appearance, and documentation must facilitate the understanding of the program.
3. Efficiency. The program should operate as fast as possible and use as little memory as possible if these resources are expensive or limited.

CONCLUSION

For all those who want to learn how to program effectively, there is one essential recommendation: practice. There is no substitute for it. All other rules relating to program design simply provide overall guidance for the mental process. And no amount of reading can substitute for the actual design of programs. Be aware that the overwhelming majority of programs fail the first time they are executed. Also, almost no large program is ever entirely correct. Because of the complexity involved in the design of a program, the possibilities for errors are almost endless. A program generally qualifies as being correct when it behaves correctly in all *conceivable* cases. This does not mean that it will not fail some day when some condition will have changed. To become an effective programmer, write a number of programs, and experience all of the usual failures until you are able to correct them by becoming more knowledgeable and by developing good programming habits.

For those readers who wish to learn more about Pascal, several books are available that will provide additional help, guidance and examples. They are listed at the end of this book.

As a final point, the author welcomes suggestions from readers regarding additional help or guidance they would like to receive, as well as all constructive criticism. Every suggestion will be acknowledged, and will be taken into account in successive editions of this book.

PASCAL OPERATORS

STANDARD PASCAL OPERATORS

	TYPE	FUNCTION	TYPE OF OPERAND(S)	TYPE OF RESULT
:=		assignment	any except file	
+	arithmetic	unary plus	integer, real	integer, real
−	arithmetic	minus sign	integer, real	integer, real
+	arithmetic	addition	integer, real	integer, real
+	set	union	set	set
−	arithmetic	subtraction	integer, real	integer, real
−	set	difference	set	set
*	arithmetic	multiplication	integer, real	integer, real
*	set	intersection	set	set
DIV	arithmetic	integer division	integer	integer
/	arithmetic	real division	integer, real	real
MOD	arithmetic	modulus	integer	integer
=	relational	equality	scalar, set, string, pointer	Boolean
<>	relational	inequality	scalar, set, string, pointer	Boolean
<	relational	less than	scalar, string	Boolean
<=	relational	less than or equal to	scalar, string	Boolean
<=	relational	set inclusion	set	Boolean
>	relational	greater than	scalar, string	Boolean
>=	relational	greater than or equal to	scalar, string	Boolean
>=	relational	set inclusion	set	Boolean
IN	relational	set membership	scalar IN set	Boolean
AND	logical	and	Boolean	Boolean
NOT	logical	negation	Boolean	Boolean
OR	logical	or	Boolean	Boolean

TURBO PASCAL OPERATORS

	TYPE	FUNCTION	TYPE OF OPERAND(S)	TYPE OF RESULT
+	string	concatenation	string, char	string
XOR	logical	exclusive or	Boolean	Boolean

RESERVED WORDS

RESERVED WORDS

AND	NIL
ARRAY	NOT
BEGIN	OF
CASE	OR
CONST	PACKED
DIV	PROCEDURE
DO	PROGRAM
DOWNTO	RECORD
ELSE	REPEAT
END	SET
FILE	THEN
FOR	TO
FUNCTION	TYPE
GOTO	UNTIL
IF	VAR
IN	WHILE
LABEL	WITH
MOD	

TURBO PASCAL RESERVED WORDS

ABSOLUTE	SHR
EXTERNAL	STRING
INLINE	XOR
OVERLAY	
SHL	

STANDARD FUNCTIONS
AND PROCEDURES

The italicized functions and procedures are not supported in Turbo Pascal.

FILE OPERATIONS	ARITHMETIC	PREDICATES
GET (F)	ABS (X)	EOF (F)
PAGE (F)	ARCTAN (X)	EOLN (F)
PUT (F)	COS (X)	ODD (X)
READ	EXP (X)	
READLN	LN (X)	
RESET (F)	SIN (X)	
REWRITE (F)	SQR (X)	
WRITE	SQRT (X)	
WRITELN		

TRANSFER	MEMORY MANAGEMENT	ORDERING
CHR (X)	*PACK (A,I,Z)*	PRED (X)
ORD (X)	*UNPACK (Z,A,I)*	SUCC (X)
ROUND (X)	NEW (P)	
	DISPOSE (P)	
TRUNC (X)	*NEW (P,T_1...T_N)*	
	DISPOSE (P,T_1,T_2..T_N)	

STANDARD
IDENTIFIERS

	CONSTANT	TYPE	FUNCTION	PROCEDURE	FILE
ABS			X		
ARCTAN			X		
BOOLEAN		X			
CHAR		X			
CHR			X		
COS			X		
EOF			X		
EOLN			X		
EXP			X		
FALSE	X				
GET				X	
INPUT					X
INTEGER		X			
LN			X		
MAXINT	X				
NEW				X	
ODD			X		
ORD			X		
OUTPUT					X
PACK				X	
PAGE				X	
PRED			X		
PUT				X	
READ				X	
READLN				X	
REAL		X			
RESET				X	
REWRITE				X	
ROUND			X		
SIN			X		
SQR			X		
SQRT			X		
TEXT		X			
TRUE	X				
TRUNC			X		
UNPACK				X	
WRITE				X	
WRITELN				X	

OPERATOR
PRECEDENCE

TURBO PASCAL PRECEDENCE

Level 3 (highest)	NOT
Level 2	* / DIV MOD AND
Level 1	+ − OR XOR (+ includes string concatenation)
Level 0	= < > <= >= <> IN

STANDARD PASCAL PRECEDENCE

Level 3 (highest)	NOT
Level 2	* / DIV MOD AND
Level 1	+ − OR
Level 0	= < > <= >= <> IN

SYNTAX DIAGRAMS

block

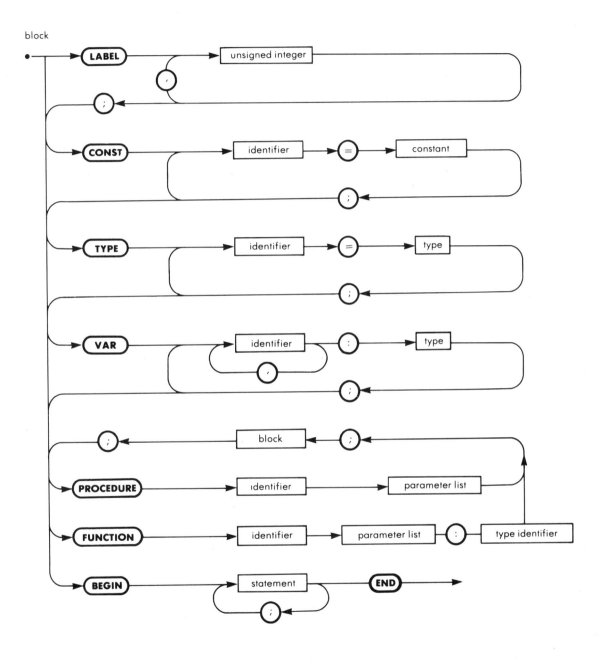

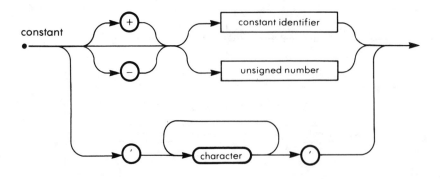

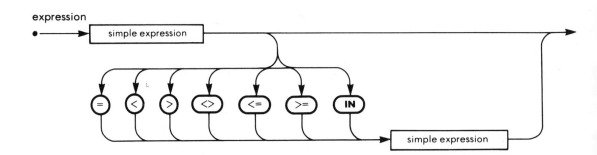

factor

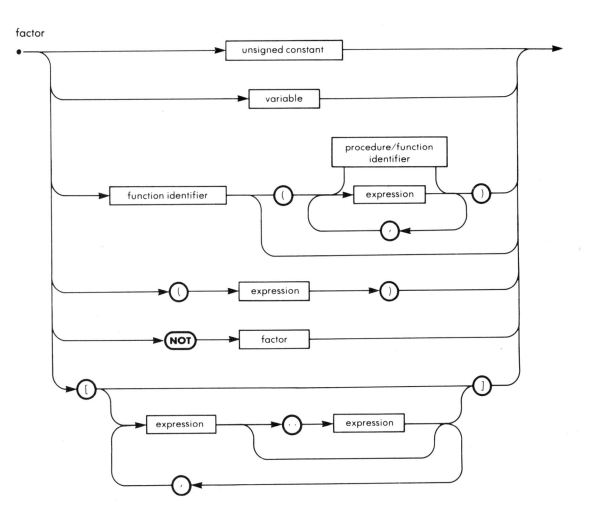

field list

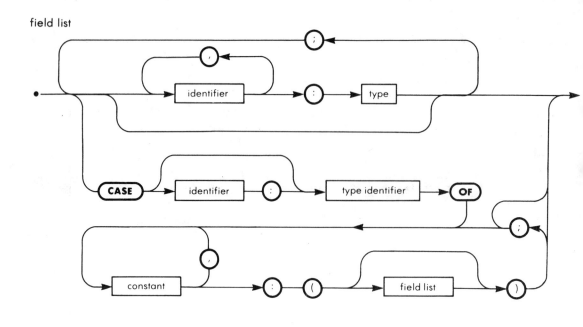

identifier

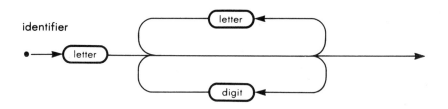

parameter list

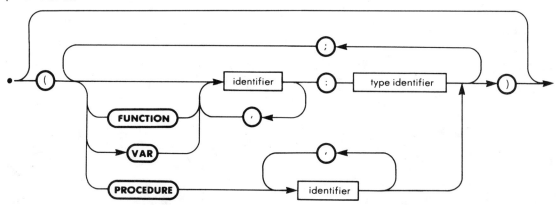

program

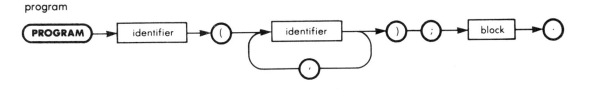

simple expression

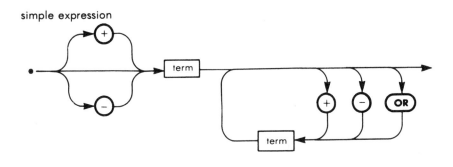

simple type

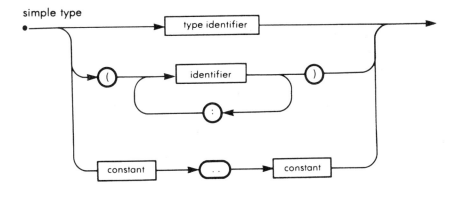

statement

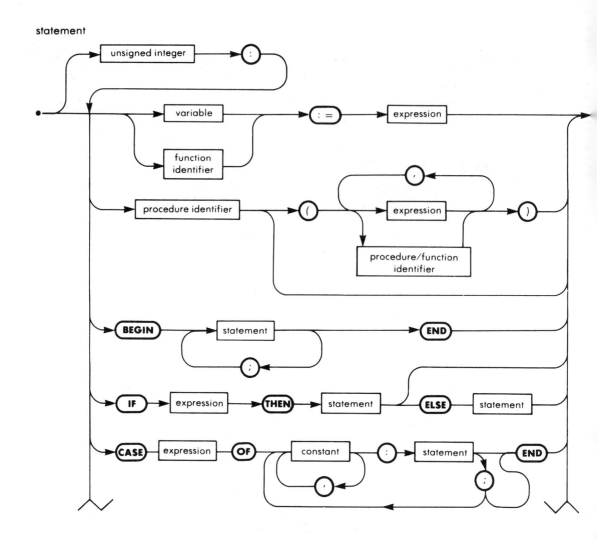

statement (cont.)

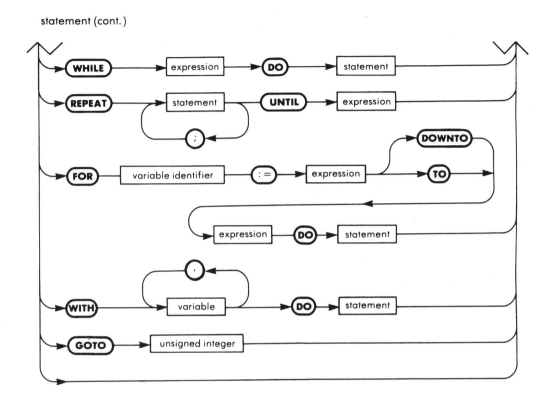

term

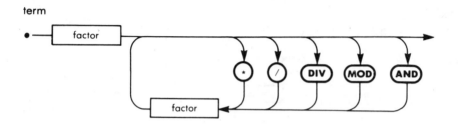

type

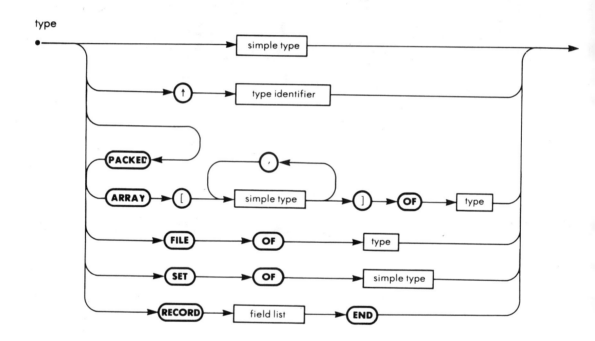

unsigned constant

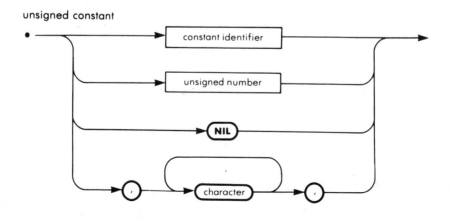

unsigned integer

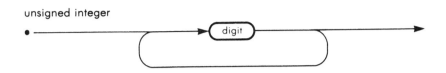

unsigned number

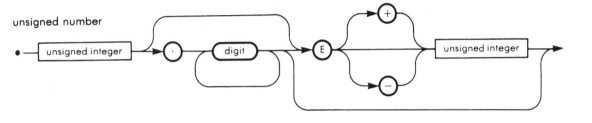

variable

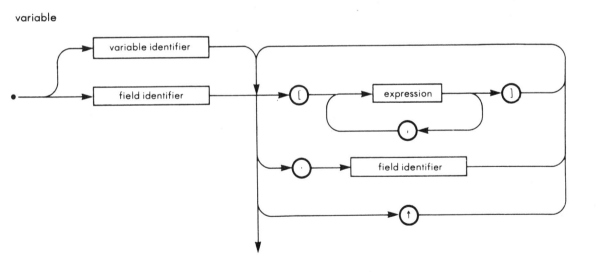

APPENDIX **G**

ASCII CODE

THE ASCII SYMBOLS

NUL — Null	VT — Vertical Tabulation	CAN — Cancel
SOH — Start of Heading	FF — Form Feed	EM — End of Medium
STX — Start of Text	CR — Carriage Return	SUB — Substitute
ETX — End of Text	SO — Shift Out	ESC — Escape
EOT — End of Transmission	SI — Shift In	FS — File Separator
ENQ — Enquiry	DLE — Data Link Escape	GS — Group Separator
ACK — Acknowledge	DC — Device Control	RS — Record Separator
BEL — Bell	NAK — Negative Acknowledge	US — Unit Separator
BS — Backspace	SYN — Synchronous Idle	SP — Space (Black)
HT — Horizontal Tabulation	ETB — End of Transmission Block	DEL — Delete
LF — Line Feed		

ASCII IN DECIMAL, OCTAL, HEXADECIMAL

#	OCTAL	HEX	CHAR	#	OCTAL	HEX	CHAR	#	OCTAL	HEX	CHAR	#	OCTAL	HEX	CHAR
0	000	00	NUL	32	040	20	SP	64	100	40	@	96	140	60	`
1	001	01	SOH	33	041	21	!	65	101	41	A	97	141	61	a
2	002	02	STX	34	042	22	"	66	102	42	B	98	142	62	b
3	003	03	ETX	35	043	23	#	67	103	43	C	99	143	63	c
4	004	04	EOT	36	044	24	$	68	104	44	D	100	144	64	d
5	005	05	ENQ	37	045	25	%	69	105	45	E	101	145	65	e
6	006	06	ACK	38	046	26	&	70	106	46	F	102	146	66	f
7	007	07	BEL	39	047	27	'	71	107	47	G	103	147	67	g
8	010	08	BS	40	050	28	(	72	110	48	H	104	150	68	h
9	011	09	HT	41	051	29	)	73	111	49	I	105	151	69	i
10	012	0A	LF	42	052	2A	*	74	112	4A	J	106	152	6A	j
11	013	0B	VT	43	053	2B	+	75	113	4B	K	107	153	6B	k
12	014	0C	FF	44	054	2C	,	76	114	4C	L	108	154	6C	l
13	015	0D	CR	45	055	2D	-	77	115	4D	M	109	155	6D	m
14	016	0E	SO	46	056	2E	.	78	116	4E	N	110	156	6E	n
15	017	0F	SI	47	057	2F	/	79	117	4F	O	111	157	6F	o
16	020	10	DLE	48	060	30	0	80	120	50	P	112	160	70	p
17	021	11	DC1	49	061	31	1	81	121	51	Q	113	161	71	q
18	022	12	DC2	50	062	32	2	82	122	52	R	114	162	72	r
19	023	13	DC3	51	063	33	3	83	123	53	S	115	163	73	s
20	024	14	DC4	52	064	34	4	84	124	54	T	116	164	74	t
21	025	15	NAK	53	065	35	5	85	125	55	U	117	165	75	u
22	026	16	SYN	54	066	36	6	86	126	56	V	118	166	76	v
23	027	17	ETB	55	067	37	7	87	127	57	W	119	167	77	w
24	030	18	CAN	56	070	38	8	88	130	58	X	120	170	78	x
25	031	19	EM	57	071	39	9	89	131	59	Y	121	171	79	y
26	032	1A	SUB	58	072	3A	:	90	132	5A	Z	122	172	7A	z
27	033	1B	ESC	59	073	3B	;	91	133	5B	[	123	173	7B	{
28	034	1C	FS	60	074	3C	<	92	134	5C	\	124	174	7C	¦
29	035	1D	GS	61	075	3D	=	93	135	5D	]	125	175	7D	}
30	036	1E	RS	62	076	3E	>	94	136	5E	↑	126	176	7E	~
31	037	1F	US	63	077	3F	?	95	137	5F	__	127	177	7F	DEL

Note: bit 7 (parity bit) is set to zero in this table.

ASCII AND EXTENDED GRAPHICS CODES

This section provides charts for the standard 128 character ASCII codes, and for the extended graphics codes available on the IBM PC and compatible computers. These screen graphics codes may be used in Turbo Pascal and some other IBM PC versions of Pascal.

The first extended character chart shows those characters available when using the WRITE and WRITELN statements with the CHR( ) procedure. The second table shows the characters available when accessing the IBM PC's screen memory directly. (For example, CHR(013) is a carriage return when used with WRITE and WRITELN, but the same code produces a music note when placed directly in screen memory.)

ASCII Value	Character	Control Character	ASCII Value	Character
000	(null)	NUL	032	(space)
001	☺	SOH	033	!
002	☻	STX	034	''
003	♥	ETX	035	#
004	♦	EOT	036	$
005	♣	ENQ	037	%
006	♠	ACK	038	&
007	(beep)	BEL	039	'
008	■	BS	040	(
009	(tab)	HT	041	)
010	(line feed)	LF	042	*
011	(home)	VT	043	+
012	(form feed)	FF	044	,
013	(carriage return)	CR	045	-
014	♫	SO	046	.
015	☼	SI	047	/
016	►	DLE	048	0
017	◄	DC1	049	1
018	↕	DC2	050	2
019	‼	DC3	051	3
020	¶	DC4	052	4
021	§	NAK	053	5
022	▬	SYN	054	6
023	↨	ETB	055	7
024	↑	CAN	056	8
025	↓	EM	057	9
026	→	SUB	058	:
027	←	ESC	059	;
028	(cursor right)	FS	060	<
029	(cursor left)	GS	061	=
030	(cursor up)	RS	062	>
031	(cursor down)	US	063	?

ASCII Value	Character	ASCII Value	Character
064	@	096	`
065	A	097	a
066	B	098	b
067	C	099	c
068	D	100	d
069	E	101	e
070	F	102	f
071	G	103	g
072	H	104	h
073	I	105	i
074	J	106	j
075	K	107	k
076	L	108	l
077	M	109	m
078	N	110	n
079	O	111	o
080	P	112	p
081	Q	113	q
082	R	114	r
083	S	115	s
084	T	116	t
085	U	117	u
086	V	118	v
087	W	119	w
088	X	120	x
089	Y	121	y
090	Z	122	z
091	[	123	{
092	\	124		
093	]	125	}
094	∧	126	~
095	—	127	△

ASCII Value	Character	ASCII Value	Character
128	Ç	160	á
129	ü	161	í
130	é	162	ó
131	â	163	ú
132	ä	164	ñ
133	à	165	Ñ
134	å	166	ª
135	ç	167	º
136	ê	168	¿
137	ë	169	⌐
138	è	170	¬
139	ï	171	½
140	î	172	¼
141	ì	173	¡
142	Ä	174	«
143	Å	175	»
144	É	176	▒
145	æ	177	▒
146	Æ	178	▓
147	ô	179	│
148	ö	180	┤
149	ò	181	╡
150	û	182	╢
151	ù	183	╖
152	ÿ	184	╕
153	Ö	185	╣
154	Ü	186	║
155	¢	187	╗
156	£	188	╝
157	¥	189	╜
158	Pt	190	╛
159	ƒ	191	┐

ASCII Value	Character	ASCII Value	Character
192	└	224	α
193	┴	225	β
194	┬	226	Γ
195	├	227	π
196	─	228	Σ
197	┼	229	σ
198	╞	230	μ
199	╟	231	τ
200	╚	232	Φ
201	╔	233	θ
202	╩	234	Ω
203	╦	235	δ
204	╠	236	∞
205	═	237	$\emptyset$
206	╬	238	ϵ
207	╧	239	$\cap$
208	╨	240	$\equiv$
209	╤	241	$\pm$
210	╥	242	$\geq$
211	╙	243	$\leq$
212	╘	244	$\lceil$
213	╒	245	$\rfloor$
214	╓	246	$\div$
215	╫	247	$\approx$
216	╪	248	°
217	┘	249	•
218	┌	250	·
219	█	251	$\sqrt{}$
220	▄	252	ⁿ
221	▌	253	^{2}
222	▐	254	■
223	▀	255	(blank 'FF')

Character Set (00-7F) Quick Reference

DECIMAL VALUE ➡	HEXA DECIMAL VALUE	0	16	32	48	64	80	96	112
⬇		0	1	2	3	4	5	6	7
0	0	BLANK (NULL)	►	BLANK (SPACE)	0	@	P	`	p
1	1	☺	◄	!	1	A	Q	a	q
2	2	☻	↕	"	2	B	R	b	r
3	3	♥	‼	#	3	C	S	c	s
4	4	♦	¶	$	4	D	T	d	t
5	5	♣	§	%	5	E	U	e	u
6	6	♠	▬	&	6	F	V	f	v
7	7	•	↨	'	7	G	W	g	w
8	8	◘	↑	(	8	H	X	h	x
9	9	○	↓	)	9	I	Y	i	y
10	A	◙	→	*	:	J	Z	j	z
11	B	♂	←	+	;	K	[	k	{
12	C	♀	∟	,	<	L	\	l	|
13	D	♪	↔	—	=	M	]	m	}
14	E	♫	▲	.	>	N	^	n	~
15	F	☼	▼	/	?	O	_	o	△

Character Set (88-FF) Quick Reference

DECIMAL VALUE ➡	HEXA DECIMAL VALUE ⬇	128 / 8	144 / 9	160 / A	176 / B	192 / C	208 / D	224 / E	240 / F
0	0	Ç	É	á	▓	└	╨	∝	≡
1	1	ü	æ	í	▒	┴	╤	β	±
2	2	é	Æ	ó	▓	┬	╥	Γ	≥
3	3	â	ô	ú	│	├	╙	π	≤
4	4	ä	ö	ñ	┤	─	╘	Σ	∫
5	5	à	ò	Ñ	╡	┼	╒	σ	∫
6	6	å	û	ª	╢	╞	╓	µ	÷
7	7	ç	ù	º	╖	╟	╫	τ	≈
8	8	ê	ÿ	¿	╕	╚	╪	Φ	°
9	9	ë	Ö	⌐	╣	╔	┘	θ	•
10	A	è	Ü	¬	║	╩	┌	Ω	·
11	B	ï	¢	½	╗	╦	█	δ	√
12	C	î	£	¼	╝	╠	▄	∞	ⁿ
13	D	ì	¥	¡	╜	═	▌	φ	²
14	E	Ä	₧	«	╛	╬	▐	∈	■
15	F	Å	ƒ	»	┐	╧	▀	∩	BLANK 'FF'

IBM PC Technical Reference Manual, pp. 7-12–7-13, © 1984 International Business Machines Corporation.

TURBO PASCAL
SYNTAX DIAGRAMS

block

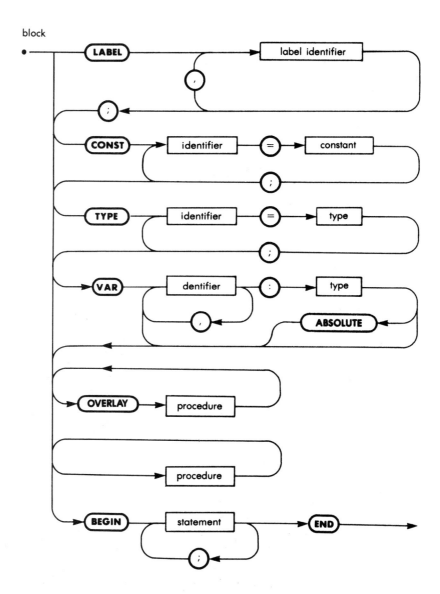

constant

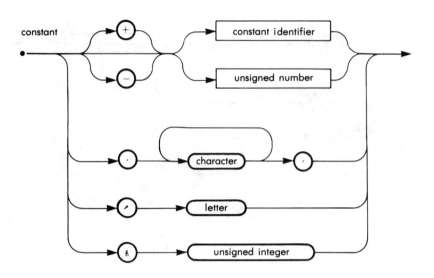

expression

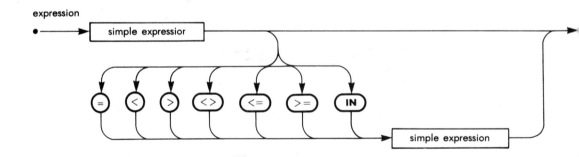

factor

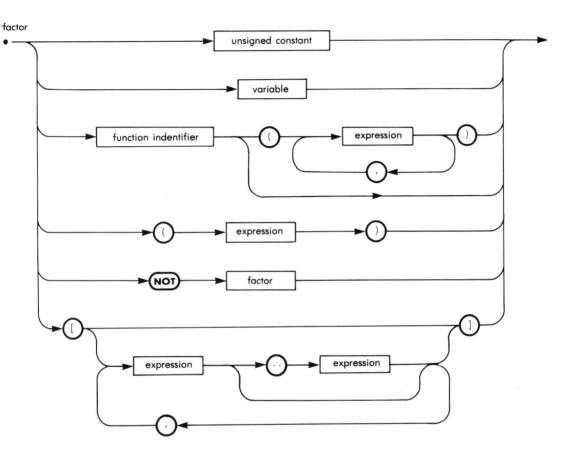

field list

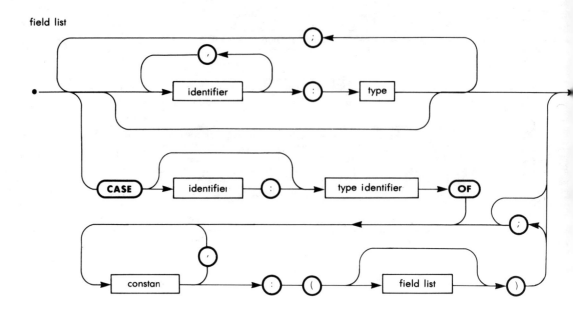

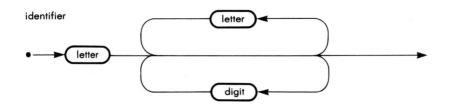

identifier

label identifier

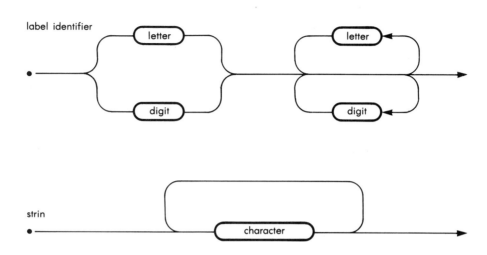

strin

parameter list

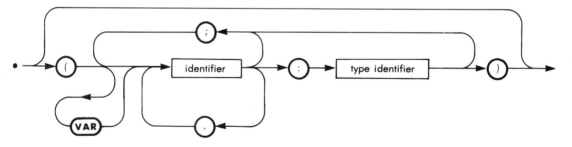

program

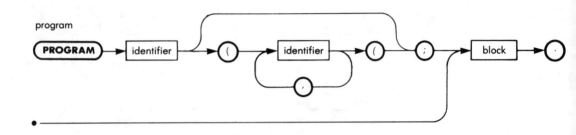

proce

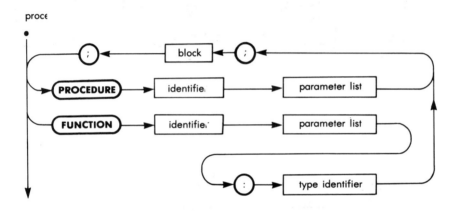

simple expression

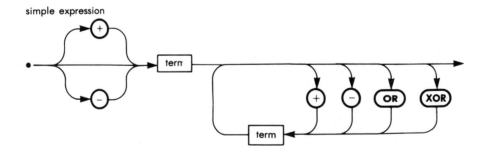

simple type

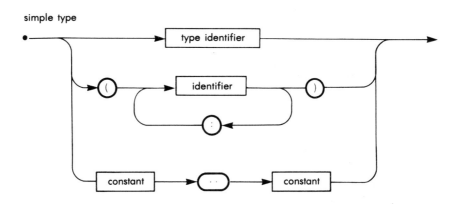

statement

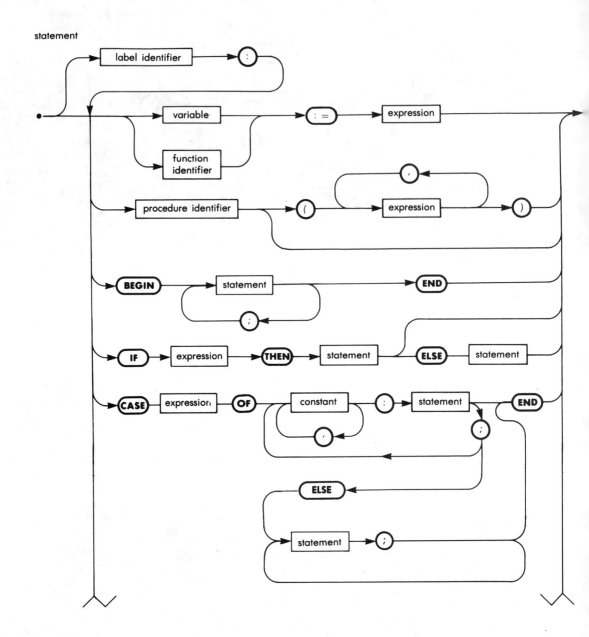

statement (cont.)

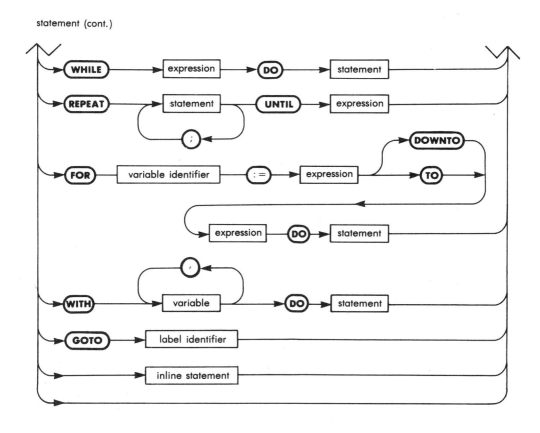

term

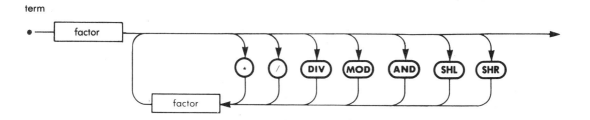

type

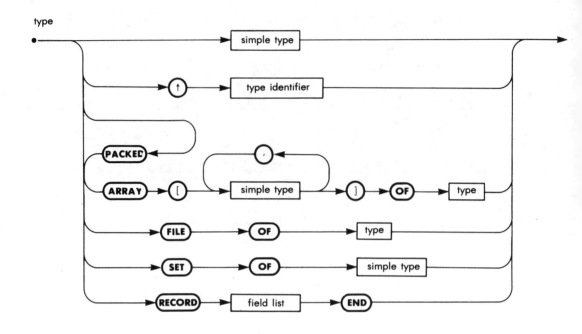

unsigned constant

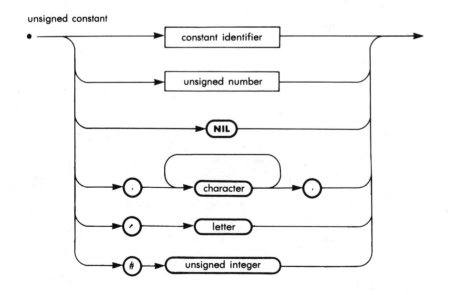

unsigned integer

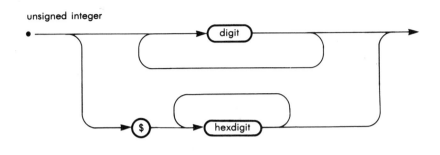

unsigned number

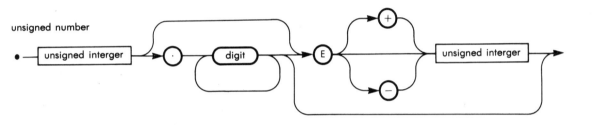

variable

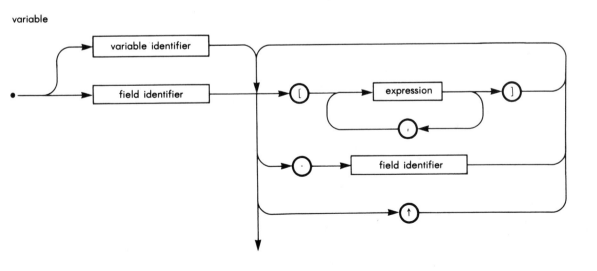

inline statement

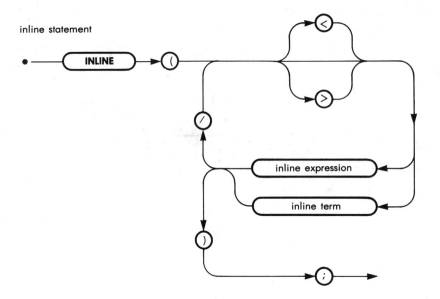

inline expression

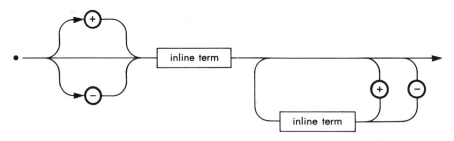

inline term

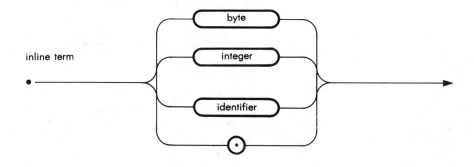

TURBO PASCAL
LIMITATIONS

# characters in a	STRING	255
# elements in a	SET	256
Maximum value of a	REAL	1E + 38, 11 digits
Minimum value of a	REAL	1E – 38, 11 digits
Maximum nesting of	WITH	9
Maximum code size	BYTES	64K *
Maximum variable	BYTES	64K *
Maximum open	FILES	16 - MS/PC-DOS 2.0 +

*CP/M 80 maximum 64k total for program and variables combined.

TURBO PASCAL
INTRINSICS

INTRINSIC	TYPE	VERSION(S)
ADDR	FUNCTION	ALL
APPEND	PROCEDURE	3.0 +
ASSIGN	PROCEDURE	ALL
AUX	STDFILE	ALL
AUXINPTR	SYSPTR	ALL
AUXOUTPTR	SYSPTR	ALL
BIOS	PROCEDURE	CP/M
BDOS	PROCEDURE	CP/M
BLACK	SYSCONST	IBM 2.0 +
BLUE	SYSCONST	IBM 2.0 +
BLOCKREAD	PROCEDURE	ALL
BLOCKWRITE	PROCEDURE	ALL
BROWN	SYSCONST	IBM 2.0 +
BUFLEN	SYSVAR	ALL
BW40	SYSCONST	IBM 2.0 +
BW80	SYSCONST	IBM 2.0 +
BYTE	TYPE	ALL
C40	SYSCONST	IBM 2.0 +
C80	SYSCONST	IBM 2.0 +
CHAIN	PROCEDURE	ALL
CHDIR	PROCEDURE	IBM 3.0 +
CLOSE	PROCEDURE	ALL
CLREOL	PROCEDURE	ALL
CLRSCR	PROCEDURE	ALL
CON	STDFILE	ALL
CONCAT	FUNCTION	ALL
CONINPTR	SYSPTR	ALL
CONOUTPTR	SYSPTR	ALL
CONSTPTR	SYSPTR	ALL
COPY	FUNCTION	ALL
CRTEXIT	PROCEDURE	ALL
CRTINIT	PROCEDURE	ALL
CSEG	FUNCTION	16-bit
CYAN	SYSCONST	IBM 2.0 +
DARKGRAY	SYSCONST	IBM 2.0 +
DELAY	PROCEDURE	ALL

INTRINSIC	TYPE	VERSION(S)
DELETE	PROCEDURE	ALL
DELLINE	PROCEDURE	ALL
DRAW	PROCEDURE	IBM 2.0+
DSEG	FUNCTION	16-bit
ERASE	PROCEDURE	ALL
EXECUTE	PROCEDURE	CP/M
EXIT	PROCEDURE	3.0+
FILEPOS	FUNCTION	MS/PC-DOS
FILESIZE	FUNCTION	MS/PC-DOS
FILLCHAR	PROCEDURE	ALL
FLUSH	PROCEDURE	MS/PC-DOS
FRAC	FUNCTION	ALL
FREEMEM	PROCEDURE	2.0+
GETDIR	PROCEDURE	IBM 3.0+
GETMEM	PROCEDURE	ALL
GOTOXY	PROCEDURE	ALL
GRAPHBACKGROUND	PROCEDURE	IBM 2.0+
GRAPHCOLORMODE	PROCEDURE	IBM 2.0+
GRAPHMODE	PROCEDURE	IBM 2.0+
GRAPHWINDOW	PROCEDURE	IBM 2.0+
GREEN	SYSCONST	IBM 2.0+
HALT	PROCEDURE	3.0+
HEAPPTR	SYSPTR	ALL
HI	FUNCTION	ALL
HIRES	PROCEDURE	IBM 2.0+
HIRESCOLOR	PROCEDURE	IBM 2.0+
INSERT	PROCEDURE	ALL
INSLINE	PROCEDURE	ALL
INTR	PROCEDURE	16-bit
IORESULT	SYSVAR	ALL
KBD	STDFILE	ALL
KEYPRESSED	FUNCTION	ALL
LENGTH	FUNCTION	ALL
LIGHTBLUE	SYSCONST	IBM 2.0+
LIGHTCYAN	SYSCONST	IBM 2.0+
LIGHTGRAY	SYSCONST	IBM 2.0+

INTRINSIC	TYPE	VERSION(S)
LIGHTGREEN	SYSCONST	IBM 2.0 +
LIGHTMAGENTA	SYSCONST	IBM 2.0 +
LIGHTRED	SYSCONST	IBM 2.0 +
LO	FUNCTION	ALL
LONGFILESIZE	FUNCTION	IBM 3.0 +
LONGFILEPOS	FUNCTION	IBM 3.0 +
LONGSEEK	PROCEDURE	IBM 3.0 +
LOWVIDEO	PROCEDURE	ALL
LST	STDFILE	ALL
LSTOUTPTR	STDPTR	ALL
MAGENTA	SYSCONST	IBM 2.0 +
MARK	PROCEDURE	ALL
MAXAVAIL	FUNCTION	ALL
MEM	SYSARRAY	ALL
MEMAVAIL	FUNCTION	ALL
MEMW	SYSARRAY	16-bit
MKDIR	PROCEDURE	IBM 3.0 +
MOVE	PROCEDURE	ALL
MSDOS	PROCEDURE	MS/PC-DOS
NORMVIDEO	PROCEDURE	ALL
NOSOUND	PROCEDURE	IBM 2.0 +
OFS	FUNCTION	16-bit
OVRDRIVE	PROCEDURE	CP/M-86
OVRPATH	PROCEDURE	IBM 3.0 +
PALETTE	PROCEDURE	IBM 2.0 +
PARAMCOUNT	FUNCTION	3.0 +
PARAMSTR	FUNCTION	3.0 +
PI	SYSCONST	ALL
PLOT	PROCEDURE	ALL
PORT	SYSARRAY	ALL
PORTW	SYSARRAY	16-bit
POS	FUNCTION	ALL
PTR	FUNCTION	ALL
RANDOM	FUNCTION	ALL
RANDOMIZE	PROCEDURE	ALL
RED	SYSCONST	IBM 2.0 +

INTRINSIC	TYPE	VERSION(S)
RELEASE	PROCEDURE	ALL
RENAME	PROCEDURE	ALL
RMDIR	PROCEDURE	IBM 3.0+
SEEK	PROCEDURE	MS/PC-DOS
SEG	FUNCTION	16-bit
SIZEOF	FUNCTION	ALL
SOUND	PROCEDURE	IBM 2.0+
SSEG	FUNCTION	16-bit
STR	PROCEDURE	ALL
SWAP	FUNCTION	ALL
TEXTBACKGROUND	PROCEDURE	IBM 2.0+
TEXTCOLOR	PROCEDURE	IBM 2.0+
TEXTMODE	PROCEDURE	IBM 2.0+
TRM	STDFILE	ALL
TRUNCATE	PROCEDURE	IBM 3.0+
UPCASE	FUNCTION	ALL
USR	STDFILE	ALL
USRINPTR	SYSPTR	ALL
USROUTPTR	SYSPTR	ALL
VAL	PROCEDURE	ALL
WHEREX	FUNCTION	2.0+
WHEREY	FUNCTION	2.0+
WHITE	SYSCONST	IBM 2.0+
WINDOW	PROCEDURE	2.0+
YELLOW	SYSCONST	IBM 2.0+

The list above does not include the Turtle Graphics and IBM Extended Graphics intrinsics in Turbo Pascal 3.0.

REFERENCES

[1]   **Pascal User Manual and Report.** Kathleen Jensen and Niklaus Wirth.
      Springer-Verlag (1974-Revised Edition 1978).

[2]   **A Primer on Pascal.** R. Conway, D. Gries, E.C. Zimmerman.
      Winthrop Publishers (1976).

[3]   **Microcomputer Problem Solving Using Pascal.** Kenneth L. Bowles.
      Springer-Verlag (1977).

[4]   **Pascal—An Introduction to Methodical Programming.** W. Findlay, D.A. Watt.
      Computer Science Press (1978).

[5]   **An Introduction to Programming and Problem Solving with Pascal.**
      M. Schneider, S. Weingart, D. Perlman.
      John Wiley & Sons (1978).

[6]   **Programming in Pascal.** P. Grogono.
      Addison Wesley (1978-Revised Edition 1980).

[7]   **A Practical Introduction to Pascal.** I.R. Wilson and A.M. Addyman.
      Springer-Verlag (1978).

[8]   **Turbo Pascal Version 3.0 Reference Manual.**
      Borland International (1983, 1984, 1985).

[9]   **Structured Programming and Problem-Solving with Pascal.** Richard B. Kieburtz.
      Prentice Hall (1978).

[10] **Beginner's Manual for the UCSD Pascal System.** Kenneth L. Bowles.
      Byte Books, McGraw-Hill (1979).

[11] **Pascal with Style: Programming Proverbs.** M. Ledgard, J. Hueras, P. Nagin.
      Hayden (1979).

[12] **The Pascal Handbook.** Jacques Tiberghien.
      Sybex (1980).

[13] **A Discipline of Programming.** E.W. Dijkstra.
      Prentice Hall (1976).

[14] **Structured Programming.** O.J. Dahl, E.W. Dijkstra, C.A.R. Hoare.
      Academic Press (1972).

[15] **Systematic Programming—An Introduction.** N. Wirth.
      Prentice Hall (1973).

[16] **Introduction to Pascal.** J. Welsh, J. Elder.
      Prentice Hall (1979).

[17] **Techniques of Program Structure and Design.** E. Yourdon.
      Prentice Hall (1975).

[18] **The Art of Computer Programming, Vol. III (Searching and Sorting).**
      D. Knuth.
      Addison Wesley (1973)

[19] **Pascal Programs for Scientists and Engineers.** A. Miller.
      Sybex (1981).

[20] **Fifty Pascal Programs.** R. Zaks and R. Langer.
      Sybex (1981).

[21] **Algorithms + Data Structures = Programs.** N. Wirth.
Prentice-Hall (1976).

[22] **A Primer on Pascal.** R. Conway, D. Gries, and E. Zimmerman.
Winthrop (1976).

[23] **The Elements of Programming Style.** B. Kernighan and P. Plauger.
McGraw-Hill (1974, 1978).

[24] **The Byte Book of Pascal.** B. Liffick (ed).
BYTE Books (1979).

[25] **Pascal.** P. Chirlian.
Matrix Publishers (1980).

[26] **Software Tools in Pascal.** B. Kernighan and P. Plauger.
Addison Wesley (1981).

[27] **From Basic to Pascal.** R. Anderson.
TAB Books (1982).

[28] **Some Common Pascal Programs.**
Osborne/McGraw-Hill (1982).

[29] **Elementary Pascal.** H. Ledgard and A. Singer.
Vintage Press (1982).

[30] **Fundamentals of Microcomputer Programming, Including Pascal.** D. R. McGlynn.
Wiley - Interscience (1982).

[31] **Practical Pascal Programs.** G. Davidson.
Osborne/McGraw-Hill (1982).

[32] **Standard Pascal User Reference Manual.** D. Cooper.
Norton (1983).

[33] **Doing Business with Pascal.** R. Hergert and D. Hergert.
Sybex (1983).

[34] **Fundamentals of Data Structures in Pascal.** E. Horowitz and S. Sahni.
Computer Science Press (1976 rev 1984).

[35] **Pascal for Programmers.** O. Lecarme and J. Nebut.
McGraw-Hill (1984).

[36] **Common Algorithms in Pascal.** D. Moffat.
Prentice-Hall (1984).

[37] **Advanced Pascal Programming Techniques.** P. Sand.
Osborne/McGraw-Hill (1984).

[38] **Programming Your Own Adventure Games in Pascal.** R. C. Vile Jr.
TAB Books (1984).

[39] **Introduction to Turbo Pascal.** D. Stivison.
Sybex (1985).

[40] **Using Turbo Pascal.** S. Wood.
Osborne/McGraw-Hill (1985).

[41] **Complete Turbo Pascal.** J. Duntemann.
       Scott, Foresman & Co. (1985).

[42] **Programming with Turbo Pascal.** D. Carroll.
       BYTE/McGraw-Hill (1985).

ANSWERS TO SELECTED EXERCISES

"Console-toi, tu ne me chercherais pas si tu ne m'avais trouvé."

"Don't worry, you wouldn't be looking for me if you hadn't already found me."

Pascal, **Pensées**, *553 (Brunsehvieg edition).*

The program listings in this appendix are written in Standard Pascal. As some Standard Pascal I/O operations are not compatible with Turbo Pascal, those sections of code that must be modified for use with Turbo Pascal are boxed, and the replacement Turbo Pascal code (if needed) is provided immediately following each exercise.

CHAPTER 1 BASIC CONCEPTS

Exercise 1-1:

```
PROGRAM PROD(INPUT,OUTPUT);
VAR
  A,B, PRODUCT : INTEGER;

BEGIN
  WRITELN('Enter two numbers ... ');
  READLN(A,B);
  PRODUCT := A * B ;
  WRITELN('The product of ',A,' and ',B,' is ',PRODUCT)
END.
```

Exercise 1-2:

```
PROGRAM SUM3(INPUT,OUTPUT);
VAR
  A,B,C,TOTAL : INTEGER;

BEGIN
  WRITELN('Enter 3 numbers ... ');
  READLN(A,B,C);
  TOTAL := A + B + C;
  WRITELN('The sum of ',A,' and ',B,' and ',C,' is ',TOTAL)
END.
```

Exercise 1-3:

No.

Exercise 1-5:

Yes. Comments may be placed anywhere and are completely ignored during execution.

Exercise 1-6:

No. An algorithm is an unambiguous, step-by-step description of the solution to a problem. (It must terminate in a finite number of steps). An algorithm may be presented in any language and is not written in a programming language. However, a well-written algorithm can be easily translated into computer instructions.

CHAPTER 2 PROGRAMMING IN PASCAL

Exercise 2-1:

1. Yes   2. No   3. Yes   4. No   5. No

Exercise 2-2:

All three will be considered as the same identifier (PERSONNO) since only the first eight characters are considered.

See p.26.

CHAPTER 3 SCALARS AND OPERATORS

Exercise 3-2:

No. It may be a constant or another type.

Exercise 3-3:

1. Yes   2. Yes   3. No (comma)   4. No (period)

Exercise 3-4:

1. 32   2. 1   3. 32

Exercise 3-5:

1. No (period missing)   2. No (comma)   3. Yes   4. No

Exercise 3-7:

1. FALSE   2. TRUE   3. TRUE

Exercise 3-8:

TWENTY FOUR must be declared as a constant and assigned a value or TWENTY FOUR must be declared as a variable and assigned a value.

```
CONST    TWENTYFOUR = 24;              VAR TWENTYFOUR : INTEGER
BEGIN                          or      BEGIN
        A :=    TWENTYFOUR;                    A : = TWENTYFOUR
```

Exercise 3-9:

None

Exercise 3-10:

1. Boolean   2. real   3. Boolean   4. integer

Exercise 3-11:

1. 1   2. 2   3. 2   4. 2

Exercise 3-12:

integer : 1, − 5,3
real   : 2.0,3.6,5.75
Boolean : TRUE,FALSE
char   : A,b,c,H,w,?

CHAPTER 4 EXPRESSIONS AND STATEMENTS

Exercise 4-1:

1. 3   2. − 2.2   3. 196

Exercise 4-2:

1. 9   2. 0   3. − 6.0   4. 32

Exercise 4-3:

1. Yes (real)   2. No (should be B := A + 2;)
3. No (assignment to a constant)   4. No (= missing)

Exercise 4-4:

1. No (should be A := 2 * (− 3))
2. No (should be (− 6.73) * 2)
3. Yes (Boolean expression)
4. No (DIV is for integers)
5. No (only one := per statement)

Exercise 4-5:

1. (3 * SQR(X)) + (2/SQR(X))
2. ABS(4 * A)
3. SQRT((6 * A) - (2 * SQR(X))
Note: can you remove some parentheses, using the rules of precedence?

Exercise 4-6:

```
FALSE
TRUE
TRUE
FALSE
FALSE
TRUE
```

CHAPTER 5 INPUT AND OUTPUT

Exercise 5-1:

```
PROGRAM SQUARES(OUTPUT);
VAR
   INT1 : INTEGER;

BEGIN
   WRITELN('Integer','   ','Square');
   INT1 := 1;
   WRITELN(INT1: 7,'   ',SQR(INT1): 7);
   INT1 := 2;
   WRITELN(INT1: 7,'   ',SQR(INT1): 7);
   INT1 := 3;
   WRITELN(INT1: 7,'   ',SQR(INT1): 7);
   INT1 := 4;
   WRITELN(INT1: 7,'   ',SQR(INT1): 7);
   INT1 := 5;
   WRITELN(INT1: 7,'   ',SQR(INT1): 7);

   INT1 := 6;
   WRITELN(INT1: 7,'   ',SQR(INT1): 7);
   INT1 := 7;
   WRITELN(INT1: 7,'   ',SQR(INT1): 7);
   INT1 := 8;
   WRITELN(INT1: 7,'   ',SQR(INT1): 7);
   INT1 := 9;
   WRITELN(INT1: 7,'   ',SQR(INT1): 7);
   INT1 := 10;
   WRITELN(INT1: 7,'   ',SQR(INT1): 7)
END.
```

Exercise 5-2:

```
PROGRAM REALREAD(INPUT,OUTPUT);
VAR
   REAL1,REAL2,REAL3,REAL4,REAL5,REAL6,REAL7,REAL8,REAL9,REAL10:REAL;

BEGIN
   WRITELN('Enter 10 reals: ');
   READLN(REAL1,REAL2,REAL3,REAL4,REAL5,REAL6,REAL7,REAL8,REAL9,REAL10);
   WRITELN(REAL10,REAL9,REAL8,REAL7,REAL6,REAL5,REAL4,REAL3,REAL2,REAL1)
END.
```

Exercise 5-4:

```
PROGRAM SQRSANDSQRTS(OUTPUT);
VAR
  INT1 : INTEGER;

BEGIN
  WRITELN('|--------|---------|----------------------|');
  WRITELN('| INTEGER | SQUARE | SQR ROOT             |');
  WRITELN('|--------|---------|----------------------|');

  INT1 := 1;
  WRITELN('| ',INT1:7,' | ',SQR(INT1):7,' | ',SQRT(INT1),'      |');
  WRITELN('|--------|---------|----------------------|');

  INT1 := 2;
  WRITELN('| ',INT1:7,' | ',SQR(INT1):7,' | ',SQRT(INT1),'      |');
  WRITELN('|--------|---------|----------------------|');

  INT1 := 3;
  WRITELN('| ',INT1:7,' | ',SQR(INT1):7,' | ',SQRT(INT1),'      |');
  WRITELN('|--------|---------|----------------------|');

  INT1 := 4;
  WRITELN('| ',INT1:7,' | ',SQR(INT1):7,' | ',SQRT(INT1),'      |');
  WRITELN('|--------|---------|----------------------|');

  INT1 := 5;
  WRITELN('| ',INT1:7,' | ',SQR(INT1):7,' | ',SQRT(INT1),'      |');
  WRITELN('|--------|---------|----------------------|');

  INT1 := 6;
  WRITELN('| ',INT1:7,' | ',SQR(INT1):7,' | ',SQRT(INT1),'      |');
  WRITELN('|--------|---------|----------------------|');

  INT1 := 7;
  WRITELN('| ',INT1:7,' | ',SQR(INT1):7,' | ',SQRT(INT1),'      |');
  WRITELN('|--------|---------|----------------------|');

  INT1 := 8;
  WRITELN('| ',INT1:7,' | ',SQR(INT1):7,' | ',SQRT(INT1),'      |');
  WRITELN('|--------|---------|----------------------|');

  INT1 := 9;
  WRITELN('| ',INT1:7,' | ',SQR(INT1):7,' | ',SQRT(INT1),'      |');
  WRITELN('|--------|---------|----------------------|');

  INT1 := 10;
  WRITELN('| ',INT1:7,' | ',SQR(INT1):7,' | ',SQRT(INT1),'      |');
  WRITELN('|--------|---------|----------------------|')
END.
```

Exercise 5-7:

1.1	6.49	17.260	27	2
2.3	8.60	5.154	1	2
3.2	7.50	4.108	8	− 10

CHAPTER 6 CONTROL STRUCTURES

Exercise 6-1:

```
PROGRAM SUM(INPUT,OUTPUT);
VAR
  I,J,N : INTEGER;

BEGIN
  WRITE('Enter an integer: ');
  READLN(N);
  J := 0;
  FOR I := 1 TO N DO
    J := J + I;
  WRITELN('The sum of the first ',N:0,' integers is ',J:0,'.');

  {Notice how using a field width of 0 forces integer N to be printed
   without any blank spaces in front of it. This makes it possible to
   put its value in the middle of a sentence and not have strange gaps.}

  WRITELN;
  WRITELN;
  WRITELN
END.
```

Exercise 6-5:

```
PROGRAM AVERAGE(OUTPUT);
VAR
  SUM, NUMBER : INTEGER;
  AVERAGE : REAL;

BEGIN
  SUM := 0;
  NUMBER := 1;

  REPEAT
    SUM := SUM + NUMBER;
    NUMBER := NUMBER + 1
  UNTIL NUMBER > 25;

  AVERAGE := SUM/25;

  WRITELN('The average of the first 25 integers is ',AVERAGE:0:1,'.');

  WRITELN;
  WRITELN;
  WRITELN
END.
```

Exercise 6-7:

```
PROGRAM AVERAGE(INPUT,OUTPUT);
VAR
  SUM, NUMBER, MAX : INTEGER;
  AVERAGE : REAL;

BEGIN
  SUM := 0;
  NUMBER := 0;

  WRITE('Enter an integer: ');
  READLN(MAX);

  REPEAT
    NUMBER := NUMBER + 1
    SUM := SUM + NUMBER;
  UNTIL NUMBER >= MAX;

  AVERAGE := SUM/NUMBER;

  WRITELN('The average of the first ',MAX,' integers is ',AVERAGE:0:1,'.');

  WRITELN;
  WRITELN;
  WRITELN
END.
```

Exercise 6-8:

```
PROGRAM AVERAGEINPUT(INPUT,OUTPUT);
VAR
  SUM, NUMBER, INT1, N : INTEGER;
  AVERAGE : REAL;

BEGIN
  SUM := 0;
  NUMBER := 0;

  WRITE('Enter the number of integers you wish to average: ');
  READLN(N);

  WRITELN;
  WRITELN;
```

```
    WRITELN('Enter the integers. More than one line of input OK: ');

    WHILE NUMBER < N DO
    BEGIN
      IF NOT EOLN THEN
      BEGIN
        READ(INT1);
        SUM := SUM + INT1;
        NUMBER := NUMBER + 1
      END;
      IF EOLN THEN
        READLN
    END;
```

```
      AVERAGE := SUM/N;

      WRITELN;
      WRITELN('The average of the entered numbers is ',AVERAGE:0:1,'.');

      WRITELN;
      WRITELN;
      WRITELN
END.
```

Replacement Turbo Pascal Code:

```
      WRITELN ('Enter the integers, one to a line.');
      WHILE NUMBER < N DO
      BEGIN
        READLN(INT1);
        SUM := SUM + INT1;
        NUMBER := NUMBER + 1
      END;
```

Exercise 6-10:

```
PROGRAM FILTER(INPUT,OUTPUT);
VAR
   NUMBER, COUNTA, COUNTR, LOW, HIGH : INTEGER;

BEGIN
   REPEAT
     WRITELN;
     WRITELN;
     WRITELN('Enter the MAX value followed by the MIN value for the filter.');
     WRITE('Enter two integers separated by a space: ');

     READLN(HIGH,LOW);
     IF HIGH <= LOW THEN WRITELN('Entry error!')

   UNTIL HIGH > LOW;

   COUNTA := 0;
   COUNTR := 0;

   WRITELN;
   WRITELN;
   WRITELN('Enter a series of numbers, one to a line. Halt by inputting a 0.');

   REPEAT
     READLN(NUMBER);
     IF NUMBER < > 0 THEN
     IF (NUMBER < LOW) OR (NUMBER > HIGH) THEN
     BEGIN
       COUNTR := COUNTR + 1;
       WRITELN('Illegal entry.')
     END
     ELSE
       COUNTA := COUNTA + 1
   UNTIL NUMBER = 0;

   WRITELN;
   WRITELN;
   WRITELN('Number of illegal entries is ',COUNTR,'.');
   WRITELN;
   WRITELN('Number of legal entries is ',COUNTA,'.')
END.
```

Exercise 6-11:

```
PROGRAM CONVERTDATE(INPUT,OUTPUT);
VAR
  MONTH, DAY, YEAR : INTEGER;

BEGIN
  REPEAT
    WRITE('Enter a date in the form MM DD YYYY: ');

    READLN(MONTH, DAY, YEAR);

    IF (MONTH > 12) OR (MONTH < 1) THEN
        WRITELN('ERROR - NO SUCH MONTH')
    ELSE
      CASE MONTH OF
         1: WRITE('January ');
         2: WRITE('February ');
         3: WRITE('March ');
         4: WRITE('April ');
         5: WRITE('May ');
         6: WRITE('June ');
         7: WRITE('July ');
         8: WRITE('August ');
         9: WRITE('September ');
        10: WRITE('October ');
        11: WRITE('November ');
        12: WRITE('December ')
      END;

    IF (DAY > 31) OR (DAY < 1) THEN
      WRITE('ERROR - no such day!')
    ELSE
      WRITE(DAY:0,', ');

    WRITE(ABS(YEAR):0);
    IF YEAR < 0 THEN
      WRITE(' B.C.');

    WRITELN;
  UNTIL (month = 0) or (day = 0) or (year = 0);
  WRITELN
END.
```

Exercise 6-12:

```
PROGRAM WRITEMONTH(INPUT,OUTPUT);
VAR
   MONTH, SECONDCHAR, THIRDCHAR : CHAR;
   MONTHLETTERS : SET OF CHAR;

BEGIN

   MONTHLETTERS := ['J','F','M','A','S','O','N','D'];
   WRITE('Enter the first three letters of a month in uppercase: ');

   READ(MONTH, SECONDCHAR, THIRDCHAR);

   IF NOT (MONTH IN MONTHLETTERS) THEN
   BEGIN
      WRITELN;
      WRITELN('Error. No such month.')
   END
   ELSE
      CASE MONTH OF
      'J'    : IF SECONDCHAR = 'A' THEN WRITE('UARY ')
                  ELSE IF THIRDCHAR = 'N' THEN WRITE('E ')
                  ELSE WRITE('Y ');

      'F'    : WRITE('RUARY ');
      'M'    : IF THIRDCHAR = 'R' THEN WRITE('CH ');
      'A'    : IF SECONDCHAR = 'P' THEN WRITE('IL ')
                  ELSE WRITE('UST ');

      'S'    : WRITE('TEMBER ');
      'O'    : WRITE('OBER ');
      'N','D' : WRITE('EMBER ')
   END;
   WRITELN
END.
```

Exercise 6-13:

```
PROGRAM TEMPERATURE(INPUT,OUTPUT);
VAR
   TEMP,TEMP1,TEMP2, I : INTEGER;
   COLUMN1,COLUMN2 : REAL;
   SCALE : CHAR;

BEGIN
   WRITELN('Temperature conversion table program');
   REPEAT
      WRITELN;
      WRITELN('Enter two numbers and a letter.');
      WRITELN('The two numbers are the temperature range for the table.');
      WRITELN('The letter must be either a "C" or "F" representing the ');
      WRITELN('correct scale (Celsius or Farenheit) for the input numbers.');
```

```
WRITE('Enter data in the form: NN NN L: ');
READLN(TEMP1,TEMP2,SCALE)
```

```
   UNTIL (SCALE = 'C') OR (SCALE = 'F');

   WRITELN;
   WRITELN;
   WRITELN;

   IF TEMP1 > TEMP2 THEN
   BEGIN
     TEMP := TEMP1;
     TEMP1 := TEMP2;
     TEMP2 := TEMP
   END;

   WRITELN;
   IF SCALE = 'C' THEN
     WRITELN('  Celsius':9,'Farenheit':13)
   ELSE WRITELN('Farenheit':9,'Celsius':13);
   WRITELN;

   FOR I := TEMP1 TO TEMP2 DO
   BEGIN
     COLUMN1 := I;
     IF SCALE = 'C' THEN
       COLUMN2 := (I * 9/5)+32
     ELSE
       COLUMN2 := (I-32)* 5/9;
     WRITELN(COLUMN1:9:2,'  ',COLUMN2:9:2)
   END;

   WRITELN;
   WRITELN
END.
```

Replacement Turbo Pascal Code:

```
WRITE('TEMP1 >> ');
READLN(TEMP1);
WRITE('TEMP2 >> ');
READLN(TEMP2);
WRITE('SCALE >> ');
READLN(SCALE);
SCALE := UPCASE(SCALE)
```

Exercise 6-14:

```
PROGRAM GRAPHSINE(OUTPUT);
CONST
  ASTERISK = '*';
  BLANK = ' ';
  DASH = '-';
  LINE = '|';
  PI = 3.14159265;          {not required if PI is a system constant}
  LINELEN = 75;             {width of page}
  TOP = 12;                 {height of half-screen}
  DEGREESPERPOINT = 6;      {number of degrees / point in graph}

VAR
  I1,I2,SINEVALUE : INTEGER;
  PRINTVAR : CHAR;

BEGIN     {do upper (Y>0) half or curve}
  FOR I1 := TOP DOWNTO 1 DO
  BEGIN
    FOR I2 := 0 TO LINELEN DO
    BEGIN
      SINEVALUE := ROUND(SIN(DEGREESPERPOINT * I2 * PI/180) * TOP);

        { We have:
        (fact * I2) since we are plotting one point every
                    DEGREESPERPOINT degrees.
        (... * PI/180) to convert radians to degrees.
        (... * top) to scale the graph for our display size. }

      IF SINEVALUE = I1 THEN
        PRINTVAR := ASTERISK
      ELSE
        PRINTVAR := BLANK;

      IF (I2 = 0) THEN
        PRINTVAR := LINE;
      IF (I2 = 0) AND  (I1 = TOP) THEN
        PRINTVAR := '1';
      WRITE(PRINTVAR)
    END;
    WRITELN
  END;

  FOR I2 := 0 TO LINELEN DO  {center (Y=0) line}
  BEGIN
    IF (I2 MOD 10 = 0) THEN PRINTVAR := LINE;
    IF ROUND(SIN(DEGREESPERPOINT * I2 * PI/180) * TOP) = 0 THEN
      PRINTVAR := ASTERISK
    ELSE
      PRINTVAR := DASH;
    IF I2 = 0 THEN
      PRINTVAR := '0';
    WRITE(PRINTVAR)
  END;
  WRITELN;
```

```
        FOR Il := 1 TO TOP DO
        BEGIN
          FOR I2 := 0 TO LINELEN DO
          BEGIN
            SINEVALUE := ROUND(SIN(DEGREESPERPOINT * I2 * PI/180) * TOP);

            IF SINEVALUE = (-Il) THEN
              PRINTVAR := ASTERISK
            ELSE
              PRINTVAR := BLANK;

            IF (I2 = 0) THEN
              PRINTVAR := LINE;
            IF (I2 = 0) AND  (Il = TOP) THEN
              PRINTVAR := '1';
            WRITE(PRINTVAR)
          END;
          WRITELN
        END
      END.
```

(Alternate Solution):

```
PROGRAM GRAPHSINE(OUTPUT);
CONST
  ASTERISK = '*';
  BLANK = ' ';
  DASH = '-';
  LINE = '|';
  PI = 3.14159265;          {not required if PI is a system constant}
  LINELEN = 80;             {display width}
  DEGREESPERPOINT = 6;      {degrees / point to plot}

VAR
  X,Y,I,J : INTEGER;

BEGIN
  FOR X := -45 TO 45 DO
  BEGIN
    Y := ROUND(SIN(DEGREESPERPOINT * X * PI/180) *
               (LINELEN DIV 2 - 1)) + (LINELEN DIV 2);
    IF X = 0 THEN
      FOR I := 1 TO LINELEN DO
        IF I = Y THEN
          WRITE(ASTERISK)
        ELSE
          WRITE(DASH)
    ELSE
    BEGIN
      IF (LINELEN DIV 2) > Y THEN J := (LINELEN DIV 2)
      ELSE J := Y;
      FOR I := 1 TO J DO
        IF I = Y THEN
          WRITE(ASTERISK)
        ELSE
          IF I = (LINELEN DIV 2) THEN
            WRITE(LINE)
          ELSE WRITE(BLANK)
    END;
    WRITELN
  END
END.
```

Exercise 6-15:

```
PROGRAM SECRETCODE(INPUT,OUTPUT);
VAR
   INDEX : INTEGER;
   CH : CHAR;

BEGIN
   CH := ' ';
   INDEX := 0;
   WRITELN('Enter message: ');
   WHILE  NOT (EOLN AND EOF) AND (CH <> 'S') DO
      IF EOLN THEN
      BEGIN
         READLN;
         INDEX := 0
      END
      ELSE
      BEGIN
         READ(CH);
         INDEX := INDEX + 1
      END;

   WHILE NOT (EOLN AND EOF) AND (CH <> 'T') DO
      IF EOLN THEN
      BEGIN
         READLN;
         INDEX := 0
      END
      ELSE
      BEGIN
         READ(CH);
         INDEX := INDEX + 1
      END;

   WHILE NOT (EOLN AND EOF) AND (CH <> 'O') DO
      IF EOLN THEN
      BEGIN
         READLN;
         INDEX := 0
      END
      ELSE
      BEGIN
         READ(CH);
         INDEX := INDEX + 1
      END;

   WHILE NOT (EOLN AND EOF) AND (CH <> 'P') DO
      IF EOLN THEN
      BEGIN
         READLN;
         INDEX := 0
      END
      ELSE
      BEGIN
         READ(CH);
         INDEX := INDEX + 1
      END;

   WRITELN;
   WRITELN(' ':(INDEX-1),'^ Message completed');
   WRITELN(' ':(INDEX-1),'  at arrow.')
END.
```

Replacement Turbo Pascal Code:
(Replace entire program.)

```
PROGRAM SECRETCODE;
CONST
  EOL = #013;

VAR
  INDEX : INTEGER;
  CH : CHAR;

BEGIN
  CH := CHR(0);
  INDEX := 0;
  WRITELN('Enter message: ');
  WHILE  (UPCASE(CH) <> 'S') DO
    IF CH = EOL THEN
    BEGIN
      WRITELN;
      INDEX := 0
    END
    ELSE
    BEGIN
      READ(KBD,CH);
      WRITE(CH);
      INDEX := INDEX + 1
    END;
  WHILE (UPCASE(CH) <> 'T') DO
    IF CH = EOL THEN
    BEGIN
      WRITELN;
      INDEX := 0
    END
    ELSE
    BEGIN
      READ(KBD,CH);
      WRITE(CH);
      INDEX := INDEX + 1
    END;
  WHILE (UPCASE(CH) <> 'O') DO
    IF CH = EOL THEN
    BEGIN
      WRITELN;
      INDEX := 0
    END
    ELSE
    BEGIN
      READ(KBD,CH);
      WRITE(CH);
      INDEX := INDEX + 1
    END;
  WHILE (UPCASE(CH) <> 'P') DO
    IF CH = EOL THEN
    BEGIN
      WRITELN;
      INDEX := 0
    END
    ELSE
    BEGIN
      READ(KBD,CH);
      WRITE(CH);
      INDEX := INDEX + 1
    END;
```

```
   WRITELN;
   WRITELN(' ':(INDEX-1),'^ Message completed');
   WRITELN(' ':(INDEX-1),'  at arrow.')
END.
```

Exercise 6-16:

The ';' after THEN means that nothing will ever happen as a result of the IF clause. (This is called the empty statement). The following compound statement, delimited by BEGIN and END, will always be executed.

CHAPTER 7 DATA TYPES

Exercise 7-1:

```
PROGRAM PRINTCHARS(INPUT, OUTPUT);

PROCEDURE READANDPRINT;
VAR
   INDEX, NUMBER : INTEGER;
   CH : CHAR;

BEGIN     {READANDPRINT}
   WRITELN;
   WRITELN;
   WRITE('Enter a letter and a number: ');
   READLN(CH,NUMBER);
   WRITELN('Output is:  ');
   IF (NUMBER <= 80) AND (NUMBER > 0) THEN
     FOR INDEX := 1 TO NUMBER DO
       WRITE(CH)
   ELSE
     WRITELN('Illegal number.');
   WRITELN;
   WRITELN
END;      {READANDPRINT}

BEGIN     {MAIN}
   READANDPRINT
END.      {MAIN}
```

Exercise 7-2:

```
PROGRAM READINCHARS(INPUT,OUTPUT);
CONST
  BLANK = ' ';

VAR
  CHAR1,CHAR2,CHAR3,CHAR4,CHAR5,CHAR6,CHAR7,CHAR8,
  CHAR9,CHAR10 : CHAR;

PROCEDURE READCHARS;
```

```
  FUNCTION READIN : CHAR;
  VAR
    ONECHAR : CHAR;

  BEGIN     {READIN}
    REPEAT
      READ(ONECHAR)
    UNTIL (ONECHAR <> BLANK);

            {Reads blank spaces between characters until a non-blank
             one is reached, then that character is returned}

    READIN := ONECHAR
  END;      {READIN}
```

```
BEGIN  {READCHARS}
  WRITE('Enter ten characters: ');
  CHAR1 := READIN;
  CHAR2 := READIN;
  CHAR3 := READIN;
  CHAR4 := READIN;
  CHAR5 := READIN;
  CHAR6 := READIN;
  CHAR7 := READIN;
  CHAR8 := READIN;
  CHAR9 := READIN;
  CHAR10 := READIN
END;    {READCHARS}

PROCEDURE PRINTRESULT;
VAR
  NUMBEROFBLANKS : INTEGER;

PROCEDURE PRINTCHARS(THISCHAR : CHAR; NUMBER : INTEGER);
VAR
  I1 : INTEGER;

BEGIN    {PRINTCHARS}
  FOR I1 := 1 TO NUMBER DO
    WRITE(BLANK);

  FOR I1 := 1 TO 10 DO
```

```
      WRITE(THISCHAR);

   WRITELN
END;     {PRINTCHARS}

BEGIN    {PRINTRESULT}
   WRITELN;

   NUMBEROFBLANKS := 0;

   PRINTCHARS(CHAR1,NUMBEROFBLANKS);
   NUMBEROFBLANKS := 1;

   PRINTCHARS(CHAR2,NUMBEROFBLANKS);
   NUMBEROFBLANKS := 2;

   PRINTCHARS(CHAR3,NUMBEROFBLANKS);
   NUMBEROFBLANKS := 3;

   PRINTCHARS(CHAR4,NUMBEROFBLANKS);
   NUMBEROFBLANKS := 4;

   PRINTCHARS(CHAR5,NUMBEROFBLANKS);
   NUMBEROFBLANKS := 5;

   PRINTCHARS(CHAR6,NUMBEROFBLANKS);
   NUMBEROFBLANKS := 6;

   PRINTCHARS(CHAR7,NUMBEROFBLANKS);
   NUMBEROFBLANKS := 7;

   PRINTCHARS(CHAR8,NUMBEROFBLANKS);
   NUMBEROFBLANKS := 8;

   PRINTCHARS(CHAR9,NUMBEROFBLANKS);
   NUMBEROFBLANKS := 9;

   PRINTCHARS(CHAR10,NUMBEROFBLANKS)

END;     {PRINTRESULT}

BEGIN    {MAIN}
   READCHARS;
   PRINTRESULT
END.     {MAIN}
```

Replacement Turbo Pascal Code:

```
FUNCTION READIN : CHAR;
VAR
   ONECHAR : CHAR;
BEGIN
   REPEAT
     READ(KBD,ONECHAR)
   UNTIL (ONECHAR <> BLANK) AND (ONECHAR <> CHR(13) {EOL} );
   WRITE(ONECHAR);
   READIN := ONECHAR
END;
```

Exercise 7-3:

```
PROGRAM GIVEANINCH(INPUT,OUTPUT);
VAR
   INCHES : INTEGER;

{Note: if MAXINT in your Pascal is less than 65535, the
 CONVERT procedure shown must be modified to work correctly.}

PROCEDURE CONVERT(VAR INCHES : INTEGER);
VAR
  MILES, YARDS, FEET : INTEGER;

BEGIN   {CONVERT}
  MILES := INCHES DIV (12 * 5280);   {MODIFY if MAXINT < 65535}
  INCHES := INCHES MOD (12 * 5280);  {MODIFY if MAXINT < 65535}
  WRITE('Miles: ',MILES:0);

  YARDS := INCHES DIV (12 * 3);
  INCHES := INCHES MOD (12 * 3);
  WRITE(',   Yards: ',YARDS:0);

  FEET := INCHES DIV 12;
  INCHES := INCHES MOD 12;
  WRITE(',   feet: ',FEET:0);

  WRITE(',   inches: ',INCHES:0);
  WRITELN;
  WRITELN
END;    {CONVERT}

BEGIN   {MAIN}
  WRITE('Enter a distance in inches: ');
  READLN(INCHES);
  WRITELN;
  WRITELN;
  CONVERT(INCHES)
END.    {MAIN}
```

Replacement Turbo Pascal Code:

(Replace entire program.)

```
PROGRAM GIVEANINCH;
VAR
  INCHES : REAL;

PROCEDURE CONVERT(VAR RINCHES : REAL);
VAR
  INCHES, MILES, YARDS, FEET : INTEGER;

BEGIN
  MILES := ROUND(RINCHES / (12 * 5280.0));
  INCHES := ROUND(FRAC(RINCHES / (12 * 5280.0)) * (12 * 5280.0));
  WRITE('Miles: ',MILES);

  YARDS := INCHES DIV (12 * 3);
  INCHES := INCHES MOD (12 * 3);
  WRITE(',   Yards: ',YARDS);

  FEET := INCHES DIV 12;
  INCHES := INCHES MOD 12;
  WRITE(',   feet: ',FEET);
```

```
  WRITE(',   inches: ',INCHES);
  WRITELN;
  WRITELN
END;

BEGIN
  WRITE('Enter a distance in inches: ');
  READLN(INCHES);
  WRITELN;
  WRITELN;
  CONVERT(INCHES)
END.
```

Exercise 7-5:

G1 and G2 are global variables. Only G2 can be used in both VARVAL and SHOWSCOPE. G1 can only be used in VARVAL.

The program output is:

1
5
3
0
1
0

Exercise 7-8:

This program reverses text:

TYPE A WORD IN RESPONSE TO THE PROMPT ">".
TO STOP TYPE A BLANK.
> REDRO
  ORDER

Answers to Exercises 8.1 — 8.4!

CHAPTER 9 ARRAYS

Exercise 9-2:

```
PROGRAM WORDTODIGIT(INPUT,OUTPUT);
CONST
  BLANK = ' ';
  MAXWORDLEN = 10;
  NUMCOMPAREWORD = 11;

TYPE
  WORDINDEX = 1..MAXWORDLEN;
  WORDTYPE = ARRAY[WORDINDEX] OF CHAR;
  COMPARETYPE = ARRAY[1..NUMCOMPAREWORD] OF WORDTYPE;

VAR
  COMPAREWORD : COMPARETYPE;
  WORD : WORDTYPE;
  FINISHED : BOOLEAN;

PROCEDURE GETWORD(VAR WORD:WORDTYPE; VAR FINISHED : BOOLEAN);
VAR
  CHARINDEX,BLANKINDEX : WORDINDEX;
  CH : CHAR;
```

```
BEGIN   {GETWORD}
  CHARINDEX := 1;
  WHILE NOT EOLN DO
  BEGIN
    READ(CH);
    IF (CH = 'X') THEN
      FINISHED := TRUE
    ELSE IF (CHARINDEX < MAXWORDLEN) THEN
      BEGIN
        WORD[CHARINDEX] := CH;
        CHARINDEX := CHARINDEX + 1
      END
  END;
  IF CHARINDEX < MAXWORDLEN THEN
    FOR BLANKINDEX := CHARINDEX TO MAXWORDLEN DO
      WORD[BLANKINDEX] := BLANK
END;     {GETWORD}
```

```
PROCEDURE CHECKWORD(COMPAREWORD : COMPARETYPE; WORD : WORDTYPE);
VAR
  COMPAREWORDFOUND : BOOLEAN;
  COMPAREWDINDEX : INTEGER;

BEGIN    {CHECKWORD}
  READLN;
  COMPAREWORDFOUND := FALSE;
  COMPAREWDINDEX := 1;
  REPEAT

    IF WORD = COMPAREWORD[COMPAREWDINDEX] THEN
      COMPAREWORDFOUND := TRUE;
    COMPAREWDINDEX := COMPAREWDINDEX + 1
  UNTIL COMPAREWORDFOUND OR (COMPAREWDINDEX > NUMCOMPAREWORD);
  IF COMPAREWORDFOUND THEN WRITELN(COMPAREWDINDEX - 1)
    ELSE WRITELN('Error in input.')
END;      {CHECKWORD}
```

```
PROCEDURE ENTERCOMPAREWORDS(VAR COMPAREWORD : COMPARETYPE);
VAR
   CHARINDEX : INTEGER;

BEGIN
   COMPAREWORD[1][1] := 'O';
   COMPAREWORD[1][2] := 'N';
   COMPAREWORD[1][3] := 'E';
   FOR CHARINDEX := 4 TO MAXWORDLEN DO COMPAREWORD[1][CHARINDEX] := BLANK;

   COMPAREWORD[2][1] := 'T';
   COMPAREWORD[2][2] := 'W';
   COMPAREWORD[2][3] := 'O';
   FOR CHARINDEX := 4 TO MAXWORDLEN DO COMPAREWORD[2][CHARINDEX] := BLANK;

   COMPAREWORD[3][1] := 'T';
   COMPAREWORD[3][2] := 'H';
   COMPAREWORD[3][3] := 'R';
   COMPAREWORD[3][4] := 'E';
   COMPAREWORD[3][5] := 'E';
   FOR CHARINDEX := 6 TO MAXWORDLEN DO COMPAREWORD[3][CHARINDEX] := BLANK;

   COMPAREWORD[4][1] := 'F';
   COMPAREWORD[4][2] := 'O';
   COMPAREWORD[4][3] := 'U';
   COMPAREWORD[4][4] := 'R';
   FOR CHARINDEX := 5 TO MAXWORDLEN DO COMPAREWORD[4][CHARINDEX] := BLANK;

   COMPAREWORD[5][1] := 'F';
   COMPAREWORD[5][2] := 'I';
   COMPAREWORD[5][3] := 'V';
   COMPAREWORD[5][4] := 'E';
   FOR CHARINDEX := 5 TO MAXWORDLEN DO COMPAREWORD[5][CHARINDEX] := BLANK;

   COMPAREWORD[6][1] := 'S';
   COMPAREWORD[6][2] := 'I';
   COMPAREWORD[6][3] := 'X';
   FOR CHARINDEX := 4 TO MAXWORDLEN DO COMPAREWORD[6][CHARINDEX] := BLANK;

   COMPAREWORD[7][1] := 'S';
   COMPAREWORD[7][2] := 'E';

   COMPAREWORD[7][3] := 'V';
   COMPAREWORD[7][4] := 'E';
   COMPAREWORD[7][5] := 'N';
   FOR CHARINDEX := 6 TO MAXWORDLEN DO COMPAREWORD[7][CHARINDEX] := BLANK;

   COMPAREWORD[8][1] := 'E';
   COMPAREWORD[8][2] := 'I';
   COMPAREWORD[8][3] := 'G';
   COMPAREWORD[8][4] := 'H';
   COMPAREWORD[8][5] := 'T';
   FOR CHARINDEX := 6 TO MAXWORDLEN DO COMPAREWORD[8][CHARINDEX] := BLANK;

   COMPAREWORD[9][1] := 'N';
   COMPAREWORD[9][2] := 'I';
   COMPAREWORD[9][3] := 'N';
   COMPAREWORD[9][4] := 'E';
   FOR CHARINDEX := 5 TO MAXWORDLEN DO COMPAREWORD[9][CHARINDEX] := BLANK;
```

```
      COMPAREWORD[10][1] := 'T';
      COMPAREWORD[10][2] := 'E';
      COMPAREWORD[10][3] := 'N';
      FOR CHARINDEX := 4 TO MAXWORDLEN DO COMPAREWORD[10][CHARINDEX] := BLANK
  END;    {ENTERCOMPAREWORDS}

BEGIN    {MAIN}
    ENTERCOMPAREWORDS(COMPAREWORD);
    FINISHED := FALSE;
    WRITELN('Enter a written number, ex: "ONE", from 1 - 10. ');
    WRITELN('To halt enter "X" by itself.');
    WRITELN;
    WHILE NOT FINISHED DO
    BEGIN
      GETWORD(WORD,FINISHED);
      CHECKWORD(COMPAREWORD,WORD)
    END
END.     {MAIN}
```

Replacement Turbo Pascal Code:

```
PROCEDURE GETWORD(VAR WORD:WORDTYPE; VAR FINISHED : BOOLEAN);
CONST
  EOL = #013;

VAR
  CHARINDEX,BLANKINDEX : WORDINDEX;
  CH : CHAR;

BEGIN    {GETWORD}
  CH := CHR(0);
  CHARINDEX := 1;
  WHILE CH <> EOL DO
  BEGIN
    READ(KBD,CH);
    CH := UPCASE(CH);
    IF (CH = 'X') OR (CH = EOL) THEN
      FINISHED := TRUE
    ELSE IF (CHARINDEX < MAXWORDLEN) THEN
      BEGIN
        WORD[CHARINDEX] := CH;
        WRITE(CH);
        CHARINDEX := CHARINDEX + 1
      END
  END;
  IF CHARINDEX < MAXWORDLEN THEN
    FOR BLANKINDEX := CHARINDEX TO MAXWORDLEN DO
      WORD[BLANKINDEX] := BLANK
END;       {GETWORD}
```

Exercise 9-5:

```
PROGRAM ALPHANAMES(INPUT,OUTPUT);
CONST
  ONENAMELENGTH = 10;
  BLANK = ' ';
  MAXNAMES = 10;
  TOTALNAMELENGTH = 23;
  COMMA = ',';

TYPE
  NUMNAMES = 1..MAXNAMES;
  WORDLENGTH = 1..TOTALNAMELENGTH;
  NAME = ARRAY[WORDLENGTH] OF CHAR;
  NAMEARRAY = ARRAY[NUMNAMES] OF NAME;

VAR
  NAMESTORAGE : NAMEARRAY;
```

```
  PROCEDURE READNAMES(VAR THENAMES : NAMEARRAY);
  VAR
    COUNTER,NAMECOUNTER : INTEGER;
    ANAME : NAME;

  PROCEDURE ENTERANAME(VAR ANAME : NAME);
  VAR
    COUNTER : INTEGER;

  BEGIN   {ENTERANAME}
    IF NOT EOLN AND NOT EOF THEN
      FOR COUNTER := 1 TO TOTALNAMELENGTH DO
        IF NOT EOLN AND NOT EOF THEN
          READ(ANAME[COUNTER])
        ELSE
          ANAME[COUNTER] := BLANK;
    READLN
  END;    {ENTERANAME}

  BEGIN   {READNAMES}
    FOR NAMECOUNTER := 1 TO MAXNAMES DO
    BEGIN
      WRITELN;
      WRITE('Enter the last name of person #',NAMECOUNTER,':        ');
      ENTERANAME(ANAME);
      THENAMES[NAMECOUNTER] := ANAME;
      THENAMES[NAMECOUNTER][ONENAMELENGTH + 1] := COMMA;

      WRITE('        Enter first name:        ');
      ENTERANAME(ANAME);
      FOR COUNTER := (ONENAMELENGTH + 2) TO (TOTALNAMELENGTH - 2) DO
        THENAMES[NAMECOUNTER][COUNTER] := ANAME[COUNTER - (ONENAMELENGTH + 1)];
      THENAMES[NAMECOUNTER][TOTALNAMELENGTH - 1] := COMMA;

      WRITE('   Enter middle initial:        ');
```

```
        READ(THENAMES[NAMECOUNTER][TOTALNAMELENGTH]);
        READLN
    END
END;     {READNAMES}
```

```
PROCEDURE ALPHABETIZE(VAR NAMES : NAMEARRAY);
{Uses a simple bubble sort.}

VAR
    NAMEINDEX, CHARINDEX : INTEGER;
    FINISHED : BOOLEAN;
    DUMMYARRAY : NAME;

BEGIN   {ALPHABETIZE}
    REPEAT
        FINISHED := TRUE;          {If any two names are switched then
                                    FINISHED is set to FALSE and we keep
                                    repeating until the array is in order
                                    (i.e. no names are switched).}

        FOR NAMEINDEX := 1 TO (MAXNAMES - 1) DO    {Only N-1 comparisons needed
                                                    for a bubble sort of a list
                                                    composed of N elements}


        BEGIN
            CHARINDEX := 1;
            WHILE (NAMES[NAMEINDEX][CHARINDEX] =
                    NAMES[NAMEINDEX + 1][CHARINDEX]) AND
                    (CHARINDEX < TOTALNAMELENGTH) DO
                    CHARINDEX := CHARINDEX + 1;

            IF (NAMES[NAMEINDEX][CHARINDEX] > NAMES[NAMEINDEX + 1][CHARINDEX]) THEN
            BEGIN
                DUMMYARRAY := NAMES[NAMEINDEX];
                NAMES[NAMEINDEX] := NAMES[NAMEINDEX + 1];
                NAMES[NAMEINDEX + 1] := DUMMYARRAY;
                FINISHED := FALSE
            END
        END
    UNTIL FINISHED
END;     {ALPHABETIZE}

PROCEDURE PRINTNAMES(NAMES : NAMEARRAY);
VAR
    CHARINDEX, NAMEINDEX : INTEGER;

BEGIN
    WRITELN;
    WRITELN;
    WRITELN;
    WRITELN('The alphabetized list is:');
```

```
    WRITELN;
    FOR NAMEINDEX := 1 TO MAXNAMES DO
    BEGIN
       FOR CHARINDEX := 1 TO TOTALNAMELENGTH DO
       BEGIN
          IF (NAMES[NAMEINDEX][CHARINDEX] <> BLANK) THEN
             WRITE(NAMES[NAMEINDEX][CHARINDEX])
       END;
       WRITELN
    END
END;     {PRINTNAMES}

BEGIN     {MAIN}
   WRITELN('This program alphabetizes a list of 10 names.');
   WRITELN('The program will prompt for names.');
   READNAMES(NAMESTORAGE);
   ALPHABETIZE(NAMESTORAGE);
   PRINTNAMES(NAMESTORAGE)
END.     {MAIN}
```

Replacement Turbo Pascal Code:

```
PROCEDURE READNAMES(VAR THENAMES : NAMEARRAY);
VAR
   COUNTER,NAMECOUNTER : INTEGER;
   ANAME : NAME;
   CH : CHAR;

PROCEDURE ENTERANAME(VAR ANAME : NAME);
CONST
   EOL = #013;
   EF = #026;

VAR
   COUNTER : INTEGER;
   CH : CHAR;

BEGIN     {ENTERANAME}
   CH := CHR(0);
   FOR COUNTER := 1 TO TOTALNAMELENGTH DO
      IF (CH <> EOL) AND (CH <> EF) THEN
      BEGIN
         READ(KBD,CH);
         IF CH IN ['A'..'Z','a'..'z','-'] THEN
         BEGIN
            ANAME[COUNTER] := UPCASE(CH);
            WRITE(CH)
         END
         ELSE
            ANAME[COUNTER] := BLANK;
      END
      ELSE
            ANAME[COUNTER] := BLANK;
   WRITELN;
END;     {ENTERANAME}

BEGIN     {READNAMES}
   FOR NAMECOUNTER := 1 TO MAXNAMES DO
   BEGIN
```

```
        WRITELN;
        WRITE('Enter the last name of person #',NAMECOUNTER,':           ');
        ENTERANAME(ANAME);
        THENAMES[NAMECOUNTER] := ANAME;
        THENAMES[NAMECOUNTER][ONENAMELENGTH + 1] := COMMA;
        WRITE('          Enter first name:           ');
        ENTERANAME(ANAME);
        FOR COUNTER := (ONENAMELENGTH + 2) TO (TOTALNAMELENGTH - 2) DO
          THENAMES[NAMECOUNTER][COUNTER] := ANAME[COUNTER - (ONENAMELENGTH + 1)];
        THENAMES[NAMECOUNTER][TOTALNAMELENGTH - 1] := COMMA;
        WRITE('     Enter middle initial:          ');
        READ(KBD,CH);
        WRITE(CH);
        THENAMES[NAMECOUNTER][TOTALNAMELENGTH] := UPCASE(CH);
      END
  END;     {READNAMES}
```

Exercise 9-6:

```
        PROGRAM SENTENCEALPH(INPUT,OUTPUT);
        CONST
          WORDLENGTH = 20;
          SENTLENGTH = 30;
          BLANK = ' ';
          COMMA = ',';
          PERIOD = '.';

        TYPE
          WORDSPAN = 1..WORDLENGTH;
          SENTENCESPAN = 1..SENTLENGTH;
          WORD = ARRAY[WORDSPAN] OF CHAR;
          WORDARRAY = ARRAY[SENTENCESPAN] OF WORD;

        VAR
          WORDS : WORDARRAY;
          WORDINDEX : INTEGER;
```

```
        PROCEDURE ENTERSENTENCE(VAR THEWORDS : WORDARRAY);
        VAR
          AWORD : WORD;

        PROCEDURE ENTERAWORD(VAR AWORD : WORD);
        VAR
          COUNTER : INTEGER;
          CH : CHAR;

        BEGIN   {ENTERAWORD}
          REPEAT
            READ(CH)
          UNTIL NOT ((((CH = BLANK) OR (CH = PERIOD)) OR (CH = COMMA)) OR
                      (EOF OR EOLN));
          COUNTER := 1;
          IF NOT EOLN AND NOT EOF THEN
          REPEAT
            AWORD[COUNTER] := CH;
            COUNTER := COUNTER + 1;
            READ(CH)
```

```
            UNTIL ((((CH = BLANK) OR (CH = PERIOD)) OR (CH = COMMA)) OR
                    (EOF OR EOLN));
            AWORD[COUNTER] := CH;
            COUNTER := COUNTER + 1;
            FOR COUNTER := COUNTER TO WORDLENGTH DO
              AWORD[COUNTER] := BLANK;
            IF EOLN THEN
              READLN
        END;    {ENTERAWORD}

    BEGIN    {ENTERSENTENCE}
        WORDINDEX := 1;
        WHILE NOT EOF AND (WORDINDEX <= SENTLENGTH) DO
        BEGIN
           IF NOT EOF THEN
             ENTERAWORD(AWORD);
           THEWORDS[WORDINDEX] := AWORD;
           WORDINDEX := WORDINDEX + 1
        END;
        WORDINDEX := WORDINDEX - 1
    END;    {ENTERSENTENCE}
```

```
PROCEDURE ALPHABETIZE(VAR WORDS : WORDARRAY);

{Uses a simple bubble sort.}

VAR
   LOCALWORDINDEX, CHARINDEX : INTEGER;
   FINISHED : BOOLEAN;
   DUMMYARRAY : WORD;

BEGIN    {ALPHABETIZE}
   WRITELN;
   WRITELN(WORDINDEX,' words');
   REPEAT
     FINISHED := TRUE;
     FOR LOCALWORDINDEX := 1 TO (WORDINDEX - 1) DO
     BEGIN
        CHARINDEX := 1;
        WHILE (WORDS[LOCALWORDINDEX][CHARINDEX] =
               WORDS[LOCALWORDINDEX + 1][CHARINDEX]) AND
               (CHARINDEX < WORDLENGTH) DO
               CHARINDEX := CHARINDEX + 1;

        IF CHARINDEX = WORDLENGTH THEN
          FOR CHARINDEX := 1 TO WORDLENGTH DO
            WORDS[LOCALWORDINDEX][CHARINDEX] := BLANK   {remove duplicates}
        ELSE
        IF (WORDS[LOCALWORDINDEX][CHARINDEX] >
            WORDS[LOCALWORDINDEX + 1][CHARINDEX]) THEN
        BEGIN
           DUMMYARRAY := WORDS[LOCALWORDINDEX];
           WORDS[LOCALWORDINDEX] := WORDS[LOCALWORDINDEX + 1];
           WORDS[LOCALWORDINDEX + 1] := DUMMYARRAY;
           FINISHED := FALSE
        END
     END
   UNTIL FINISHED
END;    {ALPHABETIZE}
```

```
PROCEDURE PRINT(WORDS : WORDARRAY);
VAR
  CHARINDEX, LOCALWORDINDEX : INTEGER;

BEGIN   {PRINT}
  WRITELN;
  WRITELN;
  WRITELN;
  WRITELN('The alphabetized list is:');
  WRITELN;
  FOR LOCALWORDINDEX := 1 TO (WORDINDEX) DO
  BEGIN
    IF (WORDS[LOCALWORDINDEX][1] <> BLANK) THEN
      FOR CHARINDEX := 1 TO WORDLENGTH DO
        WRITE(WORDS[LOCALWORDINDEX][CHARINDEX]);
    WRITELN
  END
END;    {PRINT}

PROCEDURE PRINT1(WORDS : WORDARRAY);
VAR
  CHARINDEX, LOCALWORDINDEX : INTEGER;

BEGIN   {PRINT1}
  WRITELN;
  WRITELN;
  WRITELN;
  WRITELN('The input list is:');
  WRITELN;
  FOR LOCALWORDINDEX := 1 TO (WORDINDEX) DO
  BEGIN
      WRITE(LOCALWORDINDEX,'. ');
      FOR CHARINDEX := 1 TO WORDLENGTH DO
        WRITE(WORDS[LOCALWORDINDEX][CHARINDEX]);
    WRITELN
  END
END;    {PRINT1}


BEGIN   {MAIN}
  WRITELN('Type in a sentence on some lines. Stop by typing an EOF');
  WRITELN('character on a new line. Thirty words max. Enter uppercase ');
  WRITELN('or lowercase only: ');
  ENTERSENTENCE(WORDS);
  PRINT1(WORDS);
  ALPHABETIZE(WORDS);
  PRINT(WORDS)
END.    {MAIN}
```

Replacement Turbo Pascal Code:

```
PROCEDURE ENTERSENTENCE(VAR THEWORDS : WORDARRAY);
CONST
  EOL = #013;
  EF = #026;

VAR
  AWORD : WORD;
  CH : CHAR;
```

```
PROCEDURE ENTERAWORD(VAR AWORD : WORD);
VAR
   COUNTER : INTEGER;

BEGIN     {ENTERAWORD}
   REPEAT
     READ(KBD,CH);
   UNTIL NOT ((CH = BLANK) OR (CH = PERIOD) OR (CH = COMMA) OR
              (CH = EF) OR (CH = EOL));
   COUNTER := 1;
   IF NOT ((CH = EF) OR (CH = EOL)) THEN
   REPEAT
     WRITE(CH);
     AWORD[COUNTER] := UPCASE(CH);
     READ(KBD,CH);
     COUNTER := COUNTER + 1;
   UNTIL (CH = BLANK) OR (CH = PERIOD) OR (CH = COMMA) OR
         (CH = EF) OR (CH = EOL);
   IF (CH = BLANK) OR (CH = PERIOD) OR (CH = COMMA) THEN
   BEGIN
     AWORD[COUNTER] := UPCASE(CH);
     WRITE(UPCASE(CH))
   END;
   FOR COUNTER := COUNTER TO WORDLENGTH DO
     AWORD[COUNTER] := BLANK;
   IF (CH = EF) OR (CH = EOL) THEN
     WRITELN
END;      {ENTERAWORD}

BEGIN     {ENTERASENTENCE}
   WORDINDEX := 1;
   CH := CHR(0);
   WHILE (CH <> EF) AND (WORDINDEX <= SENTLENGTH) DO
   BEGIN
     ENTERAWORD(AWORD);
     THEWORDS[WORDINDEX] := AWORD;
     WORDINDEX := WORDINDEX + 1
   END;
   WORDINDEX := WORDINDEX - 1
END;      {ENTERASENTENCE}
```

Exercise 9-7:

```
PROGRAM COUNTLETTER(INPUT,OUTPUT);
TYPE
   LETTERS = 'A'..'Z';
   LETTERARRAY = ARRAY[LETTERS] OF INTEGER;

VAR
   LETFREQ : LETTERARRAY;
   CH : CHAR;
```

```
PROCEDURE READINLETTERS(VAR LETFREQR : LETTERARRAY);
VAR
   CH : CHAR;

FUNCTION UPPERCASE(CH : CHAR): CHAR;
BEGIN
   IF (ORD(CH) >= ORD('a')) AND (ORD(CH) <= ORD('z')) THEN
      UPPERCASE := CHR(ORD(CH) + ORD('A') - ORD('a'))
   ELSE
      UPPERCASE := CH
END;     {UPPERCASE}

BEGIN    {READINLETTERS}
   CH := ' ';
   WHILE NOT EOF AND (CH <> '*') DO
   BEGIN
      WHILE NOT EOLN AND (CH <> '*') DO
      BEGIN
         READ(CH);
         CH := UPCASE(CH);
         IF (CH >= 'A') AND (CH <= 'Z') THEN
            LETFREQR[CH] := LETFREQR[CH] + 1
      END;
      IF EOLN THEN
         READLN
   END
END;     {READINLETTERS}
```

```
PROCEDURE PRINTRESULT (LETFREQP : LETTERARRAY);
VAR
  CH : CHAR;

BEGIN    {PRINTRESULT}
  WRITELN;
  WRITELN('The letter count is as follows:');
  WRITELN;
  FOR CH := 'A' TO 'M' DO
    WRITE(CH:6);
  WRITELN;
  FOR CH := 'A' TO 'M' DO
    WRITE(LETFREQP[CH]:6);
  WRITELN;
  WRITELN;
  FOR CH := 'N' TO 'Z' DO
    WRITE(CH:6);
  WRITELN;
  FOR CH := 'N' TO 'Z' DO
    WRITE(LETFREQP[CH]:6);
  WRITELN;
  WRITELN
END;     {PRINTRESULT}

BEGIN    {MAIN}
  FOR CH := 'A' TO 'Z' DO
    LETFREQ[CH] := 0;
  WRITELN('Enter text. Halt input with "**" or EOF.');
  READINLETTERS(LETFREQ);
  PRINTRESULT(LETFREQ)
END.     {MAIN}
```

Replacement Turbo Pascal Code:

```
PROCEDURE READINLETTERS(VAR LETFREQR : LETTERARRAY);
CONST
  EOL = #013;
  EF = #026;
  BS = #008;

VAR
  CH : CHAR;

BEGIN
  CH := CHR(0);
  WHILE (CH <> EF) AND (CH <> '*') DO
  BEGIN
    WHILE (CH <> EOL) AND (CH <> EF) AND (CH <> '*') DO
    BEGIN
      READ(KBD,CH);
      CH := UPCASE(CH);
      IF (CH >= 'A') AND (CH <= 'Z') THEN
      BEGIN
        WRITE(CH);
        LETFREQR[CH] := LETFREQR[CH] + 1
      END
      ELSE
        IF (CH <> EOL) AND (CH <> EF) AND (CH <> BS) THEN
          WRITE(CH)
    END;
    IF CH = EOL THEN
    BEGIN
      WRITELN;
      CH := CHR(0)
    END
  END
END;
```

Exercise 9-8:

```
PROGRAM INTEGERFILTER(INPUT,OUTPUT);
CONST
  NUM = 1;
  FREQ = 2;

VAR
  LARGEST, SMALLEST: ARRAY [1..2] OF INTEGER;
  NUMBER : INTEGER;
  MININT : INTEGER;              {Not required if MININT is defined in your Pascal}

BEGIN
  MININT := -(MAXINT+1);        {Not required if MININT is defined in your Pascal}
  LARGEST[NUM] := MININT;
  LARGEST[FREQ] := 0;
  SMALLEST[NUM] := MAXINT;
  SMALLEST[FREQ] := 0;
  WRITELN('Enter some integers < ',MAXINT,' and > ',
          MININT,'. ');

  WHILE NOT EOF AND NOT EOLN DO
  BEGIN
    WRITELN;
    WRITE('Number: ');
    READLN(NUMBER);
    IF NUMBER > LARGEST[NUM] THEN
    BEGIN
      LARGEST[NUM]  := NUMBER;
      LARGEST[FREQ] := 1
    END
    ELSE
    IF NUMBER = LARGEST[NUM] THEN
      LARGEST[FREQ] := LARGEST[FREQ] + 1;

    IF NUMBER < SMALLEST[NUM] THEN
    BEGIN
      SMALLEST[NUM]  := NUMBER;
      SMALLEST[FREQ] := 1
    END
    ELSE
    IF NUMBER = SMALLEST[NUM] THEN
      SMALLEST[FREQ] := SMALLEST[FREQ] + 1;
    IF EOLN AND NOT EOF THEN
      READLN
  END;

  WRITELN;
  WRITELN;
  WRITELN(LARGEST[NUM]:0,', the largest number, was entered ',
          LARGEST[FREQ]:0,' times.');
  WRITELN;
  WRITELN(SMALLEST[NUM]:0,', the smallest number, was entered ',
          SMALLEST[FREQ]:0,' times.');
  WRITELN;
  WRITELN
END.
```

Replacement Turbo Pascal Code:
(Replace entire program.)

```pascal
PROGRAM INTEGERFILTER(INPUT,OUTPUT);
CONST
  NUM = 1;
  FREQ = 2;

VAR
  LARGEST, SMALLEST: ARRAY [1..2] OF INTEGER;
  NUMBER : INTEGER;
  MININT : INTEGER;
  MORE : BOOLEAN;
  CH : CHAR;

BEGIN
  MININT := NOT MAXINT;
  LARGEST[NUM] := MININT;
  LARGEST[FREQ] := 0;
  SMALLEST[NUM] := MAXINT;
  SMALLEST[FREQ] := 0;
  WRITELN('Enter some integers < ',MAXINT,' and > ',
          MININT,'. ');
  MORE := TRUE;
  WHILE MORE DO
  BEGIN
    WRITELN;
    WRITE('Number: ');
    READLN(NUMBER);
    IF NUMBER > LARGEST[NUM] THEN
    BEGIN
      LARGEST[NUM] := NUMBER;
      LARGEST[FREQ] := 1
    END
    ELSE
    IF NUMBER = LARGEST[NUM] THEN
      LARGEST[FREQ] := LARGEST[FREQ] + 1;

    IF NUMBER < SMALLEST[NUM] THEN
    BEGIN
      SMALLEST[NUM] := NUMBER;
      SMALLEST[FREQ] := 1
    END
    ELSE
    IF NUMBER = SMALLEST[NUM] THEN
      SMALLEST[FREQ] := SMALLEST[FREQ] + 1;
    WRITE('More? Y/N - ');
    READ(KBD,CH);
    WRITELN(CH);
    MORE := UPCASE(CH) = 'Y'
  END;
  WRITELN;
  WRITELN;
  WRITELN(LARGEST[NUM],', the largest number, was entered ',
          LARGEST[FREQ],' times.');
  WRITELN;
  WRITELN(SMALLEST[NUM],', the smallest number, was entered ',
          SMALLEST[FREQ],' times.');
  WRITELN;
  WRITELN
END.
```

Exercise 9-9:

```
PROGRAM DICTONARY(INPUT,OUTPUT);
CONST
  BLANK = ' ';
  NUMWORDS = 20;
  MAXWORDLENGTH = 10;
  STOPCHAR = '1';

TYPE
  WORDLENGTH = 1..MAXWORDLENGTH;
  DICTSPAN = 1..NUMWORDS;
  WORD = ARRAY[WORDLENGTH] OF CHAR;
  DICTIONARY = ARRAY[DICTSPAN] OF WORD;

VAR
  FRENCHWORDS, ENGLISHWORDS : DICTIONARY;
```

```
  PROCEDURE ENTERWORD(VAR AWORD : WORD);
  VAR
    COUNTER : INTEGER;
    CH: CHAR;

  BEGIN   {ENTERWORD}
    IF NOT (EOLN OR EOF) THEN
      WHILE ((CH = BLANK) AND NOT (EOLN OR EOF)) DO
        READ(CH);                   {deletes leading blanks}
    FOR COUNTER := 1 TO MAXWORDLENGTH DO
      IF NOT EOLN THEN
        READ(AWORD[COUNTER])
      ELSE
        AWORD[COUNTER] := BLANK;
    READLN
  END;    {ENTERWORD}
```

```
PROCEDURE BUILDDICT(VAR FRENCH, ENGLISH : DICTIONARY);
VAR
  WORDINDEX : INTEGER;

BEGIN   {BUILDDICT}
  FOR WORDINDEX := 1 TO NUMWORDS DO
  BEGIN
    WRITE('Enter French word #',WORDINDEX,': ');
    ENTERWORD(FRENCH[WORDINDEX]);
    WRITE('Enter English equivalent: ');
    ENTERWORD(ENGLISH[WORDINDEX]);
    WRITELN
  END
END;    {BUILDDICT}

PROCEDURE READANDCOMPARE(FWORDS,EWORDS : DICTIONARY);
VAR
  TRANSWORD : WORD;
  WINDEX : INTEGER;

PROCEDURE PRINTTRANS(OUTWORD: WORD);
VAR
  CHARIND : INTEGER;
```

```
BEGIN    {PRINTTRANS}
  WRITE('French word is: ');
  FOR CHARIND := 1 TO MAXWORDLENGTH DO
    WRITE(OUTWORD[CHARIND]);
  WRITELN
END;     {PRINTTRANS}

BEGIN    {READANDCOMPARE}
  WHILE TRANSWORD[1] <> STOPCHAR DO
  BEGIN
    WRITE('Enter English word: ');
    ENTERWORD(TRANSWORD);
    IF TRANSWORD[1] <> STOPCHAR THEN
    BEGIN
      WINDEX := 0;
      REPEAT
        WINDEX := WINDEX + 1
      UNTIL (EWORDS[WINDEX] = TRANSWORD) OR (WINDEX = NUMWORDS);
      IF (WINDEX = NUMWORDS) AND (EWORDS[WINDEX] <> TRANSWORD) THEN
        WRITELN('Word not found.')
      ELSE
        PRINTTRANS(FWORDS[WINDEX])
    END;
    WRITELN
  END
END;     {READANDCOMPARE}

BEGIN    {MAIN}
  WRITELN('Entering dictionary mode...');
  BUILDDICT(FRENCHWORDS,ENGLISHWORDS);
  WRITELN('Entering translation mode...');
  WRITELN('Stop by entering a "1" as the first character.');
  READANDCOMPARE(FRENCHWORDS,ENGLISHWORDS)
END.     {MAIN}
```

Replacement Turbo Pascal Code:

```
PROCEDURE ENTERWORD(VAR AWORD : WORD);
VAR
  COUNTER : INTEGER;
  STR1 : STRING[MAXWORDLENGTH];

BEGIN
  READLN(STR1);
  FOR COUNTER := 1 TO LENGTH(STR1) DO
    AWORD[COUNTER] := STR1[COUNTER];
  FOR COUNTER := LENGTH(STR1)+1 TO MAXWORDLENGTH DO
    AWORD[COUNTER] := BLANK
END;
```

Exercise 9-10:

```
PROGRAM TRANSSENT(INPUT,OUTPUT);

{This program expands upon Exercise 9-9 using similar procedures to
 illustrate the uses of modular program design and expansion. Note that
 the dictionary can be lengthened by changing the constant NUMWORDS below.}

{DATA STRUCTURES:
     Each WORD type is stored in an array of CHAR. The dictionary type
     is an array in which each element is a WORD (which is an array of
     CHAR). Each sentence type is an array of WORD similar to type
     dictionary but of different length.}

CONST
  BLANK = ' ';
  NUMWORDS = 20;
  MAXWORDLENGTH = 10;
  STOPCHAR = 'N';
  SENTLENGTH = 10;

TYPE
  WORDLENGTH = 1..MAXWORDLENGTH;
  DICTSPAN = 1..NUMWORDS;
  SENTRANGE = 1..SENTLENGTH;
  WORD = ARRAY[WORDLENGTH] OF CHAR;
  DICTIONARY = ARRAY[DICTSPAN] OF WORD;
  SENTENCE = ARRAY[SENTRANGE] OF WORD;

VAR
  EPHRASE : SENTENCE;
  EWORDS, FWORDS : DICTIONARY;
  WORDINDEX : INTEGER;
  CONTINUE : CHAR;

PROCEDURE PRINTWORD(OUTWORD : WORD);
VAR
  CHARIND : INTEGER;

BEGIN    {PRINTWORD}
  FOR CHARIND := 1 TO MAXWORDLENGTH DO
    IF OUTWORD[CHARIND] <> BLANK THEN WRITE(OUTWORD[CHARIND])
END;     {PRINTWORD}
```

```
PROCEDURE ENTERWORD(VAR AWORD : WORD);

{Procedure ENTERWORD has been changed so that it no longer does
a READLN after every word, as we must now read in sentences and the
Standard Pascal INPUT^ has been used for error checking. INPUT^
(see Chap. 11) is the next character to be read from the INPUT file,
in this case, standard input. Thus we can look at the next character
without having to read it in yet. GET(INPUT) advances INPUT^ along the
INPUT file when we don't want to read in the current character: in this
case, a blank. Note that it is difficult to perform a WRITE immediately
after checking INPUT^ because Pascal is expecting the program to execute
a GET, READ, or READLN.}
```

```
    VAR
      COUNTER : INTEGER;

    BEGIN     {ENTERWORD}
      IF NOT (EOLN OR EOF) THEN
        WHILE (INPUT^ = BLANK) AND NOT (EOLN OR EOF) DO
          GET(INPUT);                {deletes leading blanks}
      FOR COUNTER := 1 TO MAXWORDLENGTH DO
        IF NOT (EOLN OR (INPUT^ = BLANK)) THEN
          READ(AWORD[COUNTER])
        ELSE
          AWORD[COUNTER] := BLANK
    END;      {ENTERWORD}

    PROCEDURE ENTERSENTENCE(VAR ENGPHRASE : SENTENCE; VAR WORDINDEX : INTEGER);

    BEGIN     {ENTERSENTENCE}
      WRITELN('ENTER ENGLISH SENTENCE, NO PUNCTUATION: ');
      WORDINDEX := 0;
      WHILE NOT EOLN AND NOT EOF DO
      BEGIN
        WORDINDEX := WORDINDEX + 1;
        ENTERWORD(ENGPHRASE[WORDINDEX])
      END;
      IF EOLN THEN
        READLN
    END;      {ENTERSENTENCE}

    PROCEDURE BUILDDICT(VAR ENGLISH, FRENCH : DICTIONARY);
    VAR
      WORDINDEX : INTEGER;

    BEGIN     {BUILDDICT}
      FOR WORDINDEX := 1 TO NUMWORDS DO
      BEGIN
        WRITE('ENTER FRENCH WORD #',WORDINDEX:0,': ');
        ENTERWORD(FRENCH[WORDINDEX]);
        WRITE('ENTER ENGILSH EQUIVALENT: ');
        ENTERWORD(ENGLISH[WORDINDEX]);
        READLN
      END
    END;      {BUILDDICT}
```

```
PROCEDURE BUILDFRENCHPHRASE(VAR EPHRASE : SENTENCE; WORDSINPUT : INTEGER;
                           EWORDS,FWORDS : DICTIONARY);
```

{Procedure BUILDFRENCHPHRASE checks a word in the EPHRASE array against
each word in the EWORDS dictionary array until the two words match or
until the EWORDS array is exhausted. If an input word is found, the French
equivalent in FWORDS with the same WDINDEX value is printed. Otherwise,
"UNKNOWN" is printed. This process continues until all the entered words
have been attempted.}

```
VAR
  LOOKUPINDEX, WDINDEX : INTEGER;

BEGIN     {BUILDFRENCHPHRASE}
  FOR LOOKUPINDEX := 1 TO WORDSINPUT DO
  BEGIN
    WDINDEX := 0;
    REPEAT
      WDINDEX := WDINDEX + 1
    UNTIL (EPHRASE[LOOKUPINDEX] = EWORDS[WDINDEX]) OR (WDINDEX = NUMWORDS);
    IF  (WDINDEX = NUMWORDS) AND (EWORDS[WDINDEX] <> EPHRASE[LOOKUPINDEX]) THEN
      WRITE('UNKNOWN')
    ELSE
      PRINTWORD(FWORDS[WDINDEX]);
    WRITE(BLANK)
  END;
  WRITELN
END;     {BUILDFRENCHPHRASE}

BEGIN     {MAIN}
  WRITELN('ENTERING DICTIONARY MODE...');
  BUILDDICT(EWORDS,FWORDS);
  WRITELN('ENTERING TRANSLATION MODE...');
  REPEAT
    WRITELN;
    ENTERSENTENCE(EPHRASE,WORDINDEX);
    WRITELN;
    WRITELN('TRANSLATION IS: ');
    BUILDFRENCHPHRASE(EPHRASE,WORDINDEX,EWORDS,FWORDS);
    WRITE('DO YOU WANT TO CONTINUE? Y/N - ');
    READLN(CONTINUE)
  UNTIL CONTINUE = STOPCHAR
END.     {MAIN}
```

Replacement Turbo Pascal Code:

```
PROCEDURE ENTERSENTENCE(VAR ENGPHRASE : SENTENCE; VAR WORDINDEX : INTEGER);
TYPE
  LONGSTR = STRING[80];
VAR
  CHINDEX : INTEGER;
  STR2 : LONGSTR;

PROCEDURE ENTERWORD2(VAR AWORD : WORD; VAR INDEX : INTEGER; STR1 : LONGSTR);
VAR
  COUNTER : INTEGER;

BEGIN     {ENTERWORD2}

  FOR COUNTER := 1 TO MAXWORDLENGTH DO
    IF NOT ((CHINDEX > LENGTH(STR1)) OR
            (STR1[CHINDEX] = BLANK)) THEN
    BEGIN
      AWORD[COUNTER] := STR1[CHINDEX];
      CHINDEX := CHINDEX + 1
    END
    ELSE
      AWORD[COUNTER] := BLANK;
  CHINDEX := CHINDEX + 1
END;     {ENTERWORD2}
```

```
BEGIN    {ENTERSENTENCE}
  WRITELN('ENTER ENGLISH SENTENCE, NO PUNCTUATION: ');
  WORDINDEX := 0;
  CHINDEX := 1;
  READLN(STR2);
  WHILE CHINDEX < LENGTH(STR2) DO
  BEGIN
    WORDINDEX := WORDINDEX + 1;
    ENTERWORD2(ENGPHRASE[WORDINDEX],CHINDEX,STR2)
  END
END;     {ENTERSENTENCE}

PROCEDURE ENTERWORD(VAR AWORD : WORD);
VAR
  COUNTER : INTEGER;
  STR4 : STRING[MAXWORDLENGTH];

BEGIN
  READLN(STR4);
  FOR COUNTER := 1 TO LENGTH(STR4) DO
    AWORD[COUNTER] := STR4[COUNTER];
  FOR COUNTER := LENGTH(STR4) + 1 TO MAXWORDLENGTH DO
    AWORD[COUNTER] := BLANK
END;

PROCEDURE BUILDDICT(VAR ENGLISH, FRENCH : DICTIONARY);
VAR
  WORDINDEX : INTEGER;

BEGIN    {BUILDDICT}
  FOR WORDINDEX := 1 TO NUMWORDS DO
  BEGIN
    WRITE('ENTER FRENCH WORD #',WORDINDEX:0,': ');
    ENTERWORD(FRENCH[WORDINDEX]);
    WRITE('ENTER ENGLISH EQUIVALENT: ');
    ENTERWORD(ENGLISH[WORDINDEX])
  END
END;     {BUILDDICT}
```

Exercise 9-12:

```
PROGRAM MULMATX(INPUT,OUTPUT);
CONST
  SQUARESIZE = 5;     {This program only supports square matricies.}
                      {This value multiplies 5 x 5 matricies.}

TYPE
  MATRIX = ARRAY[1..SQUARESIZE,1..SQUARESIZE] OF INTEGER;

VAR
  RESULTANT,          {Resultant matrix}
  LFT,
  RGT : MATRIX;       {Input matricies}
  SUMIN,              {Summation index}
  ROWIN,              {Row index}
  COLIN : INTEGER;    {Column index}
```

```
PROCEDURE INMATX(VAR MATX : MATRIX);

BEGIN    {INMATX}
  FOR ROWIN := 1 TO SQUARESIZE DO
    FOR COLIN := 1 TO SQUARESIZE - 1 DO
      READ(MATX[ROWIN,COLIN])
END;      {INMATX}
```

```
BEGIN    {MAIN}
  INMATX(LFT);
  INMATX(RGT);

  { For each element in the resultant matrix, initialize to zero }
  { and sum (ROW ELEMENT * COLUMN ELEMENT)

  FOR ROWIN := 1 TO SQUARESIZE DO
    FOR COLIN := 1 TO SQUARESIZE DO
    BEGIN
      RESULTANT[ROWIN,COLIN] := 0;
      FOR SUMIN := 1 TO SQUARESIZE DO
        RESULTANT[ROWIN,COLIN] := RESULTANT[ROWIN,COLIN] +
          LFT[ROWIN,SUMIN] * RGT[SUMIN,COLIN]
    END;

  { Print results }

  WRITELN;
  WRITELN;
  FOR ROWIN := 1 TO SQUARESIZE DO
  BEGIN
    FOR COLIN := 1 TO SQUARESIZE DO
      WRITE(RESULTANT[ROWIN,COLIN]:3);
    WRITELN
  END;
  WRITELN;

  WRITELN
END.     {MAIN}
```

Replacement Turbo Pascal Code:

Use {$B-} compiler directive before beginning of program.

```
PROCEDURE INMATX(VAR MATX : MATRIX);
BEGIN
  FOR ROWIN := 1 TO SQUARESIZE DO
  BEGIN
    FOR COLIN := 1 TO SQUARESIZE - 1 DO
      READ(MATX[ROWIN,COLIN]);
    READLN(MATX[ROWIN,SQUARESIZE])
  END
END;
```

Exercise 9-13:

```
PROGRAM SPELL(INPUT,OUTPUT);
CONST
  BLANK = ' ';
  MAXWORDLEN = 10;
  NUMCOMPAREWORD = 11;

TYPE
  WORDINDEX = 1..MAXWORDLEN;
  WORDTYPE = ARRAY[WORDINDEX] OF CHAR;
  COMPARETYPE = ARRAY[1..NUMCOMPAREWORD] OF WORDTYPE;

VAR
  COMPAREWORD : COMPARETYPE;
  WORD : WORDTYPE;
  FINISHED : BOOLEAN;


PROCEDURE GETWORD(VAR WORD: WORDTYPE; VAR FINISHED : BOOLEAN);
VAR
  CHARINDEX, BLANKINDEX: WORDINDEX;
  CH : CHAR;

BEGIN    {GETWORD}
  CHARINDEX := 1;

  { Now begin to read in a word.}

  WHILE NOT EOLN DO    { If EOLN then we've finished the word.}
  BEGIN
    READ(CII);
    IF CH = 'X' THEN
      FINISHED := TRUE
    ELSE
      IF (CHARINDEX < MAXWORDLEN) THEN
      BEGIN
        WORD[CHARINDEX] := CH;
        CHARINDEX := CHARINDEX + 1
      END
  END;
  IF CHARINDEX < MAXWORDLEN THEN
    FOR BLANKINDEX := CHARINDEX TO MAXWORDLEN DO
      WORD[BLANKINDEX] := BLANK
END;      {GETWORD}


PROCEDURE CHECKWORD(COMPAREWORD : COMPARETYPE; WORD : WORDTYPE);
VAR
  COMPAREWORDFOUND : BOOLEAN;
  COMPAREWDINDEX : INTEGER;

{Check for compareword now.}

BEGIN    {CHECKWORD}
READLN;
COMPAREWORDFOUND := FALSE;
COMPAREWDINDEX := 1;
REPEAT
  IF WORD = COMPAREWORD[COMPAREWDINDEX] THEN
    COMPAREWORDFOUND := TRUE;
  COMPAREWDINDEX := COMPAREWDINDEX + 1
UNTIL COMPAREWORDFOUND OR (COMPAREWDINDEX > NUMCOMPAREWORD);
```

```
    IF COMPAREWORDFOUND THEN
      WRITELN(COMPAREWDINDEX - 1)
    ELSE
      WRITELN('ERROR IN INPUT.')
  END;    {CHECKWORD}

PROCEDURE ENTERCOMPAREWORDS(VAR COMPAREWORD : COMPARETYPE);
VAR
  COMPAREWDINDEX : INTEGER;
  FINISHED : BOOLEAN;
  WORD : WORDTYPE;

BEGIN    {ENTERCOMPAREWORDS}
  COMPAREWDINDEX := 1;
  FINISHED := FALSE;
  WRITELN('ENTER THE BASE WORDS NOW, ONE TO A LINE. TO STOP, ENTER "X" ');
  WRITELN('ALONE ON A LINE.');
  WHILE NOT FINISHED DO
  BEGIN
    GETWORD(WORD,FINISHED);
    IF NOT FINISHED THEN
      COMPAREWORD[COMPAREWDINDEX] := WORD;
    COMPAREWDINDEX := COMPAREWDINDEX + 1;
    READLN
  END
END;    {ENTERCOMPAREWORDS}

BEGIN    {MAIN}
  ENTERCOMPAREWORDS(COMPAREWORD);
  FINISHED := FALSE;
  WRITELN('ENTER THE COMPARISON WORDS NOW. TO HALT ENTER "X" BY ITSELF.');
  WHILE NOT FINISHED DO
  BEGIN
    GETWORD(WORD, FINISHED);
    CHECKWORD(COMPAREWORD,WORD)
  END
END.    {MAIN}
```

Replacement Turbo Pascal Code:

```
PROCEDURE GETWORD(VAR WORD: WORDTYPE; VAR FINISHED : BOOLEAN);
VAR
  CHARINDEX,BLANKINDEX : WORDINDEX;
  STR1 : STRING[MAXWORDLEN];

BEGIN
  READLN(STR1);
  IF (UPCHAR(STR1[1]) = 'X') AND (LENGTH(STR1) = 1) THEN
  BEGIN
    FINISHED := TRUE;
    FOR BLANKINDEX := 1 TO MAXWORDLEN DO
      WORD[BLANKINDEX] := BLANK
  END
  ELSE
  BEGIN
    FOR CHARINDEX := 1 TO LENGTH(STR1) DO
      WORD[CHARINDEX] := STR1[CHARINDEX];
    FOR BLANKINDEX := LENGTH(STR1) + 1 TO MAXWORDLEN DO
      WORD[BLANKINDEX] := BLANK
  END
END;
```

Exercise 9-15:

```
PROGRAM NAMESS(INPUT,OUTPUT);
CONST
   NAMELN = 20;          {length of names}
   SSLN = 9;             {length of social secutity number}
   NUMNAMES = 10;        {number of names to read in }

VAR
   NAMES: ARRAY[1..NUMNAMES,1..NAMELN] OF CHAR;      {holds names}
   SSNO: ARRAY[1..NUMNAMES,1..SSLN] OF CHAR;         {holds soc sec no}
   COLIN,                                            {row and column indices}
   ROWIN : INTEGER;

BEGIN

   { read names }
   FOR ROWIN := 1 TO NUMNAMES DO
   BEGIN
     FOR COLIN := 1 TO NAMELN DO
       READ(NAMES[ROWIN,COLIN]);
     READLN
   END;

   {read social secutity numbers}
   FOR ROWIN := 1 TO NUMNAMES DO
   BEGIN
     FOR COLIN := 1 TO SSLN DO
       READ(SSNO[ROWIN,COLIN]);
     READLN
   END;

   WRITELN;
   WRITELN;

   {output names and numbers}
   FOR ROWIN := 1 TO NUMNAMES DO
   BEGIN
     FOR COLIN := 1 TO NAMELN DO
       WRITE(NAMES[ROWIN,COLIN]);
     WRITELN;
     FOR COLIN := 1 TO SSLN DO
     BEGIN
       IF (COLIN = 4) OR (COLIN = 6) THEN WRITE('-');
       WRITE(SSNO[ROWIN,COLIN])
     END;
     WRITELN;
     WRITELN;
     WRITELN
   END
END.
```

Replacement Turbo Pascal Code:
(Replace entire program.)

```
PROGRAM NAMESS(INPUT,OUTPUT);
CONST
   NAMELN = 20;          {length of names}
   SSLN = 9;             {length of social secutity number}
   NUMNAMES = 10;        {number of names to read in }
```

```
VAR
   NAMES: ARRAY[1..NUMNAMES] OF STRING[NAMELN];
   SSNO: ARRAY[1..NUMNAMES] OF STRING[SSLN];
   COLIN,
   ROWIN : INTEGER;

BEGIN
   WRITELN('Enter names: ');
   FOR ROWIN := 1 TO NUMNAMES DO
   BEGIN
      WRITE(ROWIN,'. ');
      READLN(NAMES[ROWIN])
   END;
   WRITELN('Enter 9 digit SS numbers: ');
   FOR ROWIN := 1 TO NUMNAMES DO
   REPEAT
      WRITE(ROWIN,'. ');
      READLN(SSNO[ROWIN]);
      IF LENGTH(SSNO[ROWIN]) <> 9 THEN
         WRITELN('WRONG LENGTH SS NO!'^G)
   UNTIL LENGTH(SSNO[ROWIN]) = 9;
   WRITELN;
   WRITELN;

   FOR ROWIN := 1 TO NUMNAMES DO
   BEGIN
      WRITE(NAMES[ROWIN]);
      WRITELN;
      FOR COLIN := 1 TO SSLN DO
      BEGIN
         IF (COLIN = 4) OR (COLIN = 6) THEN WRITE('-');
         WRITE(SSNO[ROWIN][COLIN])
      END;
      WRITELN;
      WRITELN
   END
END.
```

CHAPTER 10 RECORDS AND VARIANTS:

Exercise 10-2:

```
PROGRAM NAMEANDBIRTH(INPUT,OUTPUT);
CONST
   BLANK = ' ';
   DASH = '-';
   SLASH = '/';
   MAXNAMELENGTH = 30;
   MAXNAMES = 20;
   THISYEAR = 86;
   ASCIIOFFSET = 48;   {The difference between a digit and its ASCII
                        code: 0 is 48 ASCII.}

TYPE
   NAMETYPE = ARRAY[1..MAXNAMELENGTH] OF CHAR;   {person's name}
   PERSON = RECORD                               {person's data record}
              NAME : NAMETYPE;
              MONTH, DAY, YEAR : INTEGER
            END;

   PERSONARRAY = ARRAY[1..MAXNAMES] OF PERSON;   {master data structure}

VAR
   PEOPLE : PERSONARRAY;
   ONEPERSON : PERSON;
   FIRSTTIME, ERROR : BOOLEAN;
   NAMEINDEX : INTEGER;
```

```
   PROCEDURE READITEM(VAR ONENAME: PERSON; VAR ERROR : BOOLEAN);

   {Procedure READITEM prompts and reads in a person and birthdate.
    It checks to make sure that the birthdate is a reasonable one. If
    an error is detected, it returns an error message and waits for
    the user to try again.}

   PROCEDURE ENTERNAME(VAR ANAME: NAMETYPE);

   {Procedure ENTERNAME reads the persons name, and pads the remainder
    of the ANAME array of CHAR with blanks.}

   VAR
      CHARINDEX : INTEGER;
      CH : CHAR;

   BEGIN   {ENTERNAME}
     IF NOT (EOLN OR EOF) THEN
     BEGIN
       CHARINDEX := 0;
       WHILE (INPUT^ = BLANK) AND NOT (EOF OR EOLN) DO
         GET(INPUT);
       FOR CHARINDEX := 1 TO MAXNAMELENGTH DO
         IF NOT (EOLN) OR (INPUT^ = DASH) THEN
           READ(ANAME[CHARINDEX])
         ELSE
           ANAME[CHARINDEX] := BLANK;
       WHILE (INPUT^ = DASH) OR (INPUT^ = BLANK) DO
         GET(INPUT)
     END
   END;   {ENTERNAME}
```

```
PROCEDURE ENTERNUMBER(VAR MDORYEAR: INTEGER; KEY: INTEGER;
                     VAR ERROR: BOOLEAN);

{Procedure ENTERNUMBER reads in the numerical data between the
 "/../" on the input line. It is called by READITEM three times,
 once each for the MONTH, DAY, and YEAR. It reads in a number
 as a character and then converst it to an integer, which makes
 inputting data more error proof.}

VAR
  NUMBER : INTEGER;
  CH : CHAR;

BEGIN     {ENTERNUMBER}
  IF NOT EOLN THEN
    READ(CH);
  NUMBER := (ORD(CH) - ASCIIOFFSET);

  {Read in a character then convert it to an integer. This code may be
   implementation dependent due to different charset mapping. In this
   case, 0 is assumed to be ASCII 48. After conversion, the number is
   checked to insure it was indeed a number and not a typo.}

  IF NUMBER <= 9 THEN
    MDORYEAR := NUMBER
  ELSE
    ERROR := TRUE;
  IF NOT ERROR AND NOT EOLN THEN     {Read second digit in input field
                                      if there is one. (e.g. the MONTH
                                      and YEAR fields in: 3/12/86).}
  BEGIN

    {If there is a second digit, then read it in and add it to
     the units place of (NUMBER * 10). As usual, check for blanks
     or a slash.}

    READ(CH);
    IF (CH <> SLASH) AND (CH <> BLANK) THEN
    BEGIN
      NUMBER := ORD(CH) - ASCIIOFFSET;
      MDORYEAR := MDORYEAR * 10 + NUMBER
    END;
    IF MDORYEAR > KEY THEN
      ERROR := TRUE;

      WHILE NOT EOLN AND (INPUT^ = BLANK) OR (INPUT^ = SLASH) DO
        GET(INPUT)
  END
  END;      {ENTERNUMBER}

BEGIN     {READITEM}
  ENTERNAME(ONENAME.NAME);
  ENTERNUMBER(ONENAME.MONTH,12,ERROR);
  ENTERNUMBER(ONENAME.DAY,31,ERROR);
  ENTERNUMBER(ONENAME.YEAR,THISYEAR,ERROR);
```

```
{Now check for impossible birthdates. February 30, for example,
 or FEB 29 when not a leap year.}

IF NOT ERROR THEN
WITH ONENAME DO
  CASE MONTH OF

    2: IF NOT (DAY > 0) AND (DAY <= 29) THEN
         ERROR := TRUE
       ELSE
         IF (YEAR MOD 4 <> 0) AND (DAY >= 29) THEN
         BEGIN
           WRITELN('Error in input, probably day');
           ERROR := TRUE
         END;

    4,9,6,11:
         IF NOT (DAY > 0) AND (DAY <= 30) THEN
           BEGIN
             WRITELN('Error in input, probably day');
             ERROR := TRUE
           END;

    1,3,5,7,8,10,12:
         IF NOT (DAY > 0) AND (DAY <= 31) THEN
           BEGIN
             WRITELN('Error in input, probably day');
             ERROR := TRUE
           END
    END
END;    {READITEM}


PROCEDURE SORTBYBIRTH(VAR PEOPLE: PERSONARRAY; NAMESREADIN : INTEGER);

{Uses a simple bubble sort to sort PEOPLE into oldest first order.
 This procedure uses the fact that for any birthday,
 ((YEAR * 10000) + (MONTH * 100) +  DAY) with be greater than
 ((YEAR * 10000) + (MONTH * 100) +  DAY) for any other birthday
 which is later than it.}

{NOTE: The value (YEAR * 10000) will create an integer overflow on
 most microcomputer systems. This value must be type real to avoid
 this problem, so all of the computed packed date values are type real.}

VAR
  LOCALINDEX : INTEGER;
  DUMMYPERSON : PERSON;
  FINISHED : BOOLEAN;

BEGIN    {SORTBYBIRTH}
  REPEAT
    FINISHED := TRUE;       {If no names are switched then FINISHED
                             will remain true and the routine will exit.}
    FOR LOCALINDEX := 1 TO (NAMESREADIN - 1) DO
    BEGIN
      IF PEOPLE[LOCALINDEX].YEAR * 10000.0 +
         PEOPLE[LOCALINDEX].MONTH * 100.0 +
         PEOPLE[LOCALINDEX].DAY  >
         PEOPLE[LOCALINDEX + 1].YEAR * 10000.0 +
         PEOPLE[LOCALINDEX + 1].MONTH * 100.0 +
         PEOPLE[LOCALINDEX + 1].DAY THEN
```

```
            BEGIN
               DUMMYPERSON := PEOPLE[LOCALINDEX];
               PEOPLE[LOCALINDEX] := PEOPLE[LOCALINDEX + 1];
               PEOPLE[LOCALINDEX + 1] := DUMMYPERSON;
               FINISHED := FALSE
            END
      END
   UNTIL FINISHED
END;    {SORTBYBIRTH}

PROCEDURE PRINTOUT(WEEBLES: PERSONARRAY; NAMESREADIN: INTEGER);
VAR
   CHINDEX : 1..MAXNAMELENGTH;
   NAMEINDEX : 1..MAXNAMES;

BEGIN    {PRINTOUT}
   WRITELN;
   WRITELN;
   WRITELN;
   FOR NAMEINDEX := 1 TO NAMESREADIN DO      {For each element in PEOPLE array
                                              in whch data was entered, do the
                                              followng: }
   BEGIN
      WRITELN;
      WRITE('Person #',NAMEINDEX,' is ');
      FOR CHINDEX := 1 TO MAXNAMELENGTH DO
         WRITE(WEEBLES[NAMEINDEX].NAME[CHINDEX]);
      WRITE(' - ',WEEBLES[NAMEINDEX].MONTH:2,'/');
      WRITE(WEEBLES[NAMEINDEX].DAY:2,'/');
      WRITE(WEEBLES[NAMEINDEX].YEAR:2);
      WRITELN
   END;
   WRITELN;
   WRITELN;
   WRITELN
END;    {PRINTOUT}
```

```
BEGIN    {MAIN}
   ERROR := FALSE;
   NAMEINDEX := 0;
   FIRSTTIME := TRUE;
   WRITELN('Enter info in form: FARR, MICHAEL-1/03/61 ');
   REPEAT
      IF NOT FIRSTTIME THEN
         READLN;

      {This code finishes reading from line before. If no line before,
       FIRSTTIME will equal true and the READLN won't be
       executed. The READLN must also be done after the EOF check
       below at the end of the loop. Otherwise the EOF test will
       wait until the user has typed in the next input line.
       Unfortunately, the prompt is not written in that case until
       after the information is entered. Note that this is a common
       error in Standard Pascal programs.}

      FIRSTTIME := FALSE;
      WRITE('ENTER A NAME AND BIRTHDATE OR EOF TO STOP: ');
      IF NOT EOF THEN
      BEGIN
         READITEM(ONEPERSON,ERROR);
         NAMEINDEX := NAMEINDEX + 1
      END;
```

```
        IF NOT ERROR THEN
          PEOPLE[NAMEINDEX] := ONEPERSON

        {If there is an error in input, then we must re-initialize
         all of the variables and try again. NAMEINDEX is decremented
         because we want to substitute the corrected entry for the
         presently incorrect one.}

        ELSE
        BEGIN
          NAMEINDEX := NAMEINDEX - 1;
          WRITELN('TRY AGAIN, ERROR IN INPUT.');
          ONEPERSON.MONTH := 0;
          ONEPERSON.DAY := 0;
          ONEPERSON.YEAR := 0;      {Re-initialize oneperson}
          ERROR := FALSE
        END
      UNTIL EOF;
      SORTBYBIRTH(PEOPLE,NAMEINDEX);
      PRINTOUT(PEOPLE,NAMEINDEX)
    END.    {MAIN}
```

Replacement Turbo Pascal Code:
(Replace two sections of code)

Section 1:

```
PROCEDURE READITEM(VAR ONENAME: PERSON; VAR DONE, ERROR : BOOLEAN);
TYPE
  INSTR = STRING[80];

VAR
  STR1 : INSTR;

PROCEDURE ENTERNAME(VAR ANAME: NAMETYPE;VAR STR2 : INSTR);
VAR
  STARTCH,
  CHARINDEX : INTEGER;
  NAMSTR : STRING[MAXNAMELENGTH];

BEGIN
  STARTCH := 1;
  WHILE STR2[STARTCH] = BLANK DO
    STARTCH := STARTCH + 1;
  NAMSTR := COPY(STR2,STARTCH,POS(DASH,STR2)-1);
  FOR CHARINDEX := 1 TO LENGTH(NAMSTR) DO
    ANAME[CHARINDEX] := NAMSTR[CHARINDEX];
  FOR CHARINDEX := LENGTH(NAMSTR)+1 TO MAXNAMELENGTH DO
    ANAME[CHARINDEX] := BLANK;
  DELETE(STR2,1,POS(DASH,STR2))
END;

PROCEDURE ENTERNUMBER(VAR MDORYEAR: INTEGER; KEY: INTEGER;
                      VAR ERROR: BOOLEAN; VAR STR2 : INSTR);
VAR
  INDEX,
  NUMBER : INTEGER;
  CH : CHAR;
```

```
BEGIN
  ERROR := FALSE;
  CH := STR2[1];
  NUMBER := (ORD(CH) - ASCIIOFFSET);
  IF (NUMBER < = 9) AND (LENGTH (STR2) > 0) THEN
    MDORYEAR := NUMBER
  ELSE
    ERROR := TRUE;

  IF NOT ERROR AND (LENGTH(STR2) > 1) THEN
  BEGIN
    CH := STR2[2];
    IF (CH <> SLASH) AND (CH <> BLANK) THEN
    BEGIN
      NUMBER := ORD(CH) - ASCIIOFFSET;
      MDORYEAR := MDORYEAR *  10 + NUMBER
    END;
    IF MDORYEAR > KEY THEN
      ERROR := TRUE;
    IF (CH = SLASH) OR (CH = BLANK) THEN
      DELETE(STR2,1,2)
    ELSE
      IF (LENGTH(STR2) > 2) AND ((STR2[3] = SLASH) OR (STR2[3] = BLANK)) THEN
        DELETE(STR2,1,3)
  END
  ELSE
    DELETE(STR2,1,1)
END;


BEGIN
  READLN(STR1);
  ENTERNAME(ONENAME.NAME,STR1);
  ENTERNUMBER(ONENAME.MONTH,12,ERROR,STR1);
  ENTERNUMBER(ONENAME.DAY,31,ERROR,STR1);
  ENTERNUMBER(ONENAME.YEAR,THISYEAR,ERROR,STR1);
```

Section 2:

```
BEGIN  {MAIN}
  NAMEINDEX := 0;
  WRITELN('Enter info in form: FARR, MICHAEL-1/03/61 ');
  REPEAT
    WRITE('Enter a name and birthdate or BLANK to stop: ');
    READITEM(ONEPERSON,DONE,ERROR);
    IF NOT DONE THEN
    BEGIN
      NAMEINDEX := NAMEINDEX + 1;
      IF NOT ERROR THEN
        PEOPLE[NAMEINDEX] := ONEPERSON
      ELSE
      BEGIN
        NAMEINDEX := NAMEINDEX - 1;
        WRITELN('Try again, error in input.');
        ONEPERSON.MONTH := 0;
        ONEPERSON.DAY := 0;
        ONEPERSON.YEAR := 0;
        ERROR := FALSE
      END
    END
  UNTIL DONE;
  SORTBYBIRTH(PEOPLE,NAMEINDEX);
  PRINTOUT(PEOPLE,NAMEINDEX)
END. {MAIN}
```

CHAPTER 11 FILES

Exercise 11-3:

```
PROGRAM PRINTLINES(INPUT,OUTPUT,INFILE);
CONST
  MAXONPAGE = 60;
  MAXNAMELEN = 20;
  BLANK = ' ';

TYPE
  PAGEINDEX = 1..MAXONPAGE;
  NAMEINDEX = 1..MAXNAMELEN;
  NAMETYPE = ARRAY [NAMEINDEX] OF CHAR;

VAR
  INFILE : TEXT;
  FILENAME : NAMETYPE;
  SPACEINDEX, SPACING : 1..3;
  PAGEPOSITION, CURRENTLINE : INTEGER;
  CH : CHAR;
  INDEX : NAMEINDEX;
  PAGENUM : PAGEINDEX;


BEGIN
  WRITE('From what file do you want the text taken? ');
  FOR INDEX := 1 TO MAXNAMELEN DO
  BEGIN
    FILENAME[INDEX] := BLANK;
    IF NOT EOLN THEN
      READ(FILENAME[INDEX])
  END;
  READLN;
  RESET(INFILE, FILENAME);

  PAGENUM := 1;
  CURRENTLINE := 1;
  PAGEPOSITION := 11;   {Room for the page heading.}

  WRITE('How shall the output be spaced? 1-3: ');
  READLN(SPACING);
  PAGE(OUTPUT);
  WRITELN;
  WRITELN;
  WRITELN;
  WRITELN;
  WRITELN;
  WRITELN('The following is a listing of file: ',FILENAME,'  PAGE 1');
  WRITELN;
  WRITELN;
  WRITELN;
  WRITELN;
WHILE NOT EOF(INFILE) DO
BEGIN
  WRITE(CURRENTLINE:3);
  WRITE(BLANK:2);
  CURRENTLINE := CURRENTLINE + 1;
  PAGEPOSITION := PAGEPOSITION + SPACING;
  WHILE NOT EOF(INFILE) AND NOT EOLN(INFILE) DO
  BEGIN
```

```
        READ(INFILE,CH);
        WRITE(CH)
      END;
    IF EOLN(INFILE) THEN
    BEGIN
      READLN(INFILE);
      FOR SPACEINDEX := 1 TO SPACING DO
        WRITELN;
      IF (PAGEPOSITION > MAXONPAGE) AND NOT EOF(INFILE) THEN
      BEGIN
        PAGENUM := PAGENUM + 1;
        PAGE(OUTPUT);
        WRITELN;
        WRITELN;
        WRITELN;
        WRITELN;
        WRITELN(BLANK:35,'PAGE ',PAGENUM:3);
        WRITELN;
        WRITELN;
        WRITELN;
        WRITELN;
        PAGEPOSITION := 10
      END
    END
  END
END.
```

Replacement Turbo Pascal Code:

(Replace entire program.)

```
PROGRAM PRINTLINES;
CONST
  MAXONPAGE = 60;
  MAXNAMELEN = 20;
  BLANK = ' ';

TYPE
  PAGEINDEX = 1..MAXONPAGE;
  NAMEINDEX = 1..MAXNAMELEN;
  NAMETYPE = STRING[20];

VAR
  INFILE : TEXT;
  FILENAME : NAMETYPE;
  SPACEINDEX, SPACING : 1..3;
  PAGEPOSITION, CURRENTLINE : INTEGER;
  CH : CHAR;
  INDEX : NAMEINDEX;
  PAGENUM : PAGEINDEX;


BEGIN
  WRITE('From what file do you want the text taken? ');
  READLN(FILENAME);
  ASSIGN(INFILE,FILENAME);
  RESET(INFILE);

  PAGENUM := 1;
  CURRENTLINE := 1;
  PAGEPOSITION := 11;   {Room for the page heading.}
```

```
    WRITE('How shall the output be spaced? 1-3: ');
    READLN(SPACING);
    WRITE(LST,CHR(12));   {TOP OF PAGE}
    WRITELN(LST);
    WRITELN(LST);
    WRITELN(LST);
    WRITELN(LST);
    WRITELN(LST);
    WRITELN(LST,'The following is a listing of file: ',FILENAME,'  PAGE 1');
    WRITELN(LST);
    WRITELN(LST);
    WRITELN(LST);
    WRITELN(LST);

    WHILE NOT EOF(INFILE) DO
    BEGIN
      WRITE(LST,CURRENTLINE:3);
      WRITE(LST,BLANK:2);
      CURRENTLINE := CURRENTLINE + 1;
      PAGEPOSITION := PAGEPOSITION + SPACING;
      WHILE NOT EOF(INFILE) AND NOT EOLN(INFILE) DO
      BEGIN
        READ(INFILE,CH);
        WRITE(LST,CH)
      END;
      IF EOLN(INFILE) THEN
      BEGIN
        READLN(INFILE);
        FOR SPACEINDEX := 1 TO SPACING DO
          WRITELN(LST);
        IF (PAGEPOSITION > MAXONPAGE) AND NOT EOF(INFILE) THEN
        BEGIN
          PAGENUM := PAGENUM + 1;
          WRITE(LST,CHR(12));            {TOP OF PAGE}
          WRITELN(LST);
          WRITELN(LST);
          WRITELN(LST);
          WRITELN(LST);
          WRITELN(LST,BLANK:35,'PAGE ',PAGENUM:3);
          WRITELN(LST);
          WRITELN(LST);
          WRITELN(LST);
          WRITELN(LST);
          PAGEPOSITION := 10
        END
      END
    END;
    WRITE(LST,CHR(12));
    CLOSE(INFILE)
END.
```

Exercise 11-7:

```
PROGRAM DIVIDEFILE (INPUT,OUTPUT,INFILE,CREDITFILE,DEBITFILE);
CONST
  NAMELEN = 20;
  ADDRLEN = 15;
TYPE
  CUSTREC = RECORD
              NAME:     ARRAY[1..NAMELEN] OF CHAR;
              NO:       INTEGER;
              AMT:      REAL;
```

```
                        KEY:        INTEGER;
                        ADDRESS:    ARRAY[1..ADDRLEN] OF CHAR;
                        CITY:       ARRAY[1..ADDRLEN] OF CHAR;
                        ST:         ARRAY[1..2] OF CHAR;
                        ZIP:        ARRAY[1..5] OF CHAR
                      END;

    VAR
      CUSTOMER : CUSTREC;
      INFILE,
      CREDITFILE,
      DEBITFILE : TEXT;

    PROCEDURE READREC;
    VAR
      INDX : INTEGER;

    BEGIN
      WITH CUSTOMER DO
      BEGIN
        FOR INDX := 1 TO NAMELEN DO
          READ(INFILE, NAME[INDX]);
        READ(INFILE, NO);
        READ(INFILE, AMT);
        READLN(INFILE, KEY);
        FOR INDX := 1 TO ADDRLEN DO
          READ(INFILE, ADDRESS[INDX]);
        FOR INDX := 1 TO ADDRLEN DO
          READ(INFILE, CITY[INDX]);
        FOR INDX := 1 TO 2 DO
          READ(INFILE, ST[INDX]);
        FOR INDX := 1 TO 5 DO
          READ(INFILE, ZIP[INDX]);
        READLN(INFILE)
      END
    END;


    PROCEDURE WRITEREC(VAR OUTFILE : TEXT);
    VAR
      INDX : INTEGER;

    BEGIN
      WITH CUSTOMER DO
      BEGIN
        FOR INDX := 1 TO NAMELEN DO
          WRITE(OUTFILE, NAME[INDX]);
        WRITELN(OUTFILE);
        FOR INDX := 1 TO ADDRLEN DO
          WRITE(OUTFILE, ADDRESS[INDX]);
        FOR INDX := 1 TO ADDRLEN DO
          WRITE(OUTFILE, CITY[INDX]);
        FOR INDX := 1 TO 2 DO
          WRITE(OUTFILE, ST[INDX]);
        FOR INDX := 1 TO 5 DO
          WRITE(OUTFILE, ZIP[INDX]);
        WRITELN(OUTFILE)
      END
    END;
```

```
BEGIN
  RESET(INFILE);
  REWRITE(CREDITFILE);
  REWRITE(DEBITFILE);

  READREC;
  WHILE NOT EOF(INFILE) DO
  BEGIN
    IF CUSTOMER.KEY = 1 THEN
      WRITEREC(CREDITFILE)
    ELSE
      WRITEREC(DEBITFILE);
    READREC
  END
END.
```

Replacement Turbo Pascal Code:

(Replace entire program.)

```
PROGRAM DIVIDEFILE;
CONST
  NAMELEN = 20;
  ADDRLEN = 15;
TYPE
  CUSTREC = RECORD
                NAME:     STRING[NAMELEN];
                NO:       INTEGER;
                AMT:      REAL;
                KEY:      INTEGER;
                ADDRESS:  STRING[ADDRLEN];
                CITY:     STRING[ADDRLEN];
                ST:       STRING[2];
                ZIP:      STRING[5]
              END;

VAR
  CUSTOMER : CUSTREC;
  CLOSE(CREDITFILE);
  CLOSE(DEBITFILE)
END.

  INFILE,
  CREDITFILE,
  DEBITFILE : TEXT;

PROCEDURE READREC;
VAR
  INDX : INTEGER;

BEGIN
  WITH CUSTOMER DO
  BEGIN
    READLN(INFILE, NAME);
    READLN(INFILE, NO);
    READLN(INFILE, AMT);
    READLN(INFILE, KEY);
    READLN(INFILE, ADDRESS);
    READLN(INFILE, CITY);
    READLN(INFILE, ST);
    READLN(INFILE, ZIP)
  END
END;
```

```
      PROCEDURE WRITEREC(VAR OUTFILE : TEXT);

      BEGIN
        WITH CUSTOMER DO
        BEGIN
            WRITELN(OUTFILE, NAME);
            WRITELN(OUTFILE, ADDRESS);
            WRITELN(OUTFILE, CITY);
            WRITELN(OUTFILE, ST);
            WRITELN(OUTFILE, ZIP)
        END
      END;

      BEGIN
        ASSIGN(INFILE,'INDAT');
        RESET(INFILE);
        ASSIGN(CREDITFILE,'CREDITDAT');
        REWRITE(CREDITFILE);
        ASSIGN(DEBITFILE,'DEBITDAT');
        REWRITE(DEBITFILE);

        WHILE NOT EOF(INFILE) DO
        BEGIN
          READREC;
          IF CUSTOMER.KEY = 1 THEN
            WRITEREC(CREDITFILE)
          ELSE
            WRITEREC(DEBITFILE)
        END;
        CLOSE(INFILE);
```

CHAPTER 12 SETS :

Exercise 12-3:

```
PROGRAM LIKENESS(INPUT,OUTPUT);
CONST
    BLANK = ' ';
    STOPCHAR = '/';
    MAXNAMELENGTH = 20;
    MAXNAMES = 20;
    FEMALE = 'F';
    MALE = 'M';
    BLONDE = 'L';       {Second letter in word.}
    BRUNETTE = 'R';
    REDHEAD = 'E';

TYPE
    NAMETYPE = ARRAY[1..MAXNAMELENGTH] OF CHAR;
    PERSON = RECORD
                NAME : NAMETYPE;
                AGE : INTEGER;
                SEX, HAIRCOLOR : CHAR
             END;

    PERSONARRAY = ARRAY[1..MAXNAMES] OF PERSON;
```

```
VAR
  LETTERS, DIGITS, SEXES, HAIRCLRS : SET OF CHAR;
  {Used for error checking; without sets error checking is very verbose.}

  PEOPLE : PERSONARRAY;
  FIRSTTIME, ERROR : BOOLEAN;
  LOWERBOUND, UPPERBOUND, PERSONINDEX : INTEGER;

  {LOWERBOUND and UPPERBOUND are variables used in procedure
   COMPAREINFO, to hold the values of the AGE boundries.
   PERSONINDEX is used to index the PERSONARRAY.}

  ENTERSEX : CHAR;
  ENTERCOLOR : CHAR;

  {ENTERSEX and ENTERCOLOR are variables used as keys to search
   the PERSONARRAY. They correspond to fields in the record PERSON
   of PERSONARRAY. They contain the desired sex and hair color
   characteristics.}

PROCEDURE ENTERNAME(VAR ANAME : NAMETYPE);

{This procedure enters name char by char and uses INPUT^ to
 check the next character to be read off the input line.}

VAR
  CHARINDEX : INTEGER;

BEGIN    {ENTERNAME}
  IF NOT (EOLN OR EOF) THEN
  BEGIN
    CHARINDEX := 0;
    WHILE (INPUT^ = BLANK) AND NOT (EOF OR EOLN) DO
      GET(INPUT);
    FOR CHARINDEX := 1 TO MAXNAMELENGTH DO
      IF (NOT EOLN) THEN
        READ(ANAME[CHARINDEX])
      ELSE
        ANAME[CHARINDEX] := BLANK
  END;
  READLN
END;    {ENTERNAME}

PROCEDURE BUILDITEM(VAR ONEPERSON: PERSON; VAR ERROR: BOOLEAN);

{This procedure enters the information into the person record
 of the present element in the PERSONARRAY PEOPLE. FLUSH(Filemane)
 is a non-standard predefined procedure which empties the buffer
 of the specified file. In this case, it allows the previous WRITE
 statement to complete before any 'GET's take place. Normally, any
 READ statement performs a FLUSH(OUTPUT) implicitly. These details
 are implementation dependent. }

BEGIN    {BUILDITEM}
  ENTERNAME (ONEPERSON.NAME);
  WRITE('Enter age of person: ');
  FLUSH(OUTPUT);
  WHILE NOT (INPUT^ IN DIGITS) AND (NOT EOLN) DO
    GET(INPUT);
```

```
     IF .(NOT EOLN) THEN
        READLN(ONEPERSON.AGE)
     ELSE
        ERROR := TRUE;

     IF NOT ERROR THEN
     BEGIN
        WRITE('Enter sex; Male/Female: ');
        FLUSH(OUTPUT);
        WHILE NOT (INPUT^ IN SEXES) AND (NOT EOLN) DO
           GET(INPUT);
        IF (NOT EOLN) AND (INPUT^ IN SEXES) THEN
           READLN(ONEPERSON.SEX)
        ELSE
           ERROR := TRUE;

        WRITE('Enter hair color; BLONDE, BRUNETTE or REDHEAD: ');

        {Though the user is asked to type in an entire word, only
         the first two characters are read. }

        FLUSH(OUTPUT);
        WHILE NOT (INPUT^ IN LETTERS) DO
           GET(INPUT);
        IF NOT EOLN THEN
           GET(INPUT);
        IF (NOT EOLN) AND (INPUT^ IN HAIRCLRS) THEN
           READ(ONEPERSON.HAIRCOLOR)
        ELSE
           ERROR := TRUE
     END
END;      {BUILDITEM}

PROCEDURE COMPAREINFO(VAR UPPERBOUND, LOWERBOUND : INTEGER;
                      VAR SEX, HAIRCOLOR : CHAR; VAR ERROR : BOOLEAN);

{Gets comparison limits for selecting stored records.}

BEGIN     {COMPAREINFO}
   WHILE NOT (INPUT^ IN DIGITS) AND (NOT EOLN) DO
      GET(INPUT);

   {This statement gets rid of all possible garbage before the first
    integer is read and also makes sure a character is not read in
    as a number. If the information needed isn't on the line then
    EOLN will be read before the upper and lower bounds are read in.
    A check is also done to insure that UPPERBOUND and LOWERBOUND
    are between 0 and 100 (years). }

   IF NOT EOLN THEN
      READ(LOWERBOUND)
   ELSE
      ERROR := TRUE;

   WHILE NOT (INPUT^ IN DIGITS) AND (NOT EOLN) DO
      GET(INPUT);
   IF NOT EOLN THEN
      READ(UPPERBOUND)
   ELSE
      ERROR := TRUE;
```

```
    IF NOT (LOWERBOUND > 0) AND (UPPERBOUND <= 100) THEN
      ERROR := TRUE;

    IF NOT ERROR THEN
    BEGIN
      WRITE('ENTER SEX; MALE/FEMALE: ');
      FLUSH(OUTPUT);
      WHILE NOT (INPUT^ IN SEXES) AND (NOT EOLN) DO
        GET(INPUT);
      IF (NOT EOLN) AND (INPUT^ IN SEXES) THEN
        READLN(SEX)
      ELSE
        ERROR := TRUE;
        WRITE('ENTER HAIR COLOR; BLONDE, BRUNETTE OR REDHEAD: ');

        {Though the user is asked to type in an entire word, only
         the first two characters are read. }

        FLUSH(OUTPUT);
        WHILE NOT (INPUT^ IN LETTERS) DO
          GET(INPUT);
        IF NOT EOLN THEN
          GET(INPUT);
        IF (NOT EOLN) AND (INPUT^ IN HAIRCLRS) THEN
          READ(HAIRCOLOR)
        ELSE
          ERROR := TRUE
    END
  END;    {COMPAREINFO}
```

```
PROCEDURE PRINTITEM(ONEPERSON : PERSON);
VAR
  CHINDEX : INTEGER;

BEGIN   {PRINTITEM}
  CHINDEX := 1;
  FOR CHINDEX := 1 TO MAXNAMELENGTH DO
    WRITE(ONEPERSON.NAME[CHINDEX]);
  WRITE('   AGE: ',ONEPERSON.AGE:0);
  WRITELN
END;    {PRINTITEM}

PROCEDURE FINDLUCKYONES(PEOPLE: PERSONARRAY; NAMESREADIN: INTEGER);

{This procedure searches through the PERSONARRAY comparing fields
 of the PERSON record containing the age, hair, and sex data. }

VAR
  NAMEINDEX : INTEGER;
  FOUND : BOOLEAN;

BEGIN   {FINDLUCKYONES}
  FOUND := FALSE;
  WRITELN;
  WRITELN;
  FOR NAMEINDEX := 1 TO NAMESREADIN DO   {for each element of PERSONARRAY}
```

```
                IF (PEOPLE[NAMEINDEX].SEX = ENTERSEX) AND
                   (PEOPLE[NAMEINDEX].HAIRCOLOR = ENTERCOLOR) THEN
                 IF (PEOPLE[NAMEINDEX].AGE <= UPPERBOUND) AND
                    (PEOPLE[NAMEINDEX].AGE >= LOWERBOUND) THEN

                 { If the kind of person specified is found, print out the record. }

                 BEGIN
                   PRINTITEM(PEOPLE[NAMEINDEX]);
                       FOUND := TRUE
                     END;
               IF NOT FOUND THEN
                 WRITELN('NONE WITH THAT DESCRIPTION WERE FOUND.')
              END;    {FINDLUCKYONES}

          PROCEDURE CHARACTERISTICS(UPPERBOUND, LOWERBOUND : INTEGER;
                                    SEX, HAIRCOLOR: CHAR);
          BEGIN    {CHARACTERISTICS}

          {This procedure prints the heading on the output. }

          WRITELN('*************************************************');
          WRITELN('THOSE PEOPLE WITH THE FOLLOWING CHARACTERISTICS: ');
          WRITELN;
          WRITE('   AGE FROM ',LOWERBOUND:0,' TO ', UPPERBOUND:0,', SEX: ');
          IF SEX = FEMALE THEN
            WRITE('FEMALE AND ')
          ELSE
            WRITE('MALE AND ');
          WRITE('HAIRCOLOR: ');
            CASE HAIRCOLOR OF
              BRUNETTE: WRITELN('BRUNETTE ARE: ');
              BLONDE  : WRITELN('BLONDE ARE: ');
              REDHEAD : WRITELN('REDHEAD ARE: ')
            END
          END;    {CHARACTERISTICS}
```

```
BEGIN    {MAIN}
  SEXES := [MALE, FEMALE];
  HAIRCLRS := [REDHEAD, BLONDE, BRUNETTE];
  DIGITS := ['0'..'9'];
  LETTERS := ['A'..'Z','A'..'Z'];
  PERSONINDEX := 0;
  FIRSTTIME := TRUE;
  ERROR := FALSE;
  WRITELN('ENTER PEOPLE AND THEIR CHARACTERISTICS, ENTER "',STOPCHAR,
          '" TO STOP.');
  REPEAT
    WRITE('ENTER PERSON''S NAME: ');
    IF NOT FIRSTTIME THEN
      READLN;

    {Finish reading from previous line. Necessary to do the
     READLN  after the EOF check below. }

    FIRSTTIME := FALSE;
    IF NOT (INPUT^ = STOPCHAR) THEN

    { Call BUILDITEM to read NAME and BIRTHDATE. }

    BEGIN
```

```
         PERSONINDEX := PERSONINDEX + 1;
         BUILDITEM(PEOPLE[PERSONINDEX], ERROR);
         PRINTITEM(PEOPLE[PERSONINDEX])
      END;
      IF ERROR AND NOT (INPUT^ = STOPCHAR) THEN
      BEGIN
         PERSONINDEX := PERSONINDEX - 1;
         WRITELN('TRY AGAIN, ERROR IN INPUT.');
         ERROR := FALSE
      END
   UNTIL (INPUT^ = STOPCHAR) OR (PERSONINDEX >= MAXNAMES);
   WRITELN('ENTERING COMPARISON...');
   WRITELN;
   REPEAT
      WRITE('ENTER AGE SPAN, (E.G. 18 TO 24): ');
      READLN;
      IF NOT ERROR AND NOT EOF THEN
         COMPAREINFO(UPPERBOUND, LOWERBOUND, ENTERSEX, ENTERCOLOR, ERROR);
      IF ERROR THEN
      BEGIN
         ERROR := FALSE;
         WRITELN('ERROR IN CHARACTERISTICS. TRY AGAIN.')
      END
      ELSE
         IF NOT EOF THEN
         BEGIN
            CHARACTERISTICS(UPPERBOUND, LOWERBOUND, ENTERSEX, ENTERCOLOR);
            FINDLUCKYONES(PEOPLE,PERSONINDEX)
         END
   UNTIL EOF;
   WRITELN;
   WRITELN
END.     {MAIN}
```

Replacement Turbo Pascal Code:
(Replace two sections of code)

Section 1:

```
VAR
   LETTERS, DIGITS, SEXES, HAIRCLRS : SET OF CHAR;
   VALIDAGE : SET OF BYTE;
   PEOPLE : PERSONARRAY;
   DONE, ERROR : BOOLEAN;
   LOWERBOUND, UPPERBOUND, PERSONINDEX : INTEGER;
   ENTERSEX : CHAR;
   ENTERCOLOR : CHAR;
   ANS,
   CH :CHAR;

PROCEDURE ENTERNAME(VAR ANAME : NAMETYPE);
VAR

   CHARINDEX : INTEGER;
   STR1 : STRING[80];
```

```
BEGIN
  READLN(STR1);
  CH := STR1[1];
  FOR CHARINDEX := 1 TO LENGTH(STR1) DO
    ANAME[CHARINDEX] := STR1[CHARINDEX];
  FOR CHARINDEX := LENGTH(STR1) + 1 TO MAXNAMELENGTH DO
    ANAME[CHARINDEX] := BLANK
END;

PROCEDURE BUILDITEM(VAR ONEPERSON: PERSON; VAR ERROR: BOOLEAN);
BEGIN
  ERROR := FALSE;
  ENTERNAME (ONEPERSON.NAME);
  IF NOT (CH = STOPCHAR) THEN
  BEGIN
    WRITE('Enter age of person: ');
    READLN(ONEPERSON.AGE);
    IF NOT (ONEPERSON.AGE IN VALIDAGE) THEN
      ERROR := TRUE;
  END
  ELSE
    WRITELN('END OF INPUT DATA');

  IF (NOT ERROR) AND NOT (CH = STOPCHAR) THEN
  BEGIN
    WRITE('Enter sex; Male/Female: ');
    REPEAT
      READ(KBD,ONEPERSON.SEX)
    UNTIL UPCASE (ONEPERSON.SEX) IN SEXES;
    WRITELN(ONEPERSON.SEX);

    WRITE('Enter haircolor - bLond, bRunette, or rEdhead: ');
    REPEAT
      READ(KBD,ONEPERSON.HAIRCOLOR)
    UNTIL UPCASE (ONEPERSON.HAIRCOLOR) IN HAIRCLRS;
    WRITELN(ONEPERSON.HAIRCOLOR)
  END
END;

PROCEDURE COMPAREINFO(VAR UPPERBOUND, LOWERBOUND : INTEGER;
                      VAR SEX, HAIRCOLOR : CHAR; VAR ERROR : BOOLEAN);
BEGIN
  WRITE('Enter LOWER BOUND: ');
  READLN(LOWERBOUND);
  IF NOT (LOWERBOUND IN VALIDAGE) THEN
    ERROR := TRUE;
  WRITE('Enter UPPER BOUND: ');
  READLN(UPPERBOUND);
  IF NOT (UPPERBOUND IN VALIDAGE) THEN
    ERROR := TRUE;
  IF NOT ERROR THEN
  BEGIN
    WRITE('Enter sex; Male/Female: ');
    REPEAT
      READ(KBD,SEX)
    UNTIL UPCASE (SEX) IN SEXES;
    WRITELN(SEX);

    WRITE('Enter haircolor - bLond, bRunette, or rEdhead: ');
    REPEAT
      READ(KBD,HAIRCOLOR)
    UNTIL UPCASE (HAIRCOLOR) IN HAIRCLRS;
    WRITELN(HAIRCOLOR)
  END
END;
```

Section 2:

```
BEGIN  {MAIN}
  SEXES := [MALE, FEMALE];
  HAIRCLRS := [REDHEAD, BLONDE, BRUNETTE];
  DIGITS := ['0'..'9'];
  LETTERS := ['A'..'Z','a'..'z'];
  VALIDAGE := [1..100];
  PERSONINDEX := 0;
  DONE := FALSE;
  ERROR := FALSE;
  CH := ' ';
  WRITELN('Enter people and their characteristics, enter "',STOPCHAR,
          '" to stop.');
  REPEAT
    WRITE('Enter person''s name: ');
    IF NOT (CH = STOPCHAR) THEN
    BEGIN
      PERSONINDEX := PERSONINDEX + 1;
      BUILDITEM(PEOPLE[PERSONINDEX], ERROR);
      IF NOT (CH = STOPCHAR) THEN
        PRINTITEM(PEOPLE[PERSONINDEX])
    END;
    IF CH = STOPCHAR THEN
      PERSONINDEX := PERSONINDEX - 1;
    IF ERROR AND NOT (CH = STOPCHAR) THEN
    BEGIN
      PERSONINDEX := PERSONINDEX - 1;
      WRITELN('Try again, error in input.');
      ERROR := FALSE
    END
  UNTIL (CH = STOPCHAR) OR (PERSONINDEX >= MAXNAMES);
  WRITELN('Entering comparison...');
  WRITELN;
  REPEAT
    WRITELN('Enter age span, (e.g. 18 to 24): ');
    COMPAREINFO(UPPERBOUND, LOWERBOUND, ENTERSEX, ENTERCOLOR, ERROR);
    IF ERROR THEN
    BEGIN
      ERROR := FALSE;
      WRITELN('Error in characteristics. Try again.')
    END
    ELSE
    BEGIN
      CHARACTERISTICS(UPPERBOUND, LOWERBOUND, ENTERSEX, ENTERCOLOR);
      FINDLUCKYONES(PEOPLE,PERSONINDEX)
    END;
    WRITELN;
    REPEAT
      WRITE('Quit? (Y/N) ');
      READ(KBD,ANS);
    UNTIL UPCASE(ANS) IN ['Y','N'];
    DONE := UPCASE(ANS) = 'Y';
    WRITELN(UPCASE(ANS));
    WRITELN
  UNTIL DONE;
  WRITELN;
  WRITELN
END.  {MAIN}
```

CHAPTER 13 POINTERS AND LISTS:

Exercise 13-2:

```
PROGRAM APPOINTMENTBOOK(INPUT,OUTPUT);
CONST
  MAXREMINDERMSGLENGTH = 80;
  PROMPT = 'ENTER COMMAND >';
  BLANK = ' ';

TYPE
  REMINDERENTRYPTR = ^REMINDERENTRY;
  REMINDERENTRY = RECORD
                    DATE : REAL;        {Real type used to prevent overflow}
                    TIME : INTEGER;
                    REMINDERSTRING : ARRAY[1..MAXREMINDERMSGLENGTH] OF CHAR;
                    REMINDERSTRINGLEN : INTEGER;
                    NEXTREMINDER : REMINDERENTRYPTR;
                  END;

VAR
  FIRSTTIMEINENTER,
  QUIT : BOOLEAN;
  REMINDERHEAD : REMINDERENTRYPTR;

PROCEDURE DELETEREMINDER;

{Remove a reminder from linked list.}

VAR
  I, NUMOFENTRYTODELETE : INTEGER;
  DEAD, REM : REMINDERENTRYPTR;

BEGIN    {DELETEREMINDER}
  WRITE('Enter number of appointment to delete: ');
  READLN(NUMOFENTRYTODELETE);
  IF (NUMOFENTRYTODELETE < 1) OR (REMINDERHEAD = NIL) THEN
    WRITELN('Bad appointment number or list is empty.')
  ELSE
  BEGIN
    IF NUMOFENTRYTODELETE = 1 THEN
    BEGIN
      DEAD := REMINDERHEAD;
      REMINDERHEAD := REMINDERHEAD^.NEXTREMINDER;
      DISPOSE(DEAD)
    END
    ELSE
    BEGIN
      REM := REMINDERHEAD;
      I := 1;
      WHILE (REM <> NIL) AND (I < NUMOFENTRYTODELETE - 1) DO
      BEGIN
        REM := REM^.NEXTREMINDER;
        I := I + 1
      END;
      IF (REM = NIL) OR (REM^.NEXTREMINDER = NIL) THEN
        WRITELN('No such entry')
      ELSE
      BEGIN
```

```
            DEAD := REM^.NEXTREMINDER;
            REM^.NEXTREMINDER := DEAD^.NEXTREMINDER;
            DISPOSE(DEAD)
          END
        END
    END
  END
END;     {DELETEREMINDER}


PROCEDURE INSERTREMINDER(REMINDER : REMINDERENTRYPTR);

{ Do the 'dirty work' of insertion sorting new reminder records
  into pointer list structure. }

VAR
  REM, PREV : REMINDERENTRYPTR;
  INSERTED : BOOLEAN;

PROCEDURE INSERT(AFTER,NEWENTRY : REMINDERENTRYPTR);

{Relink ponters to insert new entry in list after given entry. }

BEGIN     {INSERT}
  IF AFTER = NIL THEN
  BEGIN
    NEWENTRY^.NEXTREMINDER := REMINDERHEAD;
    REMINDERHEAD := NEWENTRY
  END
  ELSE
  BEGIN
    NEWENTRY^.NEXTREMINDER := AFTER^.NEXTREMINDER;
    AFTER^.NEXTREMINDER := NEWENTRY
  END
END;     {INSERT}


FUNCTION GREATERTHAN(REMINDERREC1, REMINDERREC2 : REMINDERENTRYPTR):BOOLEAN;

{Compare packed dates and times to determine earliest reminder record. }

BEGIN    {GREATERTHAN}
  IF REMINDERREC1^.DATE = REMINDERREC2^.DATE THEN
    GREATERTHAN := REMINDERREC1^.TIME > REMINDERREC2^.TIME
  ELSE
    GREATERTHAN := REMINDERREC1^.DATE > REMINDERREC2^.DATE
END;     {GREATERTHAN}


BEGIN     {INSERTREMINDER}
  IF REMINDERHEAD = NIL THEN
    INSERT(NIL,REMINDER)
  ELSE

    PARAMETERERROR := TRUE;
    WRITELN('Hour or minute out of range')
  END
  ELSE
    PACKTIME := HOUR * 100 + MINUTE
END;     {PACKTIME}


BEGIN     {ENTERREMINDER}

{Build a reminder record, and call insertion routine.}
```

```
       PARAMETERERROR := FALSE;
       NEW(REMINDER);
       WRITE('Enter date: ');
       IF FIRSTTIMEINENTER THEN WRITE('e.g. 4 10 80 ');

       {Give user example if it is his first time.}

       READLN(MONTH, DAY, YEAR);
       REMINDER^.DATE := PACKDATE(MONTH,DAY,YEAR);
       IF NOT PARAMETERERROR THEN
       BEGIN
         WRITE('Enter time: ');
         IF FIRSTTIMEINENTER THEN WRITE('e.g. 17 50 for 5:50 PM ');
         READLN(HOUR, MINUTE);
         REMINDER^.TIME := PACKTIME(HOUR,MINUTE);
```

```
      IF NOT PARAMETERERROR THEN
      BEGIN
        WRITELN('Enter 1 sentence reminder: ');
        IF NOT EOF THEN
        BEGIN
          WHILE EOLN DO READLN;
          R := 0;
          REPEAT
            R := R + 1;
            READ(REMINDER^.REMINDERSTRING[R])
          UNTIL EOLN;
          IF EOLN THEN
            READLN;
          REMINDER^.REMINDERSTRINGLEN := R;
          INSERTREMINDER(REMINDER);
          FIRSTTIMEINENTER := FALSE
        END
      END
  END
END;    {ENTERREMINDER}
```

```
 PROCEDURE PRINTDATE(THEDATE : REAL);
 VAR
   THEDAY, THEMONTH, THEYEAR, YEARREM : INTEGER;
   BEGIN
     REM := REMINDERHEAD;
     PREV := NIL;
     REPEAT
       IF GREATERTHAN(REMINDER,REM) THEN
       BEGIN
         INSERTED := FALSE;
         PREV := REM;
         REM := REM^.NEXTREMINDER
       END
       ELSE
       BEGIN
         INSERTED := TRUE;
         INSERT(PREV,REMINDER)
       END
     UNTIL (REM = NIL) OR INSERTED;
     IF NOT INSERTED THEN INSERT(PREV,REMINDER)
   END
 END;    {INSERTREMINDER}
```

```
PROCEDURE ENTERREMINDER;
VAR
   REMINDER : REMINDERENTRYPTR;
   HOUR, MINUTE, R, MONTH, DAY, YEAR : INTEGER;
   PARAMETERERROR : BOOLEAN;

FUNCTION PACKDATE(MONTH, DAY, YEAR : INTEGER) :REAL;

{Functon PACKDATE takes three integers (MONTH, DAY, YEAR) and creates
one real number from them. (A real type is used to pervent integer
overflow.) For example, to see what year it is (after PACKing)
just check the value in the ten thousands place. This technique is
used to avoid keeping individual integer values for MONTH, DAY, and
YEAR (or HOUR and SECOND). Only two values are required, real type
PACKDATE and a similar integer type PACKTIME. }

BEGIN   {PACKDATE}
   IF (MONTH < 1) OR (MONTH > 12) OR (DAY < 1) OR (DAY > 31) OR
      (YEAR < 1) OR (YEAR > 99) THEN
   BEGIN
      PARAMETERERROR := TRUE;
      WRITELN('Month, day, or year out of range')
   END
   ELSE
      PACKDATE := YEAR * 10000.0 + MONTH * 100.0 + DAY
END;    {PACKDATE}


FUNCTION PACKTIME(HOUR, MINUTE : INTEGER) : INTEGER;

BEGIN   {PACKTIME}
   IF (HOUR < 0) OR (HOUR > 23) OR (MINUTE < 0) OR (MINUTE > 59) THEN
   BEGIN
   BEGIN   {PRINTHELP}
      WRITELN(' E : Enter a reminder, a sentence of < ',MAXREMINDERMSGLENGTH:0,
              ' chars;');
      WRITELN(' D : Delete a reminder;');
      WRITELN(' L : List appointment book; ');
      WRITELN(' Q : Quit program; ');
      WRITELN(' ? : Print this help message. ')
   END;    {PRINTHELP}
```

```
   PROCEDURE APPOINTMENTCOMMAND;

   {Read a single character from the user and calls the appropriate
   procedure to execute the command designated by the input char. }

   VAR
      COMMANDCH : CHAR;

   BEGIN   {APPOINTMENTCOMMAND}
      IF NOT EOLN THEN
      BEGIN
         READLN(COMMANDCH);
         WRITELN;
         IF COMMANDCH IN ['?','E','e','D','d','L','l','Q','q'] THEN
```

```
        CASE COMMANDCH OF
          '?'     :   PRINTHELP;
          'E','e' :   ENTERREMINDER;
          'D','d' :   DELETEREMINDER;
          'L','l' :   LISTREMINDERS;
          'Q','q' :   QUIT := TRUE
        END
      ELSE
        WRITELN('Unknown appointment command "',COMMANDCH,'".')
    END
END;     {APPOINTMENTCOMMAND}

BEGIN   {MAIN}
  REMINDERHEAD := NIL;
  WRITELN('Appointment book.');
  WRITELN('Type ? for help.');
  WRITELN;
  QUIT := FALSE;
  FIRSTTIMEINENTER := TRUE;
  REPEAT
    WRITE(PROMPT);
    IF EOF THEN
      QUIT := TRUE
    ELSE
      APPOINTMENTCOMMAND
  UNTIL QUIT
END.    {MAIN}
```

```
BEGIN    {PRINTDATE}

{Unpack THEDATE and print it.}

  THEYEAR := ROUND(THEDATE / 10000.0);
  YEARREM := ROUND((THEDATE - ROUND(THEDATE/10000.0))* 10000.0);
  THEMONTH := YEARREM DIV 100;
  THEDAY := YEARREM MOD 100;
  WRITE(THEMONTH:2,'/',THEDAY:2,'/',THEYEAR:2)
END;  {PRINTDATE}

PROCEDURE PRINTTIME(THETIME : INTEGER);

{Unpack THETIME and print it.}

BEGIN   {PRINTTIME}
  WRITE(THETIME DIV 100:2,':',THETIME MOD 100:2)
END;    {PRINTTIME}

PROCEDURE LISTREMINDERS;
VAR
  REMINDER : REMINDERENTRYPTR;
  R, SEQUENCENUM : INTEGER;

  {SEQUENCENUM is the number of the item in the list currently being
   processed.}

BEGIN    {LISTREMINDERS}
  IF REMINDERHEAD = NIL THEN
    WRITELN('Appointment book empty.')
  ELSE
```

```
BEGIN
  REMINDER := REMINDERHEAD;
  SEQUENCENUM := 0;
  WHILE REMINDER <> NIL DO
  BEGIN
    SEQUENCENUM := SEQUENCENUM + 1;
    WRITE(SEQUENCENUM:5,BLANK:3);
    PRINTDATE(REMINDER^.DATE);
    WRITE(BLANK:2);
    PRINTTIME(REMINDER^.TIME);
    WRITE(BLANK:4);
    FOR R := 1 TO REMINDER^.REMINDERSTRINGLEN DO
      WRITE(REMINDER^.REMINDERSTRING[R]);
    WRITELN;
    REMINDER := REMINDER^.NEXTREMINDER
  END
  END
END;    {LISTREMINDERS}

PROCEDURE PRINTHELP;
```

Replacement Turbo Pascal Code:
(Replace two sections of code)

Section 1:

```
IF NOT PARAMETERERROR THEN
BEGIN
  WRITELN('Enter 1 sentence reminder: ');
  READLN(STR1);
  FOR R := 1 TO LENGTH(STR1) DO
      REMINDER^.REMINDERSTRING[R] := STR1[R];
  REMINDER^.REMINDERSTRINGLEN := R;
  INSERTREMINDER(REMINDER);
  FIRSTTIMEINENTER := FALSE
END
  END
END;
```

Section 2:

```
PROCEDURE APPOINTMENTCOMMAND;
VAR
  COMMANDCH : CHAR;

BEGIN
  READLN(COMMANDCH);
  WRITELN;
  COMMANDCH := UPCASE(COMMANDCH);
  CASE COMMANDCH OF
      '?' :  PRINTHELP;
      'E' :  ENTERREMINDER;
      'D' :  DELETEREMINDER;
      'L' :  LISTREMINDERS;
      'Q' :  QUIT := TRUE
  ELSE
```

```
           WRITELN('Unknown appointment command "',COMMANDCH,'".')
      END
END;

BEGIN {MAIN}
  REMINDERHEAD := NIL;
  WRITELN('Appointment book.');
  WRITELN('Type ? for help.');
  WRITELN;
  QUIT := FALSE;
  FIRSTTIMEINENTER := TRUE;
  REPEAT
    WRITE(PROMPT);
    APPOINTMENTCOMMAND;
    WRITELN
  UNTIL QUIT
END. {MAIN}
```

Index

Selections from The SYBEX Library

Languages

BASIC

YOUR FIRST BASIC PROGRAM
by Rodnay Zaks
182 pp., illustr. in color, Ref. 0-092
A "how-to-program" book for the first time computer user, aged 8 to 88.

FIFTY BASIC EXERCISES
by J. P. Lamoitier
232 pp., 90 illustr., Ref. 0-056
Teaches BASIC through actual practice, using graduated exercises drawn from everyday applications. Programs written in Microsoft BASIC.

BASIC FOR BUSINESS
by Douglas Hergert
224 pp., 15 illustr., Ref. 0-080
A logically organized, no-nonsense introduction to BASIC programming for business applications. Includes many fully-explained accounting programs, and shows you how to write your own.

EXECUTIVE PLANNING WITH BASIC
by X. T. Bui
196 pp., 19 illustr., Ref. 0-083
An important collection of business management decision models in BASIC, including inventory management (EOQ), critical path analysis and PERT, financial ratio analysis, portfolio management, and much more.

BASIC PROGRAMS FOR SCIENTISTS AND ENGINEERS
by Alan R. Miller
318 pp., 120 illustr., Ref. 0-073
This book from the "Programs for Scientists and Engineers" series provides a library of problem-solving programs while developing the reader's proficiency in BASIC.

Pascal

INTRODUCTION TO PASCAL
(Including UCSD Pascal™)
by Rodnay Zaks
420 pp., 130 illustr., Ref. 0-066
A step-by-step introduction for anyone who wants to learn the Pascal language. Describes UCSD and Standard Pascals. No technical background is assumed.

THE PASCAL HANDBOOK
by Jacques Tiberghien
486 pp., 270 illustr., Ref. 0-053
A dictionary of the Pascal language, defining every reserved word, operator, procedure, and function found in all major versions of Pascal.

APPLE® PASCAL GAMES
by Douglas Hergert and Joseph T. Kalash
372 pp., 40 illustr., Ref. 0-074
A collection of the most popular computer games in Pascal, challenging the reader not only to play but to investigate how games are implemented on the computer.

PASCAL PROGRAMS FOR SCIENTISTS AND ENGINEERS
by Alan R. Miller
374 pp., 120 illustr., Ref. 0-058
A comprehensive collection of frequently used algorithms for scientific and technical applications, programmed in Pascal. Includes programs for curve-fitting, integrals, statistical techniques, and more.

DOING BUSINESS WITH PASCAL
by Richard Hergert and Douglas Hergert
371 pp., illustr., Ref. 0-091
Practical tips for using Pascal programming in business. Covers design considerations, language extensions, and applications examples.

Other Languages

FORTRAN PROGRAMS FOR SCIENTISTS AND ENGINEERS
by Alan R. Miller
280 pp., 120 illustr., Ref. 0-082
This book from the "Programs for Scientists and Engineers" series provides a library of problem-solving programs while developing the reader's proficiency in FORTRAN.

A MICROPROGRAMMED APL IMPLEMENTATION
by Rodnay Zaks
350 pp., Ref. 0-005
An expert-level text presenting the complete conceptual analysis and design of an APL interpreter, and actual listing of the microcode.

UNDERSTANDING C
by Bruce H. Hunter
320 pp., Ref 0-123
Explains how to program in powerful C language for a variety of applications. Some programming experience assumed.

FIFTY PASCAL PROGRAMS
by Bruce H. Hunter
338 pp., illustr., Ref. 0-110
More than just a collection of useful programs! Structured programming techniques are emphasized and concepts such as data type creation and array manipulation are clearly illustrated.

Technical

Assembly Language

PROGRAMMING THE 6502
by Rodnay Zaks
386 pp., 160 illustr., Ref. 0-135
Assembly language programming for the 6502, from basic concepts to advanced data structures.

6502 APPLICATIONS
by Rodnay Zaks
278 pp., 200 illustr., Ref. 0-015
Real-life application techniques: the input/output book for the 6502.

ADVANCED 6502 PROGRAMMING
by Rodnay Zaks
292 pp., 140 illustr., Ref. 0-089
Third in the 6502 series. Teaches more advanced programming techniques, using games as a framework for learning.

PROGRAMMING THE Z80®
by Rodnay Zaks
624 pp., 200 illustr., Ref. 0-069
A complete course in programming the Z80 microprocessor and a thorough introduction to assembly language.

PROGRAMMING THE 6809
by Rodnay Zaks and William Labiak
362 pp., 150 illustr., Ref. 0-078
This book explains how to program the 6809 microprocessor in assembly language. No prior programming knowledge required.

PROGRAMMING THE 8086™/8088™
by James W. Coffron
300 pp., illustr., Ref. 0-120
This book explains how to program the 8086 and 8088 microprocessors in assembly language. No prior programming knowledge required.

PROGRAMMING THE 68000™
by Steve Williams
250 pp., illustr., Ref. 0-133
This book introduces you to microprocessor operation, writing application programs, and the basics of I/O programming. Especially helpful for owners of the Apple Macintosh or Lisa.

Hardware

FROM CHIPS TO SYSTEMS: AN INTRODUCTION TO MICROPROCESSORS
by Rodnay Zaks
552 pp., 400 illustr., Ref. 0-063
A simple and comprehensive introduction to microprocessors from both a hardware and software standpoint: what they are, how they operate, how to assemble them into a complete system.

MICROPROCESSOR INTERFACING TECHNIQUES
by Rodnay Zaks and Austin Lesea
456 pp., 400 illustr., Ref. 0-029
Complete hardware and software interfacing techniques, including D to A conversion, peripherals, bus standards and troubleshooting.

THE RS-232 SOLUTION
by Joe Campbell
194 pp., illustr., Ref. 0-140
Finally, a book that will show you how to correctly interface your computer to any RS-232-C peripheral.

MASTERING SERIAL COMMUNICATIONS
by Joe Campbell
250 pp., illustr., Ref. 0-180
This sequel to *The RS-232 Solution* guides the reader to mastery of more complex interfacing techniques.

Operating Systems

SYSTEMS PROGRAMMING IN C
by David Smith
275 pp., illustr., Ref. 0-266
This intermediate text is written for the person who wants to get beyond the basics of C and capture its great efficiencies in space and time.

THE PROGRAMMER'S GUIDE TO UNIX SYSTEM V
by Chuck Hickev/Tim Levin
300 pp., illustr., Re.f 0-268
This book is a guide to all steps involved in setting up a typical programming task in a UNIX systems environment.

REAL WORLD UNIX™
by John D. Halamka
209 pp., Ref. 0-093
This book is written for the beginning and intermediate UNIX user in a practical, straightforward manner, with specific instructions given for many business applications.

Software Specific

Spreadsheets

DOING BUSINESS WITH MULTIPLAN™
by Richard Allen King and Stanley R. Trost
250 pp., illustr., Ref. 0-148
This book will show you how using Multiplan can be nearly as easy as learning to use a pocket calculator. It presents a collection of templates for business applications.

DOING BUSINESS WITH SUPERCALC™
by Stanley R. Trost
248 pp., illustr., Ref. 0-095
Presents accounting and management planning applications—from financial statements to master budgets; from pricing models to investment strategies.

MULTIPLAN™ ON THE COMMODORE 64™
by Richard Allen King
260 pp., illustr., Ref. 0-231
This clear, straighforward guide will give you a firm grasp on Multiplan's functions, as well as provide a collection of useful template programs.

Word Processing

INTRODUCTION TO WORDSTAR®
by Arthur Naiman
202 pp., 30 illustr., Ref. 0-134
Makes it easy to learn WordStar, a powerful word processing program for personal computers.

PRACTICAL WORDSTAR® USES
by Julie Anne Arca
303 pp., illustr., Ref. 0-107
Pick your most time-consuming office tasks and this book will show you how to streamline them with WordStar.

THE COMPLETE GUIDE TO MULTIMATE™
by Carol Holcomb Dreger
250 pp., illustr., Ref. 0-229
A concise introduction to the many practical applications of this powerful word processing program.

THE THINKTANK™ BOOK
by Jonathan Kamin
200 pp., illustr., Ref. 0-224
Learn how the ThinkTank program can help you organize your thoughts, plans, and activities.

Data Base Management Systems

UNDERSTANDING dBASE III™
by Alan Simpson
250 pp., illustr., Ref. 0-267
For experienced dBASE II programmers, data base and program design are covered in detail; with many examples and illustrations.

UNDERSTANDING dBASE II™
by Alan Simpson
260 pp., illustr., Ref. 0-147
Learn programming techniques for mailing label systems, bookkeeping, and data management, as well as ways to interface dBASE II with other software systems.

ADVANCED TECHNIQUES in dBASE II™

by Alan Simpson

250 pp., illustr., Ref. 0-228

If you are an experienced dBASE II programmer and would like to begin customizing your own programs, this book is for you. It is a well-structured tutorial that offers programming techniques applicable to a wide variety of situations. Data base and program design are covered in detail, and the many examples and illustrations clarify the text.

Integrated Software

MASTERING SYMPHONY™

by Douglas Cobb

763 pp., illustr., Ref. 0-244

This bestselling book provides all the information you will need to put Symphony to work for you right away. Packed with practical models for the business user.

SYMPHONY™ ENCORE: PROGRAM NOTES

by Dick Andersen

325 pp., illustr., Ref. 0-247

Organized as a reference tool, this book gives shortcuts for using Symphony commands and functions, with troubleshooting advice.

JAZZ ON THE MACINTOSH™

by Joseph Caggiano and Michael McCarthy

400 pp., illustr., Ref. 0-265

The complete tutorial on the ins and outs of the season's hottest software, with tips on integrating its functions into efficient business projects.

MASTERING FRAMEWORK™

by Doug Hergert

450 pp., illustr., Ref. 0-248

This tutorial guides the beginning user through all the functions and features of this integrated software package, geared to the business environment.

ADVANCED TECHNIQUES IN FRAMEWORK™

by Alan Simpson

250 pp., illustr., Ref. 0-267

In order to begin customizing your own models with Framework, you'll need a thorough knowledge of Fred programming languages, and this book provides this information in a complete, well-organized form.

ADVANCED BUSINESS MODELS WITH 1-2-3™

by Stanley R. Trost

250 pp., illustr., Ref. 0-159

If you are a business professional using the 1-2-3 software package, you will find the spreadsheet and graphics models provided in this book easy to use "as is" in everyday business situations.

THE ABC'S OF 1-2-3™

by Chris Gilbert and Laurie Williams

225 pp., illustr., Ref. 0-168

For those new to the LOTUS 1-2-3 program, this book offers step-by-step instructions in mastering its spreadsheet, data base, and graphing capabilities.

MASTERING APPLEWORKS™

by Elna Tymes

250 pp., illustr., Ref. 0-240

Here is a business-oriented introduction to AppleWorks, the new integrated software package from Apple. No experience with computers is assumed.

Computer Specific

Apple II—Macintosh

THE PRO-DOS HANDBOOK

by Timothy Rice/Karen Rice

225 pp., illustr., Ref. 0-230

All Pro-DOS users, from beginning to advanced, will find this book packed with vital information. The book covers the basics, and then addresses itself to the Apple II user who needs to interface with

Pro-DOS when programming in BASIC. Learn how Pro-DOS uses memory, and how it handles text files, binary files, graphics, and sound. Includes a chapter on machine language programming.

THE MACINTOSH™ TOOLBOX
by Huxham, Burnard, and Takatsuka
300 pp., illustr., Ref. 0-249
This tutorial on the advanced features of the Macintosh toolbox is an ideal companion to The Macintosh BASIC Handbook.

THE MACINTOSH™ BASIC HANDBOOK
by Thomas Blackadar/Jonathan Kamin
800 pp., illustr., Ref. 0-257
This desk-side reference book for the Macintosh programmer covers the BASIC statements and toolbox commands, organized like a dictionary.

PROGRAMMING THE MACINTOSH™ IN ASSEMBLY LANGUAGE
by Steve Williams
400 pp., illustr., Ref. 0-263
Information, examples, and guidelines for programming the 68000 microprocessor are given, including details of its entire instruction set.

THE EASY GUIDE TO YOUR APPLE II®
by Joseph Kascmer
147 pp., illustr., Ref. 0-122
A friendly introduction to the Apple II, II plus, and the IIe.

BASIC EXERCISES FOR THE APPLE®
by J.P. Lamoitier
250 pp., 90 illustr., Ref. 0-084
Teaches Applesoft BASIC through actual practice, using graduated exercises drawn from everyday applications.

THE APPLE II® BASIC HANDBOOK
by Douglas Hergert
250 pp., illustr., Ref. 0-115
A complete listing with descriptions and instructive examples of each of the Apple II BASIC keywords and functions. A handy reference guide, organized like a dictionary.

APPLE II® BASIC PROGRAMS IN MINUTES
by Stanley R. Trost
150 pp., illustr., Ref. 0-121
A collection of ready-to-run programs for financial calculations, investment analysis, record keeping, and many more home and office applications. These programs can be entered on your Apple II plus or IIe in minutes!

YOUR FIRST APPLE II® PROGRAM
by Rodnay Zaks
182 pp., illustr., Ref. 0-136
This fully illustrated, easy-to-use introduction to Applesoft BASIC programming will have the reader programming in a matter of hours.

THE APPLE® CONNECTION
by James W. Coffron
264 pp., 120 illustr., Ref. 0-085
Teaches elementary interfacing and BASIC programming of the Apple for connection to external devices and household appliances.

THE APPLE IIc™: A PRACTICAL GUIDE
by Thomas Blackadar
175 pp., illustr., Ref. 0-241
Learn all you need to know about the Apple IIc! This jargon-free companion gives you a guided tour of Apple's new machine.

THE BEST OF EDUCATIONAL SOFTWARE FOR APPLE II® COMPUTERS

by Gary G. Bitter, Ph.D. and Kay Gore

300 pp., Ref. 0-206

Here is a handy guide for parents and an invaluable reference for educators who must make decisions about software purchases.

YOUR SECOND APPLE II® PROGRAM

by Gary Lippman

250 pp., illustr., Ref. 0-208

The many colorful illustrations in this book make it a delight for children and fun for adults who are mastering programming on any of the Apple II line of computers, including the new IIc.

THE MACINTOSH™: A PRACTICAL GUIDE

by Joseph Caggiano

280 pp., illustr., Ref. 0-216

This easy-to-read guide takes you all the way from set-up to more advanced activities such as using Macwrite, Macpaint, and Multiplan.

MACINTOSH™ FOR COLLEGE STUDENTS

by Bryan Pfaffenberger

250 pp., illustr., Ref. 0-227

Find out how to give yourself an edge in the race to get papers in on time and prepare for exams. This book covers everything you need to know about how to use the Macintosh for college study.

BASIC EXERCISES FOR THE ATARI®

by J.P. Lamoitier

251 pp., illustr., Ref. 0-101

Teaches ATARI BASIC through actual practice, using graduated exercises drawn from everyday applications.

THE EASY GUIDE TO YOUR ATARI® 600XL/800XL

by Thomas Blackadar

175 pp., illustr., Ref. 0-125

This jargon-free companion will help you get started on the right foot with your new 600XL or 800XL ATARI computer.

ATARI® BASIC PROGRAMS IN MINUTES

by Stanley R. Trost

170 pp., illustr., Ref. 0-143

You can use this practical set of programs without any prior knowledge of BASIC! Application examples are taken from a wide variety of fields, including business, home management, and real estate.

YOUR SECOND ATARI® PROGRAM

by Gary Lippman

250 pp., illustr., Ref. 0-232

The many colorful illustrations in this book make it a delight for children and fun for adults who are mastering BASIC programming on the ATARI 400, 800, or XL series computers.

Atari

YOUR FIRST ATARI® PROGRAM

by Rodnay Zaks

182 pp., illustr., Ref. 0-130

This fully illustrated, easy-to-use introduction to ATARI BASIC programming will have the reader programming in a matter of hours.

Coleco

WORD PROCESSING WITH YOUR COLECO ADAM™

by Carole Jelen Alden

140 pp., illustr., Ref. 0-182

This is an in-depth tutorial covering the word processing system of the Adam.

THE EASY GUIDE TO YOUR COLECO ADAM™
by Thomas Blackadar
175 pp., illustr., Ref. 0-181
This quick reference guide shows you how to get started on your Coleco Adam using a minimum of technical jargon.

Commodore 64/VIC-20

THE BEST OF COMMODORE 64™ SOFTWARE
by Thomas Blackadar
150 pp., illustr., Ref. 0-194
Save yourself time and frustration with this buyer's guide to Commodore 64 software. Find the best game, music, education, and home management programs on the market today.

THE BEST OF VIC-20™ SOFTWARE
by Thomas Blackadar
150 pp., illustr., Ref. 0-139
Save yourself time and frustration with this buyer's guide to VIC-20 software. Find the best game, music, education, and home management programs on the market today.

THE COMMODORE 64™/VIC-20™ BASIC HANDBOOK
by Douglas Hergert
144 pp., illustr., Ref. 0-116
A complete listing with descriptions and instructive examples of each of the Commodore 64 BASIC keywords and functions. A handy reference guide, organized like a dictionary.

THE EASY GUIDE TO YOUR COMMODORE 64™
by Joseph Kascmer
126 pp., illustr., Ref. 0-126
A friendly introduction to the Commodore 64.

YOUR FIRST VIC-20™ PROGRAM
by Rodnay Zaks
182 pp., illustr., Ref. 0-129
This fully illustrated, easy-to-use introduction to VIC-20 BASIC programming will have the reader programming in a matter of hours.

THE VIC-20™ CONNECTION
by James W. Coffron
260 pp., 120 illustr., Ref. 0-128
Teaches elementary interfacing and BASIC programming of the VIC-20 for connection to external devices and household appliances.

YOUR FIRST COMMODORE 64™ PROGRAM
by Rodnay Zaks
182 pp., illustr., Ref. 0-172
You can learn to write simple programs without any prior knowledge of mathematics or computers! Guided by colorful illustrations and step-by-step instructions, you'll be constructing programs within an hour or two.

COMMODORE 64™ BASIC PROGRAMS IN MINUTES
by Stanley R. Trost
170 pp., illustr., Ref. 0-154
Here is a practical set of programs for business, finance, real estate, data analysis, record keeping, and educational applications.

GRAPHICS GUIDE TO THE COMMODORE 64™
by Charles Platt
261 pp., illustr., Ref. 0-138
This easy-to-understand book will appeal to anyone who wants to master the Commodore 64's powerful graphics features.

THE BEST OF EDUCATIONAL SOFTWARE FOR THE COMMODORE 64
by Gary G. Bitter, Ph.D. and Kay Gore
250 pp., Ref. 0-223
Here is a handy guide for parents and an indispensable reference for educators

who must make decisions about software purchases for the Commodore 64.

COMMODORE 64™ FREE SOFTWARE
by Gary Phillips
300 pp., Ref. 0-201
Find out what "free software" is all about and how to find the specific programs you need.

YOUR SECOND COMMODORE 64™ PROGRAM
by Gary Lippman
240 pp., illustr., Ref. 0-152
A sequel to *Your First Commodore 64 Program*, this book follows the same patient, detailed approach and brings you to the next level of programming skill.

THE COMMODORE 64™ CONNECTION
by James W. Coffron
250 pp., illustr., Ref. 0-192
Learn to control lights, electricity, burglar alarm systems, and other non-computer devices with your Commodore 64.

PARENTS, KIDS, AND THE COMMODORE 64™
by Lynne Alper and Meg Holmberg
110 pp., illustr., Ref. 0-234
This book answers parents' questions about the educational possibilities of the Commodore 64.

CP/M Systems

THE CP/M® HANDBOOK
by Rodnay Zaks
320 pp., 100 illustr., Ref 0-048
An indispensable reference and guide to CP/M—the most widely-used operating system for small computers.

MASTERING CP/M®
by Alan R. Miller
398 pp., illustr., Ref. 0-068
For advanced CP/M users or systems programmers who want maximum use of the CP/M operating system . . . takes up where our *CP/M Handbook* leaves off.

THE BEST OF CP/M® SOFTWARE
by John D. Halamka
250 pp., Ref. 0-100
This book reviews tried-and-tested, commercially available software for your CP/M system.

THE CP/M PLUS™ HANDBOOK
by Alan R. Miller
250 pp., illustr., Ref. 0-158
This guide is easy for beginners to understand, yet contains valuable information for advanced users of CP/M Plus (Version 3).

IBM PC and Compatibles

THE ABC'S OF THE IBM® PC
by Joan Lasselle and Carol Ramsay
143 pp., illustr., Ref. 0-102
This book will take you through the first crucial steps in learning to use the IBM PC.

THE BEST OF IBM® PC SOFTWARE
by Stanley R. Trost
351 pp., Ref. 0-104
Separates the wheat from the chaff in the world of IBM PC software. Tells you what to expect from the best available IBM PC programs.

THE IBM® PC-DOS HANDBOOK
by Richard Allen King
296 pp., Ref. 0-103
Explains the PC disk operating system. Get the most out of your PC by adapting its capabilities to your specific needs.

BUSINESS GRAPHICS FOR THE IBM® PC
by Nelson Ford
259 pp., illustr., Ref. 0-124
Ready-to-run programs for creating line graphs, multiple bar graphs, pie charts, and more. An ideal way to use your PC's business capabilities!

THE IBM® PC CONNECTION
by James W. Coffron
264 pp., illustr., Ref. 0-127
Teaches elementary interfacing and BASIC programming of the IBM PC for connection to external devices and household appliances.

BASIC EXERCISES FOR THE IBM® PERSONAL COMPUTER
by J.P. Lamoitier
252 pp., 90 illustr., Ref. 0-088
Teaches IBM BASIC through actual practice, using graduated exercises drawn from everyday applications.

USEFUL BASIC PROGRAMS FOR THE IBM® PC
by Stanley R. Trost
144 pp., illustr., Ref. 0-111
This collection of programs takes full advantage of the interactive capabilities of your IBM Personal Computer. Financial calculations, investment analysis, record keeping, and math practice—made easier on your IBM PC.

YOUR FIRST IBM® PC PROGRAM
by Rodnay Zaks
182 pp., illustr., Ref. 0-171
This well-illustrated book makes programming easy for children and adults.

DATA FILE PROGRAMMING ON YOUR IBM® PC
by Alan Simpson
219 pp., illustr., Ref. 0-146
This book provides instructions and examples for managing data files in BASIC. Programming design and development are extensively discussed.

SELECTING THE RIGHT DATA BASE SOFTWARE FOR THE IBM® PC
SELECTING THE RIGHT WORD PROCESSING SOFTWARE FOR THE IBM® PC
SELECTING THE RIGHT SPREADSHEET SOFTWARE FOR THE IBM® PC
by Kathleen McHugh and Veronica Corchado
100 pp., illustr., Ref. 0-174, 0-177, 0-178
This series on selecting the right business software offers the busy professional concise, informative reviews of the best available software packages.

THE MS™-DOS HANDBOOK
by Richard Allen King
320 pp., illustr., Ref. 0-185
The differences between the various versions and manufacturer's implementations of MS-DOS are covered in a clear, straightforward manner. Tables, maps, and numerous examples make this the most complete book on MS-DOS available.

ESSENTIAL PC-DOS
by Myril and Susan Shaw
300 pp., illustr., Ref. 0-176
Whether you work with the IBM PC, XT, PCjr, or the portable PC, this book will be invaluable both for learning PC-DOS and for later reference.

IBM PCjr

IBM® PCjr™ BASIC PROGRAMS IN MINUTES
by Stanley R. Trost
175 pp., illustr., Ref. 0-205
Here is a practical set of BASIC programs for business, financial, real estate, data analysis, record keeping, and educational applications, ready to enter on your PCjr.

THE COMPLETE GUIDE TO YOUR IBM® PC*jr*™

by Douglas Herbert

625 pp., illustr., Ref. 0-179
Learn to master the new hardware and DOS features that IBM has introduced with the PC*jr*. A fold-out reference poster is included.

THE EASY GUIDE TO YOUR IBM® PC*jr*™

by Thomas Blackadar

175 pp., illustr., Ref. 0-217
This jargon-free companion is designed to give you a practical working knowledge of your machine—no prior knowledge of computers or programming is needed.

BASIC EXERCISES FOR THE IBM® PC*jr*™

by J.P. Lamoitier

250 pp., illustr., Ref. 0-218
PC*jr* BASIC is easy when you learn by doing! The graduated exercises in this book were chosen for their educational value and application to a variety of fields.

TI 99/4A

THE BEST OF TI 99/4A™ CARTRIDGES

by Thomas Blackadar

150 pp., illustr., Ref. 0-137
Save yourself time and frustration when buying TI 99/4A software. This buyer's guide gives an overview of the best available programs, with information on how to set up the computer to run them.

YOUR FIRST TI 99/4A™ PROGRAM

by Rodnay Zaks

182 pp., illustr., Ref. 0-157
Colorfully illustrated, this book concentrates on the essentials of programming in a clear, entertaining fashion.

Timex

YOUR TIMEX/SINCLAIR 1000® AND ZX81™

by Douglas Hergert

159 pp., illustr., Ref. 0-099
This book explains the set-up, operation, and capabilities of the Timex/Sinclair 1000 and ZX81. Covers how to interface peripheral devices and introduces BASIC programming.

THE TIMEX/SINCLAIR 1000® BASIC HANDBOOK

by Douglas Hergert

170 pp., illustr., Ref. 0-113
This complete alphabetical listing with explanations and examples of each word in the T/S 1000 BASIC vocabulary will allow you quick, error-free programming of your T/S 1000.

TIMEX/SINCLAIR 1000® BASIC PROGRAMS IN MINUTES

by Stanley R. Trost

150 pp., illustr., Ref. 0-119
A collection of ready-to-run programs for financial calculations, investment analysis, record keeping, and many more home and office applications. These programs can be entered on your T/S 1000 in minutes!

MORE USES FOR YOUR TIMEX/SINCLAIR 1000®
Astronomy on Your Computer

by Eric Burgess and Howard J. Burgess

176 pp., illustr., Ref. 0-112
Ready-to-run programs that turn your TV into a planetarium.

TRS-80

YOUR COLOR COMPUTER

by Doug Mosher

350 pp., illustr., Ref. 0-097
Patience and humor guide the reader through purchasing, setting up, programming, and using the Radio Shack TRS-80 Color Computer. A complete introduction.

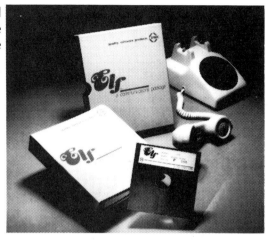

SYBEX COMPUTER BOOKS

are different.

Here is why . . .

At SYBEX, each book is designed with you in mind. Every manuscript is carefully selected and supervised by our editors, who are themselves computer experts. We publish the best authors, whose technical expertise is matched by an ability to write clearly and to communicate effectively. Programs are thoroughly tested for accuracy by our technical staff. Our computerized production department goes to great lengths to make sure that each book is well-designed.

In the pursuit of timeliness, SYBEX has achieved many publishing firsts. SYBEX was among the first to integrate personal computers used by authors and staff into the publishing process. SYBEX was the first to publish books on the CP/M operating system, microprocessor interfacing techniques, word processing, and many more topics.

Expertise in computers and dedication to the highest quality product have made SYBEX a world leader in computer book publishing. Translated into fourteen languages, SYBEX books have helped millions of people around the world to get the most from their computers. We hope we have helped you, too.

For a complete catalog of our publications:

SYBEX, Inc. 2344 Sixth Street, Berkeley, California 94710
Tel: (415) 848-8233   Telex: 336311

Introduction to Pascal: Including Turbo Pascal
Programs on Disk

If you'd like to use the same programs in this book but don't want to type them in yourself, you can send for them on disk. The disk contains all the programs in the book on a Turbo Pascal compatible disk. To obtain this disk, complete the order form and return it along with a check or money order for $20.

Amador Computer Services
P.O. Box 699
Pine Grove, CA 95665

Name _____

Address _____

City/State/ZIP _____

Enclosed is my check or money order.
(Make check payable to *Amador Computer Services*.)
Price includes applicable taxes and postage within the
United States.